"A highly perceptive analysis of the ground
of free speech. It both retains and goes bey
theoretical discussion enriches and is in tu
cases. A most welcome and timely book."
— Lord :
The Future of Multi-Ethnic Britain and *Rethinking Multiculturalism*'

"In contrast to much journalism and commentary on these issues, this is an important,
reasoned and patient account of these inflammatory matters. Mondal's book is crucial
reading for those interested not only in the work and impact of Salman Rushdie, not
only for those working in contemporary literature more widely, but also those with a
concern for issues of freedom, expression and the future of cosmopolitan and multicultural democracy."
— Professor Robert Eaglestone, Professor of Contemporary
Literature and Thought, Royal Holloway, University of London

"Anshuman Mondal has performed the considerable service of puncturing the unex-
amined clichés and self-serving cant that characterise the freedom of speech debate.
He refuses to accept at face value the assumed contention between liberal secular
notions of free speech and the supposed censorious strictures of Muslim intolerance,
as played out in numerous recent controversies. Instead, he strips the discussion back
to first principles, pointing out how all speech and writing is a dialogic act of communication that anticipates a response from its recipient. Offence is seen as the product
of the relationship between speaker, addressee and all-important contextual power
relations. In an era when 'liberals' from both the right and left have come together
to denounce Islam as an intolerant force and a geopolitical enemy, Mondal reveals
how professions of liberal reasonableness and neutrality mask an absolutist cultural
supremacism wherein the 'right to offend' is separated from its consequences. He
demonstrates how the central traditions of Western liberalism are each blind to the
power relations which mark all societies and which take a particularly intractable form
in multicultural ones.
     At the heart of the book is the question, what is free speech for? Is it an end in itself?
Or does it serve a higher purpose, such as safeguarding democracy, as is often claimed?
In a brilliant, forensic analysis of some of the rhetoric around freedom and offence,
Mondal asks how notions of a good and fair society can possibly be furthered by the
deliberate denigration of a portion of its membership. Recognising ethics as central to
the proper exercise of rights, he calls for an 'ethics of propriety' in writing and reading
where mutual obligations are acknowledged. Through detailed readings of controversies such as the *Satanic Verses* affair, the Danish cartoon controversy, the outrage
caused by the novel, *The Jewel of Medina*, and comedy films which have flirted with the
sacred and the blasphemous, Mondal charts the dead-ends reached by conventional
interpretations, while suggesting more fruitful ways to write, read and understand.
     This book is an important clarion call for care and sensitivity in our fraught multi-
cultural world, while still emphasising a critical robustness that makes demands of all
those who engage in public utterance."
— Peter Morey, Professor of English and Postcolonial Studies,
University of East London, UK

Also by Anshuman A. Mondal

AMITAV GHOSH

NATIONALISM AND POST-COLONIAL IDENTITY:
Culture and Ideology in India and Egypt

YOUNG BRITISH MUSLIM VOICES

Islam and Controversy

The Politics of Free Speech After Rushdie

Anshuman A. Mondal
Reader in English, Brunel University, UK

First published 2014 by
PALGRAVE MACMILLAN

Palgrave Macmillan in the UK is an imprint of Macmillan Publishers Limited, registered in England, company number 785998, of Houndmills, Basingstoke, Hampshire RG21 6XS.

Palgrave Macmillan in the US is a division of St Martin's Press LLC, 175 Fifth Avenue, New York, NY 10010.

Palgrave Macmillan is the global academic imprint of the above companies and has companies and representatives throughout the world.

Palgrave® and Macmillan® are registered trademarks in the United States, the United Kingdom, Europe and other countries.

ISBN 978–1–137–46607–5   hardback
ISBN 978–1–137–47167–3   paperback

This book is printed on paper suitable for recycling and made from fully managed and sustained forest sources. Logging, pulping and manufacturing processes are expected to conform to the environmental regulations of the country of origin.

A catalogue record for this book is available from the British Library.

Library of Congress Cataloging-in-Publication Data
Mondal, Anshuman A. (Anshuman Ahmed), 1972– author.
Islam and controversy : the politics of free speech after Rushdie / by Anshuman Mondal, Reader in English, Brunel University, UK.
pages cm
Summary: "Was Salman Rushdie right to have written The Satanic Verses? Were the protestors right to have protested? What about the Danish cartoons? Is giving offence simply about the right to freedom of expression, and what is really happening when people take offence? Using case studies of a number of Muslim-related freedom of speech controversies surrounding (in)famous, controversial texts such as The Satanic Verses, The Jewel of Medina, the Danish cartoons of Muhammed and the film Submission by Theo van Gogh, this book examines the moral questions raised by such controversies, questions that are often set aside at the time, such as whether the authors and artists involved were right to have done what they did and whether those who protested against them were right to have responded in such a way. In so doing, it argues that the giving and taking of offence are political performances that struggle to define and re-define freedom, and suggests that any attempt to establish a language of inter-cultural communication appropriate to multicultural societies is an ethical as opposed to merely political or legal task, involving dialogue and negotiation over fundamental values and principles. Overall, this important book constitutes a sustained critique of liberal arguments for freedom of speech, in particular of the liberal discourse that took shape in response to the Rushdie controversy and has, in the twenty-five years since, become almost an orthodoxy for many intellectuals, artists, journalists and politicians living and working in Britain (and elsewhere in the West) today. "— Provided by publisher.
Includes bibliographical references and index.
ISBN 978–1–137–46607–5 (hardback)
1. Islam and literature.   2. Freedom of speech in literature.   3. Freedom of the press—History—20th century.   4. Freedom of the press—History—21st century.   5. Rushdie, Salman. Satanic verses.   6. Literature and society.   7. Censorship.   8. East and West in literature.   I. Title.
PN605.I8M66 2014
809'.9338297—dc23   2014026278

Typeset by MPS Limited, Chennai, India.

For Leo and Leila

Contents

Acknowledgements

This book began as part of an idea for another book before it took on a life of its own, and, like a giant tree under whose shade all other forms of life wither and die, that other project has long since been consigned to oblivion. Nevertheless, it is only right that I acknowledge Brunel University for awarding me a period of research leave in 2008–9 for that other work. The seed of this book grew in response to an invitation by Elleke Boehmer and Ankhi Mukherjee to present a seminar at the Oxford Postcolonial Seminar at Wadham College in January 2009. The lively discussion that ensued convinced me that it was an idea worth pursuing.

On the other hand, the book would probably still not be complete had it not been for the generous support of the Arts and Humanities Research Council, which awarded me a Research Fellowship in 2012–13. During that time, I was also able to take up a Visiting Research Fellowship at the University of Melbourne and I am sincerely grateful to Ken Gelder and Rachel Fensham for giving my family an opportunity to reside in that wonderful city for three months, and for giving me the opportunity to research and write in the English Library; having an entire library at hand's reach is an unforgettable experience. I would also like to thank the staff and students of the English programme in the School of Culture and Communication at Melbourne for their stimulating responses to my seminars, and to Andrew Smith in particular for his highly congenial and relaxed company.

In the course of the five long years it has taken to complete this project, many others have given me a helping hand. Bob Eaglestone, in particular, has been tremendously supportive throughout, and I wish to acknowledge my debt of gratitude to him. Towards the end of the project, I was invited by Abdulrazak Gurnah to deliver a seminar at the University of Kent's School of English in March 2014, which enabled me to test some of the ideas in the last chapter while it was still hot off the press, as it were. My sincere thanks are due to Abdulrazak and the staff and students at the seminar for their engaged and astute comments and feedback. I have been fortunate, over the past few years, to have been able to work closely with a number of scholars who share many of my research interests. Together, we constitute a small research group called 'Multicultural Textualities' and my discussions and exchanges with Rehana Ahmed, Claire Chambers, Peter Morey, Stephen Morton and Amina Yaqin have enriched this book, and their friendship and collegiality has been a great boon to me. I would like to thank Rehana, Claire and Stephen in particular for reading several parts of this book and making their incisive but supportive comments, and Amina and Peter for inviting me to contribute to their 'Framing Muslims' and 'Muslims, Multiculturalism and Trust' projects, which have helped over the years to clarify much of my thinking.

Ben Doyle at Palgrave Macmillan has offered nothing but enthusiasm and support for this book, and has been incredibly efficient in expediting the reviewing and editorial process. In particular, the way he managed to secure readers' reports so quickly is, in my publishing experience, a first. I would like to thank all the readers and respondents who have, in their various ways, contributed to the shaping of the book although, of course, the responsibility for any errors that remain is mine alone.

From my childhood, a group of friends have provided me with vital emotional sustenance and, when necessary, welcome distraction from the cares and frustrations of academic life and research. In particular, I would like to thank the Reverends Stephen Griffith and Nigel Dawkins for bringing their faith, knowledge, experience and wisdom to bear on an illuminating exchange that helped me clarify my ideas on Monty Python's *Life of Brian* in the final chapter.

Finally, I must acknowledge the love and support of my family. My mother, Anjulika Mondal, remains a rock, and she always will be; sadly, however, this was the first book I have written without the encouragement of my late father, Ansar Ali, who died shortly before I began this project. In another sense, however, his presence can be felt in every sentence because our perennial discussions and arguments over *The Satanic Verses*, Islam and Muslims have been, in hindsight, enormously formative in numerous though impalpable ways. To my wife, Joanna, I cannot adequately express my gratitude for her astonishing forbearance, especially during the latter stages when she lost me to my study most evenings; I cannot fathom the depth and extent of that sacrifice and I am overwhelmed by my luck in being able to share our lives together – hopefully we can now share much more. My children, Leo and Leila, were not even born when this work began, but they will soon become readers and writers themselves, and I hope they will absorb the moral lesson that one must write and read with care and precision because words are powerful and can do much harm as well as great good. I dedicate this book to them for all the joy they have brought me.

The epigraph is from 'Martin Amis' by Patrick McGrath commissioned by and first published in BOMB 18/Winter 1987. © Bomb Magazine, New Art Publications, and its Contributors. All rights reserved. The BOMB Digital Archive can be viewed at www.bombmagazine.org.

Parts of Chapter 4 were first published as '"Representing the very ethic he battled": Islam(ism), Secularism and Self-Transgression in *The Satanic Verses*', in a special issue of *Textual Practice* edited by Lucienne Loh and Malcolm Sen, 27:3, 2013, pp. 419–37; and 'Re-visiting the *The Satanic Verses*: the *fatwa* and its legacies' in Robert Eaglestone and Martin McQuillian, eds. *Salman*

Rushdie: Contemporary Critical Perspectives (Bloomsbury, 2013) pp. 59–71. I gratefully acknowledge Bloomsbury Academic and Taylor and Francis Journals for granting permission to re-use this material here.

What does [the accountability of the author in fiction] mean morally? Is one accountable for it?

Martin Amis

Not one of you truly believes until you love for the other what is loved for the self.

Prophet Muhammad

Introduction

In 1990, as the controversy over *The Satanic Verses* rumbled on, Simon Lee published a brave little book called *The Cost of Free Speech*, which ran against the grain of a liberal consensus that saw no merit whatsoever in the Muslim protests against the novel. In the Preface, he wrote, 'so many of those who purport to value free speech betray their ideals by failing to analyse exactly why freedom of expression is important, or from whom threats to free speech arise, or when it is wrong to exercise the right to free speech'. He went on to state his belief that 'free speech is under threat mostly from ourselves and, in particular, from our refusal to face up to the weaknesses in our own reasoning and to changes in the world'.[1]

This book is written in much the same spirit and it takes up Lee's challenge to rethink and re-evaluate why freedom of speech is important in a changed world. As I show in Chapter 1, the changes to which Lee alluded have been dramatic and perhaps even epochal. The increasing pace of globalization and the continuing shrinkage of the world through advances in media and communications technology that have intensified the conflicted intimacy with which different communities and cultures rub up against one another; 11 September 2001, and other atrocities perpetrated by terrorists in the name of a particular interpretation of Islam, and the subsequent 'war on terror' and US-led military invasions; the mobilization of the 'security state' and its arsenal of surveillance techniques against perceived 'fifth columns', principally Muslim populations in the West but also, increasingly, entire civilian populations; the purported failure of multiculturalism as a means of integrating immigrant communities in western liberal democracies; all of these irrevocably distance our own period from that in which the 'Rushdie affair' broke. And yet with regards to the liberal discourse about freedom of speech, very little has changed. Indeed, the arguments advanced then have, if anything, become further entrenched in the course of a series of Muslim-related freedom of speech controversies – some of which I examine in this book – and the weaknesses apparent then have become more pronounced now in a world in which 'the West' is no longer so unquestionably domi-nant over, and can no longer afford to be so parochial about and aloof from, 'the Rest'.

Whereas Lee wrote in the context of the Rushdie controversy itself, this book was galvanized by the liberal rhetoric displayed during the media coverage of the twentieth anniversary of the *fatwa* in 2009. Although cer-tain Muslim positions in the various controversies treated here did seek to further authoritarian political agendas and to narrow the scope of expres-sive liberty, and they did so not so much to 'protect' Islam as to shore up their own authority as self-appointed spokespersons for 'true' Islam, I would nevertheless suggest that their arguments are evidently weak and incoherent and have been convincingly exposed and dismantled by their critics, both liberal and non-liberal (including other Muslims). In contrast, the liberal defence of freedom of speech appears to be strong and coherent, and to many it appears self-evident. And yet this is far from the case, so this book constitutes a sustained critique of liberal arguments for freedom of speech, in particular of that liberal discourse (which I call 'absolutist') that took shape in response to the Rushdie controversy and has, in the years since, become almost an orthodoxy for many intellectuals, artists, journalists and politicians living and working in Britain (and elsewhere in the West) today.

Some critiques of liberal positions on freedom of speech, from both Muslim and non-Muslim perspectives, are very pointed and have much merit not only because they make a more or less persuasive case for restraint or restriction of expression in the service of some greater good, such as bet-ter community or intercultural relations, or because of their re-statement of the greater value of civility over and above individual liberty (an accepted premise within other, older strands of liberalism, particularly with respect to democracy), but also because their critiques implicitly constitute alternative conceptualizations of liberty, thereby decoupling the concept from liberal-ism. In so doing, there is the possibility that we may begin to reinvigorate the concept of freedom (especially expressive freedom) by unshackling it from the slogans and tired clichés which have smothered it within contem-porary liberal discourse; and we may begin to reconceptualize it in a man-ner more 'adequate to the predicament' of a globalized world in which the universal reach of a particular cultural formation can no longer be taken for granted.[2]

In this respect, the central aim and argument of the book is to endorse and amplify the idea that moral restraint and even, sometimes, legal restric-tion is not inimical to freedom of expression as most, if not all, varieties of liberal thought would have it: even pragmatic liberals see restraints on free-dom as a regrettable necessity, which implies that *in principle* it is antitheti-cal to liberty. Restraint, on this view, is external to the concept of freedom itself, its Other. I would argue, on the contrary, that restraint is *constitutive* of liberty, that it supplements liberty in the Derridean sense, and is therefore not exterior to the concept but secreted, inevitably and inseparably, within it. Other conceptions of liberty advocated by, for instance, Gandhi in his theorization of *swaraj* as self-control (which he derived from his reading of the *Bhagavad-Gita*), or the Muslim feminist thinker Amina Wadud (derived from her reading of the *Qur'an*) are able to accommodate this paradox, but post-Enlightenment secular rationalism, with its focus on linear logic, does not seem able to grasp it.

The fact that these alternatives have been repeatedly dismissed not so much by argument and engagement as through the repeated incantation of certain liberal axioms such as 'fight speech with speech' in the open 'marketplace of ideas' is an indication of the limits of liberalism in meeting the challenge of cultural difference. In particular, this book argues that the liberal discourse of rights – which is the ground that both absolutist and more pragmatic liberalisms share – is inadequate in meeting the challenge of controversies in which at least one of the protagonists is speaking from a non-liberal perspective. This is because it vacates wider questions of ethical responsibility in favour of the narrower ethical framework of codified law – and assumes that the law is consistent with liberal principles. Even the most sophisticated liberal arguments usually bracket the wider questions of moral responsibility and accountability, leaving aside what might be termed a 'moral remainder' that non-liberal arguments often assume to be absolutely central.[3] It is this 'moral remainder' that I am concerned with; if I abjure the discourse of rights, it is not because I want to argue against the right to freedom of speech, far from it (this is worth saying lest I be misunderstood) but because I am more concerned with right and wrong and, as Lee also observes, talking about legal rights is one way to *avoid* talking about morality. I am not, however, interested in assigning or apportioning blame, although it should go without saying that I unequivocally condemn those who inflict or threaten physical violence against those who offend them. Rather, I am interested in establishing a framework for discussing the difficult ethical questions that are raised by controversial intellectual and creative work. I am aware, of course, that if it is exceedingly difficult to establish legal responsibility for offensive speech, the task of determining moral accountability seems almost insuperable, especially with regard to complex discursive articulations. Nevertheless, this book is an effort to do just that.

At the heart of this book are two very simple questions: were these authors/artists/film-makers right to have done what they did in the manner that they did it? And were the Muslims who opposed them right to have interpreted these texts as 'offensive'? These two simple questions in fact demand very complex responses that revolve around the ethics of representation, on the one hand, and the ethics of reading on the other. In the course of outlining what I have called an 'ethics of propriety' that seeks to encompass both, I have nevertheless focused much more on the ethics of representation not least because it is more appropriate for a literary-critical-cum-theoretical work such as this one, and because a responsible and proper evaluation of the (im)proprieties of reading controversial texts demands a methodology more oriented towards the sociology of reading, which I shall offer in a forthcoming work. *Islam and Controversy* therefore largely concentrates on examining and evaluating the ethical merits of four textual works produced by non-Muslims (even though two, Salman Rushdie and Ayaan Hirsi Ali, are of Muslim background) that have generated controversy amongst Muslim audiences and readerships.

However, the reader must be forewarned that this is not a book 'about' the Rushdie controversy or other Muslim-related freedom of speech controversies. Rather, it is a meditation on the value of freedom of speech within the context of the larger problem of cultural difference and inter-cultural communication, between 'western' and Muslim communities in particular. I hope it provokes questions and offers insights that are germane to other difficult intercultural dialogues, not least because the value of freedom of speech rests, as I argue in Chapter 3, on the furtherance of mutual understanding. In that spirit of *dialogue*, then, one is entitled to ask 'What can the West learn from others?' If you read much of the contemporary liberal discourse on freedom of speech, the answer for many liberals seems clear: nothing. I would suggest, however, that it could learn something about liberty itself, to augment those insights that have emerged from within the liberal tradition. The idea that self-restraint can be a basis for liberty (conceived of as self-mastery rather than autonomy) can be found in Islamic traditions, and in Vedic ones such as Hinduism, Jainism and Buddhism (to mention only those with which I am familiar). One might also add various marginalized strands of western thought, such as the communistic traditions and even Burkean conservatism. Without the influence of liberal ideas of liberty (e.g. personal autonomy) such ideas might gravitate towards authoritarianism and conformism (although the heterodoxies found in all of these discursive traditions suggest countervailing tendencies as well), but, in the context of a globally dominant hyper-capitalist consumerism that takes its cue from liberal ideas of negative liberty as freedom from restraint, such alternative conceptions of liberty may well provide a valuable corrective that might temper the corrosive effects of unrestrained liberty on the self, one's relationships with others, social trust and solidarity; they might thereby help to promote ways of thinking that go beyond self-interest, the law of the market and the rule of contract. Such dialogues are not conducted in a neutral space, of course, and this book emphasizes throughout the ways in which power relationships shape and mediate the relationships established by discourse. But just as freedom of speech is not an end in itself but a means towards achieving mutual understanding, so too is dialogue only a means towards the achievement of social justice, which is a goal that lies beyond discourse even if it is nevertheless only conceivable within and through it.

Throughout this book I speak a great deal about the responsibilities attendant upon authors towards their readers, which involves responsiveness to readers' expectations – expectations that are shaped by the proprieties established by history, culture, custom and, of course, form. Whereas all authors hope that all their readers begin reading at the beginning and finish at the end, this is not always the case and even less so for academic works which make certain demands on readers that must be reciprocated by indicating to them the shape and structure of my argument.

There are three parts to this book, the first of which establishes a contextual and theoretical frame for the readings to be found in Part II. Chapter 1 outlines the emergence of the historical conjuncture established by the controversy over *The Satanic Verses*, which frames not just that controversy but also each of the successive ones that are analysed in Part II; it also identifies two significant aspects that have considerable bearing on the discussion that follows: first, the emergence of the absolutist liberal discourse to which I devote the greater part of Chapter 2 and some of Chapter 3, and the shift in the idiom of protest from blasphemy to offensiveness. This shift is pivotal to what I call the politics of controversy insofar as the giving and taking of offence is a performative gesture which positions the offender/offendee within a relation of power. Drawing on the work of J.L. Austin and Judith Butler, I argue that offensiveness does not inhere in speech itself because offensive speech acts are not 'constative' statements that merely describe or refer to the world; rather, since not everyone who hears an 'offensive' statement will, in fact, be offended, the offensiveness cannot inhere in the words themselves, but is instead *produced* by the relationship established between the speaker, the recipient and the power relations that underlie their encounter. Offensive speech acts are therefore 'performative' statements that do work in the world by establishing a relation of domination and subordination within a 'total speech situation', as are speech acts that respond to them by 'taking' offence. As such, controversies are invariably political, not in an instrumentalist sense, but because what is being performed in the giving and taking of offence is *power* rather than simply the staking of rival truth-claims. It is within this framework of power, then, that any attempt to examine and establish the rights and wrongs of speech-acts within any given controversy must be situated.

The second chapter is a prelude to Chapter 3, comprising a detailed critique of contemporary absolutist liberal discourse on freedom of speech. I draw on extant criticisms of Millian and contractualist accounts of freedom of speech in order to demonstrate the ways in which contemporary liberal absolutism draws together several strands of liberal thought and weaves them into a powerful rhetorical tapestry that appears cogent but is, in fact, incoherent. The manner in which recent contributions to this discourse equivocate – without appearing to do so – between consequentialist and non-consequentialist arguments for freedom of speech; between Mill's 'classic argument' in favour of freedom of speech because it is a means towards desirable ends, such as happiness, progress, truth, democracy and so on, and the contractualist emphasis on freedom of speech as a fundamental right because it is a good-in-itself; between a surface emphasis on toleration and a deeper emphasis on liberal supremacy; all these reveal the conceptual fragility of a discourse that is nevertheless dominant and hegemonic. The source of this fragility is an emphasis on abstraction, proceduralism and philosophical idealism that seems to extend across the spectrum of liberal thought. Indeed, both the surface coherence and the deeper incoherence are effects of the ways in which liberalism's philosophical idealism enables contradictory and fundamentally opposed arguments to be reconciled in an apparently consistent rhetorical tapestry on the one hand, whilst, on the other, leaving such contradictions unresolved. That is, it operates as a kind of magic wand that perpetrates a rhetorical sleight of hand through an insistent series of abstractions that ignores the power relations within social life and thus fundamentally severs contemporary liberal arguments for freedom of speech from the world. Nowhere is this more apparent than in the conceptualization of speech as something distinct from 'action' because it does not have 'consequences' – which, in turn, means that *speech does not matter*. Ironically, then, in weaving together the disparate liberal arguments for freedom of speech, contemporary absolutism amplifies the weaknesses of both consequentialist and non-consequentialist arguments to the point where the value of freedom of speech itself is negated.

Chapter 3 takes up the question with which I conclude Chapter 2: what is freedom of speech for? Whilst the conclusion of Chapter 2 is that contemporary liberalism can offer no satisfactory answer to this question, this chapter is an attempt to account for the responsibilities attendant upon the acts of writing and reading, which are treated as part of a transactional social relationship that endows each participant in that relationship with a set of moral obligations towards the other. I attempt to theorize these obligations within the framework of situational ethics, drawing on the philosophy of Emmanuel Levinas but also the significant work undertaken within the field of literary ethics by critics such as Derek Attridge, Andrew Gibson, Wayne Booth, James Phelan and others. These obligations are grounded in the mutual observance, by both writers and readers, of what might be termed the proprieties of their encounter; the ethics of propriety, then, turns on whether or not producers of cultural texts do so in a manner that is appropriate to the matter they wish to treat, and conversely whether the interpretive communities with whom they enter into a relationship respond to their texts 'properly'. Both of these, in turn, are related to the 'properties' of the text that binds their relationship. At the heart of the matter, then, is the problem of textuality as it mediates social relationships, the fraught processes of encoding and decoding, which Andrew Gibson has called the 'split-space' of enunciation and reception.[4] Propriety resides within this split-space as a form of moral responsibility that is *shared* between authors and their audiences, and it operates as a limit that is established *dialogically* by producers of texts and the interpretive communities that respond to them. When those limits are observed, as they are in the vast majority of cultural transactions, the social relationships established and maintained by discourse are not disturbed or fractured. However, in case of a few texts, the limits of propriety are transgressed, either by authors or by readers or both, and it is these texts that cause controversy.

The ethics of propriety therefore provides a theoretical frame within which evaluation of the rights and wrongs of the respective acts that constitute a controversial encounter might be undertaken in the chapters that follow, but in attempting to account for these one is invariably drawn onto difficult terrain. In assigning moral responsibility, one must perforce wrestle with questions of intentionality without lapsing into intentional fallacy, and one must above all keep in mind the pressure that cultural difference brings to bear on any attempt to evaluate what is appropriate (or not) because the respective understandings of propriety are relative to the divergent expectations of the parties to the conflict. The problem of cultural difference is a notable *lacuna* in the extant work on literary ethics but it is not one that can be overlooked in a work such as this, which is fundamentally concerned with inter-cultural encounters. These are two of the reasons why the title of the chapter draws on Levinas' phrase 'a difficult freedom'. In contrast to contemporary liberal discourse, which sees the matter in absolute, almost black-and-white terms, there is nothing easy about freedom of speech or, indeed, ethics; at every turn, one is confronted by difficulty, by awkward, sometimes insuperable, questions that cannot be accounted for by a simple re-statement of principle.

Part II consists of three chapters dealing with four major cultural controversies involving Muslims. Chapter 4 examines the ethics of representation in Salman Rushdie's *The Satanic Verses*, whilst Chapters 5 and 6 respectively deal with the controversies generated by the cartoons published by the Danish newspaper *Jyllands-Posten* and the Dutch film *Submission*, and *The Jewel of the Medina*, a bio-novel about the Prophet Muhammad's wife Aisha. It is perhaps not surprising that the ethics of propriety is relatively more complex for the two literary texts as opposed to the two visual ones. This is partly because of the manner in which the visual sign operates in the cartoons and *Submission* – through what I call the logic of the 'suture' – which marshalls the ambiguity of the image and concretizes it through a form of attachment that overwhelms semantic alternatives. But the relative clarity of their respective ethical positions is determined also by context and performance: both the cartoons and the film constitute polemical interventions into an already charged and polarized political and ideological field that overdetermines their rhetorical performativity. Both novels, on the other hand, are artistic works that occupy a discursive terrain that is somewhat further removed from the directly political whilst, of course, articulating a cultural politics. Nevertheless, in unpacking what is put at stake by these two visual texts, it is possible to detect a complicity that they both share with the profoundly more complex *The Satanic Verses*. This involves the manner in which each of these texts projects a secular-liberal representation of Islam and Muslims that, at a fundamental level, not only concurs with Islamist and orthodox/conservative/masculinist interpretations of the religion, and thereby endorses them, but also obscures other possibilities of imagining Islam, such as those offered by reformist Muslims and Muslim feminists. For the editors of *Jyllands-Posten*, Theo van Gogh and Ayaan Hirsi Ali this may not be as disturbing or ironic as it might appear, situated as they are within a paradigm of 'civilization-speak' that sees 'Islam' and the 'West' locked in mortal combat;[5] for Rushdie, however, it places his text at odds with his own ethical precepts, which is why one might note that the ethical improprieties of the novel are of a different kind to those obtaining to *Submission* and the cartoons. The same might be said of *The Jewel of the Medina*, a work ostensibly respectful of the Prophet and explicitly written in support of Muslim feminist endeavours to deconstruct the patriarchal traditions of exegesis and jurisprudence that have historically subordinated women within Muslim societies. And yet, Sherry Jones' naïve attempt to represent the 'Other' woman in the form of her contemporary rendering of Aisha bint Abi Bakr within the genre of historical romantic fiction also compromises her ethical and political ambitions, subordinating her historical, cultural and religious alterity to the ideological gaze of western secular-liberal feminism, on the one hand, and the generic and cultural expectations of *western* women readers on the other.

Taken as a whole, then, each of the texts fails to observe an ethics of propriety, in some form and to some degree. It would be wrong, however, to ascribe a spurious moral equivalence between them. Each textual performance is singular: a novel like *The Satanic Verses*, immensely grand in scope and ambition, with a complex and sophisticated architecture displaying a dazzling array of literary techniques that generates a multiplicity of meanings, is clearly trying to do things with words that are very different to the more pedestrian efforts of a first-time romantic novelist, or the incendiary motivations of some cartoonists and *provocateurs*. The ethical propriety of each text is determined by their respective properties, and their specific encounters with the audiences and readerships that responded to them.

The final part of the book consists of one chapter, a reflection on the discourse that surrounded the introduction of the Racial and Religious Hatred Act 2006 into British law. This discourse illuminates some of the issues that surface consistently throughout the book in a particularly pointed manner, and as such this chapter returns to and amplifies many of the issues broached earlier in the book, in particular the vexed question within contemporary liberalism about the relationship of religion to free-dom of speech that I discuss at the beginning of Chapter 3. It undertakes a cultural critique of the ways in which contemporary liberal understandings of freedom of speech in Britain have underwritten responses to a specific issue – legislation on religious hatred – and thus brings the theoretical ideas and arguments advanced in Chapters 2 and 3 to bear on a discussion of the contemporary moment in a way that illuminates the 'state of play' as it currently stands. This chapter steps outside the frame of specific *Muslim*-related freedom of speech controversies discussed in Part II by raising more general issues of wider relevance to discussions of freedom of expression, in particular the idea of an 'ethic of care' that underwrites the ethics of propri-ety. Both of these ethics are fundamentally related to a conceptualization of language and discourse that is at odds with the philosophical idealism that underpins most liberal arguments for freedom of speech. If, for the latter, the primacy of the sovereign individual requires that discourse be conceived of in terms of the need for self-expression as an index of liberty – that the purpose of speech is, as Glen Newey puts it, to 'get it out' such that one's freedom can be measured by the extent to which one can say whatever one wants – I would argue, to the contrary, that discourse is relational rather than individual, that the point of 'speech' is communication, and that what constitutes discourse is not self-expression but dialogue: to 'get something across' rather than simply 'get it out'.[6] This returns to the question at the heart of Chapter 2, 'what is freedom of speech for?' and it suggests that its importance lies in its ability to facilitate and foster mutual understanding and thus establish and maintain relationships that are, in turn, predicated on a greater and common good, however that may be conceived.

It is for this reason that the idea of 'care' is so important to the argument of this book, and this final chapter illustrates it by addressing one possible misreading, which would suggest that I equate any offensive utterance with ethical impropriety. In this final chapter, I therefore consider those instances when offensiveness *is* appropriate by returning to the *politics* of controversy, and the power relations that determine the ethics of free speech. I am not making an argument for 'proper' behaviour, that only propriety is ethical. Indeed, the discussion of satire in this final chapter concerns itself specifi-cally with those instances where it is entirely appropriate that a writer or artist should transgress the norms of propriety. This also implies that there are instances when an 'improper' reading – such as not reading or partial reading (in both senses of the word) – is also appropriate, when taking offence strategically, as it were, is the right thing to do. To that extent one might say that an ethics of propriety is *also* an ethics of impropriety, and that both rest on an ethic of care, of taking care, because if one is to behave improperly then one should take the trouble to establish why, and to what purpose, and whether the transgression is warranted – whether there is, in fact moral value in acting improperly (it follows that acting improperly for its own sake is, *ipso facto*, unethical). This may or may not be rationally calculable (for instance, in the form of a legal responsibility), but there is in every interpersonal encounter a responsibility that exceeds reason; it is endowed upon us as living beings compelled inevitably to share our lives with other living beings and it is this intangible, incalculable responsibility that this book ultimately tries to account for.

Part I

1
From Blasphemy to Offensiveness: the Politics of Controversy

Ayatollah Khomeini pronounced his *fatwa* on Salman Rushdie over twenty-five years ago. Reviewing the 'Rushdie affair' from this vantage point reveals some fundamental continuities as well as radical discontinuities with the present situation.[1] On the one hand, on reading many of the contemporary documents chronicling the affair, it is impossible not to realize that the world we inhabit today is vastly different from that in which the controversy took place. We cannot, for example, read of the Muslim protests and the liberal response without conjuring in our minds what Paul Weller has called its 'entails': the spectres of 9/11 and 7/7, the wars in Afghanistan and Iraq and, of course, on 'terror'; the murder of the Dutch film-maker Theo van Gogh; the controversy over the Danish cartoons depicting the Prophet of Islam as a suicide bomber; the firebombing of the publishers GibsonSquare for seeking to publish *The Jewel of the Medina*; the 'failure' of multiculturalism; the 'problem' of integrating large immigrant Muslim communities into 'the West'; or the controversy surrounding the then UK Home Secretary Jack Straw's comments on the suitability of the *niqab* in modern Britain, itself an echo of the French ban on the wearing of the *hijab* in schools and other public arenas.[2] In the US, these 'cultural' issues may have been more muted, although similarly omnipresent, submerged beneath the rhetoric of the security state, but they have periodically surfaced to the forefront of American consciousness, as demonstrated by the outcry over the proposed Islamic cultural centre and mosque proximate to Ground Zero. All of this had yet to pass when 'the Rushdie affair' broke at the end of 1988, and they form a bulwark between then and now. There is a pre-lapsarian feel to the period, one determined by the relative novelty of Muslim political assertiveness, in which the language of the encounter had yet to be formulated.

However, in the absence of that language, the encounter was articulated through the existing models of a conflict between the West and Islam, an additional layer grafted onto the centuries-old discourse of antagonism between Christendom and Islam. What was remarkable was the degree to which people who might ordinarily have taken a more nuanced view of such a situation (artists and intellectuals, especially) felt compelled to take sides, and in so doing compelled others to do the same. Rana Kabbani, for example, noted how this polarizing dynamic – 'with its added ordure of vitriol and abuse' – forced her 'underground Muslim' identity 'into the open. Stung by the racial hatred which this affair unleashed . . . I needed to re-examine my allegiances.'[3] At the same time, her *Letter to Christendom* attempted to interrogate and undermine these oppositions by seeking a 'halfway house' between 'two worlds apparently incapable of meeting on common ground'.[4] It attempts the same difficult refusal to choose that, ironically, Rushdie later exhorted in his short story 'The Courter' – ironic precisely because Rushdie did not take kindly to Kabbani's defence of Islam, and her unwillingness to rush to the barricades on his behalf.[5] Almost without exception, Rushdie's liberal defenders in the West felt no such need to examine their allegiances – they seemed perfectly apparent and clear-cut.

It is this Manichean discourse that constitutes the main continuity linking our present to the events of 1988–1989. Yet those same events enumerated above are part of a *series* located squarely within a deep historical continuity, one that long predated the Rushdie affair. The 'clash of civilizations' it draws upon is an echo-chamber that reverberates into perpetuity – or, at least, since Christendom first became aware of, and confronted, Islam as a rival.[6] Samuel Huntington's famous thesis was published as an article in *Foreign Affairs* in 1993, and thence as a book in 1996, long before 9/11.[7] It preceded the attacks in Kenya and Tanzania in 1998, and on the USS *Cole* in 2000. In other words, it predated the actual emergence of radical Islamism as an emergent 'enemy'.[8] Although primarily determined by the end of the Cold War and the fall of the Berlin Wall, it also clearly registers the Rushdie affair in its construction of Islam as a particularly implacable civilizational foe. The *Foreign Affairs* article quotes Bernard Lewis' response to the Rushdie Affair in 'The Roots of Muslim Rage', and adopts its defining optic as its own:

> We are facing a need and a movement far transcending the level of issues and policies and the governments that pursue them. This is no less than a clash of civilizations – the perhaps irrational but surely historic reaction of an ancient rival against our Judeo-Christian heritage, our secular present, and the worldwide expansion of both.[9]

Huntington's text was not the origin of this discourse, of course, but it gave it a shape and currency, marshalling the amorphous mass of sentiment swirling around 'the Rushdie affair', giving it a semblance of coherence, a smattering of contemporaneity, a macro-political context, and – because of its political influence – the aura of authority.

There does not seem to have been any appreciable shift in the template laid down by 'the Rushdie affair' in the intervening years. Each successive controversy has quickly developed into a stand-off between a putative 'West' defending freedom of expression, and an 'Islam' seeking freedom from offence. The twentieth anniversary of the *fatwa*, in February 2009, was marked by extensive media coverage and commentary, but the overwhelming impression left by this retrospective appraisal was that it constituted a re-inscription, a repetition with a difference. While many of the prominent Muslim protagonists of the 'Rushdie affair' within the British context – foremost among them, Inayat Bunglawala, former spokesperson for the Muslim Council of Britain, and Ghayasuddin Siddiqui, who was then a leading member of the Tehran-backed Muslim Institute – have adapted or retracted their positions vis-á-vis the novel and the issues it raised concerning the respective limits of freedom of expression and religious liberty (as has the Islamic Republic of Iran itself, specifically with respect to Khomeini's *fatwa*), liberal positions on the controversy have not altered in any significant respect.[10] Indeed, the events of 11 September 2001 and the subsequent 'war on terror' have further entrenched them. Thus, writing in the *Observer* just before the twentieth anniversary, Andrew Anthony concluded that 'there is nothing more sacred than the freedom to question what is sacred'.[11] Likewise, on the day itself, Lisa Appignanesi invoked John Mortimer (the writer and barrister who defended Penguin during the *Lady Chatterley's Lover* case) in suggesting that 'it was almost the duty of writers to offend', a trope often reprised by contemporary liberal advocates of freedom of speech, most recently by the writers Kenan Malik and Nick Cohen.[12] Both these statements reprise, almost to the letter, the positions taken up by Rushdie and his defenders during the controversy over *The Satanic Verses*, both before and after the *fatwa*. Appignanesi echoes Rushdie's famous catechism, 'what is freedom of expression? Without the freedom to offend, it ceases to exist', and Anthony reprises Rushdie's sacralization of literature (despite his assertions to the contrary) in 'Is Nothing Sacred?' on the basis that '[l]iterature is the one place in any society . . . where we can hear *voices talking about everything in every possible way*' – where nothing *can* be sacred because to make something sacred is 'to set [it] apart', and thus remove it from that scrutiny.[13]

Rushdie himself has significantly hardened his position on Islam and Muslims, and both the emergence of what has been called the 'New Atheism' and the backlash against 'multiculturalism' have bolstered the liberal conviction that surfaced during the Rushdie affair concerning the cultural obduracy and 'backwardness' of Islam.[14] These trends have accompanied the rhetoric of the 'war on terror' and the 'clash of civilizations' articulated by a resurgent neo-liberalism and has resulted in a re-alignment of right- and left-wing liberalisms promoting a united front in the face of a common cultural foe: Islam.

The result of this re-alignment has been the fetishization of freedom of expression as a totem of western culture, and of liberalism as the register of its cultural supremacy (notwithstanding the numerous contradictions within the West that this glosses over). While right-wing neo-liberals and left-leaning social liberals make uneasy bedfellows, they have converged in the wake of the *fatwa* into a strategic alliance that identifies a fundamental conflict between the West and the so-called Islamic world. Neo-liberals identify 'Islam' as a geopolitical enemy that must be overcome to maintain the economic and military superiority of the West, whilst social liberals characterize it the *locus classicus* of illiberalism. This has been accompanied by a shift towards a more 'muscular' liberalism that has been articulated by both right and left liberals, most recently by the current British prime minister, David Cameron.[15]

Once again, this rhetoric is usually defined by its addressee: Islam. On the right the usual inflection is to exclude Muslims and Islam from 'our' cultural 'norms and values', which 'they' must 'learn' in order to demonstrate their integration into society; many left liberals have also subscribed to this culturalist turn in arguments about integration, but amongst them there is also an emphasis on an absolutist conceptualization of freedom of expression in which any limit on not just the right but the *exercise* of free speech is deemed to be an erosion of '[o]ur established and long-fought for liberties to read or not read what we like'.[16] As we have seen, this was an argument put forward by Rushdie himself in the wake of the *fatwa* and has since become common currency in liberal circles: the right to freedom of expression *ceases to exist* without the 'right' to offend. This invokes an 'all-or-nothing' argument that invariably conjures up a liberal nightmare in which 'any sentence might turn out to be a death sentence'.[17]

This 'absolutist' position on free speech has been most extensively articulated by Kenan Malik, in his best-selling account of 'the Rushdie affair' and its aftermath, *From Fatwa to Jihad* (2009), and more recently by the *Observer* columnist, Nick Cohen, in *You Can't Read This Book: Censorship in an Age of Freedom* (2012). Brian Winston, in his *A Right to Offend* (2012) has also offered a (slightly) more measured, and academic, contribution to this discourse.[18] Malik and Cohen, in particular, advocate an especially bold position: the removal of all incitement to hatred legislation, on all grounds – race, religion, gender, sexuality, disability; of laws prohibiting Holocaust denial or denial of other genocides, such as the denial of the Armenian genocide (in France); and they dismiss all feminist objections to pornography as a degradation of women. In the next chapter, I will examine the arguments, tropes and assumptions that constitute this post-Rushdie 'absolutist' discourse on free speech, but here, by way of context, it is important to note that the realignment of liberalisms in the wake of 'the Rushdie affair' has meant that this largely left-liberal discourse has accommodated antipathies and anxieties that are usually the provenance of the political

right, which in turn has helped to embed them firmly within a political consensus that, in Britain today, has acquired an almost hegemonic force. First,
it has disavowed multiculturalism as a failed experiment, a disavowal that
has accompanied and partly determined the re-signification of 'integration'
as a synonym rather than antonym of 'assimilation'.[19] Secondly, it declares
an impatience with 'political correctness', an apparently intolerable limit
on freedom of expression that it associates with multiculturalism and its
demand to 'respect' other cultures. 'Respect', then, is the third aspect of this
shift in left-liberal discourse, and it has become something of a dirty word
amongst contemporary liberal absolutists, often deployed with a sneering
sarcasm that denotes contempt for the concept. Whilst part of this shift may
have been caused by an unsurprising restatement of liberal first principles
as a response to the creeping authoritarianism of then Prime Minister Tony
Blair's 'respect agenda' (one inherited with little modification by the subsequent Brown and Coalition administrations), in which the term signals
the re-establishment of authority in the face of a supposedly feral, lawless
and 'disrespectful' underclass, it is also a response to the 'fallout' (to borrow
the title of Andrew Anthony's book, which is itself a notable articulation
of the shift in left-liberalism) of the Rushdie affair, and the sense in which
these liberals have come to see multiculturalism as a vehicle for the advance-
ment of anti-liberal, authoritarian agendas concealed beneath the rhetoric
of cultural pluralism. 'Although the fashion for relativism was growing in
Western universities in the 1980s', writes Cohen, 'leftish academics did not
say we had no right to offend the cultures of racists, misogynists and homo-
phobes, and demand that we "respect" their "equally valid" contributions
to a diverse society' – whilst going on to suggest that contemporary thinkers have now completely succumbed to 'relativism' and a politically correct
'respect' for the 'other'.[20]

What binds these strands of current political orthodoxy is a sometimes
explicit, but more often implicit, suspicion of cultural difference and equality;
or, more precisely, the *equality of cultural difference*. That much is apparent
in the discourse of the political right, even in its more liberal versions,
which has barely concealed its distaste for the equality agenda. Whilst
conservatives have embraced the 'respect agenda' as a means of uphold-
ing and reinforcing established class hierarchies, and have long rejected
multiculturalism and the supposed 'political correctness' that it requires in
the name of an avowed ethnocentrism, left-liberals have come to reject the
'respect agenda' in relation to class (whilst nevertheless often sharing
the same class prejudices) *and* culture, although for different reasons: *against*
inequality, with respect to the former, whilst affirming it with respect to
the latter – although never actually saying as much. This exposes a secular-
liberal cultural supremacism that surfaced in its current form during 'the
Rushdie affair', but which has deep historical roots within liberalism. I will
examine that supremacism in detail in the following chapter, but for now

I wish only to point out that it is one of the framing contexts in which the Muslim-related controversies that I subsequently discuss must be read.

Another frame is the tortuous, contradictory and ongoing engagements between the pre-colonial Islamic and other cultural inheritances bequeathed to modern Muslims, on the one hand, and colonial and post-colonial modernities on the other, encounters which have produced the various Islamic modernisms and revivalisms, of which Islamism is but one, albeit a highly significant one in the current conjuncture. Islamism's historical project has been to contest the terrain of global modernity to which secular-liberalism lays sole and exclusive claim (an ambition that Bernard Lewis unselfconsciously articulates in the passage from 'The Roots of Muslim Rage' quoted above). This is why Khomeini's *fatwa* must be read not as a signifier of Islam's putative medieval barbarism, as secular-liberals have been wont to do, but rather as a *counter-offensive* gesture that reveals, in its outlandish instransigence towards Western secular-liberalism's normative enterprise, alternative ways of reading human experience, history and moral value that *exceed* the paradigms of Western secular thought. The *fatwa* is only one among a multiplicity of such subaltern possibilities, but its presence as a *fissure* in dominant regimes of secular representation renders visible that which normally remains invisible because while such regimes of representation constitute western discourse as universal through their exclusion and/or domestication of 'otherness', the *fatwa's* moral and legal outrageousness as well as its unequivocal endorsement of violence *performed* a resistance to secular universalism that could be neither ignored nor assimilated. Indeed, this may be why Khomeini transgressed the due process and juridical proprieties of Islamic as well as western secular law.

Nevertheless, it should be borne in mind that the *fatwa* is distinguishable from the controversy surrounding *The Satanic Verses*, or, rather, the controversy is not reducible to the *fatwa*. Muslim protests against *The Satanic Verses* predated Khomeini's intervention by several months, there was no single Muslim position on the controversy, nor was every Muslim offended by the novel itself. At the same time, although it is generally acknowledged that Islamist movements, leaders and activists played a significant role in mobilizing and orchestrating the protests, and undoubtedly did their very best to generate as much outrage as possible, this does not mean that the pain felt by Muslim protestors and wider Muslim publics across the world (most of whom had and still have very little to do with Islamism) was simply 'manufactured' by Islamists.[21] Indeed, this characterization of the Muslim protests as *merely* political, and of Muslims' pain as nothing more than a synthetic outrage concocted by activists hoping to advance an Islamist agenda is one of the most curious elements of the contemporary liberal narrative about 'the Rushdie affair'. Such an argument is a somewhat patronizing one that rehearses standard orientalist tropes about 'ordinary' Muslims as 'unthinking sheep' susceptible to the villainous machinations of unscrupulous political leaders.[22] In any case, the fact that these protests were led and orchestrated by political activists with particular agendas is beside the point – it is the job of political actors to mobilize support for their cause, and the idea that *only* 'fundamentalists' were genuinely offended is patently untrue: Zaki Badawi, Ziauddin Sardar and Ali Mazrui, to name a few, were not 'fundamentalists' nor were the majority of Muslims participating in the protests. This 'political orchestration' motif, then, has its significance in the rhetorical work it performs by denying the legitimacy of the protests themselves on account of their unrepresentativeness or 'inauthenticity' – that they did not genuinely reflect the views of 'ordinary' Muslims.[23] But a protest does not need to be 'representative' of an entire community to be legitimate otherwise no protest would ever be legitimate. Indeed, a counter-question can be posed: were the protests *against* the protests – such as those organized by Women Against Fundamentalism – illegitimate because they, too, were not 'representative' of Muslim or non-Muslim communities?

At the same time, the fact that offence was taken by so many Muslims needs to be examined. It was, of course, not reducible to one single factor, although various heuristic candidates have been put forward in addition to political orchestration by Islamists, the concept of *izzat* being the most prominent of these.[24] Nor can we simply assume that it was somehow the 'natural' response to a clearly blasphemous text. Writing in a local newspaper during the early stages of the protest, Mohammed Siddique, a spokesperson for the Bradford Council of Mosques, argued that 'Muslims the world over are offended and hurt by such lies, and are protesting against the supposedly "fictional" novel, on the grounds that it is blasphemous.'[25] At this stage 'offence and hurt' is clearly predicated on the 'grounds' that the novel is 'blasphemous'. As the controversy developed, and as Muslim awareness grew that the UK blasphemy laws did not apply to non-Christians, a median position developed, which continued to insist on blasphemy whilst not taking for granted that the concept of blasphemy is patently obvious – rather, in making this median argument, the Muslim protestors stated their case that the concept of blasphemy should be expanded and the law extended to cover non-Christians. Eventually, the blasphemy argument was dropped altogether, and Muslim grievances gravitated solely towards the 'offence and hurt'. This has been the case in all subsequent freedom of speech controversies involving religious and non-religious issues alike.[26] Thus, blasphemy was not part of the discourse during the row over the play *Behzti* (2004–5), by the Sikh playwright Gurpreet Kaur Bhatti, but the idea of 'offensiveness' was central to it, as it was to the controversy surrounding remarks made in a live radio broadcast by the comedians Russell Brand and Jonathan Ross to the actor Andrew Sachs (2008).[27] Even the controversy surrounding the BBC's 2005 decision to screen *Jerry Springer: The Opera*, which had been running on the West End for nearly two years before that without any protest, and which *did* fall within the remit of the UK's then still extant blasphemy laws (they have since been repealed) in that it attacked figures within the Christian tradition, demonstrates the extent to which blasphemy had by then lost significance as a marker of offensiveness: an attempt to prosecute the BBC by the Christian Institute was rejected by the High Court.[28]

We can see here, in the initial instability and eventual eclipse of blasphemy as a concept by which to articulate 'offensiveness', an indicator that there is no logical relation between the two concepts. Rather, it is contingent upon the power relations operative within any given controversy, for blasphemy is the means by which a structure of power – an authorized Church, for instance – is able to mark out its authority through the interdiction of certain speech acts that are perceived to be a threat to its dominance. The equation between offensiveness and blasphemy only holds in that context; the cry of 'blasphemy!' is a performance of power, and a display of dominance. In the absence of such power the link between 'offence' and blasphemy is severed, and it is not possible to justify the offence taken in terms of blasphemy, as the protestors against both *The Satanic Verses* and *Jerry Springer: The Opera* discovered, whether or not it remained formally on the statute book as an actionable offence. In one sense, Kenan Malik is right when he states that the 'argument against offensive speech is the modern secularized version of the old idea of blasphemy, reinventing the sacred for a godless age' but to put it like this is to suggest an underlying continuity beneath the displacement of blasphemy by offensiveness.[29] However, the lack of purchase for the concept of blasphemy even in a case which clearly falls within the scope of the existing law demonstrates the extent to which the shift reveals a significant *discontinuity*, even if that rupture is ultimately a consequence of the complex forces and historical trajectories that go by the name of 'secularization'.

Since secularization, and latterly cultural pluralism, has decentred the 'sacred', it has dismantled or destabilized the 'structure of power' that the concept of the sacred was there to uphold, namely a society rooted in a single source of religiously mandated authority. In 1949, Lord Denning suggested that 'The reason for this law [of blasphemy] was because it was thought that a denial of Christianity was liable to shake the fabric of society. There is no such danger in society and the offence of blasphemy is a dead letter.'[30] 'Not only had Christianity become unwoven from the nation's social fabric', adds Malik, 'but over the next half-century other faiths and cultures wove themselves in.'[31] He goes on to conclude that 'In today's more secular age, it is culture and identity, rather than simply religion and God, that the law seeks to protect from public assault.'[32] The process of decentring, or unweaving to use Malik's metaphor, has been completed by the emergence of individualism such that religion, culture and identity is now as much a matter of individual 'feeling' as it is about collective conceptions of the 'sacred', whether secularized or not. As a result, Malik cites Monica Ali's observation that there is now a 'marketplace of outrage. And if you set up a marketplace of outrage you have to expect everyone to enter it. Everyone now wants to say, "My feelings are more hurt than yours".'[33]

At first glance, Ali seems to have a point: freedom of speech controversies are now ubiquitous whereas they had previously been few and far between: just before *The Satanic Verses* there was a controversy over Martin Scorcese's film adaptation of *The Last Temptation of Christ* (also 1988), but nearly a decade had passed since the row about *The Life of Brian* and the publication of James Kirkup's poem 'The love that dares speak its name' in *Gay News* (both 1979), which was the last successful prosecution for blasphemy (albeit a private rather than criminal prosecution). In recent years, however, in addition to the controversies examined in this book, there has been the row over the Russell Brand–Jonathan Ross–Andrew Sachs comments; over comments by the controversial comedian Frankie Boyle about disabled people (2009); the comments by the then England football manager, Glenn Hoddle, also about disabled people (1998); the furore over the author Julie Myerson's account of life with her teenage children (2009); the Home Office decision not to allow the controversial Dutch politician Geert Wilders to enter the United Kingdom to promote his film *Fitna* (2009); over the TV presenter Jeremy Clarkson's comments about public sector employees (2011); and the posting of an image of a Palestinian child in the cross-hairs of a sniper's rifle on the Instagram (2013) – to cite just a very few examples. This is not to suggest, of course, that freedom of speech controversies did not arise between 1979 and 1988, or that freedom of speech was not an issue raised in relation to struggles by political movements to tackle racism, sexism and homophobia during that period. Rather, it is to suggest that freedom of speech has become an issue in a new kind of way precisely because those 'everyday' struggles in the 1970s and 1980s were not seen as linked to questions concerning freedom of expression *in the same way* as current controversies are. Amongst liberals, in particular, they did not provoke the kind of reflection about freedom of expression in the way that post-Rushdie controversies have done. As Peter Meyer, the chief executive of Penguin Books at the time of the Rushdie affair, has said of that period, 'We had never had to think about free speech, or about why we were publishers.'[34]

The 'marketplace of outrage' metaphor needs to be unpacked, however, because it is the flipside of the 'marketplace of ideas', a concept that is revered by liberal intellectuals such as Kenan Malik and Monica Ali. According to liberal theory, if the marketplace of ideas is to do its job and 'winnow' truth from falsehood, and enable good ideas to flourish whilst discarding bad ones, then it follows that freedom of speech within the marketplace should be as unrestricted as possible and should include the freedom to offend. As such, the only surprise is that liberals are surprised that a 'marketplace of outrage' is the result, since it is only the logical conclusion of their own argument for freedom of speech. One is reminded of the philosopher Brian Klug's incisive observation that the liberals' claim that freedom of speech involves not just a right but also a 'duty' to offend seems to be accompanied by bewilderment when people actually are offended. In fact, the surprise arises, as I will show in the next chapter, from a philosophical idealism within liberal discourse that separates speech from its consequences.

Performativity and the politics of controversy

The deeper question, then, is not why people are offended but rather what taking – or indeed giving – offence actually means, or signifies, in contemporary culture. Customarily, it is seen as a 'response' to certain kinds of speech – words, phrases, tropes, gestures – that are deemed to be offensive *in themselves*. The American critic Stanley Fish has identified a taxonomical tendency in First Amendment jurisprudence, which he calls 'categorical analysis' that 'proceeds by asking essentially taxonomic questions such as "Is it speech?"'[35] If it *is* deemed to be speech then it is, under current jurisprudential practice, *ipso facto* protected by the First Amendment; if it is not, then further taxonomical questions are raised, principally '[is it] harmful to specific persons or groups?' which is analogous to asking whether the gesture or act in question is offensive. The point I am making here is that beyond the realms of First Amendment jurisprudence, where a convoluted logic strenuously and ingeniously manages to sequester speech from action, this form of categorical analysis invariably holds sway in determining whether certain forms of speech are, in fact, offensive – even amongst those who acknowledge, *contra* the US Supreme Court and certain contemporary liberals, that speech acts *do* have consequences. This in turn rests on the idea that 'offensiveness' inheres in such speech, just as it is commonly assumed that 'meaning' inheres in particular words. This apparent transparency of meaning is connected, in liberalism, to the idea that expression is self-expression, that 'Language offers a window into the hearts of our fellow human beings', that words are merely the vehicle or cipher which transports subjective ideas into the world of objects.[36] This is a corollary – and indeed a necessary one – to the fundamental principle in liberal thought, the idea that there is one 'true' self lying within each individual subjectivity.

If liberal commentators therefore interpret freedom of speech controversies in terms of competing truth-claims in the marketplace of ideas, and Muslim protestors in terms of an obvious falsehood versus an equally obvious truth, they both nevertheless share the assumption that the 'offending' discourse and the counter-utterance which signals that offence has been taken (including, sometimes, the reasons why) are both what J.L Austin called 'constative' utterances.[37] Even the idea of 'assaultive speech' as developed within critical race theory suggests that the violence of such speech inheres in the speech itself, which is perhaps not surprising since critical race theory emerged as a distinct branch of legal scholarship from within the tradition of liberal jurisprudence, even if its aim is to contest the absolutist liberalism of contemporary 'First Amendment fundamentalism'.

Since de Saussure, however, it has been understood that meaning does *not* inhere in signs, but is rather produced as an effect through the differential relation of all signs within a sign-system.[38] It is that *relationality* which produces meaning; similarly, offensiveness does not inhere in particular 'species' or categories of speech but in the *relations* governing each specific 'total speech situation'.[39] Since not all of those who hear the offensive speech will necessarily find it offensive, the offensiveness is produced not by the act of speaking certain inherently 'offensive' words, but in the *relationship* between the speaker, the manner of the speech, the recipient, and the power relations that govern this relationship within the context of a given situation.

I would suggest, therefore, that the violence of 'offensive' or 'assaultive' speech – and 'offensiveness,' as the term implies, is indeed a form of verbal and/or epistemic violence – lies not in the words themselves, but is, rather, produced as an *effect* of a certain kind of *performance* the purpose of which is to position the other to whom the speech is addressed as a subordinate, as an inferior being, a violence that resonates all the more powerfully in an era that values the idea of equality so highly as our own. Indeed, one might suggest that the idea of 'offensiveness' – both the giving and taking of it – achieves its contemporary *social* significance only in relation to the emergence of the 'equality agenda' to which it is both a reaction and a testament. The giving and taking of offence should not, therefore, be seen as 'constative' statements, because offensive statements and the counter-statements that are produced when offence is taken do not merely 'describe' or 'refer' but also do *work* in the world, and thereby change or affect it in some way, which Austin calls 'performative' statements.[40] We might therefore see the giving and taking of offence as performative speech actions, the purpose of which is to position oneself in a position of superiority or inferiority to the other. This work is invariably political, which is why the politics of controversy cannot be reduced to the instrumentalism of particular political agendas and interests, as is assumed to be the case by liberal commentators. What is being performed in the giving or taking of offence is *power* or, rather, to be more precise, the *positioning of oneself in a power relation*. To give offence is to display one's ability to do so; to take offence is to signal one's subordinate position in that power relation, to display a vulnerability that marks oneself as a victim or object of power – to perform one's powerlessness.

At first glance, this would appear to align itself with Mari Matsuda's argument that 'speech does not merely *reflect* a relation of social domination; speech *enacts* domination, becoming the vehicle through which that social structure is reinstated'.[41] As my discussion of racism below demonstrates, discourse does indeed establish and maintain hierarchies of domination and subordination – it interpellates 'subjects' within a certain structure. But precisely because the linguistic sign has an 'arbitrary' relationship to its referent, the effectivity of such speech is 'vulnerable to failure.'[42] There exists, therefore, a 'gap that separates the speech act from its future effects'.[43] It is this gap that enables not just the discursive *enactment* of power relations but also their rhetorical *reversal*. I would concur, therefore, with Judith Butler's critique of Matsuda's argument that 'injurious' speech or 'wounding' words are 'illocutionary' – that is, that the wounding takes place in the very act of speaking, which would suggest that the speech itself is injurious.[44] This would posit the view that the 'offensiveness' or 'violence' of such speech inheres in the words themselves. Nevertheless, there may be specific situations when an abusive speech act is indeed illocutionary – such as, for instance, in direct confrontation. In the instances which I have outlined below and examine throughout this book, all of which are mediated speech acts, this does not apply, and we would be better off thinking of offensive performativity as 'perlocutionary', as Butler does. However, my notion of performativity outlined here also departs slightly from Butler insofar as my interest is not so much in the performativity of speech itself, but rather the way in which speech acts signal *another* action: the act of *self-positioning* in relation to an Other or others.

Thus, for example, when the British right-wing populist television presenter Jeremy Clarkson provoked controversy in 2011 by suggesting that public sector workers participating in a strike should be 'executed . . . in front of their families', the 'offence' lay not in the expression of the sentiment itself or even in the manner of delivery (everyone recognized it was a deliberately provocative exaggeration that was not meant to be taken literally or seriously) but in the contempt he displayed towards the object of his anger. The effectivity of his 'giving offence' lay in the positioning of public sector personnel as subordinate persons; this subordination was a performative display of power, of superiority. Conversely, the reason offence was indeed taken was the recognition by such persons of their subordination, a counter-performativity that responded to the offensive gesture by highlighting the performativity of power and its effect on them. Likewise, in 2007, when contestants on the reality-television show *Celebrity Big Brother* were accused of racially abusing another contestant, the subsequent controversy turned on whether the accused were indeed racist. However, the value of this incident lies in the way the format of the show itself exposes the formation of power relations within an artificially structured social 'situation' – contestants are sequestered in a house shut off from the rest of the world and viewers are able to watch the minutiae of their social interactions, which are broadcast live. The Jade Goody–Shilpa Shetty racism incident revealed how racial abuse could be used by certain contestants in order to establish power relations within that context. In giving offence, Goody and her fellow accused were performatively attempting to establish their power over Shetty through the deployment of a discourse (racism) the main purpose of which is to establish hierarchies between groups of people.

Finally, one might also point to the response of a Muslim reader to the controversy surrounding the proposed filming of Monica Ali's *Brick Lane* in the eponymous street in 2007 in order to illustrate the performativity of 'taking offence'. In the course of their analysis of the effectivity of 'nonreading' or 'partial reading' during the controversy, Bethan Benwell, James Procter and Gemma Robinson demonstrate how the 'text' mattered only insofar as it could become a site or platform on which – and through which – such 'offence-taking' could be performed and seen to be performed (although they do not explicitly discuss it in such terms). They cite a posting on an online message forum called *Britbangla* by a 'Newbie', which quotes a passage that would appear to suggest the novel sees Bangladeshis in derogatory terms as 'illiterate, dirty little monkeys' and 'rats' (without taking into account a context that might show otherwise). At the end of the passage, 'Newbie' comments, 'If Ali had written in such a manner about the Jewish people or the blacks, I doubt she would find much succour. Yet Sylheti's [*sic*] seem to be fair game in the name of multiculturalism.'[45] 'Newbie' reads the novel not in order to contest a misrepresentation with a more truthful representation; quite the contrary, in fact (which is why s/he does not attempt to contextualize the passage): the *purpose* of the reading is to signal Sylheti powerlessness, and to accentuate that powerlessness by positioning oneself as subordinate not just to the majority white community but also in relation to other minorities, hence the comparison with 'Jews' and 'blacks'. It is from such a position of vulnerability that 'offence' can be performatively taken and morally justified.[46]

If offensiveness does not lie in words themselves, but rather in their articulation as a performance of power, it is nevertheless a performance of the power of the *discourse* within which such words signify (e.g. racism, sexism, homo- or Islamophobia) and not necessarily that of the subject who performs it. Thus the (violent) work of power is being performed when someone racially abuses someone else by calling them, for instance, a 'nigger' or a 'paki' even when the person who utters these words is not actually powerful – if they are, say, a member of a white, working class which is, in many other ways, disempowered. According to Judith Butler in *Excitable Speech*, words acquire their offensive and abusive weight through the iterative performances of power that cumulatively deploy them as vehicles of that performativity.[47] Wounding words possess the power to hurt precisely because they have a history of violence behind them, both verbal and physical. Most of the time, offence is given or taken in relation to words, phrases, and tropes that have already been used to abuse and subordinate, and are thus part of an established discourse of power. The objection, therefore, to using abusive or offensive language lies not in an objection to the words themselves, nor even to the person uttering them in any given situation, but rather to the re-iteration of a power that has been deployed before, and thus their function in a discourse that is available for any subsequent performance of subordination. Racist discourse, for instance, does not necessarily prove that the person uttering it has somehow disclosed, inadvertently or otherwise, their 'true colours', that 'deep down' s/he is a racist, although this tends to be the focal point of controversies concerning racial abuse, which is based on the premise that words are indeed 'windows into hearts of our fellow human beings', and that there is, indeed, a 'true' self.[48] In typical liberal fashion, this individualizes the problem thereby providing an alibi for the structural inequality that racism articulates. Neither does the persistence of racial invective reveal a 'natural' tendency towards racial antipathy. Rather, I would suggest that the perniciousness of racism lies in the continuing availability and purchase of racial discourse as a means of positioning oneself within established hierarchies of domination over racial others, and the reinforcement of such hierarchies in each successive iterative performance.

This is why offensive speech acts which articulate and thereby reinforce existing histories and hierarchies of domination and subordination carry such force; conversely, 'offensive' speech acts that *resist* established power formations (and thereby display their own power, even if that power is relatively weaker than the established power they challenge) are experienced very differently by those on the receiving end, that is, the powerful. The standard liberal argument for the significance and value of offensiveness as a means of 'speaking truth to power' – of offending the powerful, of attacking entrenched privilege and prevailing inequalities – posits (using a logic of abstract substitutability that pervades liberal discourse as a whole) all articulations of offensiveness as *equivalent*.[49] This is the basis of both the orthodox liberal idea that the best antidote to offensive speech is more speech, and the 'marketplace of outrage' which, like its flipside, the marketplace of ideas, is conceived as a neutral space devoid of power differentials. This evacuation of power relations underlies standard liberal tropes which rationalize the value and necessity of offensiveness as a means of contesting power, but is itself a gesture that masks the dominance of western liberalism within the global economy of power. When Nick Cohen writes that those who find something offensive should just 'learn to live with it', or David Aaronovitch suggests that people 'need to get a thicker skin', what they are in fact doing is performatively displaying that dominance through the very insouciance with which they dismiss power itself.[50] Their apparent equanimity to all forms of offensiveness is a function of their *power* and not necessarily their open-mindedness or tolerance. Western liberals very rarely 'take offence' because a dominant group can easily ignore offensive speech acts directed against it; such acts do not disturb the structural advantage they enjoy. The same was true of the fabled tolerance and openness of Muslim civilizations during the period of Islamic ascendancy and domination.

Moreover, if social hierarchies and prevailing power differentials exist as they do through the cumulative performance of discourses of power, dominant groups can not only ignore offensive speech actions more easily than subordinate groups, they can also *give* offence much more easily too. This is why, for instance, there are so few racially abusive epithets that can be directed against white people, and why they carry so little force – is 'honky' really comparable as a term of abuse to 'nigger'? On the other hand, in English – a language of dominance itself – racially abusive terms pertaining to non-white, non-European peoples come readily to hand, and new ones are easily coined, and they are much more offensive, much more wounding for the very reason that they secrete within them entire histories of subordination. Sexualized slang referring to women and homosexuals operate in much the same way: slag, slut, cunt, queer, fag, etc. Try to think of comparable terms referring to heterosexual men and the poverty of options soon becomes apparent, as does their lack of offensiveness.

In *Excitable Speech*, Butler suggests that precisely because meanings do not inhere in words, because there is a 'gap' between speech and its effects, there is the potential opening for a space of agency that might 'revalue', 'reverse', 'appropriate' or 'resignify' injurious speech through different kinds of performativity, through repetition-with-a-difference.[51] If injurious speech is indeed 'perlocutionary' then it 'works its injurious effect only to the extent that it produces a set of non-necessary effects. Only if other effects may follow from the utterance does appropriating, reversing and, and, recontextualizing such utterances become possible', and she uses the familiar example of the term 'queer' to 'suggest that speech can be "returned" to its speaker in a different form, that it can be cited against its originary purposes, and perform a reversal of effects.'[52] And yet her own argument that the power of such words to hurt derives from the historical weight that such words accrue through repetition and citation would suggest a limit to this kind of politics. Indeed, within the historical frame of previous iterations, each attempt to 'appropriate' or 'resignify' offensive terms is necessarily double-edged, as attempts by African-Africans to redeploy the term 'nigger' and by British South Asians to do likewise with 'paki' have shown: each reinscription is necessarily marked by an iteration of its previous history, which opens the door both to its normalization (that is, its apparent bleaching of its offensive freight) *and* its continued dissemination as a term of abuse – only now dominant groups can argue, as they have, that it would be hypocritical of these groups to still be offended by such words (as they are) since they use it themselves. Indeed, the very fact that African-Americans and British South Asians continue to be offended by these terms is a testament to the fact that the performative politics of reclamation does *not* liberate or even neutralize such terms.

Butler is not unaware of these risks. She recounts a story about the pedagogical difficulties she faced when exploring these issues in a summer school class at the Dartmouth School of Criticism and Theory in 1995, when an unsigned letter was sent to various students reproducing the kinds of hate speech that had been discussed in class. 'This story underscores the limits and risks of resignification as a strategy of opposition', she writes, but this comment is directed at those critical race theorists (Matsuda et al.) and feminists (MacKinnon) who seek legal remedy against hate speech and pornography: 'the censor is compelled to repeat the speech that the censor would prohibit. No matter how vehement the opposition to such speech is, its recirculation inevitably reproduces trauma as well.'[53] Such problems are, however, equally germane to the politics of performativity that she suggests as an alternative. Abigail Levin notes that Butler 'fails to discuss the all-important question of which speakers – and at what times, and under what circumstances – can perform a resignificatory . . . speech act'. She merely argues that such a politics is possible because speech is always 'vulnerable' and never 'sovereign'. Moreover, if 'speech acts still are a function of power', then it cannot be assumed that the power *to* speak is 'available to all' and so 'resignificatory speech acts . . . may reify, rather than question, the very power structure that has oppressed us'.[54]

Indeed, if, as Butler herself suggests in *Gender Trouble*, performativity is a 'dramatic and contingent construction of meaning', then the semantic instability of language means that the politics of performativity is also available to dominant groups and may, in fact, enable the powerful to appropriate the syntax of victimhood and turn advantage into disadvantage by performing their power as powerlessness.[55] This is clearly what has occurred in relation to 'offensiveness', and it more satisfactorily explains the metastasization of 'taking offence' through the body politic than the 'marketplace of outrage'. The cry of 'political correctness gone mad!' or 'health and safety gone mad!' are forms of performativity that re-order power relations by rhetorically positioning dominant groups at a disadvantage in relation to minority ethnic communities and organized labour respectively. Both tropes implicitly accept *some* limits, and thus accept that one cannot say whatever one likes about minority ethnic groups, nor can one reasonably accept no regulation with respect to workplace safety, but these are grudgingly conceded as a consequence of the principle of equality, on the one hand, and an acknowledgment of the duty of care that employers hold with regard to their employees on the other. But the tropes are equally ways of expressing dissatisfaction with the idea of equality or with the idea of employees' rights *without actually saying so*: the euphemistic nature of the performance shields the speaker from charges of hypocrisy.[56] They 'take offence' at a supposed zealousness and excess that is foisted upon them by an apparently powerful, bureaucratized elite on behalf of minorities and 'labour' even though this is nothing more than a figment of their imaginations because, first, they are themselves a part of that elite and, second, the 'authorities' therefore represent their *own* interests far more than those of minorities and the working-classes. The same process is at work in a popular complaint about immigration – 'it's not our country anymore' – which performatively positions a 'white indigenous majority' in a position of structural disadvantage in relation to (racially coded) immigrants whilst masking the structural advantage the 'majority' continues to enjoy.

This kind of performativity seems to have become a distinctive feature of freedom of speech controversies since the 'Rushdie affair'. When commentators and politicians took offence at the public incineration of a single copy of *The Satanic Verses* in Bradford in January 1989, they unhesitatingly conjured the spectre of the Nazis and thereby positioned themselves, as defenders of the novel, in a subordinate relation to the phantasmic power of a totalitarian state – a patently ludicrous and spurious equivalence was therefore established between the power of the Nazi state and that of the largely working-class Muslim protestors who had, up to this point, struggled to make anyone take their grievances seriously. As an act of performative politics, however, this comparison with the Nazis was highly effective, enabling in one symbolic stroke both a display of vulnerability (as we shall see in the next chapter, Appignanesi's trope of 'fragile freedoms' performs the same function, as does Cohen's characterization of liberalism as 'embattled') whilst claiming the moral high ground.

When Rushdie, in his 1990 Herbert Read Memorial Lecture 'Is Nothing Sacred?' conflated the protests against *The Satanic Verses* with 'an attack upon the very ideas of the novel form', and then aligned 'literature' *as such* with a very particular form of it – that is, the kinds of postmodern novel akin to his own novelistic practice – thereby suggesting that *all* literature (indeed, at times he suggests all *art*) *necessarily* contests power and authority and their 'totalized explanation[s] of the world', he obscured the fact that not all art does '[start] from this point', nor does it necessarily stand outside power and contest it; indeed, most, if not all, works of art and literature are complicit with dominant regimes of representation even if some simultaneously contest them. The performative work being done here is to position the author as the object and vicitim of power, as powerless.[57] But he conveniently overlooks the fact that (some) authors, especially highly successful ones in a secular society in which the imaginative author has supplanted and usurped the roles of shaman and priest, are powerful *subjects* able to leverage an enormous quantity of social and cultural capital. Some artists, Rushdie included, therefore have a power *to speak* that is denied others.

Similarly, when Malik, Cohen, Ali, Appignanesi and a host of other liberal writers and intellectuals argue that, as artists and intellectuals, they have 'a duty to offend' because 'The giving of offence is not just inevitable. It may also be important' they do so on the assumption that offensiveness involves the speaking of 'truth' to power and thus an important part of the struggle for liberty. But they overlook the fact that offensiveness is both more effective and, indeed, *possible* when articulated from a position of power, that offensiveness usually shores up the power of the already dominant. Again, the performative work being done is to position 'offensiveness' – and, of course, the 'offenders' i.e. themselves – outside and opposite to power and authority, and by implication in a position of (relative) powerlessness, whilst obscuring the social, cultural and political capital at their disposal.

On the other hand, when the Ayotollah Khomeini took offence at 'western imperialism and arrogance' he too performatively aligned himself with the wretched of the earth, with the poor, humiliated Muslims who had hitherto protested against *The Satanic Verses*, and he too occluded the power at *his* disposal as both a head of state and a spiritual leader, capable of mobilizing the sentiments of hundreds of thousands, if not millions, of persons across the globe, as well as the resources of a nation-state in order to aid and assist extra-judicial murder.

This is where politics and ethics converge, and the particular concerns of this book emerge. To claim one is powerless whilst enjoying the benefits of power is clearly unethical, as is the disavowal of responsibility for the consequences of one's actions. Likewise, to take offence where there are no grounds to do so, to exaggerate the offence caused or the pain felt or to manufacture it for instrumental purposes is not ethical; nor is it ethical to offend the powerless and thereby reinforce their subordination simply because it is possible to do so – that is, simply because one has the power to do so. On the other hand, nor is giving (or indeed taking) offence *necessarily* unethical; indeed, as I will argue in Chapter 7, there are occasions when giving offence can be both politically necessary and effective, and ethical. It depends on the specific performativity of giving (and taking) offence within a specific situation, on the nature of the power relations governing that situation, and the relative power and powerlessness of those giving and taking offence – although, as the above examples demonstrate, a certain vigilance is required when confronting the politics of controversy because performativity, in its very nature, is unstable and indeterminate; seldom can the positions staked out in a politics of controversy be taken at face value.

Insofar as this book is predominantly concerned with the rights and wrongs of performative actions within controversial situations, that is, insofar as it is concerned primarily with ethics, it should be remembered that power nevertheless shapes and determines the possible scope and effectivity of speech acts, and their ethical significance. That is, the ethical and the political are inseparably related. What must never be forgotten is that freedom of speech controversies are invariably *political* and not simply about competing truth-claims. The purpose of arguments which evacuate controversies of their power relations or decontextualize them or reduce them to political instrumentalism – arguments advanced from both liberal and non-liberal (in these instances, Muslim) positions – is to propose the moral rightness of a particular course of action (of the offensive speech act or its interdiction) *irrespective* of the political specificities of each encounter.

Such abstraction is inimical to the arguments put forward throughout this book, not least because I concur with the argument that the *right* to freedom of speech is necessary in order to hold the powerful to account. Within the scope of that right, the question of whether any given performative speech acts are ethically valid requires us to understand where the power lies in any given controversy, for that makes all the difference: freedom of speech is not the same as freedom to speak, and the words and actions of the powerful are not equivalent, either morally or politically, to those of the powerless.[58]

2

What is Freedom of Speech For?

Since *The Satanic Verses* a familiar and now somewhat predictable pattern of events unfolds each time a freedom of speech controversy erupts, which they appear to be doing on a more or less regular basis. First, those who have taken offence will visibly signal their outrage and call for the offending item to be withdrawn/banned/disavowed, call for an apology, and demand the offending parties be disciplined/sacked/prosecuted or otherwise chastised; the offender will either apologize or not, but seldom give ground with respect to the offending item by invoking freedom of speech as a defence; by this time the media and commentariat will be swarming around the incident like flies around a carcass: supporters of the offender(s) will not only invoke the right to freedom of speech but also, for good measure, invoke a right to offend (an entirely fictitious right that is nowhere mentioned in any of the many constitutions, charters and other legal documents where civil, political and human rights have been codified), whilst those speaking for the offended will usually invoke an equally fictitious right not to be offended apparently derived from various other fundamental rights (such as freedom of religion or privacy) that are customarily seen as bulwarks against the unrestricted right to freedom of expression.[1] And there the matter will rest, in an impasse as unbreakable as the opposing parties are implacable. Each episode usually remains unresolved, to everyone's dissatisfaction.

I sketch this somewhat typical scenario not only to highlight the dominant discourse through which freedom of speech controversies are articulated and contested, namely a legalistic discourse of rights, but also the poverty of such a discourse with respect to the end result and also in terms of the substantive content of the arguments put forward on both sides. That poverty is signalled by the invariable escalation of the idea of rights to an extreme position – the ritual invocation of rights that do not formally exist, though demonstrably incoherent, is nevertheless symptomatic of an absolutism with respect to freedom of speech that has gained enormous traction since the murderous absolutism of Ayotollah Khomeini made its decisive intervention over a quarter century ago.

Indeed, the rhetorics of both liberal and Muslim absolutisms display remarkable parallelisms. Whereas Khomeini and other Muslim absolutists fulminate about western arrogance and imperialism, their liberal opponents argue that freedom of speech is the freedom to speak truth to power, to challenge and offend the powerful. Whereas Muslim fanatics harass, intimidate, despise and even on occasion murder those Muslims who disagree with them, and characterize them as not being 'true' Muslims, free speech absolutists accuse fellow liberals (particularly academics) of selling out by accepting certain limits on expression such as laws proscribing incitement of hatred, of freedom of the press, or by advancing arguments that eschew the certainties of liberal universalism in favour of cultural relativism; there is clearly no moral equivalence between the two, but there is a similarity in their structures of thought. Hence the trope of the *trahison des clercs* deployed by both Nick Cohen and Brian Winston in their respective defences of freedom of expression, even though it is a little odd, to say the least, that they should evoke the emotive language of betrayal and appeal to group solidarity against those with whom they disagree whilst at the same time advancing John Stuart Mill's argument for freedom of expression, which insists that it is the best means for enabling a *rational* search for truth through the exchange and disputation of ideas and arguments.[2]

Cohen's rhetorical method is to speak of these treacherous academics and intellectuals as an anonymous collective. He writes, 'They [the treacherous and cowardly so-called liberals] soon found high-minded reasons to avoid it [causing offence], and redefined their failure to take on militant religion as a virtuous act. Their preferred tactic was to extend arguments against racism to cover criticism of religion', without ever identifying who 'they' are.[3] A little later, he arraigns leftist academics for being patronizing purveyors of falsehood, illusion and confusion:

Treating people as equals means treating them as adults who can handle robust argument, not as children who need to be told fairy stories and tucked up in bed. But as the culture wars raged, fairy stories were what the universities delivered. Topics and arguments were ruled off-limits; real and imagined heresies denounced with phlegm-spitting vehemence; and comforting histories promulgated on how black Egypt was responsible for the philosophies of ancient Athens, or how Amazonian tribes were noble savages living in a state of prelapsarian harmony until wicked whitey came along. Islamism came into universities whose academics had the good liberal motive that they should not discriminate against students because of their race or religion, but whose intellectual defences had been weakened by the hysterical attitudes the culture wars fostered . . . Fear caught their tongues, too: the fear of accusations of 'racism', 'neo-conservatism', 'Islamophobia' or 'orientalism'; the fear of having to admit that their vague commitments to anti-imperialist solidarity were feeding reactionary movements; and the fear of violence.[4]

Proceeding by way of smear and innuendo, and through broad generalizations, Cohen thereby spares himself the trouble of actually identifying, analysing and contesting the arguments – again, a position at odds with an espousal of Mill's argument for freedom of speech, which rests on the principle of 'thought and *discussion*'.[5]

Conversely, Cohen's other main rhetorical tactic is to select certain 'honourable' individuals – Salman Rushdie, Ayaan Hirsi Ali, and Paul Moore (a risk manager at a major UK bank) amongst others – who become heroic defenders of 'fragile freedoms', fighting a rearguard action against an amorphous mass of authoritarians and bigots, compromisers, time-servers, yes-men, hypocrites, double-dealing politicians and unthinking hordes.[6] Anyone who demonstrates less than total solidarity with these figures is sharply rebuked, again without much discussion of their actual arguments. The purpose of this tactic is to position liberalism – the pure, unsullied, classical liberalism of Mill as opposed to the modern, compromised version, with its 'contradictions and dark motives' (as if the work of Mill or other 'classical' liberals was never so much as touched by a contradiction or a dark motive) – as a precious but vulnerable beacon of truth ever at risk of becoming engulfed by the darkness of ignorance and barbarism.[7] All in all, Cohen's position is summed up in a stark and absolute opposition: 'all the enemies of liberalism [by which he means *his* kind of liberalism] are essentially the same'.[8] Needless to say, this mirrors the rhetoric of Islamists almost precisely.

As for Brian Winston's tome, which is more measured and 'academic', the tactics deployed are correspondingly more sedate and less egregious. Nevertheless, the accusations of treason and the arguments against it take up a mere seventeen pages of a 414 page book; this, in itself, is not necessarily a problem, but it is a major problem when those pages engage so superficially with the arguments, for and against both Millian and non-consequentialist arguments for freedom of expression that have exercised philosophers and legal theorists for well over a century. Of this large and still developing literature, which has expanded in scope, sophistication and ambition over the last half-century in particular (no doubt spurred by the 'culture wars' and the emergence of multiculturalism) Winston has very little to say: he rebukes Stanley Fish's brief contribution to the debate surrounding *The Jewel of the Medina*, but does not even cite his more formidable arguments in *There's No Such Thing as Free Speech and it's a Good Thing Too* never mind the work of thinkers such as Alan Haworth, Simon Lee, Susan Mendus, Bhikhu Parekh, Peter Jones, Charles Taylor, Abigail Levin, Jonathan Chaplin, Kevin Saunders, Catherine MacKinnon, Andrea Dworkin, Mari Matsuda, Richard Delgado and Jean Stefancic, all of whom have disputed, to varying degrees, the philosophical arguments in favour of freedom of speech put forward by Mill, Rawls, Dworkin, Nozick, Raz, Kymlicka and others. All of them honour the basic principle of actually examining the arguments in detail whilst developing their counter-arguments. Winston, however, simply focuses on a minor work by Tom Stoppard (a noted playwright but not a major contributor to the philosophy of freedom of speech), and conducts a very general critique of anti-Enlightenment arguments, such as those put forward by John Gray. This, he writes, can be done 'in short order because the *trahison* yields . . . no first principle to refute'.[9] The distinguished roster of thinkers cited above must feel suitably humbled by this curt dismissal of their efforts, but the claim that their formidable arguments can be disposed of 'in short order' is, in fact, nothing more than an effort to mask Winston's *lack* of argument. Winston's broader position that these critiques '[give] comfort to the enemies of free expression' demonstrates this perfectly well: in the context of Mill's defence of freedom of expression, whether arguments give 'comfort' to one's opponents is immaterial. What matters are the arguments themselves, and the coherence and competence of the counter-arguments.[10]

One particular aspect of both liberal and Muslim absolutisms strikingly reveals the isomorphism of their respective structures of thought. Both use the 'slippery slope' argument: liberals, by stating that any restriction on freedom of expression is the first step in a slide toward totalitarianism or authoritarianism; Islamists, by suggesting that even the most innocuous of offences is the gratuitous first step in a slide towards the extirpation of Islam (at the hands of western imperialism, world-wide Jewish conspiracy, or both).[11] Both draw a line and argue that to go any further is inevitably to go all the way: both argue that their respective 'freedoms' are indivisible. Moreover, so embedded is the 'slippery slope' trope in these discourses that it often appears even when not directly invoked. Thus, for instance, when Nick Cohen asserts that 'we are relearning a lesson we ought never to have forgotten: you cannot be a little bit free', he is in fact suggesting that freedom is absolute and indivisible; anything less, and it is nothing, which brings to mind Rushdie's hyberbolic statement in his essay 'One Thousand Days in a Balloon' that, 'Free speech is the whole thing, the whole ball game. Free speech is life itself'.[12] In so doing, Cohen implicitly draws a line at the top of the slippery slope, although in this case it is more of a sheer cliff than a slope. The trope also appears more obtrusively, but still surreptitiously, in statements such as, 'The resulting *slide* into relativism', or 'When the fashion in Manhattan, London and Paris is to *slide* away from universal principles, those leading the *slither* can never admit that modern liberalism contains contradictions and dark motives', where the imagery does the rhetorical work in *lieu* of an argument (the latter is particularly potent, with its insinuation of a sinister betrayal).[13]

In fact, the slippery slope argument is itself based upon a logic that is embedded even more deeply within absolutist discourse, both liberal and

Muslim. This is the logic of substitutability, whereby arguments germane to one context can be applied to others, thereby extending the reach of these arguments across *all* contexts to the point where context itself becomes immaterial. In liberal discourse, it reaches back towards Mill's 'classic defence' of freedom of expression, which means that it enjoys something of a foundational status. Alan Haworth notes that 'Mill's "prioritisation of thought and discussion" as the model for free expression in general amounts to the presupposition that the case for that way of collectively striving for truth and the case for other freedoms such as absolute "liberty of expressing and publishing opinions" *are equivalent*'.[14] This leads to the problems he identifies with Mill's (in)famous example of the 'corn dealer' as a legitimate limit on freedom of expression: 'instead of recognising . . . the possibility of there being a diversity of cases, some of which match neither a "thought and discussion" model nor that exemplified by the "corn dealer" case too closely, he is forced to treat the latter as an extreme case; that is, as an exception to a general rule which would normally apply'.[15] In other words, by substituting the 'seminar room' model across all contexts bar that of direct incitement, Mill is able to extend the argument for unrestricted freedom of expression to the 'outer limit', where there is 'clear and present danger': someone shouting 'Fire!' in a crowded movie theatre, to take only the most popular example; or national security, and so on. However, Mill's one-size-fits-all model flattens out the diversity of contexts in which freedom of speech must be considered, separately and distinctly.

This is echoed in contemporary absolutist discourse. Simon Lee has observed that 'one of the weaknesses of free speech rhetoric has been the tendency to stretch support all the way from political speech to pornographic expression, under the mistaken belief that arguments for one must apply to the other'.[16] But all such arguments rest on the idea that context is meaningless, and that any argument that is context-specific is worthless because it is apparently ad hoc and unprincipled. However, principled arguments usually involve philosophical abstractions and are not necessarily good guides for dealing with the world and its convoluted entanglements and sometimes intractable difficulties. As Nick Cohen writes towards the end of his book:

> In everyday life we accept different standards in differing circumstances. We have a right to swear when we are at home or with friends. If an employer were to dismiss us for swearing at customers or clients, we would not say that he or she was infringing our rights to freedom of speech . . . Similarly, society is entitled to say that there should be a corner in the marketplace of ideas where journalists and their managers and owners must respect notions of fairness and balance.[17]

This appears to contradict the absolutist position that he advances throughout the rest of his book, but, in fact, the phrase 'a corner of the marketplace' indicates that he is following Mill's corn-dealer example quite closely, assigning importance to context only in special, reserved or extreme cases. It is a small concession but is telling nonetheless because, as Simon Lee points out:

> The fact is that we are never at the top of the slope; we are always holding a position somewhere on the hill. It is extremely misleading to pretend that we are at the top of the hill when there are dozens of laws which already (usually with justification in terms of some other cost) restrict free speech. There are laws on patents, copyright, contracts in restraint of trade, protection of trade secrets, intellectual property, misleading or dangerous advertisements and consumer protection, libel, slander, treason, conspiracy to commit crimes, official secrets, breach of confidence and obscenity, to name a few. In many of these areas the law has been stable for many years or sometimes in retreat back up the hill. There is no automatic slide to more censorship.[18]

In other words, in the real world *there are no slippery slopes* (other than those covered in ice).[19] Rather, we must – and always do – draw lines appropriate to the context and situation in which we find ourselves. This is why slippery slope arguments are unconvincing even though they are assumed to be some kind of trump card.

I shall return to this question of context and propriety in due course, but for now I want to examine the logic of substitutability with respect to the invocations of fictitious rights such as the 'right to offend'. If one extrapolates a general 'right' to offend from a specific context in which offensiveness is, in fact, both appropriate and effective then the context is, in effect, irrelevant. Therefore, if in that instance the suppression of the offensive speech constitutes an unwarranted attack on freedom of expression, then the logic of substitutability extends this to other contexts and thence across the board. It follows that if it is right to offend in that instance, then it is right to offend in other – theoretically, all – instances. It is here that we can see the full significance of the remark by Saul Bellow, which both Cohen and Rushdie cite with approval, that 'Everybody knows there is no fineness or accuracy of suppression; if you hold down one thing, you hold down the adjoining'.[20] But 'offensiveness' is not a *species* of 'speech' which 'adjoins' other forms of speech; offensive speech, like all speech, consists of words, which are arbitrary signs that produce meaning only within the framework of an entire sign-system. Meaning does not inhere in signs, but is *produced* by each sign's differential relationship to all other signs in the system. Likewise, offensiveness cannot be said to inhere in any given utterance. Rather, it is, as I have argued in the previous chapter, an *effect* of a particular kind of verbal *performance*, one that is entirely context-specific because it is a *manner* or *way* of speaking that elicits its effect only in relation to specific addressees. It is adverbial, as it were, before it is adjectival. Instead of using the term 'offensive speech', it would be more correct to say that someone is speaking 'offensively', which is grammatically equivalent to someone speaking 'softly' or 'stupidly' or 'boringly' etc. Since not all of those who hear the offensive speech will necessarily find it offensive – just as not everyone will find someone's words 'boring' or 'stupid' – the offensiveness is produced not by the act of speaking certain inherently 'offensive' words, but in the *relationship* between the speaker, the manner of the speech, the recipient, and the power relations that govern this relationship within the context of a given *situation*. But here is the rub: to invoke a 'right' is to invoke the *law*. And if the defence of offensiveness is grounded in a 'right' then the law is extended into areas that the liberal would not want the law to reach: to put it plainly, a 'right' to speak offensively is as meaningful (that is, meaningless) as a 'right' to speak 'stupidly' or 'boringly' or any other such style of speaking. Insofar as everyone has the 'right' to speak offensively, it is because that right is predicated on the right to *speak* freely. This encompasses the right to speak offensively and all other ways of speaking within the limits set by the various laws of any given society.

Claiming a right to offend is therefore a redundant gesture, but its significance lies in the way it *performatively* signifies adherence to a particular ideological position within the discourse of freedom of speech. First articulated in its current form by Salman Rushdie and his supporters during the controversy surrounding *The Satanic Verses*, this discourse is not without its antecedents. Indeed, one of its conspicuous features is the way in which it takes several well-established but distinct – and not necessarily reconcilable – threads of mainstream liberalism and weaves them into a formidably powerful rhetorical tapestry that, at first glance, certainly appears cogent and coherent.

Central to this discourse is the idea that freedom of expression is, as Kenan Malik puts it, 'not just an important liberty, but the very foundation of liberty'.[21] It can be found, for instance, in George Orwell's *Nineteen Eighty-Four*. The final epigram of Chapter 7, an entry in Winston Smith's diary, reads: 'Freedom is the freedom to say two plus two equals four. If this is granted, *all else follows*'.[22] Orwell's vivid conceptualization of a totalitarianism so extreme and all-pervading that it controls not only expression but also penetrates subjective thought has profoundly shaped the post-war liberal imagination, and primed it towards a nightmare scenario in which the very basis of liberalism, the autonomous and sovereign individual, is fundamentally compromised. Given early liberalism's primary concern with establishing the grounds for liberty in the teeth of an over-mighty state, Orwell's vision of a state so mighty that it is capable of manipulating reality challenges the notion of an objectivity on which the idea of individuality rests; for, if the fundamental unit of liberalism is the sovereign individual, how else might the relationships between these individuals who, in Conrad's words 'live as we dream, alone' be mediated? How might a collection of such individuals, together constituting a society, arbitrate between the subjective vision of each of its members? If, as commonly assumed, this is done through 'culture' and the 'shared' values it articulates, it is nevertheless fundamentally important that culture corresponds to an 'objective' reality which might anchor such shared meanings and values to a neutral ground that exceeds the subjectivity of each individual – hence the emergence of empiricism and realism as modes of thought and representation that accompanied the ascendancy of liberalism and the sovereign individual.

Orwell perceives totalitarianism to be a threat to this nexus, and this compels him to assert the primacy of thought and conscience, and the freedom to express thought, as a first principle. His vision of an absolute power determines his understanding, present in liberal thought from its outset, that freedom is freedom *from* power. This in turn rests on an understanding of the individual as a sovereign agent who is the sole author of thoughts that originate within him/herself, and for whom expression is an extension of that subjective self into the world of objects. It follows, then, that any restriction on expression is a limit on the sovereignty of the self.

This line of thought was established by Descartes, but its most significant iteration can be found in John Stuart Mill's *On Liberty* (1859), a text that, along with Milton's *Areopagitica* (1644) and Locke's *Letter on Toleration* (1689), is one of the principal reference points for modern liberalism, especially the contemporary absolutist variant. Mill grounds his 'classic defence of freedom of speech' on the 'freedom of thought and discussion'. As a utilitarian, Mill argues that there is an overall benefit to society if each individual is at liberty to develop him or herself according to their own capacities. 'Once liberty is protected', writes Abigail Levin, 'individuality flourishes; once individuality flourishes, diversity arises; and once diversity arises, we can begin to assess competing visions of the good'.[23] This, of course, 'presupposes the notions of liberty of thought and conscience, since it is only if we have the ability to think for ourselves that we may then be able to choose "our own good in our own way,". . . So, for Mill, the idea of liberty of thought is a crucial precondition for any other liberty'.[24]

This, in turn, relates to Mill's argument for freedom of expression. For Mill, 'freedom of expression follows from freedom of thought. This move from liberty of thought to liberty of expression is a very significant one, in that it goes from the wholly individual realm, where others are not affected, to the social one, where they may be'.[25] Freedom of expression is therefore subject to Mill's harm principle (which, as we have seen, has its weaknesses) in a way that freedom of thought is not, and because of this, it must be justified in terms of its contribution to the overall good – happiness, well-being, progress, etc. – towards which liberty as a whole is oriented. This leads Mill to argue that freedom of expression – conceived as 'freedom of thought and discussion' – is valuable because it enables society to progress through the increase of knowledge and truth. In other words, the consequence of this freedom is that knowledge and truth will increase, false ideas will be weeded out, and this will in turn enable individuals (and therefore society) to develop a proper apprehension of themselves and their circumstances, and to conceive their own way of living a 'good' life accordingly.

This argument has become something of a shibboleth in contemporary liberal discourse – at least of the popularizing variety – to the point where it is used as a trump card in much the same way as the 'slippery slope'. It is, nevertheless, beset by several weaknesses. Foremost among them is the assumption that freedom of expression necessarily delivers something that might be called 'truth'. One does not have to be a Nieztschean or post-modern sceptic to understand that this assumption is flawed. This is because the 'freedom of thought and discussion' on which Mill rests his argument is, in Alan Haworth's words, 'the freedom of the seminar room' – an idealized notion of knowledge and the exchange of ideas in which 'a group of earnest and rational individuals is assembled. Their purpose is to find truth. Members of the group take turns to advance propositions – opinions – for consideration by the others. Arguments for and against are elaborated and tried out in the hope that some advance to the truth will be made. All opinions, even those which are on first appearance quite wild and extravagant, are treated with equal seriousness'.[26] As has been suggested, Mill derives from this an 'equivalent' argument for a number of related but distinct freedoms: 'liberty of expressing and publishing opinions', freedom of the press, from censorship, to hold religious beliefs, to engage in adversarial politics and so on. The assumption seems to be that either 'arguments sufficient to demonstrate the virtues of thought and discussion apply equally well to the other activities he lists or, conversely, he is assuming that those activities are themselves cases of thought and discussion'.[27] But, writes Haworth, 'the tabloid press regularly demonstrates that the liberty of a newspaper to publish as it likes and the liberty to contribute to a process of thought and discussion need hardly overlap', and, '[i]t isn't always realistic to think of what goes on in a governing assembly, such as the British parliament, as a disinterested exercise in the pursuit of truth'.[28] He goes on to cite three instances in the mid-1990s where controversies over freedom of expression had very little, if anything, to do with 'thought and discussion': the appointment of a lecturer holding anti-semitic views, another holding racist views, and a furore surrounding an election poster representing a politician (Tony Blair, as it happens) with 'demon eyes'. This is exactly what Susan Mendus, in the context of the Rushdie controversy, refers to when she writes that 'it is far from clear that the cases in which free speech is most problematic are cases in which truth is at issue'.[29]

So, it is not at all clear that 'all else follows' from the freedom to 'think' as Orwell and Mill would have it. Indeed, it is far from clear that there is any such thing as freedom of thought. An advertisement break during a television programme, a thumb through any magazine or newspaper, or a walk down the aisles of a supermarket reveals what every capitalist instinctively knows and what many left-wing thinkers have spent entire careers demonstrating, namely that the rational autonomous and sovereign individual that is the Subject of the juridico-political and philosophical discourses of modern liberal democracy is nothing but a sort of grammatical fiction around which to gather and organize all sorts of ideas about power, property, agency, responsibility and choice. Liberal and neo-liberal economists may have built, around this fiction, the still greater fiction of rational choice theory and the efficient markets hypothesis, but the great crash of 2008 ought to have put paid to that fancy (the fact that it has not suggests that the 'market place of ideas' is not the great conduit of truth it is made out to be). So should recent developments in neuroscience: whilst, on the one hand, neuroscientists are demonstrating that 'we are "predictably irrational," with our minds playing tricks on us all the time', such that we are, in effect, 'slaves to our brain chemistry more often and in more ways than we might like to admit', so too do companies 'not care whether we buy their product after making a cool, rational decision, balancing all the pros and cons. In fact they would prefer that we act out of compulsion, habit, or craving'.[30]

All of this suggests that the revered 'marketplace of ideas' is erected on shaky and unstable foundations. And yet most liberals – not just absolutists – duly trot this out as yet another of their sanctified shibboleths. It is another of the many abstractions on which liberalism rests its case. Stanley Fish has noted the curious fact that 'Liberal thought begins in the acknowledgment that faction, difference, and point of view are irreducible; but the liberal strategy is to devise (or attempt to devise) procedural mechanisms that are neutral with respect to point of view and therefore can serve to frame partisan debates in a nonpartisan manner'.[31] Alongside the notion of 'objectivity', this emphasis on procedure enables liberalism to bind its fundamental units – sovereign individuals – into some form of overall coherence, and provides a means of arbitrating between them. The value of the marketplace of ideas is, therefore, 'to regulate in a purely formal way the contest between conflicting agendas', and as such provide a means by which free 'thought and discussion' or expression thereof can lead to an increase in the number of propositions and opinions known to be true. Well, that is the theory; in reality, 'the marketplace has to be set up – its form does not exist in nature – and since the way in which it is to be set up will often be a matter of dispute, decisions about the very shape of the marketplace will involve just the ideological considerations it is meant to hold at bay'.[32] In other words, far from being a neutral and purely formal forum, both the establishment and the functioning of actually existing marketplaces of ideas – as with other markets – are a consequence and function of power. To mix metaphors somewhat, they are not 'open houses' into which anyone with an idea in their heads might enter, nor are they 'level playing fields' which treat all expressions as equal, nor are they theatres which allow everyone a platform. They are shot through with exclusions, unacknowledged hierarchies, and unspoken rules and assumptions, such that freedom *of* speech and freedom *to* speak cannot be thought of as synonymous; they are very often in tension if not in outright conflict.

Indeed, one of the most powerful arguments put forward by feminists and critical race theorists in the United States in favour of removing First Amendment protections for pornography and hate speech is that these forms of discourse not only subordinate their objects (women and ethnic and racial minorities) but silence them as well; that is, the freedom of pornographers and racists to express themselves violates the right to freedom of speech of women and ethnic minorities. This is because racist speech and pornography 'communicate ideas of the inferior moral worth of their targets', which in turn produces a cultural environment in which these persons are indeed deemed to be inferior.[33] As Catherine MacKinnon puts it:

> In the context of social inequality, so-called speech can be an exercise of power which constructs the social reality in which people live . . . Together with all its material supports, authoritatively *saying* that someone is inferior is largely how structures of status and differential treatment are demarcated and actualized. Words and images are how people are placed in hierarchies, how social stratification is made to seem inevitable and right, how feelings of inferiority and superiority are engendered, and how indifference to violence against those on the bottom is rationalized and normalized.[34]

The discrepancy in power relations which this process both produces and upholds means that those deemed inferior in the culture at large – even if they are not formally or officially subordinated, as in apartheid South Africa or pre-Civil Rights America – will not have the same opportunity to access or even enter the marketplace of ideas, and were they to be able to do so, their arguments would not be taken as seriously, or carry as much weight, as those who are deemed superior to them. As such, the 'mere granting of a formal right' – that is, equality before the law – does not in itself deliver true liberty or equality.[35]

Moreover, if this is the case, then one of the central arguments for unrestricted freedom of expression is also undermined. This is the view that the best antidote to hurtful or offensive speech is more speech. In fact, this is so central to nearly all forms of liberal discourse, absolutist or otherwise, that it really must be classified as a cliché.[36] As Stanley Fish observes, the argument 'at once acknowledges the reality of speech-related harms and trivializes them by suggesting that they are *surface* injuries that any large-minded ("liberated and humane") person should be able to bear. The possibility that speech-related injuries may be grievous and *deeply* wounding is carefully kept out of sight'.[37] The 'rebuttal' argument is, however, weakened by a number of factors. First, as we have seen, if those who have been the victims of obnoxious speech are in a subordinate position (and, as we have seen in Chapter 1, this is almost always likely to be the case if wounding words are actually wounding) then their ability to exercise their right to rebuttal will be compromised, if indeed, they are able to exercise it at all; secondly, the argument 'would only make sense if the effects of speech could be canceled out by additional speech, only if the pain and humiliation caused by racial or religious epithets could be ameliorated by saying something like "So's your old man"'. But, as Fish rightly notes, 'expression is more than a matter of proffering and receiving propositions . . . words do work in the world of a kind that cannot be confined to a purely cognitive realm of "mere" ideas'.[38] Thirdly, the critical race theorist Charles R. Lawrence III has argued that 'Assaultive racist speech functions as a preemptive strike. The racial invective is experienced as a blow, not a proffered idea, and once the blow is struck, it is unlikely that dialogue will follow'.[39] Actually, an idea *is* proffered, the idea that the victim of the insult is an inferior being and is thus worthy of contempt. But this not an idea that can be argued with or refuted because 'the perpetrator's intention is not to discover truth or initiate dialogue, but to injure the victim'.[40] All of this underscores the Cartesian philosophical idealism that lies at the core of liberal thought, behind which, suggests Fish, 'lies a vision of human life as something lived largely in the head'.[41] As such, its various abstractions are incapable of dealing with the world as it is, with the effects of power, with the consequences of words.[42]

Although many if not most liberals acknowledge that actually existing marketplaces of ideas do not work as they are meant to in theory – how could they not? – they usually argue that this is because of the many unnecessary restrictions that exist in law on freedom of expression (although they will usually be loath to argue that copyright laws, for instance, should be revoked). But these are merely the outward and formal restrictions instituted as a result of conscious thought and deliberation by governing assemblies and political authorities. By far the most effective restrictions are those imposed invisibly and silently by dominant and hegemonic ideologies, which inscribe limits on what is imaginable, thinkable, sayable without so much as the tiniest of genuflections towards the law. Censorship, for example, is criticized by liberals on the basis of it being 'an act of external interference with the internally generated communicative, expressive, artistic, or informational preferences' of a sovereign individual.[43] But if that sovereignty is an illusion, if the individual subject is not autonomous but *produced*, at least partly, as an effect of a power that is external to the subject itself, then censorship becomes a far more complex matter, to the point where a critic like Judith Butler feels the need to use the term *foreclosure* because it is by no means clear when it involves 'external interference' or is simply part of the 'internal' constitution of the individual self.[44] To use the language of liberal philosophers, there is often no clear distinction between the frustration and formation of one's preferences by an external force. If this is the case, then 'censorship is occurring both necessarily and prior to the speaker's formulation of the intent to speak', which means that the classical liberal idea that the state should be a 'neutral facilitator' of the marketplace of ideas is impossible; moreover, the marketplace itself cannot be a neutral arena.[45] The free play of ideas, then, is a mirage. In fact, it is worse than that; the 'neutrality' of the marketplace of ideas, and the formalist abstractions of liberal thought more generally, serve to mask the power relations that operate within society, and which, within western liberal democracies at least, have ensured that liberalism's own pre-eminence remains obscured. Liberal arguments for 'neutrality' or 'equality' in the marketplace of ideas have a hollow ring about them because they are far from disinterested.

Despite these many weaknesses in the 'classical' Millian defence of free expression, contemporary free speech absolutists (and more temperate liberals) seem to think that merely rehearsing Mill's arguments is enough to vouchsafe their own; ironically, Mill's own cautionary advice against adopting ideas out of habit and custom so that they become 'dead dogma' instead of 'living truth' has been ignored by many of those who have followed in his wake.[46] But alongside arguments derived from Mill, contemporary free speech absolutism also deploys arguments from other strands of liberal thought that were conceptualized precisely in order to address the weaknesses in Mill's thought, and even to contest them at a fundamental level. Foremost among these is that strand of liberal political philosophy known as 'contractualism', which tries to account for the existence of moral rights in terms of a foundational 'social contract' that binds together individuals into social relations involving reciprocal rights and obligations.[47] The social contract is said to be an extrapolation from 'nature' and 'natural law', or is established at a foundational moment in the history of a given society, a theoretical fiction to which the general assemblies of 'the people' in post-revolutionary United States and France approximate; it emerges from the deliberations and decisions of these 'conventions' as embodied in the constitutions that are issued thereof. Thus, when liberal arguments for free speech reference 'natural law' – as Brian Winston does in his book *A Right to Offend*: 'Inalienable rights, though, are generally as much the work of humanity as they are a reflection of divine authority. The ancient *jus natural*/natural law was legitimated by its universality and not its divine origin'[48] – or whenever reference is made to the American Constitution, the Founding Fathers, and the First Amendment – as Winston does only a few lines later, and as Cohen and Malik do frequently – what is being signalled is the idea that the 'right' to freedom of expression is grounded in the 'social contract'.

According to Alan Haworth, 'There is no getting away from the fact that Mill's argument is consequentialist in the sense that it purports to establish that the toleration and protection of the liberty of thought and discussion has a certain good *consequence*. That consequence is a likely increase in the number of propositions known to be true'.[49] If any 'viable' consequential-ism must 'hold at least one thing . . . to be good, not for its consequences, but "in itself" or "for its own sake"', then it is equally clear that this must be something other than the value that facilitates it; the 'goal' of liberty, for example, is not liberty itself but, say, 'equality' or 'social justice' etc.[50] For Mill the utilitarian, it is 'happiness' and 'progress'. But if this is the case, then 'rights' are instrumental not fundamental and, as a result, they are con-tingent upon their serving the higher good for which they are established. Contractualism, on the other hand, seeks to establish 'rights' as fundamen-tal for it 'was felt that consequentialist ethical positions, such as utilitarian-ism, cannot account for rights, and that they thereby violate the Kantian injunction to treat others as "ends in themselves" and never as means'.[51]

For John Locke, this means rights are 'natural' because they are 'rooted – like bodily organs – in the individual person'.[52] The 'social contract' insti-tutes these natural rights at some originary moment when the 'state of nature' becomes established as a social order (it seems Locke believed that this moment was a real historical moment).[53] But, argues Haworth, 'there is at least one alternative way to represent the relationship between persons and their rights. This also respects the Kantian injunction, but it places the necessity for coexistence and cooperation centre-stage and represents the exercise of rights and duties as a function of that necessity'.[54] This is the position adopted by John Rawls, whose seminal *A Theory of Justice* posited the establishment of the social contract not in some mythical transition from a state of nature to the social contract, but in the outcome of a hypo-thetical convention of society's representatives, 'negotiators who participate *on an equal footing* and reach agreements which define rights and duties for all'.[55] Among the fundamental rights which Rawls believes such an assembly would choose is the right to freedom of expression, in a form not dissimilar to that extant in the First Amendment of the US Constitution. It is not surprising, therefore, that contemporary free speech absolutists are attracted to contractualism for it apparently grounds the right to freedom of expression in nothing other than itself, the 'rational' outcome of a process of deliberation that any rights based society which valued the liberty and autonomy of the individual would choose, thereby making it 'inalienable' and a 'good-in-itself'.

And yet it is clear that contractualism suffers from the same abstract ideal-ism as Mill's arguments. The originary moment of the social contract is in fact nothing more than a 'logical construct' and Rawls's 'rational choosers' are 'hypothetical, timeless, abstract, rational men' stripped of anything that might impede a purely rational, formal and disinterested deliberation;[56] the 'veil of ignorance' behind which they must operate is, of course, nothing more than a logical fiction which enables Rawls to pursue a strictly logical argument; and the assumption that as negotiators they participate 'on an equal footing' exhibits once again the liberal inability to account for *power*. Indeed, the purpose of stripping down the 'rational choosers' to a disembodied Cartesian *cogito* is to dissolve anything that might create an imbalance in that equality. The point is not merely that this could never happen in practice, leading to a divergence between the theory's claims and its adequacy as an explanation of reality; rather, the point is to show how even in the most sophisticated of liberal theories, social power is set aside in favour of abstractions like 'neutrality' that, in reality, serve to reinforce the power of the already powerful.

Moreover, a further weakness of contractualism in relation to freedom of expression in particular is that its non-consequentialism invariably slips back into consequentialism. This is because any absolutely absolute right to freedom of speech is untenable. There is always a limit, not least because of other rights, some of which are also 'fundamental', and which are in tension, if not conflict, with the right to freedom of expression. If the violation of other rights is deemed to be unacceptable, then this in itself is the 'greater good' upon which the right to expressive liberty is contingent. Mill's 'harm principle', which most non-consequentialist arguments would also accept (in the form of 'clear and present danger'), is another way in which consequentalism returns through the back door, as it were, since such harms would violate other, fundamental rights such as the right to life and security of person. When Cohen writes, 'For all my liberalism, I cannot think of one honourable reason why governments should not be allowed to keep information secret that might be used by the Taliban to compile a death list', it is presumably because this exception serves the greater good of national security as well as the personal security of several individuals.[57]

It appears that the non-consequentialist arguments for the right to freedom of expression advanced by contractualism have their antecedents in the related but distinct concept of toleration.[58] Locke is clearly a key figure here insofar as he articulated both a contractual theory of rights and advocated toleration in his *A Letter Concerning Toleration*, but perhaps the more decisive convergence can be found in the First Amendment of the Constitution of the United States, 'Congress shall make no law respecting an establishment of religion, or prohibiting the free exercise thereof; or abridging the freedom of speech, or of the press'. Unsurprisingly, current free speech absolutists draw on this convergence to argue that freedom of religion is grounded in freedom of expression, 'Religious freedom – including freedom from religion – requires freedom of speech', which is consistent with their understanding of freedom of expression being the foundational liberty;[59] that is, they suggest that article 18 of the Universal Declaration of Human Rights (guaranteeing freedom of religion) is derived from (and therefore subordinate to) article 19 (freedom of expression) on the basis that if one person's divine truth is another's heresy, then the profession of all religious truths in the public sphere can only be guaranteed if each religion is guaranteed the right to freely express it.[60] Even though the First Amendment does not suggest that the one is consequent upon the other, this seems like a not unreasonable conclusion to draw. On the other hand, as Martha Nussbaum's recent discussion of the evolution of freedom of religion jurisprudence suggests, given the religious proclivities of the early American colonists (most of whom were fleeing religious persecution), it seems more plausible to suggest that freedom of speech emerged out of the need and desire for freedom of religion – and this is indeed the order in which the First Amendment frames it. From this perspective, the relation between the two liberties is very different even though the logic is the same: rather than being consequent upon and therefore subordinate to freedom of expression, religious freedom is a corollary and equal liberty.

Either way, the relationship between the two liberties is grounded on the idea of toleration. But there are three specific objections to be made about the liberal concept of toleration in relation to freedom of expression. First, Locke's conceptualization of toleration is by no means the same thing as later, secularized liberals take it to be. In particular, Locke is making his argument within the context of addressing schisms and heresies within a specifically Christian context. He assumes 'the existence of an underlying consensus between diverse Christian factions. "Christian brethren" are, as Locke goes on to say, "all agreed in the substantial and truly fundamental part of religion". So far as Locke is concerned, it seems that toleration is possible only where there is consensus'.[61] That is, there is an underlying vision of the 'good' which justifies toleration of different beliefs. It is by no means self-evident that this concept of toleration can be easily translated into either a secular context, or a multicultural, multi-religious context where what is at stake is not just a variety of conceptions of a commonly perceived and understood 'good', but rather the fundamental nature of what constitutes the common 'good' in the first place.

Secondly, it appears that for Locke '[t]he virtue of toleration is, thus, the virtue of minding your own business; of rubbing along with your neighbours, of keeping yourself to yourself and your nose out of their affairs'.[62] But this does not support an argument for freedom of speech, especially not an absolutist position. For Cohen, Malik, Winston, et al. the value of free speech is the exact opposite – it is to have the right to criticize others, to *not* mind one's own business. In the context of freedom of expression, then, criticism of others is not toleration but its opposite, a form of intolerance (which should be distinguished from the kind of intolerance that imposes itself on others, that is, intolerance as coercion). Toleration and freedom of expression are therefore at odds with each other, and it would be difficult to argue that the latter should be rooted in the former.

In any case, the idea of toleration as put forward by Locke is consistent with the idea of a privatized religion being the 'regulative principle' that arbitrates 'different conceptions of the good' (any such principle is, of course, an example of the proceduralism so central to liberal thought), which in turn means accepting the fundamental premises of the liberal conception of religion. This regulative principle is therefore decidedly not neutral, but rather privileges *one* conception of religion, one culture, above all others. And if this is what governs the public sphere (because the public/ private distinction means that alternative, non-privatized conceptions of the good must be confined to the private sphere), then it follows that liberal culture enjoys a foundational advantage – all *public* discussions within the realm of free speech must be conducted under its aegis. Liberal arguments for toleration, then, mask a far from tolerant will to power and dominance; moreover, if the price of participation in the public sphere is the privatiza-tion of one's beliefs, and if such beliefs require their profession in public, then those religious persons who do not subscribe to a liberal orthodoxy on permissible religiosity find themselves either excluded from the marketplace of ideas or suffer a profound disjunction of their public and private selves.

The third and final objection is that the argument for freedom of religion being contingent upon freedom of expression only works if it is imagined that everyone can go around blaspheming against everyone else's most fun-damental beliefs *without any consequences* – if, that is, everyone just shrugs their shoulders and minds their own business. If they did *not* just shrug their shoulders, and instead met blasphemous speech with some of their own, the assumption still remains that there are no consequences to speaking as such, that the speech merely runs, like the proverbial water, off the believer's back. There is, perhaps, no use in objecting to the elegant symmetry of this non-consequential line of thought by pointing out that in the real world this is not likely to happen.

It may well be that free speech absolutists draw on non-consequentialist arguments and tropes whilst simultaneously adhering to Mill's consequen-talism because their opponents in recent controversies, especially Muslims but also feminists and critical race theorists, deploy consequentialist argu-ments to argue for *restrictions* on the freedom of expression. Talal Asad has drawn attention to the contrast between the Christian emphasis on being a witness to the truth (of the Gospel) that will set one free (John 8:32), with the Islamic tradition in which 'what matters is the Muslim's social practices . . . not that person's internal thoughts. In contrast, the Christian tradition allows that thoughts can commit the sin of blasphemy and should therefore be subject to discipline'.[63] The Muslim concern, therefore, is not with belief per se but the social consequences of any given act.[64] The same position is held by feminists and anti-racist campaigners and critical race theorists: the problem is not the expression of a belief but the *consequences* of its expression. What is at stake, then, is not the notion of freedom itself, or even of rights to freedom, but the acceptable consequences of freedom. The point is that whereas consequentialist arguments *for* freedom of expression emphasize, like Mill, its *positive* consequences, others emphasize the *negative* consequences. In this context, one can begin to see the appeal of non-consequentialism for any absolutist discourse on free speech.

One can also begin to see the influence, too, of First Amendment jurisprudence as it has evolved in the twentieth century, for this is the only jurisprudence in the world that *institutes* the principles of contemporary liberal absolutism. Looking enviously over the Atlantic, writers such as Nick Cohen and Kenan Malik – both of whom argue for the scrapping of incitement to hatred laws (on all grounds: race, religion, gender, sexuality, disability), dismiss feminist arguments about the degrading effect on women of pornography, reject any proscriptions on Holocaust denial or denial of the Armenian genocide, and support limits only when there is 'clear and present danger' of a 'crime' resulting in physical (presumably, bodily) harm – can see in the US judicial system a jurisprudence which practises what they (Cohen and Malik) preach.[65] This could be because First Amendment jurisprudence has itself developed its non-consequentialist stance in response to campaigns based on consequentialist arguments; or it could be due to a kind of constitutional fundamentalism that respects the letter above the spirit of the First Amendment – or both.

Of all the criticisms that have been made of the way the US judicial system currently interprets the First Amendment, it is the separation of speech from action, and therefore from consequences, that is of interest here. As Stanley Fish notes, this distinction between speech and action

> is essential because no one would think to frame a First Amendment that began 'Congress shall make no law abridging freedom of action', for that would amount to saying 'Congress shall make no law', which would amount to saying 'There shall be no law', only actions uninhibited and unregulated. If the First Amendment is to make any sense, have any bite, speech must be declared not to be a species of action, or to be a special form of action lacking the aspects of action that cause it to be the object of regulation. The latter strategy is the favored one and usually involves the separation of speech from consequences.[66]

But, just as non-consequentalism slides into consequentialism in theory, so too does it succumb in practice: 'when a court invalidates legislation because it infringes on protected speech, it is not because the speech in question is without consequences but because the consequences have been discounted in relation to a good that is judged to outweigh them'.[67] Nevertheless, the courts proceed as if this were not the case, leading to 'superficially cogent but deeply incoherent' opinions that enforce a neutrality that not only 'has produced results which, by the liberal principles [of egalitarianism] . . . ought to be considered unjust', but also leads to certain absurdities and paradoxes that arise directly from the idealism that inheres in non-consequentalism.[68] On the one hand is the idea, now enshrined in legal precedent, that 'there is no such thing as a false idea' (*Gertz* v. *Robert Welch*, 1974). Fish's comment on this is witheringly on the mark: 'What this means (it couldn't possibly mean what it says, because what it says is obviously false) is that for First Amendment purposes a court will suspend its judgments as to truth and falsity or right and wrong in order to give expression the widest possible scope . . . Better instead to leave the task of winnowing the wheat from the chaff to time and the marketplace of ideas'.[69] But if there is no such thing as a false idea, then there is also no such thing as a true idea ('like the idea that women are full-fledged human beings or the idea that Jews shouldn't be killed') and therefore nothing for the marketplace to 'winnow'.

On the other hand, if freedom of speech is a primary value, as non-consequentialism appears to suggest that it is (when of course it is not), then, as with arguments for toleration, it could only be so if whatever is said *does not matter*. If words have no consequences, they also have no weight, and if they have no weight, they have no value. As Haworth notes of Speaker's Corner, in London's Hyde Park (the only place outside a US court-room where anything like absolute freedom of speech obtains): 'Anyone can go to Speakers' Corner in London's Hyde Park, stand on a box, and say anything they like. It's a tradition. However, if you try it, you will find that the fact that you are standing in that place, and on that box, is a signal to all and sundry that nothing you say is to be taken at all seriously'.[70] This is how free speech absolutism leads to the very negation of that which it holds most sacred. Again, it follows from the idealism that bedevils liberal thought at its core. The 'whole ball game' – to borrow Rushdie's phrase for a moment – rests on the belief that freedom of speech involves freedom from the restraints of power (hence the recurring trope of 'speaking truth to power'); there is no understanding that to speak is also to *exercise* power. At the core of its vision, then, is an evacuation of power relations. But if you do not take account of the power relations that 'shape' the flow of 'free' speech (the phrase is Talal Asad's), your idealized abstraction of speech will inevitably result (as a logical consequence, not because of a slippery slope) in this paradox that is physically instantiated in Speaker's Corner. Instead of enhancing truth, enabling freedom, securing justice, or whatever good you hope it might, the freedom to speak freely becomes the freedom merely to make worthless noise.

I have been arguing that contemporary absolutist discourse on freedom of speech is constituted by two fundamentally opposed – and contradictory – arguments, each with their own weaknesses. It is not surprising, then, that the discourse is, like the jurisprudence it so admires, 'superficially cogent but deeply incoherent'. Thus we find, for instance, Nick Cohen citing without comment – and thus with approval – the Supreme Court opinion that there is no such thing as a false idea.[71] On the other hand, when discussing the libel case brought against the science writer Simon

Singh by the British Chiropractic Association some pages later, he spends some time demonstrating how many claims put forward on behalf of chiropracty are, indeed, 'false'.[72] Or take this passage from Kenan Malik's *From Fatwa to Jihad*:

> The response to the Danish cartoons revealed how far the landscape of free speech had been remade. Once free speech had been seen as an *inherent good*, the fullest expression of which was a necessary condition for the elucidation of truth, the expression of moral autonomy, the maintenance of social progress and the development of other liberties.[73]

Both non-consequentialist and consequentialist understandings of freedom of speech sit alongside each other here; if it is either an 'inherent good' or a foundational principle – a 'necessary condition' – then it is a 'good-in-itself'. On the other hand, if it is important because it enables 'truth' 'moral autonomy' 'social progress' and so on, then freedom of speech is not a 'good-in-itself'. Its value lies in the realization of these higher 'values'.

It would seem, therefore, that absolutist discourse on freedom of speech can offer no coherent answer to the question, *what is freedom of expression for?* Does its value lie in itself because it is of supreme value, and therefore the consequences of free speech should be subordinated to it and dismissed as inconsequential? Or does its value lie in the way it serves some higher purpose? As we have seen, the problem with non-consequentialism lies in the way it slips back into a covert consequentialism, but the problem with consequentialism is that it cannot support a strong and absolutist commitment to freedom of speech because it must always be subordinated to the 'purpose' that it serves. This, in turn, means that forms of speech which undermine or subvert that higher purpose must be restricted. Indeed, as Stanley Fish has shown, in relation to a passage in Milton's *Areopagitica*, the exclusion of Catholics from enjoying a right to freedom of expression is not an embarrassing anomaly or contradiction but is rather *constitutive* of the freedom he (Milton) envisages because 'all affirmations of freedom of expression are, like Milton's, dependent for their force on an exception that literally carves out the space in which expression can then emerge'.[74]

In other words, far from being the antithesis of freedom of expression, against which any lover of liberty must be eternally vigilant, restraint and restriction is the very thing which makes it possible. For every discourse, there is always an originary exclusion which makes it possible to say that it is about *this* and not *that*. Ironically, this is an insight attested to by Salman Rushdie himself; 'every story' he writes in *Shame*, is an act of censorship because it 'prevents the telling of other tales'.[75] Unlike his later self, the Rushdie of *Shame* understood well enough that the arena of discourse cannot be without limits because discourse itself would be meaningless if it were. The freedom *to* discourse is dependent on those constraints and limits that produce intelligibility, understood both as 'meaning' and 'purpose'. If all restraint is eschewed, if all expression is allowed, then there is no 'purpose' or 'value' towards which freedom of expression is directed, and its 'capaciousness' in fact betokens its pointlessness. As Fish puts it, 'like expression, freedom is a coherent notion only in relation to a goal or good that limits and, by limiting, shapes its exercise'.[76]

The absolutist discourse on freedom of expression (including the later Rushdie) is not, however, willing to recognize any such limitations. As such, and despite all the contradictions that ensue, absolutists hold steadfast to the view that freedom (of speech, or liberty in general) is the ultimate value and that only freedom matters – a position that Haworth dismisses as 'at best, the expression of . . . a certain romantic posture'.[77] It is worth dwelling on some of the implications that arise from this discourse, however, not least because it is espoused by many who hold positions of power and influence, both in western Europe and America.

Nearly all the liberal writers, artists, intellectuals, editors, broadcasters, journalists and politicians who espouse the absolutist position on freedom of expression profess to do so in order to protect democracy and to enhance equality, especially the equality of women and those with alternative sexual preferences in the face of misogynistic and homophobic religious traditions. But their contradictory insistence on both consequentialist and non-consequentialist notions of freedom speech without limits undermines these values, such that their profession of them could be said to be merely rhetorical. Thus, when the editor of the Danish newspaper *Jyllands-Posten* says, 'special consideration of their [Muslims'] . . . religious feelings . . . is incompatible with contemporary democracy and freedom of speech, where you must be ready to put up with insults, mockery and abuse', he speaks for many who believe that 'insults, mockery and ridicule', are an integral part of a flourishing democratic culture.[78] For some, the tolerance of *all* forms of speech is an indicator of democratic strength, and even its necessary condition; for others, there is no harm to democracy in allowing such forms of speech, whilst, on the contrary, democracy *would* be undermined if they were curtailed. However, if freedom of expression is an 'inherent good', then its relationship to democracy is immaterial, and if that is the case, then any benefit to democracy is *incidental*. It does not follow, then, that mockery and abuse is a fundamental aspect of a healthy and flourishing democracy; it might equally facilitate an *unhealthy* democracy. Moreover, if freedom of expression is the primary value, then those who value it as such must be indifferent to its consequences, and therefore indifferent to the kind of democracy that ensues. As with other aspects of liberal thought, such as the 'marketplace of ideas', democracy is thereby reduced to a procedural mechanism, a periodically performed ritual. On the other hand, if democracy is a *consequence* of freedom of expression, it remains to be explained how abusing, insulting and demeaning sections of the citizenry contributes to an overall strengthening of the democratic culture as a whole; it is just as, if not far more, likely that those who are targeted in this manner will become increasingly marginalized, excluded and resentful, thereby *weakening* democracy, which ideally requires the active participation of all citizens striving towards a common good. Because the argument being put forward is a consequentialist one, the political and ethical value of 'insult, mockery and ridicule' *must* be determined by the speaker's objectives: is the purpose of such speech to belittle, demean and injure the marginal, weak and powerless? Or is it to puncture the pretensions and potencies of the powerful? This in turn undermines the assumption that 'insult, mockery and ridicule' contributes to a flourishing democracy because that link is a *contingent* rather than *necessary* one.

The political culture of the United States, where freedom of expression enjoys the widest latitude, demonstrates exactly why there is no necessary connection between an unqualified freedom of expression and the quality of democracy. It is arguable that the emotionalism and shrill righteousness of moral and political debates, since the advent of the 'culture wars', is the consequence of an attitude to freedom of speech that has lost sight of its purpose and deemed it to be both a good-in-itself and, somehow, a guarantor of democratic politics. But the result of this contradiction has been an almost complete breakdown in the channels of communication between US society's constituent groups, and an increasingly partisan and ghetto-ized public discourse – in which insult, mockery and ridicule is endemic and almost *de rigueur* – that has resulted in political polarization and paralysis, and the capture of the procedural mechanisms of democracy (the hollow shell that remains) by wealthy and powerful corporate and plutocratic interests.

Or take equality; although not all of those who profess an absolutist commitment to freedom of expression would agree with Malik and Cohen that incitement to hatred legislation should be lifted, they would nevertheless concur that such restrictions undermine freedom of expression in principle. They are necessary, but regrettable. And yet if, as Kevin Saunders argues, the gradual rolling back of material considered sexually obscene in contemporary western society is not, as free speech enthusiasts would argue, a sign of the inevitable march of liberty, but rather an indication of its *displacement* onto 'hate speech' because, in both cases, it is 'about degrading humankind . . . to something that is in a sense less than human', and if we are to accept that 'hatred' cannot be produced in any way other than through discourse, then the removal of restrictions on hate speech signifies an indifference, at best, to the inequality thereby produced.[79] As with so much else in liberal thought, this indifference to inequality is obscured by a rhetorical commitment to equality that amounts to nothing more than a formal abstraction – equality before the law. Even then, as

Bhikhu Parekh has wryly observed, '[i]t is a little odd for law to prohibit religious, racial or ethnic discrimination but grant more or less absolute immunity to utterances that feed the attitudes and nurture the practices leading to such discrimination'.[80]

Just as modern liberal advocates for freedom of expression are embarrassed by Milton's exclusion of Catholics from the right to liberty, so too are they embarrassed by the slaves held by the same, white American men who could otherwise piously pronounce that 'all men [!] are created equal'; just as they are discomforted by Mill's *chutzpah* in withholding liberty *in the name of liberty and progress* from the 'inferior peoples' whose destinies he oversaw in the British Colonial Office, so too do they have to confront the cultural supremacism espoused by Thomas Babington Macaulay, for whom 'a single shelf of a good European library' was worth more than 'whole native literature of India and Arabia'.[81] These are not accidental contradictions, or contingent exclusions. These are the exclusions that determine the space of liberal discourse itself, which is supremacist to its core. In a penetrating essay on liberal ideas of toleration, Jonathan Chaplin has observed that efforts by liberal philosophers such as Robert Nozick and Will Kymlicka to address cultural pluralism, betray 'a conception of cultural plurality which has a *built-in liberalising tendency*. Cultural communities may preserve their distinctiveness, but only within the limits determined by liberalism . . . It thus follows that the only kind of culture [that . . .] is valuable is, after all, precisely a liberal culture'.[82] On the other hand, Chaplin suggests that Joseph Raz's 'open acknowledgement of . . . liberalism's "liberalizing mission",' and 'the moral superiority of liberal culture over others' at least has the virtue of being honest.[83] But in so declaring his interest, as it were, Raz must also dispense with equality as one of liberalism's goals, at least at a collective, cultural level, and fall back instead on the notion of the equal moral worth of individuals, thereby displaying once more liberalism's inability to account for anything over and beyond the individual. But if, as Susan Mendus argues, culture and community constitute the very medium through which an individual feels self-worth and self-respect, if they constitute the means by which individuals are even able to evaluate those things, can a dismissal of cultural equality be kept distinct from a dismissal of equality at an *individual* level?[84] I would suggest not.

It is in this context, then, that the significance of several tropes in the absolutist discourse on freedom of speech become visible. The repetition of the phrase 'speaking truth to power'; the characterization of heroic but embattled defenders of fragile freedoms against authoritarianism; even the accusation against fellow liberals for 'selling out' or 'compromising' with the imperatives of social, cultural and religious power, where power is invariably seen as something external to liberalism, something that confronts it, not something it possesses; all of these tropes can be seen as rhetorical displacements that do the work of disavowing and deflecting the observation that liberalism itself is the dominant culture in modern western society, and that liberals are loath both to admit this privilege or concede it.[85]

This, in turn, enables us to understand the full force of liberal dismissals of religious groups who object to absolutist conceptions of freedom of speech. Not all phrase it quite as abrasively as Nick Cohen when he writes, 'Argument involves the true respect that comes from treating others as *adults* who can cope with challenging ideas', and (approvingly) 'The new atheists thought that the best argument was . . . to say bluntly that there is no God, and we should grow up'; there is, nevertheless, a consensus that religious believers are in thrall to 'fairy-tales' which cannot be rationally defended.[86] This infantilization is merely another means by which liberalism *performs* its assumption of moral superiority and subordinates those with whom it disagrees. Given that freedom of speech controversies involving Muslims involves, by definition, at least one protagonist articulating itself from outside liberalism, this assumption has the function of effectively excluding them from the marketplace of ideas in which they are supposed to state their case. If that requires a rational defence of their beliefs, and if it is assumed that such beliefs cannot be defended rationally (because they are 'fairy tales'), then the marketplace is, in effect, closed to them.

Such peremptoriness may be why Penguin did not even bother to acknowledge, let alone reply to, a letter from the British Muslim protestors which, long before the intervention of the Ayotollah, suggested a way forward might be the insertion of a disclaimer at the beginning of *The Satanic Verses* stating that the work was fictional and not historical.[87] Given that it *was* clearly a fictional text, that Rushdie was often at pains to point this out during the controversy, and also that it has been customary for nearly all feature films to include a similar kind of disclaimer in their credits, it is difficult to explain Penguin's reticence here other than by suggesting that perhaps the Muslim position was not even recognized as a viable (never mind legitimate) argument. Or it may be that Penguin may have felt that any argument advocating even the most minimal restraint on expressive liberty constituted an attack on freedom of speech per se rather than an alternative conceptualization of it. Either way, Penguin's lack of response exhibits the intellectual complacency of contemporary liberalism insofar as it is unable to conceive of freedom as anything other than indivisible, undifferentiated and absolute. The effect of such blindness is plain to see – the protests escalated, books were burnt, and an ailing Ayotollah, on the lookout for a political opportunity, seized his chance. The rest is, of course, history but the point to be drawn from this missed opportunity is that Penguin did not feel any need to debate the limits of freedom of expression with the Muslim protestors because, in their view, *there was no debate to be had.* That is, any such objections could be dealt with in even shorter order than even Brian Winston might have imagined – they could be simply ignored. Needless to say, this does not provide a conception of freedom of speech that is adequate to the task of mediating between liberal and non-liberal ideas of freedom, restraint and the common good. For that, we need a different and more coherent answer to the fundamental question: what is freedom of speech for?

3

A Difficult Freedom: Towards Mutual Understanding and the Ethics of Propriety

Almost all those who argue for the validity of legal restraints on free speech do so in relation to gender (pornography), race, sexuality and disability.[1] Very few are willing to consider restrictions on religious grounds. In the US, this may be the consequence of an intepretation of the First Amendment which sutures freedom of speech to religious freedom, and which prohibits the establishment of a state religion. Talal Asad and Saba Mahmood have advanced arguments that have problematized the discourse of free speech in relation to blasphemy and what Mahmood calls 'moral injury' but have refrained from extending them to matters of law (indeed, Mahmood explicitly cautions against juridical approaches), whilst Stanley Fish's intervention into the controversy about the (non-)publication of *The Jewel of the Medina* represents another skirmish in his ongoing battle with First Amendment 'fundamentalists', but he stops short of calling for legal restrictions.[2] In Britain, until the several attempts by the then Labour government to introduce protection from incitement to religious hatred in the first decade of the twenty-first century (first in 2001, then again in 2005 and finally in 2006), Simon Lee, Tariq Modood and Bhikhu Parekh had been the only major philosophers who had argued for extension of the incitement to hatred legislation in the wake of the Rushdie affair.[3] In the broader public sphere, however, even those far from absolutist liberals who were happy to accept limitations on speech in relation to sex, gender and race drew a line when confronted with the possibility of a restriction in relation to religious groups. Indeed, each successive attempt by the government to introduce such an offence reprised the Rushdie controversy, with a volley of protests raised in objection to the perceived erosion of freedom of speech. I will return to the discourse surrounding the UK government's attempts to introduce legislation to cover incitement to religious hatred in Chapter 7, but here I want to deal with the perceived exceptionality of religion on the grounds that what is at stake in that instance is 'belief', that it would be impossible to protect religious groups without protecting their beliefs, and that this in turn would protect religious beliefs from legitimate criticism, which would in turn substantially curtail freedom of speech. It is a perception that highlights the limits of thinking about religion and freedom not just within liberal discourse but in modern discourses more generally, including modern religious discourses themselves.

Even the most sophisticated of contemporary arguments about religion and freedom of expression deal with religious experience primarily in terms of *belief*.[4] Historically speaking, however, this conception of 'religion' is a very recent development, the effect of a secularism which has profoundly altered the understandings of what being 'religious' involves amongst both religious and non-religious persons the world over. Indeed, as Talal Asad has shown, the very idea of 'religion' itself is a consequence of this shift to a secular 'knowledge' in which 'religiosity' appears less as a set of disciplinary practices and codes which upheld the social and political authority of the medieval church and more as a set of 'propositions' in which the faithful 'believe'; this is accompanied by a transfer of authority away from the institutions in which such disciplinary practices were embedded towards the primacy of individual 'conscience'. The effect of this has been to create a 'cognitivist' understanding of religion in which religious experience is fundamentally 'about' what one believes.[5]

It is, of course, no accident that this process brought 'religion' into line with the 'rationalism' and, indeed, philosophical idealism of modern liberalism, since both liberalism and this new concept of religion emerged together and developed dialectically, triangulated by their mutual constitution in relation to post-Reformation and post-Enlightenment developments in secular thought. As a result, liberalism – *including the various religious liberalisms of modernity, such as modern Anglican liberalism, Muslim and Jewish liberalism etc.* – seems unable to conceive of religious practice in terms other than beliefs which appear to be held through 'rational' (or irrational) adherence to a set of propositions that must be verifiable according to the logics of secular knowledge. Understandably, for those of an atheistic disposition, religious belief is found wanting on this score.

But the more important implication, by far, is the separation of 'beliefs' from the person of the believer for it is this that determines the logic of exception in relation to restrictions to freedom of speech on religious grounds. Insofar as most people, including most liberals, accept limits with regard to race, or gender and sexuality, it is because these are not seen to be matters concerning one's beliefs – which are seen, in some way, to be *chosen* – but are deemed to be more fundamental and involuntary aspects of our identity over which we exercise no choice. These just 'are' part of who we are and thus not a matter for rational scrutiny. Since one must therefore distinguish, as Michael Ignatieff argues, between beliefs and the individuals who hold them, it is possible to protect individual Muslims (for example) from abuse, but not the honour of Muhammad or any other

Muslim conceptions.[6] Tariq Modood, however, has questioned whether this distinction can be upheld:

> This distinction between beliefs and the individuals who may or may not hold those beliefs may normally work, but there is at least one type of belief where it does not hold: beliefs that form the self-definition of a group, for there cannot be membership of a group without some idea of the relevant groupness. . . . A group exists only while some persons identify themselves and others in certain ways, and this cannot be done without beliefs.[7]

In fact, the distinction between 'voluntary' (with respect to religious beliefs) and 'involuntary' (race, gender, sexuality) aspects of identity does *not* 'normally work'. For it to do so, one must accept the proposition that race, gender and sexuality are fundamentally rooted in biology – that 'biology is destiny' to borrow Freud's phrase – rather than social discourses that produce the 'identity' of the object of which they speak. Feminists, anti-racists and queer theorists, for example, have developed a formidable range of insights into the many ways in which biology most certainly is *not* destiny.[8]

Conversely, the idea that an individual religious believer 'voluntarily' subscribes to a set of propositions which s/he should, in the face of rational evidence demonstrating their lack of veracity, willingly jettison in favour of other beliefs is not only to take for granted the familiar centre of liberal thought, the sovereign, autonomous individual who is the sole author and origin of him- or herself, but also to fundamentally misapprehend the nature of one's relationship to belief, religious or otherwise. Susan Mendus has argued that the liberal idea of individual 'autonomy' rests on 'the claim that we may find our own language distinct from the language of the tribe', which in turn rests on the assumption that 'values' and 'moral beliefs' are 'possible objects of choice'. This is derived from a Kantian tradition in which, 'people should be encouraged to "decide" upon their moral beliefs, meaning that the beliefs they hold ought to be the result of rational enquiry: they ought to be the consequence of active deliberation, not the consequence of prejudice, tradition or brute emotion'.[9] Such a tradition is suspicious of 'socialization [which] is understood as something which masks an individual's true nature.' For Bernard Williams, however, moral values are *not* objects of choice because they cannot *just* be the outcome of an entirely rational process of 'active deliberation':

> I suspect it to be true of moral, as it certainly is of factual convictions, that we cannot take very seriously a profession of them if we are given to understand that a speaker has just decided to adopt them . . . We see a man's genuine convictions as coming from somewhere deeper in him than that.[10]

In other words, if moral beliefs and values – whether secular or religious – are entirely voluntary and can easily be adopted and just as easily discarded, they cannot be serious convictions. It follows that 'there is a strong sense in which what we are is given rather than chosen', and, like our racial, ethnic or gender identities, 'moral and religious belief[s] . . . are equally incapable of being given up simply by an act of will or on the basis of rational deliberation'.[11]

The point is amplified by John Horton, who writes, 'Muslims or Jews, for example, are not groups of people who simply happen to share common interests or tastes, or even similar opinions . . . It is to partake of a common history and to stand in a particular relation with the group which is integral to one's sense of who one is.'[12] The point, of course, is that being part of a 'common history', and having a relation to a group (any group) are matters outside one's own control; they exceed the sovereignty of the self and thus are not in any sense 'voluntary'. Of course, one's moral beliefs and values are not static; they change and develop in relation to events and circumstances, and people convert to other systems of belief or lose faith in their own. These are not, however, simply the result of serene and disinterested rational deliberation but involve highly emotional, often painful, and at times agonizing, existential crises for both the individual and the group.[13] What matters, then, is not the distinction between beliefs and individuals, or between aspects of a person's identity that are chosen and thus ought to be defensible, and those that are not and therefore cannot be defended rationally; what matters is the difficulty of negotiating between *different* beliefs in a context of radical plurality where the secular-liberal belief that religious faith is a matter of beliefs that are supplementary to a person's 'core' identity (defined in secular terms by race, ethnicity, gender or sexuality) is itself just one belief among many.

It is this problematic that determines any adequate response to the question, 'what is freedom of speech for?' especially in a multicultural, multireligious context in which 'toleration' is not simply a matter of protecting individual autonomy, but is *also* a recognition of 'the individual's need to locate himself within a group', and therefore to mediate relationships between groups as well as individuals. This has prompted Susan Mendus to suggest that liberalism's individualistic emphasis on speech as the 'expression' of an autonomous self should be accompanied by an understanding of speech as a form of 'communication'. It follows, then, that the 'justification of free speech will be that it enhances rather than thwarts the possibilities of communication between different people', and 'increases the possibility of mutual understanding'.[14]

Tariq Modood has developed this insight by invoking a distinction between *eristic* and *dialectic* reasoning. Public discourse, he argues, is (or should be) 'structured by a goal . . . The goal is that all speech, all discourse, should use every opportunity to convert nonagreement into at least some possibility of meaningful exchange.'[15] To illustrate his point, he describes how in the early Socratic dialogues, Plato shows Socrates making no effort 'to understand his opponent, to help his opponent reach greater understanding, or to seek some constructive common ground; instead, the *logos* is used to break up the opponent's understanding, to demonstrate Socrates' intellectual superiority and to exert intellectual power over his opponent. None of these dialogues lead anywhere; they all break down in bad temper.'[16] This is *eristic* reasoning; in the context of social discourse, it is that form of discourse that 'provokes anger' and thus 'threatens the field of discourse itself'.[17] Dialectic reasoning, on the other hand, 'uses questioning and criticism carried out co-operatively and constructively. Its ideal is to share understanding and through creative difference to improve understanding.'[18] But the dialogue depends upon a built-in restraint, which is 'that arguments must not be pressed or criticisms ignored in a way that threatens the possibility of discourse' itself. For Modood, 'the ideal, as far as free speech is concerned, ought to be to create the conditions for *dialectical* enquiry and to prevent those conditions that lead to the breakdown of rational discourse into *eristical* conflict.'[19] Thus, participants in a dialogue, and by implication, any social or public discourse, hold a certain responsibility to observe those restraints that enable social discourse in the first place.

The value and significance of freedom of speech thus depends on what some absolutist liberals have come to see as something of a chimera: responsibility. They sneer at and mock the idea that rights should be accompanied by responsibilities; for them, it is a way of masking restrictions and subversions of the whole idea of liberty itself.[20] If they acknowledge a responsibility attendant upon free speech, it is the responsibility to express oneself without restraint, a self-centred notion entirely consistent with the fundamental tenets of liberalism, but which, as we have seen, is beset by weaknesses and contradictions. Modood and Mendus, on the other hand, prompt us to acknowledge a responsibility not just to ourselves but also to those to whom our discourse is addressed, and with whom we are attempting an act of communication aimed at furthering 'mutual understanding'.[21]

One might be skeptical of Modood's rationalism, and therefore less optimistic about the possibility of creating the conditions for *dialectic* as opposed to *eristic* social discourse. One might also doubt whether there should be a legal basis underwriting the principles of restraint that would make conditions more favourable for *dialectic* dialogue (Modood favours a law prohibiting group defamation; Parekh some form of communal libel law), and institutions through which it might be channelled because, for him, it cannot be 'entirely a matter of individual conscience. There must be some public forum where these issues are discussed, principles laid down, specific charges examined, defenses heard, apologies and retractions made, and commitments about future behaviour given.'[22] Maybe so, but the wider point is not about the limitations of 'individual conscience' or, indeed, of law and reason, but rather the importance of *ethics*.

This has been obscured by the legalistic discourse which has framed debates about freedom of speech and its limits. As Simon Lee has noted: 'we so often shy away from judging the rights and wrongs of exercising rights. Indeed, part of the point of rights-talk is to avoid such judgement', but without ethics freedom has no significance or value.[23] For if one way of looking at ethics is to see it not as the performance of a moral duty but rather the active moral agency that one assumes in the space *between* conflicting moral imperatives, then ethical agency requires the liberty to make a moral choice which, in turn, endows liberty with an ethical dimension which gives freedom a 'meaning' or 'purpose'. The greater the extent of liberty in a society, the more important it is that individuals exercise that liberty responsibly. Ethics is thus a correlate of liberty. All this would have been perfectly obvious to John Stuart Mill, but his contemporary acolytes insist on a legalistic notion of the 'right' to freedom of speech in such a way as to smother the ethical notion of responsibility in favour of a narrowly legalistic notion of responsibility (one cannot be held responsible for the social effects of one's speech – hence the objection to incitement laws – but one *is* responsible when accounting for speech as 'property', hence no objection to copyright laws).

Unsurprisingly, there is an ethical vacuum at the core of freedom of speech discourse, especially its absolutist form. Take this passage from Cohen's *You Can't Read This Book*:

> Do you believe in freedom of speech?
>
> Are you sure?
>
> Far be it from me to accuse you of living with illusions, but unless you are a tyrant or a lunatic – and the line between the two is thin – you will rarely speak your mind without a thought for the consequences. You would be friendless within a day if you put a belief in absolute freedom of speech into practice . . . Humans are social primates, and socialising with the rest of our species requires a fair amount of routine self-censorship and outright lying, which we dignify with names such as 'tact', 'courtesy' and 'politeness'.
>
> The appeal of censorship becomes evident when you consider whether you would be happy for others to say what they thought about you. Even if what they said was true – particularly if what they said was true – you would want to stop them saying that you were ugly, boring or smelly. You would expect them to lie to you, just as they would expect you to lie to them . . . We want our status confirmed. We want others to lie to us so that we can lie to ourselves. We want to be respected.[24]

Cohen begins this extremely skilful piece of rhetoric by admitting that absolute freedom of speech is an impossibility, and concedes all sorts of considerations that validate the need for certain restrictions which enable humans to socialize with each other. Having therefore conceded that there is an ethical basis for such restraint, Cohen then shifts tack and suggests that this is, however, something of a mirage, that there is something shameful, morally wanting, dishonest and self-deceiving in something as fundamental as, say, being sociable or wanting society to function properly. Thus, whilst the passage opens by positioning the believer in absolute freedom of speech as a *naïf* labouring under an illusion, it ends by excoriating the 'necessary' but morally deficient reality of its opposite – restraint – and thus recuperates the libertarian believer as an idealist who, despite apparently being in thrall to an illusion is, in fact, able to apprehend a deeper 'truth' which the rest of us have to conceal behind a deceptive web of repressive denial. Consequently, far from being a necessary 'reality' – or truth – the ethical basis of restraint is now, by a subtle twist of the argument, itself nothing more than an illusion, a 'lie'.

This kind of rhetorical manoeuvre (seldom performed so effortlessly) is typical of absolutist liberal discourse, which concedes the impossibility of absolute freedom of speech in order to sound more reasonable than it is (imagine, if you will, someone trying to argue that it would be fine for someone to shout 'Fire!' in a crowded theatre), only to smuggle the absolutism back in as an ideal, a truth that we can only betray by accepting the restraints that are necessary in order to muddle along in society as best we can. The purpose of these rhetorical performances is to claim a moral high ground that masks a kind of fanaticism that is as extreme, in its own way, as the Muslim absolutists to which Cohen and company are implacably opposed. This holier-than-thou puritanical idealism not only mirrors their opponents, but is likewise used as a moral trump card in order to close the argument and claim outright victory.

Such moralism, however, depends on a denial of ethics as an active moral enquiry that eschews absolute positions whilst negotiating the relative demands of conflicting values. In Cohen's passage, and in the discourse it represents more generally, it is symptomatically exposed by the dismissal of 'respect', which has, for many in the liberal intelligentsia, become something of a dirty word.[25] This begs the question of what 'respect' means for them, and if, as the title of Cohen's chapter suggests, the first rule for censors is to 'demand a respect you don't deserve', then who *does* deserve it? 'We want others to lie to us so we can lie to ourselves. We want to be respected' – whether or not all absolutist liberals would go so far as to suggest that 'respect' is a kind of necessary lie, or a self-deluding way of bolstering our egos, it does seem clear that underlying this dismissal of 'respect' as nothing more than a ruse through which opponents of freedom can narrow the scope of liberty is a vision of 'true' respect as something so rare that to 'deserve' it one has to live up to an impossible ideal – impossible because, by our very nature as social primates, we must betray it. That is, for the absolutist, 'true' respect is due either to nobody at all, or only to those who can similarly apprehend the 'lie' with which we all have to live: those who think exactly like themselves, in other words. It goes without saying that in this, as in so many other ways, the rhetoric of liberal and Muslim absolutisms shadow each other precisely.

The self-centredness of such an approach to 'respect' is immediately apparent, and totally at odds with modern ethics, in all its various manifestations, which concerns itself with the primary relation to the Other (an idea that Cohen dismisses with scorn rather than argument). The work of Emmanuel Levinas, for example, suggests that the ethical relation to the Other is prior to everything else, that it is the very condition of possibility for ethics itself. For Levinas, we begin with respect; respect is the foundation of social being, and thus the ground of self-identity; it is neither the 'necessary lie' nor a prize that is 'deserved' only by those rare individuals who somehow exceed Cohen's paltry expectations of human behaviour.

Likewise, Kenan Malik's impatience with the idea of restraint betrays his own ethical blindspot. Citing Richard Webster's plea to both sides in the Rushdie controversy to refrain from burning each other's flags, Malik dismisses such an idea as being responsible for *increased* social tension and hostility as well as the erosion of fundamental liberties, 'Not burning your enemy's flag leads, then, not to more respect for different cultures, but to a cacophonous din about why my flag is more deserving of being left unburnt than yours.'[26] As such, his view is diametrically opposed to Modood's in that he sees *restraint*, rather than the lack of it, as being responsible for the breakdown in social discourse between communities, although, without the latter's careful reasoning, Malik's position appears to be no more than a rehearsing of standard liberal arguments and presuppositions. Drawing the usual distinction between speech and action ('Most people would accept there is a distinction between words and deeds'[27]), which distances speech from its effects ('there is no direct relationship between words and deeds'), he attenuates the notion of responsibility for one's speech, and the effects it might have, by claiming that in 'blurring the distinction between speech and action, incitement laws blur the idea of human agency and moral responsibility'.[28] Quite apart from being unable to explain the point of writing, or speech or any form of communication if it does not have any 'effects' – as if it were just a form of throat-clearing – the supposedly 'clear' idea of moral agency and responsibility which is being blurred here is one that is *individual* in both orientation and origin – that is, it is *self-centred*. Malik therefore seems to be unable to come to terms with any notion of 'responsibility' that sits outside the liberal tradition, where responsibility might lie not just within and to oneself. Moreover, it is a notion of responsibility that removes responsibility from *some* individuals for their deeds (speakers, writers, etc.), whilst reserving it for others (those who receive the 'message'). If the sovereign individual who receives the message is solely responsible for his or her own response to any speech that might have provoked their 'deed', then this in turn absolves the speaker of any responsibility for the effects of their speech. In such a scenario, restraint becomes pointless, but it rather undermines the usual gesture acknowledging that there 'is nothing new in the insistence that free speech has to be used responsibly'.[29] Malik references Oliver Wendell Holmes's famous example prohibiting the shouting of 'Fire!' in a crowded theatre, but if he absolves speakers of any responsibility for the effects arising from their speech, then it is difficult to see why it would be *wrong* to shout 'Fire!' in such circumstances given that the responsibility for any consequent stampede would lie with the stampeders: his logic suggests that the stampeders would be morally culpable for any injury or death rather than the person who provoked it.

Liberal absolutists often make what Alan Haworth calls an 'appeal to science', and to the presumed lack of restraint that animates modern 'scientific culture', in order to support their arguments for freedom of speech, and it is significant that their characterization of 'science' often involves a romanticization of scientific methodology as a purely rational, disinterested pursuit of an 'objective' truth *whatever the consequences*. It is not simply that historians and sociologists of science have demonstrated that actual scientific practice bears little resemblance to such an idealized portrait; rather, the purpose of the 'appeal to science' lies in its marginalization of ethics.[30] Scientists the world over must be much relieved to know that in the world according to Nick Cohen, Kenan Malik or Richard Dawkins (these latter two really should know better) they are no longer subject to the oversight of ethics committees, or that they can now continue with their work without any accountability to their general publics or the environments in which they live.

On the other hand, not only have neuroscientists increasingly demonstrated how the idea of the sovereign individual is nothing more than a liberal myth (social scientists, who have long known this, do not seem to matter; what matters for liberal absolutists is 'hard science' – although they are not averse to utilizing social science when it suits them), so too does the work of Scott Atran, who describes his anthropological research as the 'science of the sacred', support Modood rather than Malik. For those who apparently care about such matters (like Malik and Cohen), Atran supplies plenty of 'hard data' (large quantitive surveys) as well as insightful qualititative analysis. *Contra* Malik, for whom both moral and juridical responsibility is rooted in the sovereign individual, Atran is aware that 'History says that our ancient tribal future is fired forward by faith in *groups*, their gods and glory, no matter how secular these may appear.'[31] What binds groups together 'to co-operate and to compete' are 'sacred values' and taboos that '[a]long with religious rituals and insignia . . . identify one cultural group as different from another'.[32] Values can be 'sacred' for religious and non-religious groups alike, such as 'a belief in the importance of individual morality, fairness, reciprocity, and collective identity ("justice for my people")', and because these constitute a group's core sense of 'who we are', people hold them to be 'absolute and inviolable'.[33] There is therefore a 'moral logic to seemingly intractable religious and cultural disputes that cannot be reduced to secular calculations of interest but must be dealt with on its own terms'.[34]

While, on the face of it, this would lead to the conclusion that there is no way to resolve such emotive and fundamental disputes, Atran's research suggests, on the other hand, a paradox in which sacred values are '"eternal" and morally absolute, yet widely open to interpretation'.[35] Surprisingly:

> Absolutists who violently rejected profane offers of money or peace for sacred land were much more inclined to accept deals that involved their enemies making the symbolic but difficult gesture of conceding respect for the other side's sacred values. For example, Palestinian hard-liners were more willing to consider recognizing the right of Israel to exist, if the Israelis apologized for suffering caused to Palestinian civilians in the 1948 war (which Palestinians call *Naqba'* (the Catastrophe)).[36]

The same was noted of Israeli leaders as well, and Atran concludes '[m]aking these sorts of wholly intangible "symbolic" concessions . . . aren't enough on their own, but they are the beginning; they are the things that just might make the other side willing to listen and calm the heat in their anger. Words have the extreme power to change emotions.'[37]

Atran's 'science of the sacred' is notable for the way it acknowledges the limits of reason and the influence of 'emotional' and non-rational factors that motivate people with regards to deep cultural attachments and beliefs. Since these are often at stake in freedom of speech controversies, this idea of a 'symbolic' exchange respecting the sacred values of one's opponent always-already encodes a principle of restraint which corresponds exactly to that which Richard Webster appealed when asking both sides in the Rushdie controversy not to burn each other's flags, and which Modood and Mendus suggest might form the basis of *dialectic* exchange and 'mutual understanding'.[38] In this scenario, 'responsibility' is shared *between* the interlocutors, and 'respect' is due to *everyone*, even (especially) those with whom one fundamentally disagrees. Instead of leading to mutually hostile camps shouting incomprehensibly past one another, as the absolutists claim, 'respect' – that is, the ethics of reciprocal restraint – actually offers the possibility of reframing the discourse of controversy and conflict into a productive dialogue that may, in time, lead to a form of resolution – although no one should be under any illusions about how difficult this may prove to be. It is with this in mind that I will attempt to sketch an ethical agenda that moves beyond the 'right' to freedom of expression in order to evaluate the rights and wrongs of texts and images that have provoked cultural controversies.

Responsibility to/for the other: maximal and minimal ethics

Writing, indeed *any* form of communication, is a moral act. To use language is to position oneself, and be positioned, in relation to an Other who is addressed by the speaking or writing subject. The relational character of language both bequeaths meaning and binds intersubjective relationships that in turn constitute culture and society, and the norms and values encoded in and upheld by them. Small wonder, then, that language is of crucial importance for Emmanuel Levinas' conception of ethics, both in the earlier *Totality and Infinity* (1961) and the later, post-Derridean, *Otherwise than Being* (1974). In the earlier work, the face-to-face encounter with the other which establishes ethics also 'first institutes language' so that 'the relation between the same and the other . . . is language . . . primordially enacted as conversation'.[39] In the latter work, Levinas responds to Derrida's critique of *Totality and Infinity* in his essay 'Violence and Metaphysics', which showed that 'ethics cannot exist save in language or "arche-writing", which will underlie any "pure" ethical moment: the ethical . . . is a result of language', and he conceives language as 'no longer simply the expression of my unique response to the other, but is the very condition or possibility of all ethics in general'.[40]

Although Levinas has profoundly re-shaped contemporary thought about ethics, he is not a moral philosopher in the traditional sense. His aim is to establish ethics as the ground of philosophy, and he is not so much concerned with ethics itself as with meta-ethics or the 'ethics of ethics', which is 'prior to any unique case of ethical responsibility'; he has himself noted that his 'task does not consist in constructing ethics; I only try to find its meaning'.[41] He is therefore interested in how the appeal of the other, which calls the self into a responsibility that Levinas calls 'ethical', is the basis not just of ethics, and thence philosophy, as such, but is in fact the primary 'event' – which Eaglestone characterizes as the 'quasi-transcendental (but non-divine), untotalisable (non)place from which ethics comes'[42] – that is the foundation of being. In contrast to the phenomenology which Levinas contests, being does not originate within an ego or self, but in the *relation* between the self and the other, 'The "between-the-two" [L'entre-les-deux], the interval between the I and the You, the *Zwischen*, is the site where the work of being takes place.'[43] The encounter between the self and other which establishes their relation is anterior to being and thus prior to the constitution of the self; the call of the other, and the response to it, calls the self into being, and thus responsibility to and for the other is the condition of being itself. In *Otherwise than Being* Levinas asks, 'why does the other concern me? What is Hecuba to me? Am I my brother's keeper?' and he suggests that these 'questions have meaning only if one has already supposed the ego is concerned only with itself, is only a concern for itself . . . But in the prehistory of the ego posited for itself speaks a responsibility, the self is through and through a hostage, older than the ego, prior to principles.'[44] This means that 'each of us is always already responsible for the others who people the world . . . We are fundamentally responsible for others before we can theorise this relationship . . . The otherwise than being, the totally other, comes before our being. Our unconditional responsibility . . . exists before us and we are "thrown" into it, without any choice.'[45]

There is, therefore, a utopian charge to Levinasian ethics, and an always already inscription of failure because the very posing of such a question and its answer pre-supposes the language of being, which comprehends the other in terms of the self.[46] Comprehension, suggests Levinas, involves 'taking [prendre] and . . . comprehending [comprendre], that is, the fact of englobing, of appropriating', and thus is a form 'ontological imperialism' which always comes after the event of being called to account for the other, but it is the only way through which the relation can itself be accounted for, that is, articulated.[47] As Derrida puts it, 'arche-writing is the origin of morality as of immorality. The nonethical opening of ethics. A violent opening.'[48] At the core of Levinasian ethics, then, is a lapse that cannot be reversed, an inevitable betrayal of our 'unconditional responsibility' that cannot be redeemed. This is apparent in Levinas' conceptualization of the Saying and the Said. The Levinas of *Otherwise than Being* conceives of language as 'made up of the 'transcendent' saying (*le dire*) and the 'immanent' said (*le dit*)'.[49] The Saying is 'the condition of ethics, its mode', and 'it does not communicate anything except *the desire to communicate* . . . it is the "publicness" or openness to the other upon which language is grounded'.[50] While, on the one hand, the presence of the Saying in the Said 'allows the ethical to signify "within ontological language",'[51] its necessary 'incarnation' in the language of the Said, without which there can be no ethics, closes the infinite openness to the other that is found in the Saying, and translates it into principles, categories, axioms, *doxa*: 'The saying, which is unthematisable, impossible to delimit, becomes limited, thematised, said.'[52] For Levinas, then, ethics is both necessary, indeed ineluctable, and *impossible*.

There is, therefore, a kind of intransigence in Levinas' thought towards being, and a utopian desire – which can never be realized – to account for the pre-lapsarian encounter with the other which establishes the call to responsibility, a call that can never be accounted for by the language of being, the categorical language of the Said that englobes the other and surrogates it to the imperialism of the ego. I shall return to the way in which Levinas suggests that the Saying can, in turn, interrupt the logic of the Said and thus enable ethics to 'signify' in the Said in due course, for it will touch on the critical question of 'manner(s)' in the ethics of communication. For now, one must note the profound influence that Levinas' utopian intransigence has had on what might be termed the 'postmodern turn' in ethical criticism that has accompanied and contested the return of ethical criticism since the late 1980s, which emerged in response to the hiatus imposed by the ascendancy of formalist modes of criticism in the early and mid-twentieth century.

The work of Robert Eaglestone, Andrew Gibson and Derek Attridge exhibits an awareness, derived from their close engagement with Levinas, of the necessary impossibility of ethics. Eaglestone and Gibson, in particular, take to task neo-humanist critics and philosophers such as Martha Nussbaum, Wayne Booth and David Parker, and ethical pragmatists such as Richard Rorty on the grounds that they ignore, subordinate and marginalize the characteristics of textuality in their readings; or they 'share with the whole classical tradition of ethical criticism . . . a belief that, at some level ethics is a totality or involves totalities, whether of value or perception . . . This, precisely, is an ethics that cannot allow for radical difference, heterogeneity, the thought of the incommensurable.'[53] For Gibson, this is because their ethical endeavors involve what he calls 'radical surpassing' whereby 'the given is transcended, observed from an Olympian height . . . The ethical position always exists beyond or on a different plane to its object.'[54] As a result, for such thinkers 'there must always be clarity and distinction in ethics, or, to use a common term in ethical discussions, discrimination. Such an ethics self-evidently always either relies on or produces determinations. It shrinks from imagining that there might be an ethical dimension to the relation to the indeterminable itself.'[55] The point Gibson seems to be making here, if I am reading him right, is that for all their insistence on self-reflexiveness, and their awareness of ethics as difficult and demanding, Nussbaum, Booth et al. aim to arrive at a determinate *judgment*, a 'discrimination' that ultimately must forswear the 'indeterminable' or that which resists and remains unassimilable to the terms on which their judgment rests. Such judgments assert the self's own conceptions over the other and thus amount to 'an imposition of force' that is 'unethical' – 'what lies outside me neither asks for, requires, nor justifies such an imposition'.[56] As such, '[t]he question, again, is how to heed "the work's demand', rather than making demands of it'.[57]

Echoing Gibson, Attridge makes a distinction between responsibility *to* the other, and responsibility *for* the other. 'Being responsible for the other', he suggests, 'involves assuming the other's needs (if only the need to exist), affirming it, sustaining it, being prepared to give up my own wants and satisfactions for the sake of the other.'[58] Thus, an ethical reading for Attridge is a *creative* reading that involves being taken 'hostage' by the text, 'to work against the mind's tendency to assimilate the other to the same . . . In its encounter with the other, an encounter in which existing modes of thought and evaluation falter, creative reading allows the work to take the mind . . . to the borders of its accustomed terrain.' One surrenders to the 'demands' of the text, and in so doing responds to its singularity, 'registering what is unique . . . in this particular work'.[59] Conversely, a 'creative' reading is itself a singularity, equivalent to the 'originality' of a creative work; that is, creative readings are 'original' in the sense that they respond to what is singular, original and other in the works to which they respond. As with Gibson, this involves a suspension of judgment, 'of habits' as Attridge puts it, in order to 'rethink old positions'.

I find the arguments put forward by Gibson and Attridge both compelling and logically consistent. There is undeniable rhetorical and critical power, for instance, in Gibson's notion of a 'postmodern ethics' as 'auto-deconstruction', as a resistance to the appropriations of judgment and an attention to the aporia that inhabits any thinking about alterity, indeterminacy, incommensurability and so on. But, in following Levinas and pursuing what might be termed a 'maximalist' approach to ethics, postmodern ethics generates certain problems for any ethics that attempts to account for the rights and wrongs of protagonists in freedom of speech controversies. It is not simply that the impossibility of postmodern ethics is always already inscribed into its endeavor. As Gibson acknowledges, much of the value of postmodern ethics, and of the Levinasian account from which it is derived, lies in the way it attempts to 'find productive ways of living and thinking within and through' paradox.[60] If one were to point out that Gibson's critique of the determinations and discriminations of neo-humanist ethical critics in the name of indeterminacy is itself a determinate judgment, or that the act of interpretation, even interpretations which seek to tease out indeterminacy, singularity, heterogeneity and so on, *necessarily* imposes itself on the alterity of the text rather than surrendering to its 'demands', and is therefore a form of 'mastery' that overwhelms the other, one would be correct but missing the point. In any case, Gibson anticipates just such a charge. Following Geoffrey Galt Harpham, he suggests that:

> ethics holds close to the 'yearning for convergence, rationality, closure, transcendence'. But it also 'sustains an august reticence, a principled irresolution'. Its element is 'the strictly undecidable' which 'suffers determination by morality'. Ethics is 'properly dis-interested' and, as such, precedes and governs our political and moral 'interestedness'. It is born free, but also bound everywhere by morality 'to particular communities, institutions, codes, and conventions'. This does not mean that we can or should shrug off the ordinary, difficult world of moral choices for the lofty, high-minded indeterminacies of ethics, abandoning commitments for what Bernard Williams calls the 'intellectualist satisfactions' of 'a refined indecision' . . . Harpham rightly insists that the determination of ethics by morality is to be neither slighted nor denied. We are moral as we are political because we are historical beings, and no movement 'beyond morality' is properly conceivable . . . Ethics nonetheless operates a kind of play within morality, holds it open, hopes to restrain it from violence or the will to domination, subjects it to a 'kind of auto-deconstruction'.[61]

Rather, the problem is that Levinasian ethics is not ethics as such and it therefore establishes only the call the responsibility; it does not enable us to account for particular responsibilities. The question is *how*, in any given situation, does ethics 'suffer determination' by 'interested' parties, and how might we account for that? To argue, as Gibson does, that deconstructive textual strategies, such as those accounted for in his reading of Jeanette Winterson's *Written on the Body*, constitute an ethical, if utopian – or, rather, ethical *because* utopian – praxis is fine; but the social reproduction of that praxis as a 'work' that has effects in the world involves 'determinations' that can only be assessed and evaluated in the context of its address to a given interpretive community or communities. Doing this involves putting the deconstructive and utopian praxis within the text into relation with a specific transaction or set of transactions between the 'work' and its readers/ addressees, and therefore an 'exteriority' that is always already determined by history, politics, society and culture. Such a relation necessarily draws the work away from its (utopian) relation to a singular other and into the world of embodied others, or 'other others' as Derrida puts it.[62]

For Gibson and Attridge, however, maximal ethics requires them to eschew embodied others; for them, the 'other' is either the text itself, in its irreducible singularity, which 'in its fullness is always and in principle inaccessible', or is a concept, an idea that certain texts reveal or speak to, such as indeterminacy, irreducible difference, incommensurability and singularity.[63] This much is apparent in Gibson's treatment of 'reception' where he examines certain texts that invite certain kinds of readings, and thus a certain kind of relationship of the reader to them, which he calls ethical. But the only 'reading' he offers is his own; he does not engage with other readings and assess *their* relationship to the text in question. If they do not respond to the textual invitation as *he* sees it, are they therefore unethical readings? On the other hand, what if these alternative readings interpret the textual invitation otherwise? Is this a misreading, or a valid interpretation, in which case, in what sense would it be true to speak of these readings as in some way not 'ethical'? Or take Gibson's reading of B.S. Johnson's work, where he identifies an 'ethical scrupulousness' that self-consciously approximates the singularity of the 'event' of experience, particularly the reading experience, through a dissolution of the material unity of the novel as a representational form that otherwise imposes (unethically) a unity or wholeness of being onto that which is radically incomplete (experience). But does it follow that other works, more or less representational and unified in form, are therefore more or less unethical? Likewise, one might ask of Attridge whether only 'creative' readings and 'inventive' works of literature are ethical insofar as only these, according to him, are fully responsible to the singularity and alterity they either bring into being or encounter.

It would seem, therefore, that postmodern ethics, as theorized by Gibson and Attridge, adopts a maximalism that would prioritize one form of ethical practice – criticism which eschews determinations in favour of 'auto-deconstruction' and 'play' within morality; or which responds 'fully' and 'creatively' and 'inventively' to the singularity of the other – and foreclose others, which in its own terms would be unethical given that their own conception of ethics rests on a disavowal of such totalization. Indeed, if ethics always derives from and speaks to a situation that is specific and singular – a point on which both postmodern and neo-humanist ethical critics agree – then it would surely be the case that a transcendent or universal theory of ethical *practice* – as opposed to meta-ethics – is itself a violation of this principle. If that is the case, then there must be different kinds of ethics appropriate to different situations. If one type of ethical praxis is germane to a moral dilemma which requires an evaluation of the conflicting claims of two or more moral imperatives (as dramatized, for instance, in *Antigone*), another is required for the ethics of the encounter, such as the intercultural encounter; yet another might be called for by certain types of texts, whilst others may invite different forms of ethical engagement. Likewise, the kinds of ethical criticism espoused and practiced by, say, Martha Nussbaum, Wayne Booth and others cannot be ruled out *tout court* even if their interest in particulars (or 'concretizations') lies in the way that they speak to a generality, whereas for postmoderns the singular resists all attempts to assimilate it into a general ethical system. Nevertheless, if, as Eaglestone argues, ethical criticism cannot be reduced to *a* methodology, then the methodology of the neo-humanists, which tends to focus on the 'narrative or dramatic presentation of moral questions, dilemmas, embodied in characters, imagined agents, lives, selves or subjectivities', may have some purchase in relation to *some* ethical projects though not, of course, all.[64] My reading of Gibreel Farishta's suicide in *The Satanic Verses* in chapter 3 demonstrates one such instance where the 'dramatic presentation of moral dilemmas' is particularly hospitable to a critique of the novel's ethical concerns.

Such ethical pragmatism, which might be termed ethical minimalism, sits athwart and askance the maximal position derived from Emmanuel Levinas but does not invalidate it; nor is it a matter of choosing between minimal and maximal ethics. Rather, what I have in mind is a relation between maximal and minimal ethics which simultaneously charges the latter with deconstructive energy and pulls the former towards a necessary engagement with encounters between embodied others that demand determinate judgments. It is here that two brilliant essays by Derek Attridge on Derrida's amplification and creative re-writing of Levinasian thought illuminate the inter-relationship between minimal and maximal ethics, and how they must be seen as mutually constitutive modes of ethics rather than as alternatives. In 'The Impossibility of Ethics: On Mount Moriah' Attridge considers the implications of Derrida's reading, in *The Gift of Death* (via Kierkegaard), of the tale in Genesis concerning the sacrifice of Isaac by Abraham. Derrida and Keirkegaard both note the 'monstrous' obligation under which

Abraham is placed and 'how his responsibility to the absolute Other requires that, by sacrificing his son, he sacrifice the ethical obligations he is under as father, husband, patriarch, social being', but Derrida draws a wider point which highlights the story's dramatization of the impossibility of ethics.[65] 'As soon as I enter in a relation with the other', writes Derrida, 'I know that I can respond only by sacrificing ethics, that is to say by sacrificing whatever obliges me to also respond, in the same way, in the same instant, to *all* the others.'[66] There are an 'infinite number' of these 'other others' in their quotidian multitude, '[b]ut if ethics is the simultaneous responsibility toward every other, *as singular other*, and also a call to respond to all other others 'in the same way, in the same instant' then, as Attridge notes, 'ethical behavior . . . is utterly impossible'.[67] This impossibility inscribes an insuperable *aporia* within the heart of ethics because '[m]y responsibility to the singular other . . . runs counter to my responsibility to other singular others', such that 'the act of doing justice is always also the act of doing injustice'; in singularly responding to the singular call of God, Abraham does justice to Him, but the price is a terrible injustice to Isaac.[68]

Moreover, Abraham's decision to choose one over the other is unjustifiable because, for Derrida (as for Levinas) responsibility is 'unconditional' and must therefore 'exceed any prescribable algorithm . . . there can be no fully reliable means whereby my responsibility to x can be calculated as greater or lesser than my responsibility to y'.[69] This explains Abraham's silence concerning his decision to obey God's command, 'in placing one [unconditional] responsibility . . . above another, or rather many others – to Isaac, to the family, to the state, to the human community, to the covenanted future . . . to ethics as a general system . . . the impossibility of justification, the inevitability of silence is obvious. To account for his decision in language . . . would be to cross from the unconditional to the conditional, from the incalculable to the calculable.'[70] Likewise, if we follow through one of Derrida's own comical exaggerations by which he presses home the point about ethical impossibility, 'My preference for the cat I call my "own" over all other cats in the universe is as inaccessible to the language of explanation and justification as Abraham's preference for God over Isaac.'[71]

It would seem that the implacable logic of Derrida's argument leads to one conclusion: that 'ethical acts . . . cannot happen'.[72] And yet, even though ethical obligation cannot 'finally, be explained, grounded, justified . . . it happens all the time. And it is always singular: this person, this case, this demand obliges me, here and now. My cat, and not the millions of other cats in the world.'[73] There is, however, a risk that 'obligation' – responsibility – is therefore 'capricious' and 'arbitrary', because if 'we cannot make ourselves answerable to every other in the world' and if our response, our decision, is incalculable and unjustifiable, then 'how do we choose? Of all the demands made on us by others, which are genuine and which are spurious?'[74] It is here that we can turn to the second of Attridge's essays on Derrida and

Levinas, 'Posthumous Infidelity: Derrida, Levinas and the Third', which amplifies and extends that question in a long passage during which Attridge highlights Derrida's creative re-writing of the notion of 'the third' as it appears in Levinas' work.[75] First, Attridge traces the development of the concept in Levinas, from its appearance in *Totality and Infinity* to its reformulation in *Otherwise than Being*. In the earlier text, the ethical response, for Levinas, 'is aroused by the epiphany of the face inasmuch as it attests the presence of the third party, the whole of humanity, in the eyes that look at me'.[76] Attridge comments that this 'is a remarkable way to move from the ethical – in Levinas's sense, as the singular relation of the self and the other – to the political', which in turn provokes a reprise of the question as found in 'The Impossibility of Ethics': 'How, in answering my obligation to the singular other, do I simultaneously act justly with regard to the whole of humanity?'[77] In *Otherwise than Being*, 'the third' is significantly revised, and it no longer appears as 'part and parcel of the ethical relation', 'looking at us through the eyes of the other', but rather 'as a *complication* of the face-to-face rapport':

> 'The other stands in a relationship with the third party,' writes Levinas, 'for whom I cannot entirely answer, even if I alone answer, before any question, for my neighbor.' Because the other for whom I am responsible is responsible for other others, the simply [*sic*] intimacy of the ethical relation is breached, and the one name Levinas gives to the domain that we enter when we start to take the other others into account is *justice*.[78]

Attridge then cites a passage from 'Peace and Proximity' (1984) in which Levinas asks, 'how does responsibility obligate if a third party troubles this exteriority of two . . . The third party is other than my neighbor but also another neighbor, and also a neighbor of the other . . . What am I to do?. . . Who passes before the other in my responsibility?'[79] This is, for Levinas, 'the first question in the interhuman . . . the question of justice. Henceforth, it is necessary to know, to become consciousness. Comparison is superimposed on my relation with the *unique* and the incomparable, and, in view of equity and equality, a weighing, a thinking, a calculation.'[80] According to the later Levinas, then, 'justice' emerges from the troubling of the ethical encounter by 'the third', which compels the crossing from the incalculable to the calculable, from the singularity of the ethical encounter to the generality of the ethical system – law, morality, politics, state.

It is at this point that Attridge introduces Derrida's response, a response which, he suggests, observes a fidelity to Levinas's thought through a creative infidelity that 'enriches and deepens it'.[81] Despite noting, on several different occasions, the difference between Levinas's earlier and later conceptualizations of 'the third', in his meditation on and mourning of Levinas in 'A Word of Welcome' Derrida proceeds as if there had been no shift at all. According to Attridge, he conflates the 'two kinds of thirdness' because, 'What Derrida wants from Levinas is a combination of his later account of justice – as law, as calculation, politics, rights and so on (very different, incidentally, from his own account of justice in a text like 'Force of Law') – with his earlier account of the third – as immediately apparent in the face to face.'[82] But Derrida does not stop there; instead he compounds this infidelity with an even greater one, by insisting that the face-to-face encounter, which retains its primacy in Levinas's thought as the essential moment that inaugurates ethics, 'would be a violent relation if it occurred *without* the intervention of the third, its purity threatened by the very absence of that which must compromise it'.[83] This would seem to be a gratuitous mis-reading of Levinas, for whom it is the violence of *the third* that is itself the 'first violence, violence of judgment, transformation of faces into objective and plastic forms'.[84] In Attridge's words, 'if there is a violence that poses a threat to ethics in Levinas's view, it is the violence brought onto the scene by the arrival of the third, the imperative of justice'.[85]

Why would Derrida want to misread the work of his friend in such an obvious and clearly deliberate manner? It is here that the force of the 'other others' and the impossibility of ethics is brought to bear on Levinasian thought because of Derrida's recognition 'that questions of justice and politics, of the other of the other, can't be kept out of the ethical relation'.[86] His conflation of the two kinds of thirdness would seem to be a rhetorical tracing over of the shift in Levinas's thought in order to emphasize the point he (Derrida) wants to make about the necessary emergence of politics, justice, calculation, and *accountability* from within the ethical moment itself, a moment that also simultaneously exceeds them in its absolute, unconditional singularity. This paradox is accompanied by a 'double bind' that is made visible by Derrida's greater violation of Levinas in which 'the advent of the other in its absolute singularity would be a violent assault' because, if I surrender unconditionally to the other, as I am called to by my responsibility to the other, I am then overwhelmed by the other and thus the other violates *me* because the other, too, is subject to the same responsibility; the violence of the other is, however, 'prevented by the simultaneous and necessary emergence of the third', which mediates the primary relation between self and other and, in so doing, protects each from the other. Nevertheless, as Derrida admits, 'the protecting or mediating third, in its juridico-political role, violates in its turn, the purity of the ethical desire devoted to the unique. Whence the terrible ineluctabilty of a double constraint.'[87] This double bind is both ineluctable insofar as it emerges from within the ethical relation itself, and necessary insofar as it enables the question of the 'lesser violence' to appear – as Attridge notes, 'For Derrida, it is always a question of the lesser violence.' Both the unconditional responsibility to the other, and the call of the 'other others', of justice, of politics, of law, involves a violation, but which is the greater and which the lesser is undecidable in advance of each specific and singular act of responsibility.

As I read it, then, the purpose of Derrida's twin infidelities is, on the one hand, to clear a space from within Levinas's ethical maximalism for an ethical pragmatics, for the necessary and ineluctable force of minimal ethics that is precipitated by our responsibility to other others through politics, justice and the law, and conversely to retain the pressure of our unconditional responsibility to singularity upon the minimal ethics that we must by necessity engage in, which is a way of keeping open, or always in mind, the utopian charge of the 'Good' that 'in Levinas's sense . . . has never been present, cannot be fully recalled, and therefore cannot be adequately projected in an all-encompassing positive description of the Good or of Justice', that ghost of the incalculable which insistently haunts us even as we undertake the compromises required in order to *do* justice in the realm of the calculable.[88] It is for this very reason that one might speak of 'doing justice' and the determinate judgments it demands as a *minimal* ethics, for it is necessary but insufficient; it, too, is always a failure, a provisionality, a mere approximation of the justice that is required of us by our unconditional responsibility to the other. On the other hand, the rhetorical overwriting of the shift in Levinas's discourse concerning the third might additionally be read as an attempt to expel all trace or possibility of the priority of the one over the other, of ethics over justice, of maximalism over minimalism, or *vice versa*, their mutual relation held in perpetual and undecidable suspension awaiting particularization at any given moment, in any given place, in any given encounter, in any given act.

An ethics of propriety

In accounting for the moral conduct of participants in freedom of speech controversies, in calling them to account, there is therefore a need to hold in view both the unconditional responsibility to the other that is the basis of the ethical relation between them, and the conditional responsibilities that relativize that unconditionality, that disperse it between other others, embodied others, whose 'interest' must be weighed on the scales of 'justice' in the context of a politics governing each specific encounter. In what way could it be said that the work of this writer, this text, the objections of these readers, or the endorsement of others are *justified*? To speak in such terms is to weigh, calculate, and *judge* even if, in the end, such an effort cannot fully account for the responsibilities at stake and undertaken (or not, as the case may be) by those involved.

Indeed, it is here that a further revision of Levinas is necessary, one implicit in Derrida's creative introduction of 'the third' within the ethical relation itself. If, for Levinas, the unconditional responsibility to which the self is called emerges from its relation with the other, from that which lies 'between us' (entre-nous), it is nevertheless assigned to the self (or the other-as-self).[89] Responsibility is therefore the property of one or the other, and does not lie 'between us'; that is, it is not shared.[90] It is only with the intervention of the third in the realm of the calculable, in the realm of justice, that responsibility can be thought of as shared, but it would seem that even in the primary ethical relation between self and other, responsibility ought to lie 'between us' because otherwise the very possibility of reciprocity is precluded – hence Derrida's point that 'the advent of the other in its absolute singularity would be a violent assault'. If my responsibility to the other is to surrender myself, to be taken 'hostage' by my responsibility to the other, then what obligates the other to do likewise if not the same responsibility arising from the same relation with me?

This notion of a shared and reciprocal responsibility is especially important in any attempt to account for literary and cultural controversies because literature, and communication in general, is, as Spivak suggests, 'transactional'.[91] If, as Adam Newton suggests, authority passes from author to reader via the text, then this obligates the reader to enter into a relationship with the author, again via the text, the nature of which determines the ethical basis of their encounter.[92] This is what Jean-Paul Sartre means, perhaps, when he suggests that one assumes a responsibility for a book as soon as one opens it; it is also to what Toni Morrison refers when she says 'Readers and writers both struggle to interpret and perform within a common language sharable imaginative worlds.'[93] James Phelan describes this mutual obligation as follows:

> The default ethical relation between implied author and authorial audience in narrative is one of reciprocity. Each party both gives and receives. Authors give, among other things, guidance through ethical complexity and expect to receive in return their audiences' interest and attention. Audiences give that interest and attention and expect to receive in return authorial guidance. *The default assumption, of course, need not always be in place, but deviating from it necessarily entails certain risks.* Audiences that place their own interests (ideologies, politics, ethics) at the center of their reading risk turning reading into a repetitious activity that misses the ways in which authors can extend their vision of human possibility and experience. Authors who do not provide guidance or who take aggressive stances toward their audiences risk alienating those audiences to the point of losing them.[94]

The point I would like to draw out from this description is that the ethics of this relationship depends on both author and reader observing certain *proprieties* that arise from the reciprocal obligation of each to the other, the shared calling into responsibility whereby each responds to the needs of the other. These proprieties are determined by shared aesthetic, cultural, moral and even political codes and conventions to which both writers and readers refer, and these govern and delimit what Jauss calls the 'horizon of expectations' within which literary transactions take place.[95] These expectations may be met, complicated, or frustrated, but they are always present – and, as we shall see, in the case of certain controversial texts, the 'horizon of expectations' may, in fact, be divergent and perhaps irreconcilable. But even in these instances, even when the expectations that determine the proprieties of the literary transaction are not shared, the mutual *obligation* – the shared responsibility – of the author to the reader, and the reader to the text, remains as the irreducible ethical basis for any literary encounter, beyond determination.

Within this frame, then, authors make certain textual choices which they feel to be appropriate to the matter they wish to treat. But the transactional nature of the literary encounter means that the 'propriety' of their choices – which need not be, and in fact often are not the result of conscious decisions – is not a matter of their judgment alone, nor indeed immanent in the text, but is also the effect of what Wayne Booth calls the 'actualization' of the text's potential by a reader, who will deem it to be 'appropriate' or not, a decision that is also most often not a rational or conscious one. But this judgment is itself subject to propriety; in other words, the reader's judgment about the propriety of any given text must be the outcome of a 'proper' response to the author's text if it is to observe the obligation to the other.[96] Just as for Wolfgang Iser the literary 'work' cannot be identical with the text itself nor with the concretization of it by the reader, but 'must be situated somewhere between the two', so too does propriety lie *between* author and reader, an *effect* of their relation, of their shared responsibility to each other.[97]

It is difficult to account, in theoretical terms, for what we might mean when we speak of a work being 'appropriate' to the matter that it treats, or a reading being a 'proper' response to any given encounter with any given text, not least because 'propriety' is as much *affective* as rational, an intuition, a feeling, a sensibility that exceeds knowledge and theory. Indeed, this is precisely what makes it *ethical* because, 'Knowing must always decide beforehand what will count as knowledge. . . . For knowledge to be knowledge it must turn upon itself, retrieve its project, deliberate, probe, and prove.' The ethical, on the other hand, is that 'movement that sustains knowledge while remaining outside of knowledge. . . . This is not because ethics makes some truths better and others worse, but because it disrupts the entire project of knowing with a higher call, a more severe 'condition': responsibility.'[98]

Given this, it is perhaps easier to illustrate than explain. In the process of a long critique of Hayden White and the limits of what he calls 'radical constructivism' in historical writing, Dominick LaCapra quotes White as saying, 'We can confidently presume that the facts of the matter set limits on the *kinds* of stories that can *properly* (in the sense of both veraciously and appropriately) be told about them only if we believe that the events themselves possess a "story" kind of form and "plot" kind of meaning.'[99] LaCapra then goes on:

> In light of his earlier work, one might have expected White to argue that the latter presumption is untenable . . . The reader might well do a double-take when White, contrary to expectations, writes: 'In the case of an emplotment of the events of the Third Reich in a "comic" or "pastoral" mode, we would be eminently justified in appealing to the "facts" in order to dismiss it from the lists of "competing narratives" of the Third Reich.' White goes on to make an exception for an ironic, metacritical twist on a comic or pastoral story, but how he is able to put forward the earlier dismissal as 'eminently justified' is puzzling in terms of his earlier postulates.[100]

The puzzlement derives from the way in which White's *ethical* judgment about the (im)propriety of certain forms of historically representing the Third Reich *exceeds* his ability to explain it in terms of theory. To that extent, it demonstrates the limits of theory and knowledge in the face of ethical responsibility, a responsibility that may or may not be consciously registered but which is nevertheless present each time an author searches for the 'right' form for their subject matter, whether or not they are successful in realizing it (and which La Capra himself observes: a few pages earlier, he suggests that 'one might justifiably criticize a work of art on historical as well as aesthetic and normative grounds if it treated the Third Reich *in a manner* that excluded or marginalized the Nazi genocide', and in a footnote he adds a critique of Roberto Benigni's film *Life Is Beautiful* as follows: 'The "magical realism" and humour that work wonderfully in the first, pre-concentration camp part . . . become in many ways *inappropriate in the context of the concentration camp*.'[101]) In brief, 'appropriate' is a term that exceeds knowledge because it cannot be generalized beyond each specific instance; it is ethical precisely because there can be no general theory defining what is or is not 'appropriate', even though one may – as both White and LaCapra, in their own ways, do – identify why, in each instance, some form of work may or may not be appropriate.

In a similar vein, it is perhaps easier to explain what I do *not* mean when I speak of a reader responding 'properly' to a text. By reading 'properly' I do not mean a normative standard of literary accomplishment which satisfies certain accepted criteria of literary or semiotic critical ability (whatever that might be); nor do I mean a reading that subscribes to what semioticians call the 'preferred' reading; nor do I want to imply that 'better' readings, or 'more detailed' or more 'insightful' readings, as measured on some kind of scale against 'worse' or 'sketchy' or 'banal' readings, are more ethical.

Indeed, in some cases, the 'proper' response might be not to read a text at all. In a very thought-provoking and highly original analysis of the controversy surrounding the filming of Monica Ali's *Brick Lane*, Bethan Benwell, James Procter and Gemma Robinson show how the political effects and cultural dynamics of controversies surrounding texts like *The Satanic Verses* and *Brick Lane* must take account of what they, following Aamir Mufti, call 'reception by pastiche', and also how 'reading', 'partial reading' and 'non-reading' are encoded as moral positions, 'morally invested' terms 'deployed to perform moral work in defending or attacking', the texts at the centre of such controversies.[102] Non-reading should not, they argue, be seen as the opposite of reading, but part of 'a continuum of reading' and thus a 'particular *kind* of discursive engagement' that is 'ultimately inseparable from reading'.[103] On this basis, they (rightfully) criticize the presumption that 'a closer (sometimes corrective), more detailed and rigorous reading of *Brick Lane* is the best way to resolve the current stalemate'.[104]

While I find the argument compelling as a form of cultural analysis, I would suggest that this does not negate or invalidate the reciprocal obligations that mark the relation of the author to his or her (non)readers as ethical. Even though, as I have suggested, responsibility is not indivisible in the literary transaction insofar as it cannot be assigned to either author or reader but is rather 'shared' and 'between the two', nevertheless, there can be no (non)reading without a text, so it must be acknowledged that the responsibility attendant upon the author at the level of minimal ethics is in some sense anterior to that attendant on the reader even if, at the level of maximal ethics, it is not because the shared responsibility is unconditional and therefore beyond temporality. If that author, in their textual choices, does not observe the ethics of propriety (by, for example, willfully and deliberately violating their readers' sense of propriety) then, in such instances (and, again, these can only be determined in their specificity) it may well indeed be the 'proper' response *not* to read the text.

Superficially, this would seem to corroborate Rushdie's point that 'It is very, very easy not to be offended by a book. You just have to shut it.'[105] But this rests on an assumption that the literary transaction is merely a private one between an author and each individual reader, with each transaction hermetically sealed off from all the others. It overlooks the fact that a published work is a *social* action and the performativity of offence as a public gesture thus still stands even if individual readers who might be offended do not read the work. Moreover, it also assumes that any offence given may stand – indeed *should* stand – without response. In that sense, then, it arrogates to itself a privilege to perform a particular gesture – giving offence – whilst disallowing the validity of any counter-offensive performativity. I would argue, however, that not only does the public performativity of giving offence still stand, it *warrants* an opposing performativity of 'taking offence' even if readers choose not to read the book, and that, depending on the specific determinations of each transaction, it may be ethically valid for an individual to 'take offence' whether or not he or she has read the work – indeed, it is not clear, for instance, why it is assumed that one can 'defend' *The Satanic Verses* on principle even if one has not read the book (it is clear that many of its defenders had not) but disallow any opposing position on the same grounds. In other words, the ethical validity of both giving and taking offence remains at stake whether the work is 'read' or 'not read'.

A 'proper' response, therefore, is one that *responds to the properties of the text.* The concept of textual 'property' is, of course, uncontroversial. Genre is one commonly accepted way of speaking about textual properties, but it is rather narrow in scope and, being a typological concept, is subject to the presuppositions of the typologist. What I have in mind is more encompassing, relating to what Booth has called the text's 'horizons of potentiality' derived from its 'nature', or Daniel Schwarz calls the text's 'structure of effects . . . the *doesness* of the text';[106] likewise, from the other end of the critical spectrum, Derek Attridge refers to a work's 'modus operandi'.[107] All of these are ways of speaking to what I refer to as the 'manner' of the text, which is something more than just its 'style' or 'form'. 'Manner' refers to an ensemble of textual strategies that produce the effect of its 'property' (which exceeds it), strategies that include but are not limited to those ordinarily considered 'stylistic'. So, whilst it would include tropes and turns of phrase, syntax and typographical arrangements, for example, it would also refer to the *way* in which the text handles or presents themes, episodes, plot, characters, the direction and tone of dialogue, and so on, as opposed to the 'theme', 'plot' 'characters', etc. themselves;[108] moreover, it is the *relation* of each of these 'parts' or 'aspects' of the text's 'manner' to the ensemble as a whole that is significant: some aspects of the text's manner might carry more weight than others, some might work against others, some might appear anomalous or go 'against the grain' whilst the significance of others might rest on the way they appear to be representative or dominant, that is, the way they seem to make up the 'grain' itself. The *ethical* significance of the text's 'manner' lies in its relation to the larger assemblage that is the text itself, an assemblage that is simultaneously always more than the sum of its parts and always reducible to its parts – hence its vulnerability to what Benwell et al. call 'partial' reading, or 'reception by pastiche' – but never an 'organic' and 'harmonious' unity.[109]

Propriety, then, is a limit – the limit which suggests that not all forms are appropriate for any given subject, or not all interpretations are permissible of any given text, that not all possibilities are open in any given encounter. Although, as Derrida suggests, texts, as forms of signification, are subject to *différance* so that their meaning is never exhausted, that they are always 'open' to new interpretations, this does not mean that they are infinitely open or limitless in their hospitality; if that were so, then there would not be even the semblance of a meaning, just marks on a page or noise in the air. At the ethical level, propriety is, as Modood suggests, the limit that enables discourse itself to continue. But such a notion confronts a contemporary dogma that prevails amongst certain (powerful and influential) artists, writers, intellectuals and journalists, that in the realm of discourse nothing should be off-limits, that the freedom of the imagination should be unlimited, that speech should be as limitless as possible. For this dogma the concept of 'propriety' would be – probably *is* – suspect, a conservative idea that obstructs liberty, enlightenment and progress. It is true that in its colloquial sense propriety has acquired a pejorative inflection precisely because, like the cognate term *decorum*, it has been used to uphold certain hierarchies and privileges, to maintain a certain existing way of doing things, and the dominance of particular groups by narrowing the scope of discourse and action. But it is also true that propriety would seem to be a fundamentally constitutive part of all human relationships, a structural necessity in all forms of discourse and in all scenarios, insofar as it is not only that limit which enables discourse itself to continue but also that limit that gives any given discourse its identity by marking out what is proper and improper to it. Beyond that, of course, it is part of the ethical relation, of the unconditional shared responsibility that constitutes inter-subjectivity. Of course, in practice, it is determined by power relations in every scenario, every situation. Propriety is, like speech itself, never neutral;[110] but it is not an *inherently* conservative, or suspect, concept.

It is for this reason that the ethics of propriety is not a roundabout argument for self-censorship, which many might imagine it to be. In any case, self-censorship is itself something of a dubious concept notwithstanding its currency in certain liberal circles as the new front in the fight for expressive liberty. As suggested in Chapter 2, if theorists such as Judith Butler have abjured the term 'censorship' in favour of 'foreclosure' precisely because the distinction between 'internal' and 'external' restraints on thought do not hold, then the deconstruction of this distinction, from which the distinction between censorship and self-censorship is derived, would render self-censorship, at least, conceptually redundant. Even if we accept the concept of 'censorship', and the internal/external distinction on which it rests, it does not follow that self-censorship is a necessary corollary. If someone holds their tongue, or makes different artistic choices, because they fear the consequences, or reprisals, then this is the effect of an *external* coercion, and is, therefore, no different from censorship. If, on the other hand, something cannot be thought or said prior to its rationalization, that is, if a particular limit is internalized so thoroughly that it is un-sayable or unthinkable – which is another common way of characterizing self-censorship, and is central to Kenan Malik's argument that the protestors against *The Satanic Verses* 'lost the battle' but 'won the war' because liberals had become sensitized to 'the dangers of cultural and religious provocation' and thus 'internalized the *fatwa*'[111] – in what way would this amount to *self*-censorship as opposed to the 'repression' that Freud saw as necessary to the constitution of civilization itself – the 'taboos' that all societies possess, which are the limits that define that society through that which it excludes; or the 'hegemony' or 'ideology' which Marxist thought sees as crucial in maintaining the dominance of the ruling class through the internalization of a world-view and its norms and values, the purpose of which is to rule-out the thinkability of others? The point, of course, is that all of these are not forms of *self*-censorship because all are generalized limits at large across societies and cultures that cross, and thereby deconstruct, the permeable border between the self and others, the internal *cogito* and the external world of objects, or the *ego* and the *id*.

Nor is propriety as I have conceived it here the basis for immunity against criticism, as some contemporary liberals who dismiss the idea of 'respect' might think. Because the unconditional responsibility of the self to the other is *shared* and reciprocal, neither can violate the other, but equally neither can insist on its inviolability. To do so would be to sever the *relation* which would constitute a violation of the shared responsibility to the other that is the basis of ethics itself. There is no 'absolute' Other because, as Derek Attridge puts it, 'for two entitities to exist in relation to one another' they must 'share some general framework, however minimal'. Therefore, the other in its 'relating' to me 'is always, and constitutively, in the process of turning from the unknown into the known'. Conversely, 'my own singularity, too, is thus not a walled-in uniqueness'.[112] If propriety is the coming into a 'proper' relation with the other on the basis of a shared responsibility to each other, then the encounter with alterity is always a negotiation, a reciprocation, a to-ing and fro-ing, a give-and-take.[113] Within the frame of such a negotiation, I need not refrain from criticism of the other if the terms of the relation lead to it (indeed, if one considers, as Attridge does, the 'text' to be an 'other' then all 'interpretation' and 'criticism' would be negated if I did) as long as that criticism does not itself violate my responsibility to the other. Allison Weir puts it slightly differently and in so doing reconceptualizes the very notion of critique itself in a way that would accommodate what I am trying to say here. She suggests that 'critique' and criticism within secular-liberal thought is invariably conceived in terms of opposing or resisting 'norms'. This in turn rests on the notion that those norms are 'other' to the self, that they are external to an autonomous individual subject. For Weir, however, critique and criticism could be re-conceptualized as a 'reworking' of the terms of one's relationship to the other.[114] This view rests on the dialogic relationality and interpenetration of the self and other, which leads us once more back to the question of 'manner(s)'.

Literary and cultural controversies arise because the limits of propriety are transgressed by certain works. The vast majority of works observe these limits, as established in their specific encounters with specific readerships and audiences, and are thus quite uncontroversial. Whatever provocations to thought or ethical self-reflection they might generate are nevertheless within the bounds of the tacit shared understandings that determine the horizon of expectations framing the encounter. Even the 'singular' and creatively 'original' works which Attridge thinks constitute properly ethical forms of literature insofar as they provoke readers to go 'beyond existing conventions' by articulating 'thoughts that have not yet even been formulated as thoughts, feelings that as yet have no objective correlative', for the most part remain within these bounds and cause no controversy.[115] Certain works, by design or in effect, transgress the limits of propriety tolerable by certain interpretive communities. These are exceptional works, the ones that provoke controversy. Their exceptionality either lies in their attempt, deliberately, to test the limits of propriety; or in their accidental transgression through clumsiness or insensitivity; or in their desire to knowingly provoke as hostile a reaction as possible from a particular interpretive community – or even a combination of all of these. And there may certainly be some texts which transgress the limits of propriety not because of their composition but because of their reception. These texts may be deemed transgressive by readers unable or unwilling to read them 'properly'; that is, not only those who just misunderstand it, but also those who wilfully misunderstand it. Indeed, in some cases, 'understanding' may not be the issue at all; either the author, or those provoked by the author, may seek to generate controversy by severing their ethical relation to the other in order to perform a morally encoded positioning of superiority or inferiority.

The limits of propriety, it goes without saying, are specific to each interpretive community and thus a text that remains within the bounds of propriety according to one interpretive community may wildly exceed it according to another. Rare is the text that is read by one interpretive community (apart, perhaps, from academic monographs, where it is the rule). If there is a multiplicity of readerships, it may or may not matter depending on the fractures within and between these readerships, and how the text relates to those fractures. But when there are multiple readerships, and those readerships are fractured by culture, history, ethnicity, race, and profound differences in worldview (e.g. secular-liberal and Islamic), then a text stands in a very precarious ethical position. As more than one commentator at the time noted, Rushdie occupied a very special position with respect to his readerships. His liminality, which had prompted him to write *The Satanic Verses* just as it had his previous novels, carried with it a responsibility to 'weigh the impact of his words in both [the western and Islamic] worlds'.[116] According to Modood's schema, it obliged him to enable a *dialectical* communication between his Islamic and western readerships, 'to share . . . and . . . improve understanding'.[117] Arguably, too, his ethical and political task, within the context of centuries of misrepresentation and misunderstanding, was to do justice to those readerships – especially those the novel 'represents' in both political and discursive senses of the term. But there was a responsibility attendant upon his readers, too, to respond to the properties of his text and to do justice to it. The same is true of every subsequent controversy that this book examines, which is why (non)reading, or reception by pastiche, however significant in terms of the social and political performativity of 'offence' and the deployment of moral registers to that end, is always *potentially* problematic from an ethical point of view.

Responsibility and textuality: authorship, readerships and cultural difference

So how can we tell if authors and readers, in their singular encounters with each other, have undertaken their ethical responsibility to the other? This is a question at the heart of my critical agenda, that minimal ethics that I call the ethics of propriety. To return to Levinas, briefly, we are here in the position of the third and we might recall here the question that I omitted in the ellipsis within the quotation from 'Peace and Proximity' above, 'What am I to do? *What have they already done to one another*? Who passes before the other in my responsibility?' As third parties we are, both you and I, subject to the same shared responsibility that binds the authors and readers on whom we gaze, those controversialists who constitute the object of our attention. We are thus responsible for and to them, so the genitive of the ethics of propriety is doubled – we are subject, as much as they, to the propriety that we examine. This means a further doubling: the ethics of propriety, as undertaken here, is an ethics of both writing *and* reading. And yet, in the corpus of ethical criticism since its re-emergence as a serious critical field in the later 1980s, the latter has been extensively treated by both neo-humanists (Wayne Booth, Daniel Schwarz, Martha Nussbaum, David Parker, et al.), and postmoderns (J. Hillis Miller, Andrew Gibson, Derek Attridge, Robert Eaglestone) and those who fall somewhere between the camps (James Phelan, Adam Newton), whereas Séan Burke's *The Ethics of Writing* stands in magnificent isolation on the other side of the chasm.[118] Quite why this should be is beyond the scope of this chapter, but one must suggest – if only because it is pertinent to what follows – that ever since the twin notions of the 'intentional fallacy' and the 'death of the author' became general amongst scholarly literary critics, there has been a reticence to assign authorial responsibility to *writing* because, as Burke reminds us, *contra* the assumption that the 'author' is a 'transcendental signfier' or a figure denoting the 'metaphysics of presence', authorship involves *absence* since, by definition, it 'allows words to take on a life and destination beyond the originator's recall'.[119] If writing exceeds the writer's intentions how, then, are we to hold the writer responsible for that which eludes, exceeds, or turns against him or her?

And yet, as the persistence of literary controversy demonstrates, outside the university non-professional readers, even professional ones such as reviewers, and certainly the law, all insist on calling authors 'back along the ethical path that tracks a text to a proper name, to a person, a biography and a set of intentions'.[120] As such, for Burke, there is a need to affirm 'the continuing moral relevance of assessing the authorial acts in terms of their historical outcomes'.[121] It must be noted, however, that his principal concern is with theorizing what might be called the ethics of the signature, and thus a meditation on the responsibility attendant upon writing in general – what Derrida calls 'arche-writing' – whereas my concern is with that particular aspect of writing we call 'representation', that is, with the ethics of representation or, rather, the ethics of *representing*: representation as praxis, a form of action, as opposed to a 'thing' or artefact.

But the fact that Burke's book – as he himself acknowledges – is called the *Ethics of Writing* and not 'the ethics of authorship' attests to the radical complication that textuality – especially literary textuality, which is more or less polysemous, heterogeneous, semantically unstable and polyvalent – inscribes into the ethical task of assigning responsibility for the performance of writing. Any ethics of propriety will therefore have to come to terms with the textuality that mediates the relationship between author and reader whilst attempting to account for the responsibilities attendant upon and governing that relationship in each specific encounter. At a methodological level (the level of criticism), then, one might agree with Booth that we must distinguish between the flesh-and-blood author 'whose intentions, whether or not recorded outside the work, are only loosely relevant to one's reading of the work, and the actualized text's intentions: what one can infer from the collection of choices' made by the 'the author implied by those choices'.[122] And even though we might also agree with him that, at the methodological level, it is the implied as opposed to the flesh-and-blood author who is responsible for the text, at the ethical level (the level of evaluation) one is compelled to account for the text's 'signature' by tracing responsibility back to a 'proper name, to a person', if only because that proper name accepts responsibility for its signature in law, as the recipient of royalties and other benefits.[123]

For any ethical criticism there *must* be a reckoning with 'intentionality' even if that can only be the intentionality of the implied author as inferred from the sum of all the textual strategies and effects which each reader, in the singularity of their encounter with each text (and each reading is always singular, even if that same reader has read the same text before), attributes to the implied author who signs for them. But if, as I have suggested, the textual address for which the implied author takes responsibility is itself only produced by its reading, then its intentionality – its invitation to the reader – is not simply 'there' waiting to be decoded by the other to whom it is addressed. It, too, is produced by the recursive relationship between the implied author and the reader, the other, so that a text's intentions are not its alone. This, of course, complicates the question of responsibility, and disperses it *between* the authorial/textual and reading subjects.

But who exactly does the implied author address? Who is the other into which it enters a relation, to whom it is responsible? If one of the distinctive features of writing, according to Burke, is that it has 'no power of selection over who receives its words', then it is simultaneously addressed to everybody and nobody.[124] The 'other' to whom a work is addressed cannot be a singular person, or even a particular group of persons. Writing's vagabondage, its promiscuity, ensures that the 'other' that receives the address can be nothing other than an ideal other, which narratology gives the name of 'implied reader' or, following various technical refinements, the 'authorial audience'. James Phelan defines it thus: '*The authorial audience takes on the beliefs and knowledge that the [implied] author assumes it has*, including the knowledge that it is reading a constructed text. Joining the authorial audience is crucial for our experience of all the invitations offered by the different components of the text.'[125] It seems, then, that the distinction between authorial audience and flesh-and-blood reader/audience rests on the fact that entering the 'authorial audience' is a necessary condition for flesh-and-blood readers to be able to 'experience . . . all the invitations offered by the different components of the text'. In a later passage, Phelan expands upon this by remarking that 'entering the authorial audience' enables 'flesh-and-blood readers' to 'recognize the ethical and ideological bases of the author's invitations', so it is the *first step* in any attempt to evaluate the text, and thus necessary (if not sufficient) for any ethical response to it, that is, to do justice to those invitations.[126] But if the implied reader assumes all the values of the implied author, then there is, in fact, no difference between the two.[127] Thus, a text cannot but address itself, and the implied reader is a kind of conceptual fiction rendered necessary by the fact that writing has no specific address. If a *text* is narcissistic and intransitive, however, as a 'work' it is indeed oriented towards an 'other', which I have called an 'embodied' rather than conceptual other, with all its personal, cultural, social and historical freight. For the ethics of the literary transaction, then, the implied reader is redundant; what matters is the relation between the implied author as the surrogate signatory of the text's intentionality and therefore its invitation, and the actual reader who responds to that invitation. There is, therefore, no 'first step', there is only one step. And if the invitation is itself co-produced by the reader, what is at issue are precisely those historically weighted accumulations and circumstances that frame the work's reception by particular interpretive communities, which narratological concepts such as the 'implied reader' overlook.

It is here that the problem of inter-cultural incommensurability complicates such models of reading for what if, as *The Satanic Verses* controversy demonstrated, a particular interpretative community does *not* share 'the beliefs and knowledge the author assumes it has'? What if, in certain cases, these assumptions are symptomatic of a violation of the otherness of these readers that is encoded in the textual invitation itself? And if they do not share the assumptions that lie behind the invitation, how should – could – such readers respond in order to do justice to the invitation being extended to them, especially if that invitation both addresses them (at the level of content) but *also* excludes them? In that case, there is clearly a dual (or even multiple) invitation, and if there are several 'others' to which the work is addressed, to which is it responsible? All of them or just some of them? In terms of maximal ethics, the answer is clear: it is to all of its 'others'; but in terms of minimal ethics, can we infer from the intentionality of a work an audience to which it is *primarily* addressed and a *secondary* addressee? And what if the invitation issued to that primary audience is different to that issued to the secondary one? Which is of greater ethical importance and significance? Are such texts speaking with forked tongues? Is their dual register an indicator of duplicitousness?

These are the questions, amongst others, that are provoked by an ethics of propriety, especially one that orients itself towards intercultural controversies. Indeed, for all the richness and insight of the ethical criticism that has been produced over the years, there is one yawning absence in that literature: the problem of cultural difference. All of the ethical criticism thus far assumes a shared cultural frame of reference, even when they attempt to grapple with or account for what Phelan calls, 'the consequences of difference'.[128] Intercultural controversies pose, with a vengeance, that problem of difference because the *ethoi* of authors and readers involved in them diverge, often irreconcilably. Neither the unitary ethos of 'community' presumed by Nussbaum, nor the 'webs of interlocution' offered by Charles Taylor account for the multiple, fractured and irreducible heterogeneity of global mediascapes and audiences that are a constitutive feature of contemporary modernity and were nascent at the time of the *fatwa*.[129] Such fractures problematize Booth's assumption that (implied) authors and readers share what he calls 'nonce' beliefs and 'fixed' norms, 'fixed only in the sense that the implied author and implied reader share them as normal both for the fictional world and for their world'.[130]

On the other hand, postmodern ethics is similarly troubled by cultural difference even though it would seem to explicitly address it. Gibson's 'split-space of reception', for example, registers its pressure but his subsequent reading of *The Satanic Verses* illustrates the way in which it is elided by a reading frame that fails to acknowledge the very incommensurability it attempts to account for. For Gibson, *The Satanic Verses* 'in its multiplicity, as in its plurality . . . is radically at odds with . . . "terrifying singularity"' – by which, of course, he means 'unicity' rather than 'singularity' in the postmodern sense – and, 'in its self-transformations or self-refashionings, its will to become another novel, *The Satanic Verses* is peculiarly ethical'.[131] This is because it confronts the reader, in its constant metamorphoses, with 'the singularity [in the postmodern sense] and specificity of the text and the textual event', by resisting the reader's (phenomenological) desire to 'impose order on the text-as-becoming'.[132] It also resists this through its plurality of 'worlds, cultures, languages, voices, styles', so that it has 'no single foundation [and thus] in Docherty's terms, it makes of reading an encounter with a succession of singular and specific events . . . most blatantly obvious in the movements in the novel between realism and fantasy or counter-myth'.[133] It thus constitutes a split-space, of enunciation and reception, confronting the reader with several disjunct narrative temporalities that 'resist' a unitary reading or interpretive coherence.

Within the terms of Gibson's project to outline a postmodern ethics, all this is very well, but as my own reading of the novel in Chapter 4 shows, this is to go entirely with the grain of the text, and to assume that the text is ethical because it embodies postmodern ethics whilst failing to acknowledge that such ethics are themselves specific to a particular cultural formation, and that for many Muslim readers, it was precisely those elements of the novel that Gibson celebrates for being 'peculiarly ethical' that were most ethically troubling. Paradoxically, therefore, Gibson universalizes his own, postmodern, values in the name of heterogeneity, incommensurability and radical difference; one suspects he falls into this contradiction – a 'foundational' paradox that cannot be lived with and 'worked through' because it destabilizes the anti-foundational claims of postmodern ethics – because, for him, the 'other' of cultural difference remains merely conceptual.

More recently, Derek Attridge has examined the ways in which 'cultural distance' complicates any 'responsible reading' that seeks to account for the 'inventiveness' that arises from a work produced by and from within a different culture to that of the reader's own. He acknowledges that cultural difference is, in fact, both translatable and untranslatable, and so a reader encountering a text from another culture is 'almost always, then, operating in a realm of *relative* cultural distance, somewhere between complete coincidence and total difference'.[134] This leads him to conclude that 'the ethics of reading literary works from other cultures is not, it turns out, significantly different from the ethics of reading works from one's own culture, which are always distanced to some degree or other. That distance is part of what makes the work valuable, and a responsible reading is one that will take full account of it'.[135] This conclusion rests, however, on Attridge's more general concern with the 'singularity' of 'literature' – that which marks a text as 'literary'. Such texts 'may contain important information about other cultures . . . which [they] share with other kinds of document,' but Attridge sets to one side the ethics of representation (and of responding to representations) – that is, the responsibility to 'embodied others' – in order to focus on the conceptual otherness that constitutes the 'singularity' of *any* 'inventive' literary work.[136] In so doing he effectively negates the fact of cultural difference itself: is it true that the ethics of reading a text from a different culture is more or less the same as the ethics of reading a text produced in one's own culture? If, as I have argued, cultural difference introduces a radical (but not absolute) divergence between the author's and reader's horizons of expectations, and if this in turn means that they may not share the same sense of propriety, then it is difficult to see how the ethics of reading a text produced from within one's own culture can be comparable to the ethics of reading a text from a different one – unless 'responsible reading' is conceived in abstract terms as a response to a merely *conceptual* otherness. Indeed, I would suggest that the effectivity of cultural distance *mostly* operates at the level of representation because that is how the reader principally encounters the alterity of another culture; that which makes a work 'literary' may well be transcultural (for example, an Egyptian novel may perform its literariness in ways similar to an English novel), but that which makes a culture what it is (which is represented as opposed to performed by the text) by definition is not.

As for the ethics of *writing* across cultural distance, this later essay is not concerned with it, only with 'responsible reading'. In fact, the only point at which Attridge concerns himself with it at all is in *The Singularity of Literature*, where he writes:

> a responsible response to an inventive work of art, science, or philosophy (to mention only a few possibilities) is one that brings it into being anew by allowing it, in a performance of its singularity for me, for my place and time, to refigure the ways in which I and my culture, think and feel. This may mean being willing to take on trust that it has something valuable to say when it appears obscure or objectionable, at least until several readings – and perhaps conversations or research – make an informed and just response possible.[137]

At first there does not seem to be anything particularly problematic here; Attridge's comment that we should take a work 'on trust' is entirely of a piece with an ethical openness that does not encounter it with pre-conceived notions. But throughout *The Singularity of Literature*, he seems to assume that a truly 'inventive' and thus 'singular' work of art will, by definition, be responsible for and to 'otherness' (which is what makes it 'singular' and 'inventive'), and thus its value will exceed or redeem anything that may be 'objectionable' within it. The qualification at the end of this passage is therefore rendered somewhat redundant. Since a 'responsible reading' responds to the 'singularity' and 'inventiveness' of the work, and since – in the case of those works deemed to contain 'objectionable' material – whatever is 'objectionable' in it is in fact part of what makes it singular and inventive, then a properly responsible reading *must* assume that such material is, in fact, what is valuable about the work; further 'research' would seem incidental or largely immaterial.

The problem is, once again, that Attridge's conception of responsibility is based on a 'conceptual' notion of otherness as opposed to 'embodied' others who may not be quite so willing to take on trust that the material to which they object in a work is – *of course* – what makes it 'inventive' and therefore 'ethical'. It is an aspect of Attridge's ethical maximalism, which locates ethics beyond determination. As I have argued in Chapter 1, however, embodied others usually (maybe always) encounter objectionable material within a historical frame that determines their relation to it – the material to which they object is usually an iteration of similar material to which they have already objected, and which has already been established within a discourse of domination and subordination. It would therefore not *necessarily* be unethical for them to be wary of such material. To return to the example of *The Satanic Verses* again, this is a novel that is startlingly inventive and singular, and it therefore *is*, in Attridge's terms, responsible to and for otherness in the way it brings something new into the cultural formation, and unsettles the habits of mind of at least one of its readerships; but, as will become apparent in the next chapter, it *also* conforms to certain prevailing orthodoxies and prejudices within that culture and readership with respect to certain 'embodied' others such as Islam, Muslims and religious believers in general. This divergence arises from the cultural distance that Attridge minimizes in his later essay, and accounting for it requires us to weigh up and evaluate the *relative* significance of its 'inventiveness' and its conformity, which returns us once more to the question of manner: the *ways* in which the novel achieves its 'inventiveness' and 'singularity' must be read against the *ways* in which it appears objectionable to at least some of its readers. Within an ethics of propriety – that is, ethical minimalism – accounting for its responsibilities would therefore mean *not necessarily* taking on trust that its value exceeds that which is 'objectionable' within it – at least until further research compels us to do otherwise.

Ethics as moral performativity

Throughout this chapter, I have returned at various points to the importance of what I have called 'manner(s)'. One final return is called for, via Levinas once more. In attempting to conceive how ethics might signify in a language that is always-already violently metaphysical and logocentric, a language that closes off openness towards alterity through the very categorical exclusions that produce meaning and significance, Levinas proposes his famous distinction between the Saying and the Said. For Levinas, language is amphibological, which means it is simultaneously 'logocentric, closed, finite, bound up with the thinking of essence and being', which he calls the Said, and also that which exceeds 'logos', and is 'beyond being', which he calls the Saying.[138] Each speech act, each instance of what is Said, therefore secretes within itself a Saying, which is what Simon Critchley calls a 'performative doing' that is always betrayed by the language in which it is Said but is never totally engulfed by it and thus remains as a residue, *in*

potentia.[139] If language is thus both ethical and unethical, the ethical significance of any given utterance, then, lies in the way that the Saying and
the Said relate to each other, the *manner* in which what is Said 'englobes'
and appropriates the Saying and, conversely, the way in which the Saying
disrupts and interrupts the categorical closures of the Said. This is embodied
in the style of *Otherwise than Being*, which ethically performs the resistance
to closure and 'being' and thus illustrates how 'ethics' might indeed signify
in the language of the Said. Ethics, then, is not a set of rules, or propositions, not something that is 'thought' or 'believed' but a form of conduct, a
behavior, a moral performance, and it is the nature of that performance that
is at stake in what I have called the ethics of propriety. *How* does this work
relate to the 'other' that constitutes it? With that in mind, ethics, especially
the ethics of propriety, is *nothing but* the manner(s) exhibited by each of us
in our encounter with the other.

Postscript

We are back on the summit of Mount Moriah, and the patriarch's knife is
raised above the throat of his beloved (but not only, nor even firstborn) son
when the voice says, 'Do not lay your hand upon the boy or do anything to
him, for now I know that you fear God, seeing you have not withheld your
son, your only son, from me' (Gen. 22:12). Attridge writes, 'The Bible story,
designed to reassure us of the goodness and wisdom of the divine plan, gives
us a happy ending, but it is false to everyday experience, an "ideological"
resolution, perhaps, of a real and inescapable contradiction. On our daily
Mount Moriahs, God is silent.'[140] This is the way in which modernity
habitually reads the 'happy ending' of the *Akedah*, the Binding of Isaac. It
is how Derrida reads it, but not Levinas, for whom the command to spare
Isaac is the more important of the two commandments (the first being to
sacrifice him).

In terms of the significance for ethics, I think that the Levinasian interpretation is more justified, and Derrida uncharacteristically fails to push his
reading to its logical conclusion. If the story dramatizes, as Derrida suggests,
an irresolvable conflict between our unconditional responsibility to the singular Other, symbolized by God, and our ethical obligations to other others
under the sign of 'ethics' as 'general laws of conduct and relationship', the
key point is that it is God who is the origin of *both* responsibilities.[141] It is
thus an allegory of the necessity of what I have called minimal ethics, the
necessary but insufficient response to the impossible demands of 'maximal
ethics' (God's demand for the sacrifice of Isaac). The staying of Abraham's
hand thus represents God's recognition of this paradox, and his absolving
of our responsibilities to Him over and above our responsibilities to those
other others that he Himself enjoins: his absolution, that is, of the inescapable *failure* or, more strongly, *betrayal* that this involves. This is the function
of the tropes of 'forgiveness' and God's mercy, and of posthumous reward

and '*divine* justice' in the Abrahamic monotheisms – to 'make good' that failure that is endowed upon us by divine necessity. The point is that *only* the absolute Other as represented by God can decide to absolve us of our responsibilities to Him; but also, more crucially, in the story to which all three monotheisms turn for an account of their unconditional responsibility to their God, *He resolves the paradox in favour of our responsibility to other others.*

This, of course, is of primary importance when considering the ethical obligations on Muslim readers for whom the *Qur'an*, as the Word of God, is the absolute Other to which they must unconditionally respond; but this same *Qur'an* not only rehearses the story of Abraham and Isaac (as Isma'il) within its own text, it also embodies its message in its simultaneous demand to be observed above all others, and its insistent articulation of Muslims' responsibilities towards other others. Alongside the verse 'Whether the person concerned be rich or poor, God's claim takes precedence over [the claims of] either of them' (Q4:135) one might set the *hadith* of the Prophet: 'would you serve Allah? Serve your fellow creatures (first)'.[142] To be faithful to the *Qur'an* above all other others, whether textual or human, is to be unfaithful to it, to betray one's responsibilities to those other others that the *Qur'an* and *hadith* also enjoin. As in the *Akedah*, Muslims cannot absolve *themselves* of those responsibilities in favour of a higher, singular responsibility to Allah; only Allah can do that, and in the *Qur'an*, as in Genesis, He *chooses not to*. The betrayal of those responsibilities, then, is a betrayal of the Allah to whom they profess to be faithful. What I have said here about Muslim readers applies equally to (secular) writers insofar as it applies to *everyone* (which is exactly why the mythic power of the *Akedah* carries such force). They, too, cannot absolve themselves of their responsibility to other others in the name of a higher responsibility to an absolute Other which, since the Romantics, has gone under the sign of the 'Imagination' or 'Truth'. It is of no consequence if they do not believe in God, or if, on the question of responsibility, the Imagination or Truth, unlike God, remains silent. The staying of Abraham's hand is a mythic resolution, and its 'truth' lies not in the realm of knowledge or belief – as either a 'literal' truth with an objective correlative, or with provenance over only those who profess to believe in Abraham's God – but in its articulation of that responsibility which binds all humans to each other prior to their knowing it.

Part II

4
The Self-Transgressions of Salman Rushdie: Re-Reading *The Satanic Verses*

Almost a year after Ayatollah Khomeini's 'unfunny Valentine' propelled him into hiding, Salman Rushdie published a defence of himself and his novel, *The Satanic Verses*, entitled 'In Good Faith'.[1] By turns morose and melancholic, proud and defiant, at times prickly and defensive, and at others aggressively on the offensive, the essay provides eloquent testimony to a life being lived under extreme pressure. Yet it is more than just a window into the beleaguered author's frame of mind, for in its wide-ranging discussion of the issues raised by the controversy – the respective limits of freedom of expression and religious freedom, the role of the imagination and the writer in speaking truth to power, and the respective value of secular and sacred texts to name a few – this essay (and, subsequently, the Herbert Read Memorial Lecture later published as 'Is Nothing Sacred?') can be seen as a mirror which reflects those concerns back upon the novel itself.[2] It has therefore provoked much comment in the voluminous archive of academic and journalistic responses to *The Satanic Verses* controversy. Significantly, the essay's central claim – that *The Satanic Verses* is 'a secular man's reckoning with the religious spirit', that is written 'in good faith'[3] – has not received the critical attention it deserves, a lack that speaks to the problematic which I seek to address here, namely the divergence and incommensurability of secular and non-secular interpretations of the novel.

In the polarized context of a controversy in which the very principle of freedom of expression was perceived to be under threat, readers approaching *The Satanic Verses* from a secular perspective – whether critical or supportive of Rushdie, and with few exceptions – took as axiomatic the view that it is entirely legitimate to subject religious discourses to criticism and satire regardless of the manner in which it is undertaken;[4] for these readers, the question of Rushdie's 'good faith' does not even arise since the ethical confirmation of his integrity lies in the a priori validity of the novel's speaking of a (profane) truth to (sacred) power, which is one of the ways that western secularism has historically defined itself. As such, secular perspectives on the novel accept Rushdie's claim at face value – that the novel was *self-evidently* a genuine and serious critique of Islam, not a vehicle to 'insult and abuse' its Prophet – precisely because the legitimacy of subjecting religious discourses and personalities to critical examination – regardless of one's motives or intentions – does not need to be established and therefore defended.

On the other hand, many of those readers encountering the text (or, in most cases, the controversy) from a non-secular point of view – principally Muslim, but also some from other faiths – rejected Rushdie's claim because for them the legitimacy of secular discourse is superseded by the primacy of the religious discourses that determine and shape their faith. This does not, of itself, preclude the possibility of acknowledging and even accepting criticism – many Muslim participants in the debate argued that they did not object to criticism of Islam and its Prophet *as such*, but rather the manner of it[5] – but, nevertheless, from this perspective the ethical validity of secular criticism of religious discourses requires explanation and cannot be taken for granted.

Moreover, one of the many incommensurabilities determining the controversy was between the *grounds* on which secular criticism might offer such an explanation, and those by which Muslims might have understood or accepted it. In other words, part of the difficulty in translating the controversy into a mutually productive dialogue lay in the fact that the explanations put forward by Rushdie and his secular champions were not acceptable – or even recognizable – as such to their Muslim interlocutors because the respective axioms of moral judgment concerning 'the relative value of the sacred and the profane', were divergent and irreconcilable.[6] Therefore, Muslim (non)readers by and large rejected Rushdie's claim to have written the *The Satanic Verses* in good faith, also without further examination.

This, then, is the problematic within which any attempt to address the *ethical* validity of Rushdie's endeavour must take its place, for that is what is at stake in his claim to have written 'in good faith'. In attempting to examine whether Rushdie's novel offers testimony to support his case one must situate any reading within the space vacated by these polarized critical paradigms and attempt to traffic between them. Is it possible to do justice to the secular impulse behind Rushdie's reckoning with religious faith *and* judge his efforts in terms of Islamic traditions of interpretation and moral judgment, that is, in terms other than the secular imperatives of modern literary criticism itself? This requires a methodology capable of utilizing the critical protocols and insights of secular literary criticism whilst simultaneously subjecting that criticism to the pressure of an opposing perspective that might, for instance, read the same text not only from a radically different perspective, but also from very different foundational principles – and, in so doing, also subject this *other* perspective to the same pressure as well.[7] This dual task, which, following Edward Said, I shall call 'contrapuntal criticism', seeks not to resolve or 'transcend' these divergent paradigms in some superordinate synthesis but rather to bring both into 'crisis' in the name of a critical agenda that seeks to explore the ethics (as opposed to just the politics) of a cross-cultural text.[8] This is important because *The Satanic Verses* – that 'love song to our mongrel selves'[9] – breathtakingly traverses (and travesties) multiple cultural boundaries, transgressing the boundary between the secular and the non-secular in particular. In that sense, it is a text that *invites* a contrapuntal criticism because it is a work that brings the secular and the non-secular, the sacred and the profane, into contact and crisis.

In 'In Good Faith' Rushdie writes, 'I still believe – perhaps I must – that understanding is possible, and can be achieved without the suppression of the principle of free speech. What it requires is a moment of good-will; a moment in which we may all accept that the other parties are acting, have acted, in good faith.'[10] Here Rushdie not only defends his motives, but also acknowledges the integrity of his opponents. It is an ethical gesture insofar as it seeks to transform a 'bad' situation into a 'good' one: the recognition of each other's 'good-will', Rushdie hopes, might transform mutual incomprehension and rancour into productive exchange and dialogue ('understanding is possible').

But how is one to assess the integrity of the gesture itself? Making a claim of this kind is not in itself a guarantee of its validity. Moreover, the gesture is doubly-charged; it is an once an attempt at reconciliation and an avoidance of compromise – it both reaches out to the 'other' but does not give any ground; instead, it seeks to set the problem to one side. It is also both defensive and offensive (in the sense of 'attack'). On the one hand, it responds to the charge that his intention was simply to 'insult and abuse' the Prophet Muhammad and Islam. At the same time, Rushdie challenges his Muslim opponents to live up to *their* claim that Islam is not above or beyond criticism by acknowledging his novel as a serious and genuine critique. At no point, however, does he concede the possibility that the manner of this critique might indeed justify their complaint.

As it stands, therefore, Rushdie's claim remains open to (conflicting) interpretation and rests on the vexed question of the novel's 'manner' or 'style' in relation to Islam and its Prophet. *The Satanic Verses* therefore offers the only testimony by which one might arbitrate between his claim on the one hand, and those of his Muslim opponents on the other. Whilst acknowledging that *The Satanic Verses* resists definitive readings, the critical task I want to pursue here is an examination of the novel in relation to two of the charges laid against Rushdie, which themselves encompass (as we shall see) most of the others: that *The Satanic Verses* is a 'work of bad history';[11] and that, as a Muslim-heritage author writing about Islam for a western audience, he abuses his power of description in order to perpetuate Orientalist stereotypes and revive tropes within a long tradition of Christian anti-Islamic polemics. Finally, I shall consider whether or not the novel is a genuinely contrapuntal text that effectively brings secular and non-secular experiences into a productive *melange* or 'hotch-potch' (to use Rushdie's own terms), which enables a secular sensibility to inhabit and thereby empathize with, and understand, religious experience, albeit imaginatively and temporarily, or whether, in fact, it subordinates the singularity of the one (religious experience) to the dominating perspective of the other (secularism). The validity of Rushdie's claim to have written in good faith rests on how we might read *The Satanic Verses* in the light of these concerns.

The Satanic Verses and the ethics of historical representation

Throughout the many paratexts surrounding *The Satanic Verses*, Rushdie demonstrates two particular equivocations with respect to the relationship of his novel to history. On the one hand, he acknowledges the proximity of his fiction to the historical record: 'almost everything in those sections – the dream sequences – starts from an historical or quasi-historical basis'.[12] On the other hand, he distances his novel from history, his fiction from the 'partial and ambiguous' facts: 'The section of the book in question . . . deals with a prophet who is not called Muhammad living in a highly fantasticated city . . . this entire sequence happens in a dream, the fictional dream of a fictional character . . . and one who is losing his mind, at that. How much further from history could one get?'[13]

In 'In Good Faith' he clarifies his position by dwelling at length on the relationship between 'fiction' and 'fact'. Beginning with an insistence on the 'fictionality of fiction' as a riposte to the allegation that *The Satanic Verses* is a 'work of bad history'[14] he then goes on to state that:

> I was not attempting to falsify history, but to allow a fiction to take off from history . . . the point is not whether this is 'really' supposed to be Muhammad, or whether the satanic verses incident 'really' happened; the point is to examine what such an incident might reveal about what revelation is.[15]

As Jerome de Groot has pointed out, such concerns have been germane to historical fiction since its inception, but Rushdie's particular formulation might be said to be 'postmodern' insofar as it self-consciously argues that the significance of historical 'facts' do not emerge self-evidently, but rather through the (fictional and non-fictional) *use* of that past for particular ends.[16] This problematizes the very distinction between 'fact' and 'fiction' insofar as the idea of 'facticity' being a sufficient ground for historical knowledge is called into question. Instead, facts must be 'fashioned' (the root of 'fiction', *fingere*, means 'to fashion') – whether by the historian or the novelist – into a 'meaning' through formal techniques of representation that invariably involve some form of narrativization, even when that narrativization is not outwardly apparent.[17]

This, however, raises ethical questions concerning the validity of using the past for ends which are, to use Rushdie's own words, 'tangentially historical' by means of the deliberate tampering with its material traces for it is accepted by both Rushdie's critics, and by Rushdie himself, that he 'plays' with the historical record. Such questions are, however, foreclosed almost immediately when Rushdie apparently repeats the same point on the next page: 'Fiction uses facts as a starting-place, and then spirals away to explore its real concerns . . . to treat fiction as if it were fact is to make a serious mistake of categories.'[18] On closer inspection, however, this is a totally different construction of the relationship between fact and fiction, for instead of blurring the distinction between them it emphasizes their categorical difference. This articulates a more 'empiricist' notion of history in which facts are facts, and historiography and fiction occupy radically different, even opposed, discursive terrains.

This second equivocation between postmodern and empiricist registers in relation to history accounts for the attenuated sense of responsibility he demonstrates in relation to his writing. On the one hand, he celebrates with Promethean enthusiasm the Romantic notion of an absolutely free imagination, but on the other hand, as a secularist and materialist he recoils from the metaphysical implications implicit in such an idealist sacralization of aesthetics.[19] As a result, he feels compelled to exhibit some kind of responsibility to material reality, and this he does by observing and acknowledging the notion of historical facticity whilst, at the same time, minimizing his responsibility to the 'facts' by placing it as merely a point of departure from which the unrestrained imagination might take flight.

Such equivocations stand *in lieu* of the ethical questions that arise when the very notion of 'facticity' is thrown into doubt, and Rushdie's occlusion of them is symptomatic of the relative paucity of ethical consideration within postmodernism generally about the responsibilities attendant upon historical representation, which stands in stark contrast to its extensive consideration of such epistemological issues as the grounds of historical knowledge, and the limits of representation and textuality.[20] Ironically, these are considerations that are made visible in the first place by postmodernism's critique of historical empiricism. The ethic of historical empiricism, which aims for totality, comprehensiveness, objectivity and fidelity, attenuates ethical self-awareness by reducing 'good' historical practice to a matter of method.[21] Every stage of historical practice – the selection and deselection of sources; the authorization or otherwise of such sources; the indexing of 'evidence' according to its 'value'; the inclusion or exclusion of evidence in the account; the formal organization of the material in a 'faithful' representation; and, crucially, the key concept of 'empathy' – throws up questions that are insistently ethical but which are nevertheless trumped and flattened by methodological concerns. The selection of a 'good' source, for instance, involves more than just weighing up its reliability or trustworthiness; it also involves asking questions about what purpose the source might serve, and for whom; is it morally acceptable to use such a source, and if not, why not? To what ends might the 'evidence' be legitimately put? What is a 'good' reading of the evidence? Is it acceptable to fill in the gaps through speculation – to insert one's own voice in place of the silence? To what extent might an educated guess suffice, and at what point should one refrain from going further? These are all moral as well as epistemological, ideological or political questions.

To the extent that postmodernism has rendered the processes of historical fashioning visible, it has exposed the historian and novelist to such moral dilemmas because it invites reflection on the correct relationship, within historical practice, between means and ends. But it has consistently foreclosed such questions by focusing relentlessly on the epistemology and politics of representation, but rarely, if ever, on the ethical responsibilities attendant upon the act of historical *writing*. Linda Hutcheon suggests that 'if the archive is composed of texts then it is open to all kinds of use and abuse', and if this is true (and I think it is) then surely one question that arises concerns the point at which that abuse denies the very historicity of the archive itself?[22] This is a question of degree not of kind (as suggested, for example, by the empiricist emphasis on the categorical separation of 'fact' from 'fiction'): if postmodernism enables historical 'play' by deconstructing the foundations of historical empiricism, to what extent can one play with the facts before the representation becomes not a 'historiographical metafiction', nor even a historical fiction, but merely a fantasy? That is, how far is it possible or desirable to depart from what is 'conventionally accepted' before the critique is negated by the *extent* of the distance?[23] How much can the conventional archive be violated before the violation itself becomes the issue rather than the critical re-vision of the historical record? Such questions invite us to dwell on degrees, extents and limits, which are all part of the vocabulary of ethical practice but are seldom present in the lexicon of both empiricist and postmodern theorizations of historical practice.[24]

In *The Satanic Verses*, Rushdie does not always violate the conventional historical record relating to the first years of Islam. Indeed, it may well be the relative proximity of his account of the formation of Islam to the orthodox sacred history that precipitated such emotional turbulence in contemporary Muslim (non)readers. Nevertheless, there are some clear transgressions of the orthodox narrative and some less obvious play with the available historical evidence, and the question thus arises as to whether these uphold or undermine his claim to have written 'in good faith'. Might the ambiguous position he adopts in relation to history when defending the novel be indicative of a profound, and barely acknowledged, discomfort about the integrity of his (ab)use of the sacred history of Islam and its Prophet?

If we accept the argument that the historical archive is not a residuum of data consisting of transparent 'facts' that in turn yield up a singular and 'objective' narrative about the past, that 'facts' are constructs that are semantically unstable and polysemous, and these in turn deliver a multiplicity of possible narratives, then how might we judge the integrity of any given historical narrative? We can no longer assume that it turns on the question of misrepresentation, for there is no objective standard against which to measure a writer's (in)fidelity to a given set of facts.

This is especially the case where the 'evidence', such as it is, is of a kind and quality that requires – indeed demands – the active engagement of the historian (or novelist) in reconstructing the past. As Rushdie notes, the material traces that constitute the evidence for the early years of Islam, and in particular the *sira* or biography of the Prophet Muhammad, are 'fragmented and ambiguous', consisting of – more or less – trustworthy anecdotes and reports of the Prophet's behaviour and conduct collected in canonical and non-canonical compendia known as *hadith*, as well as accounts of the major events that were pieced together from oral testimonies, eye-witness accounts and other documentation (such as the letters and treaties signed by the Prophet, the 'Constitution of Medina', etc.), from which the early Islamic historians like ibn Ishaq, at-Tabari, ibn Sa'd, and al-Waqidi pieced together narratives that converge in many respects, but diverge in others.[25]

Therefore, Rushdie's deviation (or otherwise) is, in itself, not the issue.[26] Indeed, as a passage in *The Satanic Verses* illustrates, the biography of the Prophet, and hence the early history of Islam, has been continually subject to creative re-tellings and appropriations and 'variations': 'From his mother Naima Najmuddin he [Gibreel] heard a great many stories of the Prophet, and if inaccuracies had crept into her versions he wasn't interested in knowing what they were.'[27] One might read this as a metafictional acknowledgment of Rushdie's own indifference to the inaccuracies in his own version of events, an indifference that merely replicates the creative re-tellings, appropriations and 'variations' of the Prophet's biography undertaken by both elite and subaltern agents throughout the centuries. As Annemarie Schimmel has shown, the figure of the Prophet has been radically re-worked within the idioms of popular piety, much to the chagrin of both conservative religious scholars, whose authority is challenged by such demotic discourses, and modernist reformers who cavil at the 'execrescences' that have, over the years, sedimented over the early narrative accounts of the *sira*.[28]

In such instances, 'error' operates as the signifier of a difference that exposes the work to which a history – sacred or otherwise – can be put to use: just as Rushdie's inaccuracies signal his own purposes, so too do popular rewritings 'work over' the *sira* for their own ends. As if to demonstrate that this is not peculiar to Islam, the episode with Gibreel's mother is reprised a couple of pages later in the novel in a reference to the Hindu monkey-god Hanuman. Gibreel, we are told, played the god 'in a sequence of adventure movies that owed more to a certain cheap television series emanating from Hong Kong than it did to the Ramayana'(24).[29] The discursive formations that go by the name of 'Islam' and 'Hinduism' (and any other major religion, for that matter) are constituted in their totality as much by these popular or demotic narratives, with all their 'errors' and 'inaccuracies', as by their 'orthodox' and 'authorised' counterparts, and within that formation they are, *pace* Hutcheon, no more nor less 'true' that those authorized narratives that have been stamped with the official imprimatur of truth.

The task, then, is not to judge Rushdie's responsibility to his 'evidence', and therefore his good faith, in terms of the extent of his departure (or otherwise) from some putatively unproblematic and uncontested historical 'truth' about the life of the Prophet. Rather, the task is to ascertain and interpret how Rushdie 'works' the material he draws upon, as Keith Jenkins would put it, and to what purpose.[30] To that end, there can be few better episodes to examine than the incident which gives the novel its title, known to Muslims as the affair of the *gharaniq*, or the high-flying cranes, for it perfectly illustrates the postmodernist argument about historical 'facticity' – that facts themselves, and not just the interpretations of those facts, are contentious, not least because the fact cannot speak for itself.

The episode of the *gharaniq* concerns the Prophet's temptation by a (satanically-inspired) revelation conceding that the three principal deities worshipped by the pagan Meccans could be accepted as divine intermediaries of Allah. It occupies an interstitial space within the archive of early Islam, part of a vast apocryphal store of narratives about the Prophet's sayings and conduct (*hadith*) that forms the basis for the Prophetic biographies (*sira*). Early Muslim annalists such as al-Waqidi (*c.*747–823 CE), ibn Sa'd (784–845 CE) and al-Tabari (838–923 CE) mention it in their accounts, but it was rejected as inauthentic by the compilers of the two canonical compendia of *hadith*, Bukhari (810–870 CE) and Muslim (818–874 CE). However, the great medieval *hadith* scholar al-Asqalani (1372–1448 CE) accepted its authenticity.[31] It is thus a contested fragment that stands both within and to one side of the historical record – an indeterminacy that Rushdie exploits in his novel.

The way Rushdie works this episode is to cast doubt on the divine origin of the Qur'anic revelation. All possible interpretations of Rushdie's use of this episode lead to this conclusion for we are told that 'God isn't in the picture' (111) when the *gharaniq* verses are revealed. Thus, these verses are either an expression of the Prophet's innermost desire; 'we all know how my mouth got worked' (123); or they are a conscious political expediency in order to gain some tactical advantage, 'a dream of power' (111); or they demonstrate that the Prophet was incapable of distinguishing the authentic verses of Allah from the inauthentic whisperings of Satan *because there is no such distinction* ('both times, baba, it was me' (123) says Gibreel, referring to the 'authentic' divine verses in the extant *Qur'an* and the repudiated 'satanic' verses); in which case, as Aravamudan argues, the logic of metonymy extends this doubt to the entirety of the revelation (if it is not possible to authenticate this verse, then what about the next, or any other?).[32] If we extend the metonymic logic further, then the entirety of the *Qur'an* can be seen as 'satanic' rather than 'divine'.

But are these the only readings that such an episode might yield? The episode is rendered by Tabari as follows:

> [The Prophet] longed in his soul that something would come to him from God that would reconcile him with his tribe. With his love for his tribe and his eagerness for their welfare, it would have delighted him if some of the difficulties which they made for him could have been smoothed, and he debated with himself and fervently desired such an outcome. Then God revealed [Sura 53] . . . and Satan cast on his tongue, *because of his inner debates* and what he *desired* to bring to his people, the words: 'These are the high-flying cranes; verily their intercession is to be hoped for.'[33]

Notice how the Prophet's personal desire and motivation is openly acknowledged as the basis for his temptation, and is not psychologized in the modern sense as a displacement of some ulterior cause; nor does it cast doubt on the authenticity of the Prophetic experience. Instead of the incident illustrating the Prophet's duplicity or casting doubt on the revelation, the story may instead have been seen as a parable highlighting the *ethical* basis of the Prophet's temptation, i.e. to make things 'smooth' for his tribe (the pagan Quraysh) because of his love for them and their welfare (and of the early Muslims). A desire for reconciliation – and compromise – lies beneath the temptation, one that is undertaken for honourable motives according to the story, not because of devious calculation and political expediency. What Tabari and his early Muslim readers almost certainly would *not* have done is deploy a modern rationality – religious or otherwise – that invariably translates ethical and ontological issues into epistemological ones, and the experience of faith simply into a question of belief.

Modern Muslims find the *gharaniq* episode blasphemous and offensive because they have, to a greater or lesser extent, absorbed post-Enlightenment secular rationality through colonial and thence post-colonial educational systems that have largely transformed the ways in which they encounter their own religious traditions. As such, they refute the incident itself by suggesting that there are no historical grounds for its authenticity. This counter-argument is articulated in terms of historical empiricism, both through the insistence that *The Satanic Verses* is a work of 'bad history', and the explicit distancing of 'fact' from 'fiction'.[34] In so doing, Rushdie's modern Muslim antagonists demonstrated a shared conceptual and discursive space with their opponent by arguing on the grounds of in/authenticity whilst concurring that the episode 'works', from both points of view, to undermine the existence of Allah.

Regardless of the 'authenticity' of the episode, it is likely that Tabari, Waqidi and other early Muslims would not have seen the same blasphemous implications in the incident because they are only apparent from the vantage point of a secularism they could not possibly have inhabited. Rather, the early Muslims accepted that humans were tempted by *shaitans*, who sensed their inner desires and exploited them, and they would have accepted too that the Prophet would not have been exempt from such temptations, not least because the Prophet's temptations are alluded to elsewhere in the *Qur'an* itself.[35] Nor could they possibly have understood the episode to be implying the non-existence of Allah. For them, the temptation of the Prophet by a *shaitan* would simply be the unremarkable and *prima facie* evidence that human affairs are subject to divine and supernatural power.

This example of contrapuntal analysis shows how placing divergent readings in counterpoint can simultaneously contest Rushdie's use of Islamic history *and* the refutations of his Muslim critics, thereby bringing the opposition itself into crisis: Rushdie and his Muslim critics are shown to possess more common ground than they might each acknowledge. Far from being opposed to one another, their understandings of this pivotal episode converge whilst their rhetorical opposition is maintained by the exclusion of other, subaltern possibilities. However, this does not furnish sufficient evidence for an assessment of Rushdie's 'good faith', not least because, in this instance, he sticks quite closely to the recorded script – and he can hardly be faulted for drawing the same blasphemous conclusions from the episode as his Muslim opponents, namely that the episode casts doubt on the divine origin of the *Qur'an*.

Elsewhere in *The Satanic Verses*, however, he deviates quite markedly from the conventional historical accounts of the Prophetic *sira* and the social, religious and political milieu he inhabited. Take this passage from the 'Return to Jahilia' section of the novel:

> Mahound had no time for scruples, Salman told Baal, no qualms about ends and means. The faithful lived by lawlessness, but in those years Mahound – or should one say the Archangel Gibreel? – should one say Al-Lah? – became obsessed by law. Amid the palm trees of the oasis

Gibreel appeared to the Prophet and found himself spouting rules, rules, rules, until the faithful could scarcely bear the prospect of any more revelation, Salman said, rules about every damn thing, if a man farts let him turn his face to the wind, a rule about which hand to use for the purpose of cleaning one's behind. It was as if no aspect of human existence was to be left unregulated, free. (363–4)

This is the satirical climax of the novel, the point at which its critique is most sharply focused. It operates through a mode of comic exaggeration, and deliberate, highly provocative *violation* of the historical record precisely in order to signal, as obtrusively as possible, its violations. The passage, which in its totality is a long one (363–8), proceeds to enumerate a long series of prohibitions, a couple of which are genuine, but most of which are completely fabricated, bizarre and absurd, the excessiveness of such legislation – signalling a totalitarian view of life – mimicked by narrative excess. Although an alibi of sorts is provided by the suggestion that this is being articulated by the character Salman the Persian (whom we later discover to be embittered), it is nevertheless clear that the perspective is the narrator's, if not Rushdie's himself, not least because Salman the Persian is, by Rushdie's own admission, an ironic, metafictional gesture towards the author.[36] As Nico Israel has observed, such is Rushdie's predilection towards *parabasis* that many of his characters throughout his fiction become mouthpieces for his own views.[37] This is further buttressed by the instability in the narration itself, moving as it does almost imperceptibly between reported speech, free indirect discourse, and third-person narration (e.g. 'Gibreel appeared to the Prophet *and found himself* spouting . . . ', a perspective that could not possibly have any association with Salman the Persian).

Muslim critics – and a few secular Muslims, such as Talal Asad – have pointed out the numerous errors in detail in this long passage, which is, in fact, far more radically blasphemous in the conventional sense than the title incident which it reprises; for this is the passage in which Salman inserts his own little 'errors' into the Qur'anic text, and the implication that the extant text is not the literal word of Allah but rather a human corruption is much more apparent.[38] However, my interest here is in the way the satire initially proceeds from a *secular* rather than theological basis; or, rather, in how the theological doubt that it eventually articulates emerges out of a critique of the allegedly excessive legalism of Islam/Submission. The semantic development as well as chronological progression of the passage moves from Salman's doubts about 'rules' to his eventual tampering with the Qur'anic verses. At first, Salman 'began to notice how useful and well-timed the angel's revelations tended to be . . . All those revelations of convenience' (364–5). *En passant*, he notes with distaste the new rules on marriage and rehearses a long list of other 'rules' showing how women are kept subservient in the new religion of Submission/Islam. But the passage ends with a theological rather than legal critique: 'if my poor words could not be distinguished from the Revelation by God's own messenger, then what did that mean?' (367).

It seems, therefore, that Salman's theological doubts are consequent upon a more primary concern with Islam/Submission's *secular* presence: its political and legal aspects. Rushdie's critique here rests on his apprehension of, and distaste for, what he sees as Islam's excessive and stultifying legalism, which leaves 'no aspect of human experience . . . unregulated, free' (364). This is the basis of what he takes to be the totalitarianism of contemporary Muslim societies. Ironically, however, he shares this view of Islam – albeit from a totally different perspective – with the Islamists whom he attacks, for Islamism has, since its inception in 1920s Egypt, been little concerned with theology and more concerned with Islam's secular dimensions: the state and the law.[39]

This is not necessarily a problem. In order to attack something, in order to satirize it, one must share the same terms of reference as the target, and the architecture of the novel, with its narrative about the Imam (Khomeini), clearly signals that modern Islamism – or 'fundamentalism' as it was then known – is one of Rushdie's principal concerns. The problem, however, arises in the way that the passage suggests that Islamic legalism is *directly* derived from the Qur'anic revelation, or, to put it more accurately, that the revelation is itself excessively and fundamentally legalistic, full of 'endlessly proliferating rules' (365). This is an abuse of the historical past insofar as it conflates both theological and secular critiques, thereby widening the scope of the attack to encompass both *Islam* and Islamism, and, in fact, renders any possible distinction between the two impossible through an essentializing gesture which contends that Islam, at its moment of origin, is in fact inherently Islamist.

In fact, there are relatively few legal verses in the *Qur'an*. Of the 6000 or so verses, only about 500 have legal content, and 'these prescriptions cover a limited range of human affairs'.[40] According to Montgomery Watt, during his time in Medina, the Prophet instituted extensive legal reforms only with respect to 'social security, marriage and inheritance'. He also carried out minor legal reforms with respect to slavery, usury, drinking of wine, and a prohibition on the intercalation of the lunar calendar.[41] As he drily notes, 'What he did, when the record of it is read, seems to be very little, but in the circumstances of the time, it was effective'.[42]

In presenting it otherwise, Rushdie seems to be making three distinct slippages in the 'rules, rules, rules' passage. The first is between *ahadith* and revelation. The former are reports about the Prophet's pronouncements, actions, behaviours, likes and dislikes, responses to certain situations and so on. These constitute an extensive collection of anecdotes that cover a wide range of social experience. Sami Zubaida notes that the *Sahih* of al-Bukhari, which is one of the two canonical collections of *hadith*, consists of '97 books, subdivided into 3450 chapters, adding up to 2762 *ahadith*, many repeated in different contexts. Each book contains *ahadith* pertaining to a particular subject, such as "prayer, fasting, alms, testimony, buying and selling, surety, marriage"' and so on.[43] This is clearly what Rushdie has in mind when characterizing the comprehensiveness of Islamic legalism, for *ahadith* became a principal source for Islamic jurisprudence (*fiqh*) and what is now known as the *Shari'ah*.[44] However, Islamic jurisprudence only began 'towards the end of the Ummayad period', that is, some two hundred or so years *after* the death of the Prophet.[45] In other words, the *sunna* or example of the Prophet, as recorded in the *ahadith*, did not become codified as law in any legal sense until well after the formative period of Islam. In fact, according to Zubaida (following Norman Calder), the grounding of *Shari'ah* on the foundations of the *Qur'an* and the *sunna* of the Prophet was the *last* stage in the development of the law.

> The chronology of the evolution of legal thought in the third century, according to Calder's account, is the following: the formulation of rules and reflection upon them comes first and is put forward in the terminology of *ra'y*, opinion. Eventually the justification of rules is sought in preceding juristic authority, such as Malik or Abu Hanifa. *At a subsequent stage, and driven by competition between schools to justify their particular rules, arises the appeal to prophetic precedent, now developed in the discipline of* 'ilm al-hadith, *the compilation and verification of prophetic narrative . . . The last stage is the introduction of scriptural sanction, the articulation of the rules so far developed to texts from the Quran.*[46]

Rushdie therefore not only misrepresents the origin of the *Shari'ah* in revelation, but also anachronistically posits it as having been operational during the Prophet's lifetime.

This is the basis for the second slippage, between two different kinds of normativity. Rushdie ascribes a normative *law* to a period when Islamic normativity must have been primarily based on the 'emulation' of the Prophet himself rather than 'rules' derived from the revelation and the *sunna*, which speaks to the relative lack of 'rules' (in the legalistic sense) in the *Qur'an* itself. As Salman Sayyid has put it, 'the message is manifested in the actions of the messenger. In other words, the Prophet reveals what Islam is, but Islam is also what the Prophet does.'[47] Moreover, the normativity that arises from emulation is qualitatively different to that produced by law. An ideal to be emulated is not the same as a law that cannot be transgressed. It is clear, for example, that the Muslims during the Prophet's lifetime, did not feel compelled to reproduce, in every detail, the example of the Prophet – and nor have Muslims since.[48]

The third slippage in this passage is between Islamic law and 'divine law'. The *Shari'ah* is 'largely man-made, based on exegesis, interpretations,

analogies, and extensive borrowing from customary practices . . . and existing local Middle Eastern legal traditions'.[49] The suggestion that there are
'rules about every damn thing' (363) has its corollary in the idea that 'the
shari'a . . . is the revealed law of God and is, therefore, the perfect set of rules
for human conduct, which needs no supplementation by man-made laws'.[50]
These ideas form the basis of Ayatollah Khomeini's notion of rule by jurist,
vilayat-e-faqih, which, in both Rushdie's fiction and in life, articulates the
very antithesis of hybridity. Rushdie is therefore complicit in the ideological framing of *Shari'ah* as 'divine law' by Muslim orthodoxy and Islamists,
in particular, although the notion has common currency amongst Muslims
and non-Muslims – which explains why most modern Muslim critics did
not pick Rushdie up on this point in their readings of this passage; to have
done so would have thrown the hegemonic characterization of Islamic law
as 'divine' into crisis.

What I am arguing here is that Rushdie's historical violations involve a
series of essentializing gestures which suggest that the Islamic religion, at
the moment of its origin, instituted the kind of totalitarian Islamic state
envisaged by contemporary Islamists and embodied in the Islamic Republic
of Iran. The text's architecture, which involves a series of intricate parallelisms that connect the various narratives, also buttresses the essentialism
most forcefully articulated in the 'rules, rules, rules' passage. For instance,
it is clear that the city of Jahilia is a narrative double of both Mecca *and*
Tehran, the description of the latter – 'a mountain looming over a city'
(206) – invoking the former, which is overlooked by Mount Hira/Cone. This
link between seventh-century Mecca and late twentieth-century Tehran is
reinforced in the passages suggesting that Mahound's/Muhammad's insti-
tution of Submission/Islam in Jahilia/Mecca is maintained by the coercive
apparatuses of a totalitarian state, in particular a secret police and network
of informers reminiscent of the Shah's SAVAK organization. However, as
Watt reminds us, the early Islamic social structure was not 'an impersonal
state' and the Prophet 'had no police force. The very idea of such a thing
was probably unknown among the Arabs.'[51] Furthermore, whilst the available historical evidence suggests that the dwellings of seventh-century
Mecca were 'extremely primitive',[52] the novel's contrary representation of
Jahilia as a sophisticated and bacchanalial metropolis (103, 116), full of
'piazza(s)' (117) and 'enormous palazzo(s)' (376) invites comparison with
a putatively wealthy, westernized and decadent Tehran prior to the 1979
Revolution, 'in which the riots of the starving were brutally put down by
Hind's personal police force' (361). Similarly, post-Mahound, the city's
'newly puritanical streets' (377) reflect the post-revolutionary moralism of
the Islamic Republic of Iran.

Such essentializing gestures erase fourteen hundred years of Islamic
history, and undermine the claim Rushdie makes in 'In Good Faith' that
The Satanic Verses attacks 'the narrower definitions of Islam' as opposed to

Islam as a whole.[53] Indeed, throughout that essay, he displays an insistent urge to distinguish between *some* Muslims and forms of Islam, and the wider generality of Muslims and Islam itself, with whom he says he has no quarrel; 'I knew that Islam is by no means homogeneous, or as absolutist as some of its champions make it out to be', he writes, and it 'contains the doubts of Iqbal, Ghazzali, Khayyam as well as . . . narrow certainties . . . ribaldry as well as solemnity, irreverence as well as absolutism.' Elsewhere, he asks 'that great mass of ordinary, decent, fair-minded, Muslims . . . not to let Muslim leaders make Muslims seem less tolerant than they actually are'.[54] This gesture is repeated again and again, in 'One Thousand Days in a Balloon' as well as in 'In Good Faith', and in so doing he hopes to demonstrate that he sees a distinction between Islam as a historical phenomenon in all its diversity and development, and what he sees as the attempt by certain Muslims to place it outside of history, to eternalize it by 'fixing' it forever.[55] However, there is a discrepancy between this later claim that the novel defends 'historical' Islam from the 'fundamentalists' and the textual evidence furnished by the novel itself. The space opened up by this discrepancy illuminates the unwitting complicity between Rushdie and the Islamists he is apparently attacking, for their respective essentializations rest on a mutual *foreclosure* (despite Rushdie's apparent endorsement of them) of the heterodox and subaltern possibilities that exist, and have existed, within the scriptural and apocryphal traditions of 'historical' Islam.

Furthermore, it is actually very difficult to pin down the particular Muslims or 'narrower' forms of Islam he has in mind: certainly, Khomeini and the Islamism of the Islamic Republic of Iran, and 'fundamentalists' more generally; but he also arraigns 'Muslim leaders' and 'orthodoxy' and even organized religion of any kind. The very expansiveness of this target, the way it shifts throughout his discourse, its very instability, in fact collapses the distinction he so assiduously tries to maintain between the general and the particular, for it is almost impossible to imagine how anyone could be a Muslim at all without some kind of orthodoxy, or some form of institutionalized practice. In fact, it becomes very difficult to imagine an Islam that Rushdie might approve of; the standard response amongst critics is to suggest Sufism, but it would have to be a de-institutionalized Sufism shorn of its *tariqas*, its rigid hierarchies and spiritual disciplines.[56] Indeed, it is difficult to avoid the conclusion that the only kind of Muslim Rushdie really does not have a problem with is the kind that sees his or her faith in purely secularized terms as a private, individualized spirituality. Despite asserting that his novel dissents against 'imposed orthodoxies *of all types*', Rushdie therefore imposes an orthodoxy himself, namely secular-liberalism and its version of permissible religiosity.[57] However, this orthodoxy – shall we call it 'secular fundamentalism'? – remains invisible to him because it constitutes the ideological ground on which he stands.

Neo-Orientalism

'They have the power of description, and we succumb to the pictures they construct' (168) says one of the mutants incarcerated in a facility holding illegal immigrants to Saladin Chamcha, newly transformed himself into the very embodiment of Thatcherite Britain's racially coded fantasies of 'devilish' Others. If *The Satanic Verses*, and Rushdie's work more generally, rightly occupies a major platform in the canon of post-colonial criticism, it is because his work has demonstrated an insistent concern with the politics of representation, in particular the ways in which relations between 'the West' and its (post-)colonial Others have been mediated by discourses that structure 'the East' not only as 'the West's' antithesis and subordinate, but also, in Edward Said's formulation, its 'underground self'.[58] Much Muslim criticism of the novel overlooked or obscured the fact that *The Satanic Verses* is as much concerned with contesting racism and orientalism as with the foundations of Islam and its manifestations (both in dream and reality) in the late twentieth century, but others contended that far from challenging hegemonic machineries of representation, as far as its portrayal of Islam and its Prophet was concerned, the novel in fact subscribes to and reinforces them.

The Muslim case against *The Satanic Verses* amounted to an accusation of communal libel that had 'demeaned and degraded them in their own and especially other's eyes'.[59] The libel, in their eyes, consisted of two parts: first, the abusive and insulting treatment of figures in their sacred tradition whom they revere; 'such taunts,' writes Modood, 'are not part of the healthy clash of ideas that all beliefs ought to be subject to; they are an incitement to community hatred based on an intimate knowledge of what will hurt'.[60] Secondly, the Muslim protestors argued that the novel offered a grossly inaccurate and misleading historical account of the foundation of their religion. We have dealt with the latter of these above; the former can be said to consist of three specific points: abusive and insulting language directed at the Prophet of Islam and his earliest companions; the infamous brothel scenes; and the representation of the character of the Prophet, Mahound.

The first of these accusations is relatively easy to evaluate. Muslim complaints invariably referred to the way in which the novel described the Prophet's earliest companions as a 'trinity of scum', 'fucking goons', or how they are described as drunks, and a 'bunch of riff-raff'. It almost seems pointless to point out that these are embedded in the dialogue of characters implacably hostile to the early Muslims, but it bears saying again if only to make the point that much of the literary criticism at the heart of the controversy was of a very poor standard: many of the Muslim critics seemed to be either unaware of the textual status of dialogue, the basic demands of dramatic staging, and of the difference between narrator and character (all of which is puzzling given the long traditions of drama, narrative prose and literary criticism in Muslim countries), or they did not care, in which case their criticisms were unprincipled. As Rushdie put it in his fine riposte, 'the scene in which the Prophet's companions are called "scum" and "bums" is a depiction of the early persecution of the believers . . . How, one wonders, could a book portray persecution without allowing the persecutors to be seen persecuting?'[61]

Much was made of the description of Bilal – an Abyssinian slave who was one of the first converts to Islam and, on account of his fine voice became the first Muslim *muezzin* to issue the call to prayer – as an 'enormous black monster . . . with a voice to match his size' (101). This was taken by some to be a racist slur on one of the most revered of the Prophet's early companions, but Ali Mazrui, one of the more sophisticated of the early Muslim contributors to the debate, wonders, rather, why the novel does not 'give either Bilal or Islam the *explicit* credit of being a multi-racial religion from so early a stage'.[62] Leaving aside the apparent facetiousness of such a demand (why *should* Rushdie have made this explicit rather than leave it, as he does, implicit?) Mazrui makes two substantive points about what he sees as the novel's compromised racial politics, which he magnifies through a somewhat gratuitous comparison with *Mein Kampf*; given the novel's clearly articulated anti-racist stance, these are worth considering when evaluating the novel's ethical weight. The first involves Rushdie's choice of 'Mahound' as the name of his fictional Prophet (of which more presently). Mazrui ties together a string of historical associations within what might be termed the 'white-western' tradition that connote 'the convergence between religion and racism. In Medieval Europe the ultimate religious symbol of the devil on earth was Muhammad. The ultimate racial symbol of the devil on earth was the black man.'[63] Therein, for Mazrui, lies the racial coding of Rushdie's choice of name for his Prophet, which he himself describes as the 'Devil's synonym' (93).

The second example of problematic racial coding for Mazrui is Rushdie's representation of Bilal's narrative *avatar*, Bilal X, in the Imam episode. The passage in question describes Bilal X as follows:

> The voice is rich and authoritative, a voice in the habit of being listened to; well-nourished, highly trained, the voice of American confidence, a weapon of the West turned against its makers . . . In the early days, Bilal X protested against such a description of his voice. He, too, belonged to an oppressed people, he insisted, so it was unjust to equate him with the Yankee imperialists. The Imam answered, not without gentleness: Bilal, your suffering is ours as well. But to be raised up in the house of power is to learn its ways, to soak them up, through that very skin that is the cause of your oppression. The habit of power, its timbre, its posture, its way of being with others. It is a disease, Bilal, infecting all who come near it. If the powerful trample over you, you are infected by the soles of their feet. (211)

What seems to exercize Mazrui here is the imputation that African-Americans, despite their oppression, are themselves representatives of western cultural hegemony, their victimhood compromised and corrupted by power: 'Is Rushdie making fun of African-Americans generally? Or is he satirizing Afro-american Muslims? Or is he ridiculing the significance of Malcolm X?'[64]

Notwithstanding the debates within all oppressed and minority groups about the validity and efficacy of what might be called the politics of victimhood (and the charges hurled at them for it by political opponents), Mazrui seems to overlook the possibility that Rushdie is making a serious point here about power, its mode of operation and its effects: it is not, after all, simply Malcolm X that is integrated into the figure of Bilal X (and, by metonymic extension, Afro-American Muslims), but also the African-American mainstream musical tradition (Bilal X had, we are told, 'succeeded in climbing the Everest of the hit parade, not once, but a dozen times, to the very top'), which has been appropriated as one of the representative channels of American and western cultural imperialism (another figure lurking in this composite picture is neither black, nor American, but certainly one of the highest profile Muslim converts of recent times: Yusuf Islam aka Cat Stevens).

Indeed, the full significance of the passage concerning Bilal X only becomes apparent when read in conjunction with the infamous brothel episodes. These attracted the most immediate controversy due to their explosive combination of sex, religion and satire. Even some of Rushdie's strongest defenders found the brothel scenes overly provocative. Malise Ruthven, for instance, noted that 'the savage coarseness of tone that occurs in the brothel scene' were 'questionable' and concluded that 'we may agree with Rushdie's sentiments; we may salute his courage; we may admire his literary skill, without respecting his judgement'.[65]

Aside from some of the very first criticisms (long before the controversy itself), most of the Muslim protestors did notice the clear distinction in the text between the prostitutes in the brothel taking on the names of the Prophet's wives, and the Prophet's wives themselves. What they objected to was the association between them; could Rushdie not have found another way of making his point without impugning the honour of the Prophet's wives, whom Muslims see as the 'Mothers of the Believers'? In other words, it was as if Rushdie had brought their *own* mothers' reputations into disrepute. In most Muslim countries the social structure still involves a notion of family or clan honour, called *izzat*, of which the women of the family are the custodians. That honour is upheld through strict codes of sexual propriety and any transgression of those codes, or any imputation of a transgression through illicit sexual activity, is a shameful matter, bringing the *izzat* of the family into disrepute. This sense of *izzat* is particularly strong amongst Muslims of the Indian subcontinent, who constitute the vast majority (some

70 per cent) of British Muslims. Even the *association* of illicit sexual activity with the names of the Prophet's wives – seen as Mothers of the 'tribe' of Islam – thus dishonoured the *izzat* of all Muslims.

It is only fair to point out that the brothel scenes quickly moved to the background as the controversy developed, although it remained a powerful, if somewhat muted, chord in the ensemble of Muslim protests. Very few of the later Muslim critiques dwelt at length on it, although all touched upon it in passing. Rushdie's own defence of the brothel scenes is that it served 'to dramatize certain ideas about morality; and sexuality, too, because what happens in the brothel . . . is that the men of Jahilia are enabled to act out an ancient dream of power and possession, that of possessing the queen. That men should be so aroused by the great ladies' whorish counterfeits says something about *them* not the great ladies'.[66] This defence does raise the issue of power that is at the heart of this episode and is, in fact, one of the central but under-discussed thematics of the novel as a whole. But the episode is not just about power, sexuality and possession; it is also about the resistance to power and the manner of its subversion. For the prostitutes' adoption of the identities of the Prophet's wives is clearly a parody directed against the power of the Prophet. It is significant that it is a strategy formulated by the poet, Baal, and as such this parody – which, the novel suggests, is far more effective at eroding the legitimacy of power (if inherently fragile, and provisional in its successes) than overt confrontation – encodes the logic of the *The Satanic Verses* into itself, which is an attempt to write back to power through, amongst other things, a parody of the life of the Prophet of Islam.

On the other hand, if Rushdie's tactic in juxtaposing the 'two struggling worlds, [harem and brothel] pure and impure, chaste and coarse . . . making them echoes of one another' is to show that 'no imperium is absolute, no victory complete' (378) then so too does it show, in a nicely dialectical way, how power co-opts and renders complicit even those who believe themselves to be adversarial to it. What begins as a parodic satire of the Prophet and his *harem* ends as an ersatz imitation of it, as the 'the staff of the Curtain warmed to the new task' (381) to the point where they begin to imitate the reputed behaviour of the Prophet's actual wives and then project onto Baal, as the Prophet's illicit doppelgänger, the reponsibilities of legal matrimony; 'His wives now made it plain to him that they expected to fulfil his husbandly duties in every particular' (383); in the end, 'they had grown so accustomed to their new names they couldn't remember their old ones' (390).

Can it be said, therefore, that *The Satanic Verses* is aware of its own complicity with the frames of power that it ostensibly seeks to contest? Would such an awareness provide an alibi for Rushdie against the charges that he succumbs to the seductive gaze of western power? It is a difficult question to answer; in making his point about power and the resistance to it, Rushdie not only juxtaposes the sacred and profane worlds of the *harem* and brothel but, as we have seen, he scandalously blurs the distinction between them. In so doing, the episode (as well as the earlier passage about Bilal X) demonstrates the novel's main theme about the impossibility of remaining 'pure', either in culture or in politics, but it also confirms the Muslim claim that the brothel scenes act as a lightning rod that conducts much of the novel's oppositional energy into the channel of a well-worn orientalist stereotype of the Muslim world as licentious and sexually degenerate. Moreover, one effect of this blurring is the implication that such ways of the Muslim world have their basis in the character and behaviour of its Prophet.

Norman Daniel begins his celebrated study *Islam and the West* with an unequivocal statement: 'The earliest Christian reactions to Islam were much the same as they have been until quite recently. The tradition has been continuous and it is still alive', and he concludes scarcely less equivocally that 'we need to keep in mind how mediaeval Christendom argued, because it has always been and still is part of the make-up of every Western mind brought to bear upon the subject'.[67] The fundamental elements of European attitudes towards Islam that were established by early Christian polemics against what was at first perceived to be an upstart heresy within Christianity itself have proved to be remarkably durable over the centuries, and, despite some shifts in emphasis and the secularization of approach following the Enlightenment and the rise of Orientalism, the same tropes still provide the basic grid of perception through which the West views Islam.[68] These consist of the idea that the Prophet Muhammad was a false prophet, an impostor and a schemer who used divine revelation as a justification for his worldly ambitions; that Islam is inherently a martial and violent religion that was spread at the point of a sword, which brooks no argument, and is not open to rational disputation; that Muslims are 'so zealous for their religion that wherever they hold power they mercilessly behead every man who preaches against their religion';[69] and a morally degenerate religion – an 'easy' religion that constitutes a 'broad way to perdition' that contrasts unfavourably with the moral rectitude and asceticism of Christianity – that permits self-indulgence and sexual licence. This last point has, after the advent of European Romanticism, been subtly transformed into its very opposite – that Islam is an excessively rigid and puritanical religion that *denies* sexual freedom and is particularly oppressive of women. It was the person of the Prophet himself on whom all the disparate elements of Christian anti-Islamic polemics were brought to bear in order to cohere into a general attack on Islam as a whole: '[t]he life of Muhammad was seen as an essential disproof of the Islamic claim to revelation. It was often treated as the most important disproof of all. To this end writers believed and wished to show that Muhammad was a low-born and pagan upstart, who schemed himself into power, who maintained it by pretended revelations, and who spread it both by violence and by permitting to others the same lascivious practices he indulged in himself.'[70]

With all this in mind, Rushdie's choice of Mahound as the name for his fictional Prophet is deeply problematic and provocative, and lends considerable credibility to the charge of Orientalism. Rushdie's defence is not exactly convincing. The rationale is set out clearly in the novel itself: 'To turn insults into strengths, whigs, tories, Blacks, all chose to wear with pride the names they were given in scorn; likewise, our mountain-climbing, prophet-motivated solitary is to be the medieval baby-frightener, the Devil's synonym: Mahound' (93). Rushdie later restated the argument in 'In Good Faith', pointing out that the reclamation of symbols of oppression and persecution is a theme that runs throughout the novel, and indeed, insofar as such acts constitute a means of symbolically opposing power and its ability to create pictures of the world to which the powerless must succumb, this does bind together the naming of the Prophet, the reclamation of the 'devil' symbol by the youths of Brickhall, and the brothel episode.

Nevertheless, the argument that the naming of Mahound is 'to attempt the sort of affirmation that, in the United States, transformed the word black from the standard term of racist abuse into a "beautiful" expression of cultural pride', is both disingenuous and evasive.[71] The standard term of racist abuse in the United States was not 'black' but 'nigger', and it is revealing that the other instances given in the text are also not particularly offensive insults: is he really suggesting that 'whigs' and 'tories' stand comparison with terms such as 'nigger' or 'paki'? Of course not, which is why he does not include those terms, either in the novel or, conspicuously, in his essay. Moreover, the value of such reclamation remains unclear; is he really providing a serious option for Muslims here? Should Muslims try to 'reclaim' the term 'Mahound' from the anti-Muslim polemicists? Why? What would they profit by it? In any case, the act of reclamation is one that the persecuted group must undertake themselves. As Richard Webster pointed out, 'For Rushdie, having confirmed that he is himself not a Muslim, to argue that he is reclaiming language on behalf of all Muslims is an act of quite extraordinary presumption.'[72] His argument has the appearance of being merely a debating point, one that makes logical sense but is insensitive to the wider contexts within which he is writing, and particularly to those people (i.e. Muslims) on whose behalf he claims to be acting. In this instance, therefore, Rushdie is arrogating to himself the same power to describe others that he claims to be contesting.

Rushdie's mischievous inventiveness with language means he cannot resist inserting a little pun in the section on naming Mahound which also raises questions about the tradition of writing within which he locates his novel. Mahound is referred to as 'prophet-motivated', an allusion to Muhammad's career as a merchant prior to his assuming the mantle of prophethood. As if to underline the point, in the next paragraph the Prophet is described as 'Mahound the businessman'. The 'businessman' motif is revived later in the novel when the disillusioned Salman the Persian, fed up with the rules-obsessed religion Mahound has founded, returns to Jahilia from Yahtrib and recounts to Baal his loss of faith. The narrator states, 'Salman the Persian got to wondering what manner of God this was that sounded so much like a businessman. This was when he had the idea that destroyed his faith, because he recalled that, of course, Mahound himself had been a business-man, and a damned successful one at that' (364). In medieval Christian polemics against Islam, Muhammad's earlier career as a merchant was taken to be an indicator of his worldliness, which was contrasted with the spiritual other-worldliness of Jesus Christ. The Prophet-cum-businessman was a trope that opened up other accusations, most notably that he was a schemer, on the one hand, and a fraud and impostor on the other. This is because the idea that Islam was a 'practical' religion coincided with a fundamental divergence in Islamic and Christian conceptualizations of revelation. Daniel writes that, 'Latins were genuinely scandalized by the Islamic conception of *ad hoc* revelations given in response to political or social problems of the moment. For the Muslim, a revelation that responded to the circum-stances of a particular moment was normal, whereas to the Christian mind such a thing seemed to be its own condemnation.'[73] In other words, where Muslims see the situatedness of Qur'anic verses as evidence of Allah's ability to guide and instruct those who follow His path, medieval Christians saw only expedience – the justification of Muhammad's desires through pre-tended revelations of convenience.[74]

The 'businessman' trope in *The Satanic Verses* rehearses these medieval Christian concerns almost precisely. Mahound's pragmatism – 'Mahound, most pragmatic of all Prophets' (381) – is the basis for doubting the rev-elations he receives. The full significance of the novel's use of the 'satanic verses' incident cannot be understood without an awareness of this histori-cal frame. 'The pretence to prophecy was . . . to see it as a device to obtain, or retain power', writes Daniel; 'Muhammad's religious deceit was presented as the implement of his secular ambition.'[75] But the novel goes much fur-ther, for the 'convenience' of the revelations is alluded to, and explicitly mentioned, several times:

> Salman began to notice how useful and well-timed the angel's revela-tions tended to be, so that when the faithful were disputing Mahound's views on any subject . . . the angel would turn up with an answer, and he always supported Mahound . . . It would have been different, Salman complained to Baal, if Mahound took up his positions after receiving the revelation from Gibreel; but no, he just laid down the law and the angel would confirm it afterwards . . . All those revelations of convenience . . . And after the end of the war, hey presto, there was the Archangel Gibreel instructing the surviving males to marry the widowed women . . . at once, bang, out comes the rule book, the angel starts pouring out rules about what women mustn't do . . . (364–7)

Moreover, the novel discusses the convenience of the revelations in relation to exactly the same concerns that so exercised the medieval Christian polemicists. For if power was one of the principal reasons the Prophet was thought to have fabricated justification from the Almighty, the other was his apparently limitless appetite for sex.

Three aspects of the Prophet's sexual conduct were of particular interest: one concerning his marriage to Zaynab bint Jash, the wife of his adopted son Zayd; one concerning the rumours of sexual impropriety against his wife A'ishah; and Qur'anic verses dealing with the number of wives and concubines permitted to the Prophet. The last two of these are reprised in *The Satanic Verses*:

> He told Baal about a quarrel between Mahound and Ayesha, recounting the rumour as if it were incontrovertible fact. 'That girl couldn't stomach it that her husband wanted so many other women . . . Finally, he went into – what else? – one of his trances, and out he came with the message from the archangel. Gibreel had recited verses giving him full divine support. God's own permission to fuck as many women as he liked. So there: what could poor Ayesha say against the verses of God? You know what she did say? This: 'Your God certainly jumps to it when you need him to fix things up for you.' (386)

> Salman's story: Ayesha and the Prophet had gone on an expedition to a far-flung village . . . Camp was struck before dawn. At the last moment Ayesha was obliged by a call of nature to rush out of sight into a hollow . . . Ayesha returned after relieving herself to find herself alone, and who knows what might have befallen her if a young man, a certain Safwan, had not chanced to pass by on his camel . . . Safwan brought Ayesha back to Yathrib safe and sound; at which point tongues began to wag . . . 'Same as ever. He saw his pet, the archangel, and then informed one and all that Gibreel had exonerated Ayesha . . . And this time, mister, the lady didn't complain about the convenience of the verses.' (387)

As often the case with Rushdie, the context for the first of these episodes is recounted elsewhere, in the parodic behaviour of the whores of The Curtain – 'Once he [Baal/Mahound/Muhammad] was caught with "Mary the Copt" by "Hafsah",' in 'Hafsah's quarters and on Ayesha's day . . . ' (384) – and refers to *The Qur'an* 33:51 ('You may defer any of them if you wish, and take in any of them you wish. And if you if you had desired any of those you had deferred, no blame attaches to you') in response to which Aisha is reported to have made her tart response,[76] as well as 33:49–50 ('O Prophet, we have made licit for you the wives to whom you have given their bridal money, as also the slaves that God assigned you as war booty . . . and also a believing women if she offers herself to the Prophet, provided the Prophets wishes to marry her, as a special dispensation to you only, but not the believers').

There are a couple of distancing strategies here by which Rushdie protects himself from the charge that he is responsible for the conjuring of such phantoms of medieval Christian prejudice. The first is that it – as well as the rest of the 'historical' matter in this section of the 'Return to Jahilia' narrative – is reported by Salman the Persian, who is embittered by the lack of gratitude shown to him by Mahound; the second, by the phrase 'recounting the rumour as if it were incontrovertible fact', which clearly signals that perhaps his word should not be taken altogether seriously. The point, however, is not the liberty with which Rushdie bowdlerizes the *hadith* to make his point, nor is it whether he should, as author, be held responsible for the malicious gossip of one of his characters; rather, it is the fact that the presence of these episodes in *The Satanic Verses* does strike a deep, subterranean chord that had been established centuries before, and which has shaped the tenor and timbre of western hostility towards Islam – and continues to do so. Moreover, it does so without acknowledging other evidence within the Islamic sources which suggest that far from being 'convenient' many verses of the *Qur'an* (and other revelations known as *hadith qudsi* which, though seen as such by Muslim scholars, are not included in the extant text) were, in fact, often uncongenial to the Prophet or – as in the case of those exonerating Aisha – were revealed only after extended periods of agonizing silence during which the Prophet doubted whether any more revelations would come.[77] If the intention of the novel was, indeed, to explore the human event of revelation, to portray the Prophet's revelations purely through the trope of 'convenience' is to diminish it to the singular dimension demanded of polemic, and thereby to collude in a tradition that completely rejected the very notion of Muhammad being a recipient of any revelation. This directs the reader to a single conclusion: that the Prophet Muhammad could not have been anything other than a 'false prophet': 'The closer you are to a conjuror . . . the easier to spot the trick' (363). Except, in this case, this idea is derived not from those closest to him, but from those most distant and hostile to him, many of whom knew very little about the Prophet other than he *must* have been a false prophet.

Beyond this, there are indications that the metaphysical tradition which determines the novel, and on which it draws, is not an Islamic one, but rather a Christian tradition sedimented within the *mentalité* of western secularism – and this reinforces the view that *The Satanic Verses* approaches its 'Islamic' material as an Other in a manner reminiscent of medieval Christian and, latterly, Orientalist discourses. The idea of 'Satan' and the 'satanic', for instance, which is so pivotal to the structure and dynamic of the novel, is, in fact, drawn not from Islamic concepts but from Christianized ideas about the nature of good and evil. As we have already seen, the temptation of the

Prophet by a *shaitan* would not have seemed in any way remarkable to his Companions and the early Muslims, for whom *shaitan* were, in fact, merely a kind of spirit known as *jinn*. It was the early Christian polemicists who freely translated this term into their own equivalent. Normal Daniel notes, as an aside, that 'The *jinn* having no European equivalent, Latins happily assumed them to be devils';[78] conversely, it is clear that the angel *Iblis*, who in the *Qur'an* occupies roughly the same role taken by Satan in the Christian tradition, derives his name from the Greek word for 'devil', *diabolos*.[79] Teasing out the differences between the terms 'Satan', 'devil', 'Iblis' and *jinn*, in fact, unravels the metaphysical assumptions governing *The Satanic Verses*.

As usual, Rushdie displays a flamboyant disregard for fine distinctions, and he customarily collapses these terms into equivalents of one another, only once alluding to the indeterminacy of 'Satan' in the *Qur'an* itself, 'This Shaitan was no fallen angel', reflects Gibreel during one of his visionary episodes, 'Truth was, he wasn't an angel at all! – "He was of the djinn so he transgressed." – Quran 18:50, there it was, as plain as the day' (353). The trouble is, Gibreel sees no distinction between this *jinn* called 'Shaitan' and 'Iblis' – 'Iblis/Shaitan standing for darkness, Gibreel for the light' – so he would have trouble explaining why the *Qur'an* does indeed speak of Iblis/Satan as an angel on other occasions, 'And when We told the the angels, "Prostrate yourselves before Adam!" – they all prostrated themselves, save Iblis, who refused and gloried in his arrogance: and thus he became one of those who deny the truth' (Q 2:34).[80] In general, *The Qur'an* uses *shaitan* when referring to Satan's role as a 'tempter' in the Judeo-Christian tradition (hence it *is* strictly accurate to speak of the 'satanic verses'), but uses the name 'Iblis' when referring to his refusal to obey Allah's order to bow down before humanity (Rushdie uses the term 'Shaitan' for both, except in the passage above).[81] Indeed, the verse that Rushdie cites speaks of Iblis' refusal *and* explains this by denying his angelic status. It is not surprising, then, that 'Muslim thought remains undecided as to whether he [Satan/Iblis] was an angel or a *djinn* and does not pronounce an opinion on the possibility of his being a "fallen angel".'[82]

This indeterminacy reflects both a linguistic and conceptual indeterminacy dating back to the earliest usages of the term 'satan' in the Hebrew Bible, and its subsequent development in the Christian 'New Testament'. Henry Ansgar Kelly has pointed out that:

> both Hebrew and Greek have definite articles, but they mean the opposite thing. In Hebrew, 'the satan' designates a common noun, 'the adversary' in the sense of 'an adversary.' But satan by itself, without the article, can either mean 'a satan' ('an adversary') or stand as a proper name, 'Satan.' In Greek, on the contrary, a proper name is signaled by the presence of the definite article: 'the diabolos' means either 'the devil' (that is, 'a devil'), or 'Devil,' a proper name.[83]

It is likely, therefore, that the many transactions between Greek, Latin, Syriac and Aramaic translations of the Hebrew Bible over the centuries are responsible for the conceptual indeterminacy and semantic instability of 'S/satan', which is absorbed into the metaphysics of the *Qur'an* and thence into Islam: *shaitan* speaks to that Old Testament Hebrew sense of 'an adversary', whilst Iblis draws on its Greek origins in signalling 'Satan' as '*the* Adversary', and as such the *Qur'an* displays both an 'old' (Hebrew/Jewish) concept of 'satan' (as a general adversary or opponent) and a Greek/Christian 'new' understanding of 'Satan' as 'the Devil', who is a particular being. But these 'old' and 'new' understandings of 'S/satan' do not map easily on Jewish/Christian and Old/New Testament distinctions. Satan's development is an uneven and convoluted one: 'S/satan' appears until as late as the third century CE, in both Judaism and Christianity, as an *agent* rather than *adversary* of God. In the Book of Job, 'Satan is one of the Angels of God who patrols the Earth and reports on the activities of Human Beings. In consultation with God, he proposes tests to determine their virtue and fidelity', and in later books of the Old Testament satan(s) also become(s) 'accusers' and 'obstructors', not of God, but men. S/satan's role as a 'tester' of humanity persists into the New Testament, where he is also, variously, an 'obstructor, agent provocateur, police chief, judge, jailer, and disciplinarian'.[84] He does so, however, always within and subject to the authority and permission of God. Although 'Jesus himself, as well as Paul and other New Testament writers . . . dislike him intensely' they acknowledge his 'divinely assigned duties'.[85]

On the other hand, in *both* the Old and New Testaments, there is 'no premundane fall of the Angels. There is no connection of Satan with the Serpent of Eden or the sin of Adam . . . There is no Antichrist, only anti-Christs, who are Human . . . There is no rebellious Lucifer'; in short, there are none of the features customarily associated with Satan in later times.[86] There is also one further notable omission: there is 'no speculation as to where Satan came from or how he obtained his position as tester and accuser of Humankind . . . all Angels and Heavenly Ministers in the Bible come from nowhere. They just appear.'[87] This perhaps indicates a certain attitude towards the problem and nature of 'evil', to which the name of 'Satan' has invariably become attached in all the Abrahamic monotheisms. Early in Abrahamic metaphysics, one might suggest that evil does not exist, and is not conceptualized, 'as such' but is rather the effect of humanity's failure to observe and obey the will of God, a failure that is both precipitated and proven by S/satan's tests. Moreover, this failure is accepted as being a part of existence, one that follows from the initial failure to resist the temptation in the Garden of Eden, requiring not too much enquiry into its nature or significance. But, in the light of humanity's persistent (and consistent) moral failure – that is, failure to live according to the will of God, who is Good – questions must inevitably be raised as to the cause: is this failure part of God's Will? Does he, in fact, set up humanity to fail? How can that be, if God is 'Good'?

It is here that the 'problem of evil' – and all the tricky metaphysical questions to which it gives rise again and again in the Abrahamic monotheisms (free will, predestination, original sin, etc.) – surfaces, and 'Satan' is increasingly drafted in to provide an explanation. Although Satan 'became evil by identification with his functions' (i.e. to provoke moral failure among humans), and by the Book of Chronicles he is 'held to be responsible for evil', he could not become *identified* with evil 'as such' because 'in the Old Testament there is no suggestion of any dualism . . . any philosophy of evil culled from the Bible must find room for evil within the concept of God and within his purpose'.[88] It is not until the third century CE that the Church Fathers explicitly address this problem by first implicating Satan in the fall of Adam and Eve, and then by constructing a narrative about his *rebellion* against God and his subsequent fall from Heaven in which the temptation of Adam and Eve plays a pivotal role.[89] A fourth century work, *Life of Adam and Eve*, explains that just as Satan is the cause of Man's fall from Eden, so too is Man responsible for Satan's fall from Heaven, for Satan objects to God's command to the angels to worship Man, whom God had created in His image. His next act of rebellion was to lead Adam and Eve astray. This rendering displays a remarkable convergence with the accounts of Iblis and *Shaitan* in the *Qur'an*.

But the real significance of Rushdie's 'Satan' only becomes apparent once we realize that *Qur'anic* metaphysics does not, in any way, adopt the notion first developed in the third century CE by Origen of Alexandria that 'Satan' is an 'enemy' of God, which reflects the influence of a dualism that does not exist in Islamic metaphysics. When the *Qur'an* does speak of *Shaitan* as an enemy, it explicitly states that he is an enemy of 'man' not God: 'Satan to man is a manifest enemy' (12:5; see also 7:22, 20:117 and 20:122). Although Islamic metaphysics displays striking continuities with Judeo-Christian understandings of Satan and rehearses common elements of his 'biography', it does *not* follow the turn that was initiated by Origen that subsequently became the dominant paradigm within Christian satanology. Origen suggested that Satan rebelled against God before the creation of the Cosmos. The cause of this rebellion is his 'pride' (which follows earlier antecedents within Christianity, and is absorbed by Islam) but since the cosmos had not yet come into being 'the Devil's fall was caused by internal faults that had nothing to do with Adam'.[90] Origen 'specifically says that he is answering the theory of "some" who say that Satan's original nature was Darkness', but in so doing he accommodated that view into a dialectical synthesis in which Satan *lapses* from Light (God) towards its cosmic opposite. 'The net result', notes Kelly, 'is that the Devil became much, much worse than he had been before, and the Christian religion was transformed, in effect, into a Zoroastrian system. The main difference between Iranian Dualism and the New Christian Dualism is that in the former the Principle of Evil always existed as such, whereas in post-Origen Christianity the Principle of Good created the Principle of Evil!'[91] As with Judaism, which had begun to absorb Zoroastrian dualistic influences from the Babylonian exile onwards, the effect was 'explicit monotheism' but 'implicit dualism'.[92]

Seen from this perspective, the crucial passage in *The Satanic Verses*, when Rekha Merchant's apparition says to Gibreel (more *parabasis* again: we are told that this 'speech is one of which the "real" Rekha would plainly have been incapable'), 'the separation of functions, light versus dark, evil versus good, may be straightforward enough in Islam . . . but go back a bit and you will see that it's a pretty recent fabrication' (323) is, quite simply, wrong with respect to Islamic metaphysics. The central principle in Islamic theology is *tawhid*, the irreducible Unity of God, which results in an uncompromising monotheism that Rushdie elsewhere utilizes for his own ideological purposes (see next section) but which he inexplicably overlooks here. Although *tawhid* is a technical abstract term that is not found in the *Qur'an*, the principle it articulates is insistently repeated throughout it – '13 times God is described as "sole divinity" (*ilāh wāḥid*), and 29 times it is said of Him *lā ilāha illā huwa* "[there is] no divinity other than He" (not to mention other formulae of identical meaning)' – and it forms the basis of the *shahadah*, the Muslim article of faith, '*La illahah illalahu*, There is no God but God'.[93] Being the foundational principle of Islam, the *Qur'an* condemns any perceived deviation from it as *shirk* (associationism, commonly translated as 'idolatry'), and attacks the Christian Trinity as well as pagan idolatry. Muslim theologians would spare no effort at refuting the doctrines of the dualistic cosmogonies that co-existed with Islam in the Near East – the Manicheans, the Marcionites and, of course, the Zoroastrians – and they rejected 'ontological dualism' as well as 'metaphysical' or 'cosmic' dualism. The universe was not, they claimed, composed of 'two opposing orders of reality, good or bad by nature . . . the same substance can be subjected to accidents of opposite nature and that the same subject can successively cause opposite actions; these last emanate from one and the same agent, "the living whole".'[94] Quite apart from the striking similarity, if not sympathy, of this formulation with Rushdie's conceptualization of hybridity (especially the novel's preference for Lucretian metamorphosis over Ovid's), it is noteworthy that the theologian who most forcefully pursued this point, Abd al-Jabbar (d. 1025 CE), understood that the debate with the dualists rested, ultimately, on the 'problem of evil'. He argued that dualism renders 'absurd the blame and praise . . . associated with the breaking or observance of the commandments', which is why Islamic metaphysics emphasizes 'free will' and, conversely, de-emphasizes Satan's power to effect evil, never mind embody it: 'The emphasis in Islamic thinking has always been that individuals are responsible for their own "fall", as in the case of Adam, and while the role of Satan as a tempter is real . . . he provides no excuse for evil behaviour on the part of the individual.'[95] Even more pertinently, while Rushdie draws on some characteristics of the Sufi conceptualization of Satan as 'a tragic figure, lost, hopeless and lonely', the dualistic framework within which his Satan operates, as an avowed enemy of God, is antithetical to the Sufi insistence on *tawhid*, for the Sufis, perhaps more than anyone, have pushed the concept to its logical extreme, yearning for *dissolution (fana)* into the Divine Being.[96] Indeed, even al-Hallaj's famous conceptualization of Iblis as the arch monotheist whose disobedience lay in his uncompromising adherence to *tawhid*, 'preferring the general Law which had been given ("to worship God alone") to the short-term Commandment "(bow down before Adam")', substantiates the point that Sufism is hostile to dualism.[97] For someone who has expressed his admiration for Sufism many times and exhibits an intimate familiarity with its literature, Rushdie should really have known better.

How could Rushdie have committed such a gratuitous error? Is it conceivable that there is an element of deliberation here, a signal of the unreliability and untrustworthiness of what Roger Clark calls the novel's 'satanic narrator', one that sits beside the more conventional omniscient narrator, who 'sweeps in and out of the text like an evil wind', and 'is the sworn enemy of God and Islam'?[98] Certainly, the novel's persistent deconstruction of good and evil (see 'Excluded middles' below) is at odds with the dualism within which its Satanic figure is located. But, as we shall see, this characterization of Islam as dualistic is so fundamental to the architecture of the *The Satanic Verses* that one can only concur with Roger Clark that it is more likely that it is the *deconstruction* of good and evil that is the decoy, and not the dualism, 'The satanic narrator's antagonism to God, Allie and Everest underscores the fundamental cosmic division which he does his best to disguise when he argues that good and evil are interpenetrable'.[99] The contradiction arises from what might be called the novel's metaphysical ambition to dethrone God in the name of a secularism that is apparently anti-metaphysical whilst deploying metaphysical idioms and tropes such as 'Satan' and the 'satanic'. This is typical of the 'complicitous critique' that Linda Hutcheon identifies with postmodernism, but the *aporia* can only be resolved through the construction of an opposition between a secular rejection of moral dualism on the one hand, and a religious embrace of dualism on the other. The fact that this characterization of Islam as dualistic would be unrecognizable to Muslims themselves, but is so easily accepted and recognized by western discourses is symptomatic of the manner in which *The Satanic Verses* colludes with the 'Othering' gaze of the western representations it apparently seeks to contest, a complicity that it most certainly does not critique.

At the same time, we can glimpse here, through a contrapuntal opening, another complicity between Rushdie and his Muslim readers that each disavows, one that compromises the ethics of both *The Satanic Verses* and its reception by its Muslim readers. It is clear from the critical Muslim responses to the novel that many 'educated' and 'modern' Muslims (and possibly many subaltern Muslims?) *have* absorbed, to some extent, the post-Origen view of Satan as an embodiment of evil, along with its quasi-dualistic metaphysical apparatus. This sits uneasily alongside the simple, graspable concept of *tawhid* that still remains fundamental, and retains its primacy, for all Muslims *qua* Muslims. One might speculate that this contradiction is symptomatic of the extent to which Islamic discourses do not constitute a space of pure alterity to the 'West' but have, in fact, absorbed 'western' ideas and precepts to a degree that neither modern Muslims nor non-Muslims are prepared to acknowledge. As we shall see, this bears upon the ways in which *The Satanic Verses* approaches the question of hybridity in relation to Islam.

Excluded middles and the theology of doubt

The problem of recovering and representing alterity without exercising an epistemic violence that recuperates it as merely an Other to the dominant (and dominating) logic of the Self is one of the central problematics within post-colonial studies. It is also one of the central concerns within Salman Rushdie's fictional work, and this is one of the reasons why his work is such an integral part of the post-colonial counter-canon. Moreover, it is something that Rushdie himself has spoken of as being one of the main preoccupations of *The Satanic Verses*. He states that the novel is 'a serious attempt to write about religion and revelation from the point of view of a secular person', and that 'it is by no means always hostile to faith'.[100] Indeed, he goes on to say, 'the most secular of authors ought to be capable of presenting a sympathetic portrait of a devout believer'.[101] But if, as we have seen, the criticism that the novel represents Muslims and Islam as 'Other' is largely warranted, Rushdie raises here a further question concerning its treatment of religious faith in general. The critical question, then, is whether or not Rushdie succeeds in representing the alterity of religious faith from a secular point of view.

However, this question in turn rests on whether or not the novel successfully mediates between secular and non-secular ways of thinking and being. Or, to put it slightly differently, does the text inhabit a space *in-between* the secular and the non-secular, that hybrid (Third) space where alterity can emerge as neither an extension of the Same nor as an alien Other but as something else besides, that space where 'newness enters the world'? The trope of hybridity in *The Satanic Verses* is, therefore, crucial to addressing these questions, not least because, in Rushdie's own words, the novel is 'love song to our mongrel selves'.[102]

One of the central questions framing the narratives of *The Satanic Verses*, and determining its thematic concerns, is 'What kind of idea are you?' There is another, equally important, one: 'How does newness come into the world?' Both of these converge upon the figure of the hybrid, which appears in many forms throughout the novel, beginning with its epigraph, which, by invoking Daniel Defoe's *History of the Devil* also evokes one of his other works, 'The True Born Englishman', a poem which satirically observes that such a creature is, in fact, a 'het'rogenous thing' that has emerged from the numerous migrations and conquests, the many cultural infusions and racial incursions that have punctuated British history since ancient times.[103] This is one of the main themes of a novel that addresses the racist exclusivism of British nationalist identity during the period of Thatcherite ascendancy. From the outset, therefore, Rushdie juxtaposes migration – Defoe's Satan is a vagrant with no fixed abode – with hybridity and then, in the arresting opening scene, fuses this with another of the novel's main tropes, metamorphosis. Beginning with Gibreel Farishta singing, 'To be born again . . . first you have to die', (1) followed by a song that overtly signals hybridity, '"O my shoes are Japanese," . . . "These trousers English if you please. On my head, red Russian hat; my heart's Indian for all that"' (5) the episode breathlessly concludes with the question:

> How does newness enter the world? How is it born? Of what fusions, translations, conjoinings is it made? How does it survive, extreme and dangerous though it is? What compromises, what deals, what betrayals of its secret nature must it make . . . ? (8)

As the novel progresses, the narrator periodically asks the other question, 'WHAT KIND OF IDEA ARE YOU? Are you the kind that compromises, does deals, accommodates itself to society, aims to find a niche, to survive?' (335). The echo of discourses surrounding immigration and integration in late twentieth-century Britain aligns both these questions to the phenomenon of migration. As Rushdie would later write after the *fatwa*, 'If *The Satanic Verses* is anything, it is a migrant's eye view of the world. It is written from the very experience of uprooting, disjuncture and metamorphosis . . . that is the migrant condition . . . from which, I believe, can be derived a metaphor for all humanity.'[104]

The narrative therefore rests on a set of axiomatic principles concerning the value of migration, its ability to foster change, transformation and renewal, and the necessity of compromise in order to ensure survival. Since metamorphosis, migration, and compromise all produce 'hybrid' formations in one form or another, the novel valorizes hybridity and its attendant 'ethic of impurity' as a fundamental principle of historical development that invokes Darwin's theory of natural selection: adaptability is the key to survival.[105] This ethic of impurity is the basis for the novel's exuberant dismantling of established structures of thought and patterns of belief, and its insistent interrogation of 'orthodoxies of all types', in particular those aligned to the 'ethic of purity'. Foremost among these are the cultural codes of chauvinistic nationalism (such as Thatcherite Conservatism) and the moral codes of established religion (such as Islam).

The ethic of impurity, as expressed by *The Satanic Verses*, therefore has a dual provenance, one avowedly secular and historical, the other theological and metaphysical. Whilst the former tackles the binaries of 'insider/outsider' constructed along racial, cultural and, indeed, religious lines, the latter explores the nature of good and evil and, using what Roger Clark has identified as a 'satanic narrator', upsets and confounds traditional, religiously sanctioned moral imperatives as a means of interrogating the religious beliefs that both produce and are produced by them.[106]

Thus, on the one hand, the novel clearly endorses Zeeny Vakil's 'ethic of historically validated eclecticism' against 'the confining myth of authenticity' that Saladin Chamcha espouses until he accepts and embraces his hybrid identity. On the other hand, as with other dichotomies, the novel consistently throws the distinction between good and evil into doubt, sometimes inverting them, sometimes blurring the distinction between them, and at other times insisting on their inter-relatedness, even interpenetration. The distinction between the sacred and the profane is blurred, for instance, by the mirroring of the Prophet's household by the whorehouse; a poster for the film *Mephisto* relates some lines from *Faust*, '*Part of that power, not understood/Which always wills the Bad, and always works the Good*' (417, original emphasis), and the narrator goes to some length to explain that 'the separation of functions, light versus dark, evil versus good . . . [is] a pretty recent fabrication. Amos, eight century BC, asks, "Shall there be evil in a city and the Lord hath not done it?"' (323).

Throughout the novel, this pattern is repeated in relation to both the secular and religious narratives: the 'ethic of impurity' establishes dichotomies only to collapse them again. At the same time, however, there is a contrary current running through the novel in which there is a *divergence* between the secular and religious registers with respect to the key trope of compromise, which is itself a deconstructive trope insofar as it involves the overcoming of oppositions. On the one hand, the theme of compromise and pragmatism is linked to hybridity and figured as a secular virtue with respect to history, but on the other it appears to be a symptom of religious failure – a pragmatic acknowledgement of the need to dilute the 'purity' of the faith in the face of (secular) reality.

The avowedly secular Saladin's fortunes, for example, only begin to improve after he begins to compromise his devotion to a particular myth of British national 'authenticity' in favour of a hybrid identity that accommodates both his British and Indian selves. At his lowest point he witnesses a 'chimeran graft . . . two trees that had been bred into one . . . If such a tree were possible, then so was he' (406). The closing passages of the novel, in which Saladin not only accepts his hybrid identity but recuperates it by returning to India to make peace with his father (a representative figure of Indian nationalism), not only deconstructs the insider/outsider oppositions set up by nationalism itself, but also ironically renders him 'whole' in a way denied to his rival and antagonist, Gibreel, whose quest for wholeness is predicated on a rejection of 'moral fuzziness' in favour of the 'stark, imperative oppositions' (354) that he believes constitute the true faith of a religious believer.

At no point does the novel contradict this idea that true religious faith is unambiguously aligned with the 'ethic of purity'. Acts of compromise by religious characters are shown to be signs of weakness and a betrayal of fundamental principles, and are seen as such by the characters themselves. This, in turn, throws into doubt the authenticity of the various revelations that appear in the narrative, and the divinity from which they supposedly emanate. The novel's representation of the episode of the 'satanic verses', for instance, rests on the question 'Is Allah so unbending that he will not embrace three more [goddesses] to save the human race?' (111). The answer to this profoundly moral and theological question is, as we have seen, predicated on the exigencies of power: '*Any new idea, Mahound*', says the narrator, '*is asked two questions. The first is asked when it's weak: WHAT KIND OF IDEA ARE YOU?*'. The Prophet's doubts, such as they are, are a consequence of his political marginalization and his rejection of compromise, even when weak, testifies to the view that true faith involves 'the path of purity and not of base compromise' (272). Likewise, in the 'Ayesha' narrative the 'satanic verses' episode is reprised when the modern and secular Mirza Saeed offers Ayesha a compromise at precisely the moment when her power is fragile and vulnerable. Like Mahound, she is initially tempted but eventually rejects the compromise even though she is in a position of weakness, 'His offer had contained an old question: *What kind of idea are you?* And she, in turn, had offered him an old answer: *I was tempted but now I am renewed; am uncompromising; absolute; pure*' (500).

The idea that Islam, in particular, is totally antithetical to compromise and the hybridity to which it is aligned is made explicit by the narrator:

> [Islam is] the cussed, bloody-minded, ramrod-backed type of damnfool notion that would rather break than sway with the breeze . . . The kind that will almost certainly, ninety-nine times out of a hundred, be smashed to bits; but, the hundredth time, will change the world. (335, original emphasis)

Quite apart from reprising, as we have seen, one of the key tropes of medieval anti-Islamic Christian polemics, Islam is here figured as an exception to the text's principle of historical development through hybridity. It is the one-in-a-hundred phenomenon where the ethic of purity establishes itself, survives and even thrives. This is despite the fact that Islam was founded on an act of migration, the *hijrah*. Since migration, for Rushdie, inevitably produces hybridity Islam's exceptionalism in this regard becomes all the more remarkable. Indeed, the novel contrasts Islamic/Muslim migrations with others, aligning it with a notion of 'exile' that seeks to preserve purity. The Prophet flees Jahilia/Mecca in order to resist further temptations to compromise, but returns in victory and reinstates the purity of the faith on its inhabitants; the Imam – 'An exile. Which must not be confused with, allowed to run into, all the other words people throw around: émigré, expatriate, refugee, immigrant . . . ' (205) remains impassive to the western metropolis that surrounds him, sealing himself within his apartment (behind a *purdah*); the rigid, closed mind of Hind Sufyan the believing Muslim, contrasts unfavourably with the cosmopolitan eclecticism of her husband; and then there are the Muslim pilgrims of the 'Ayesha' episode who metonymically represent the wider body of the faithful, for whom the journey to Mecca is an act of purification, the forgiving of sins figured metaphorically by Mishal Saeed's desire to cleanse her body of its cancerous cells. In Rushdie's own terms, it is as if Muslim/Islamic migrations involve merely a displacement rather than the radical 'translation' that other migrants experience.[107]

As a result, Islam is yet again essentialized as a system of belief that is 'outside' history. As we have seen, this is ironically complicit with the Islamist understanding of Islam as a 'pure' religion that transcends history, one that Rushdie avowedly contests.[108] Moreover, the text is here displaying what the anthropologist Johannes Fabian has termed 'allochronism'; that is, in portraying Islam as a religion that remains essentially unchanged, it is marked as a superseded way of life that may co-exist with modernity but is not 'co-eval' with it. Islam (and religion in general) is a remnant of 'another time', not an integral and valid way of living 'in our time'. It is part of humanity's infancy, not its maturity.[109] By suggesting religious faith is in a state of 'arrested development', *The Satanic Verses* thus rehearses a classic secularist gesture, which enables secularism itself to monopolize the ground upon which 'modern' ways of thinking and being can be realized.[110]

From this perspective, the modernization or reform of Islam that Rushdie calls for, and elsewhere acknowledges as part of its history, is rendered impossible.[111] For if newness does enter the world through 'conjoinings' and 'hotch-potch', a 'bit-of-this and a bit-of-that', then Islam's 'purity' speaks to an inability to accommodate the plurality and multiplicity on which such a process depends. As such, its renewal and reform is precluded. The opening words of the novel are, 'To be born again, first you have to die' (1). The refrain is repeated with a difference on the last page, 'if the old refused to die the new cannot be born' (547). The implication is clear: the death of Islam, or at least its Allah, is the prerequisite for a new sort of Muslim. And what could a 'born-again' Muslim look like after such a death? Only a secularized Muslim for whom faith is a matter of private belief, a reproduction of the Subject produced by western secularism.

In the context of a novel that celebrates multiplicity and hybridity, this characterization of cultural difference as a zero-sum-game – for a new culture to emerge another must die – is absurdly contradictory unless we put it into the symbolic economy of a secularism which requires the 'death' of religion in order to constitute itself – as symbolized by Gibreel Farishta's suicide at the end of the novel, which enables the secular Saladin to 'move on'. Given that the secularism to which Rushdie subscribes already takes for granted the death of the Christian God, the novel's focus on Islam becomes more significant because its late twentieth-century resurgence was perceived as a threat to secular hegemony (one that was ironically, albeit indirectly, reinforced by the novel's publication and the subsequent controversy).

Thus, a text that seeks to challenge 'orthodoxies of all kinds' reinforces a secularist orthodoxy, which believes that religion no longer has anything to contribute to human development (and, indeed, is positively obstructive). As a consequence, *The Satanic Verses* is unable to extend its dismantling of the binary oppositions that uphold established patterns of thought to those governing secularism. In a famous and oft-cited passage, the narrator asks, 'What is the opposite of faith? Not disbelief. Too final, certain, closed. Itself a kind of belief. Doubt' (92). This opposition between faith and doubt is the basis for what Malise Ruthven has called the novel's 'theology of doubt', and it is the governing structuring principle through which the text explores religious faith from a secular point of view. Like all theologies, however, the 'theology of doubt' revered by *The Satanic Verses* is a structure that rests on a foundation that must, in order to uphold the structure, lie outside the structure itself; as a result, all the oppositions *within* the structure can be dismantled, but the foundational principle or *logos* cannot; it is beyond 'play'.[112] Therefore, in the novel's 'theology of doubt' the opposition between faith and doubt is itself beyond doubt. The opposition is never dismantled within the novel *because it cannot be done*; without it the novel would not be what it is.

But what happens when the novel's 'theology of doubt' is put into doubt from an alternative critical position which does not take as axiomatic the antinomy between faith and doubt? If *The Satanic Verses* is a 'love song to our mongrel selves', what kind of reading might emerge if we 'mongrelize' the very thing it cannot, namely if we put our faith in doubting the 'theology of doubt'?

Turning Rushdie's question around, one might ask, 'what is the opposite of doubt?' It is by no means obvious that the answer should be 'faith' because that answer depends on a definition of faith that is synonymous with the more obvious and precise answer, namely 'certainty'. 'Faith' is here read purely as dogma and placed within an *epistemological* frame as opposed to an *experiential* one. This is neatly dramatized in an exchange between the Prophet Mahound and one of his followers after the former recants his concession to polytheism. Khalid the water-carrier, who had begun to doubt the Prophet after his recitation of the 'satanic verses', says, 'Messenger, I doubted you. But you were wiser than we knew . . . you were bringing us a deeper truth. You brought us the Devil himself so we could witness the working of the Evil One . . . You have enriched our faith' (125). This episode stands in counterpoint to an earlier passage ('Gibreel feels his despair: his doubts . . . What can I do? What shall I recite?' (110–11) in which Mahound's doubts are expressed through a series of searching questions that testify to his faith being tested by doubts that are, nevertheless, framed by secular concerns concerning power and compromise, 'is it just a dream of power? Must I betray myself for a seat on the council? . . . Is Allah so unbending . . . ?' (111). In the later episode, Khalid demonstrates an experiential insight that (self-)knowledge emerges as a handmaiden to a truth already perceived (darkly) through a faith that is tested and disturbed by doubt. Mahound's response undercuts this immediately, for the very person in whom Khalid rests his faith is unable to appreciate how faith might work in such a way: 'Mahound moved away from the sunlight falling through the window. '"Yes." *Bitterness, cynicism.* "It was a wonderful thing I did. Deeper truth. Bringing you the Devil. Yes, that sounds like me"' (my emphasis). The sarcasm in Mahound's words is unmissable, and it signals to the reader that his understanding of faith is one that 'has to KNOW' (122) the Truth; in the absence of epistemological proof, his experience of the Truth ('this time, the angel, no question. He wrestled me to the ground' (124)) is still open to doubt, and he finds himself unable to believe. From this point on, the novel de-emphasizes Mahound's prophetic attributes and instead emphasizes his political career. The implication of such a shift from the sacred to the secular is that, in the absence of rational proof of the revelation's divine origins, religious belief is – can only be – ultimately a vehicle for worldly concerns.

Rushdie is rehearsing what Talal Asad has called 'a modern cognitivist view of religion'.[113] In his genealogy of the concept, he shows how 'religion' emerged as a category of analysis brought about by a transformation of 'knowledge' that is one of the major causes and effects of that complex historical transformation of society that goes by the name of 'secularization'. This involved a profound shift from the medieval understandings of religiosity based on 'monastic discipline . . . the very term religious was therefore reserved for those living in monastic communities; with the later emergence of nonmonastic orders, the term came to be used for all who had taken lifelong vows by which they were set apart from the ordinary members of the Church'.[114] Religion was, at that time, *institutional* – an arrangement of authority and a means of discipline. Asad notes that '[s]everal times before the Reformation, the boundary between the religious and the secular was redrawn, but always the formal authority of the Church remained dominant'.[115] Religious dogma – the codified beliefs authorized by the Church – had a social function, namely to uphold and reinforce, through discipline and doctrine, the social and political authority of the Church.

But from the seventeenth century, attempts were made to define religion as a universal concept, part of a post-Reformation and early Enlightenment attempt at producing a universal secular knowledge. In the process, 'religion' became 'abstracted and universalized' and its very nature was reshaped as a result.[116] On the one hand, the new conceptualization of a Natural or universal Religion as involving 'beliefs', 'practices' and 'ethics', 'meant that henceforth religion could be conceived as a set of *propositions* to which believers gave assent'; on the other, 'the triumphant rise of modern science, modern production, and the modern state' – increasingly shifted 'the weight of religion more and more onto the moods and motivations of the individual believer. Discipline (intellectual and social) would, in this period, gradually abandon religious space, letting "belief", "conscience" and "sensibility" take its place.'[117]

This process has set the parameters within which modern discussions of religion take place. According to Clifford Geertz, for instance, 'The basic axiom underlying what we may perhaps call "the religious perspective" is everywhere the same: he who would know must first believe.'[118] Asad's genealogy contests this axiom by showing that 'religion' is not a transcendent, transhistorical phenomenon predicated on belief that is 'everywhere the same', but is in fact a set of historically contingent practices and ways of being that change over time and differ between cultures.[119] What may have emerged out of Christianity as a product of its specific history may not hold true for understanding Islam. If this is so, then both the meanings and the relationships between the key terms that are invariably at stake in modern discussions of religion – belief, faith, knowledge (and in this particular instance, doubt) – cannot be categorically defined once and for all. Rushdie, however, does precisely this, adopting an Olympian vantage point on 'religion' which performs exactly the kind of separation of knowledge from belief that is characteristic of modern secular thought's 'rigorous sense of boundaries, limits, and proper domains'.[120] In his fictional and non-fictional discourse, Rushdie's engagement with religious experience is invariably framed by an *opposition* between 'faith' 'belief' and 'dogma' on the one hand (treated as synonyms), and 'knowledge' and 'doubt' on the other (also treated more or less synonymously on occasion, or as distinct but related on others). Thus, he writes '[t]o choose unbelief is to choose mind over dogma . . . Imperfect human knowledge may be a bumpy, pot-holed street, but it's the only road to wisdom worth taking.'[121]

However, this understanding that knowledge and belief (and their respective correlates) are distinct, even opposing, categories is belied by the reminder that for the

> pious learned Christians of the twelfth century . . . knowledge and belief were not so clearly at odds. On the contrary, Christian belief would then have been built on knowledge – knowledge of theological doctrine, of canon law and Church courts, of the details of clerical liberties, of the powers of ecclesiastical office (over souls, bodies, properties),

of the preconditions and effects of confession, of the rules of religious orders, of the locations and virtues of shrines, of the lives of the saints, and so forth.[122]

Similarly, Caputo points out that '[w]hilst Augustine and his successors certainly distinguished faith and reason, they treated this distinction like markers or milestones on a continuous path . . . They did not think of them as two separate and distinct spheres or domains.'[123]

Once we acknowledge that Rushdie's conceptualization of faith and doubt as opposites is historically determined by a particular way of speaking about 'religious experience', we might begin to doubt the conceptual as well as historical validity of the antinomy. That is, we might begin to approach these terms from a 'post-secular' and postmodern as opposed to a secular and modern perspective. We might point out, for instance, that doubt and faith were not seen by pre-modern Muslims as well as Christians in such antinomian terms. Abedi and Fischer cite one of the many parables about the sixth Shi'ite Imam, Imam Sadiq, in which the Imam responds to a young man who doubts the existence of God by exclaiming, 'Allah-u-Akbar! This is the *beginning* of certitude and faith.'[124] The great medieval Muslim philosopher al-Ghazzali declared, in an almost uncanny inversion of Geertz's formulation, 'he who has not doubted has not believed'.[125]

From a post-secular perspective the pivotal dichotomy proposed in *The Satanic Verses* between faith and doubt is part of an ensemble of distinctions governing secular modernity – between the religious and the secular, faith and reason, public and private, and so on – that can be seen as *rhetorical* discriminations that 'invented the very categories they were discriminating, none of which had existed, and certainly not in these precise terms, before modernity'.[126] Thus, one can doubt the novel's 'theology of doubt' because, from an alternative vantage point, there is no reason to assume that doubt and faith are mutually exclusive. Indeed, there are very good reasons to think that they are in fact mutually *constitutive*.

In his meditation, *On Religion*, John Caputo sets out to 'waylay the usual distinction between religious and secular in the name of what I shall call the "post-secular" or a "religion without religion".'[127] For him, religion may be found 'with or without' religion because 'having a religious sense of life' is not (or not necessarily) about *believing* in a set of propositions authorized by bishops and mullahs, but is in fact 'a very basic structure of our lives . . . that should be placed alongside other very basic things, like having an artistic sense or political sense, experiences that belong to anyone worth their salt'.[128] Each and every one of us must confront the future, which 'pries open the present by promising us the possibility of something new', but there are different kinds of future: there is the 'relatively foreseeable future, the future for which we are planning, the future for which we are all hard at work', which Caputo calls the 'future present';[129] but there is also something he calls 'the absolute future', which is a future that is *unforeseeable* and which is not the realm of the possible but rather of the *impossible*. This 'impossible' is not the opposite of 'possible' but 'something of whose possibility we just cannot conceive':

> With the 'absolute' future we are pushed to the limits of the possible, fully extended, at our wits' end, having run up against something that is beyond us, beyond our powers and potentialities, beyond our powers of disposition, pushed to the point where only the great passions of faith and love and hope will see us through. With the 'absolute future,' I maintain, we set foot for the first time on the shore of the 'religious,' we enter the sphere of religious passion, and we hit upon a distinctively 'religious category.'[130]

This 'notion of life at the limit of the possible, on the verge of the impossible' is where the 'religious side of every one of us' can be found. It is an uncontainable *excess* that lies 'beyond the sphere in which we have some mastery, beyond the domain of sensible possibilities'.[131] It is here that *faith* begins, at that point where knowledge falters, where reason is confounded, where we cannot trust our senses. For the 'absolute future' is a 'darker and more uncertain and unforeseeable region', where our 'sense of reality and its limits is disturbed; our sense of what is possible and impossible begins to tremble, to destabilize, to become unsteady and *uncertain*'.[132] Far from being the opposite of doubt, faith is in fact predicated on a radical and unresolvable uncertainty since belief in 'what seems highly credible or even likely requires a minimum of faith, whereas to believe what seems unbelievable, what it seems impossible to believe, that really is faith'.[133]

As such, it is fraught with risk because if faith is faith in the 'chance for something completely new . . . we never know who is going to come knocking at our door; it could be Gabriel himself or it could be a devil. With the absolute future there are no guarantees.'[134] This has rather pointed significance for *The Satanic Verses*, of course, because the title incident can, from this perspective, be seen as an exemplary story of faith *as well as* doubt. If, as Caputo suggests, 'faith is not safe' because it is 'inhabited by unfaith',[135] or because it is *constituted* by doubt, then the authority of the revelation rests ultimately on a faith that *must* be subject to doubt because just as faith without doubt is not faith, so too a doubt without faith is not doubt. Doubting is an incompleteness, a lack; it is a kind of reluctance which only assumes itself through the temptation of faith: that willingness to believe even if, at present, one is not prepared or able to submit to it. Doubt cannot be a repudiation or outright rejection of faith; it must rather be a *suspension* of faith, a wavering, interstitial condition that shuttles back and forth between faith and unfaith. Without faith to complete it, doubt ironically becomes a dogmatic intransigence. To read the satanic verses incident as a signifier of doubt without admitting that it *also* dramatizes the immanence of faith in doubt itself – and if the antinomy between faith and doubt is to hold Rushdie cannot admit this – is, in fact, to negate the concept of doubt which Rushdie celebrates; if Leonard Cohen sings, ironically, that 'your faith was strong but you needed proof' so too does the *Qur'an* make a point of saying that if the faithless need the proof of a miracle, their faith is not really faith (a reproof, as it were, that is directed towards the 'hypocrites' in Medina who professed Islam only for tactical reasons): 'So why do they turn away from admonition as if they were frightened asses fleeing from a lion? No, each one of them wants a scroll (of revelation) spread before him. It will not be so . . . ' (Qur'an, 74: 50–2).[136] Likewise, for Rushdie's Muslim critics not to admit that the incident represents an exemplary demonstration of faith is to negate the faith they say they possess.

One could say that faith is an 'extreme' condition, were it not likely that such a statement would be misunderstood as suggesting that religious extremism is equivalent to faith itself, which is how Rushdie and the New Atheists present it. In fact, religious 'extremists', or 'fundamentalists' as they used to be known, do not embrace the radical uncertainty of faith, but the faithless certainty of conviction, which is merely a projection into the future ('it will be thus') of ideas or beliefs that have their origins in the present, in the *now*, our sense *now* of what the future will be like, which is to say it is concerned with the 'future present' not the 'absolute future'; unlike faith, fundamentalist belief is not open to the impossible, for the fundamentalists' future (their *eschaton*) is already conceived of as a possibility in the present. As Caputo suggests, '[a]t the core of fundamentalism . . . there lies *a repressed fear that faith is only faith and as such a risk with no guarantee of anything*, which is the truth about religion to which it testifies in the mode of repressing it'.[137] In other words, fundamentalism wants faith to be other than what it is, namely knowledge of what Caputo calls The Secret – that is why it is, perversely, a secularist formation because secularism too insistently translates faith into the (erroneous) knowledge that it ascribes to 'belief'.

Fundamentalism's literalism is merely the most obvious symptom of its faithlessness; however, less literal-minded believers may also be prone to the faithless notion that religious faith involves merely an intellectual conviction concerning a set of theological propositions or dogmas. Such people may be more or less dogmatic – it depends on where they stand in relation to the fragile line that separates belief-as-faith from belief-as-conviction, that separates openness towards the 'impossible', towards the radical uncertainty of the absolute future, from its closure. On the other hand, secular non-believers may be open to faith in the impossible in a way many religious believers are not; they too may be more or less dogmatic, more or less certain they *know* The Secret (there is no God). This is why Caputo prefers to speak of the 'religious *in* people' rather than distinguish between religious and non-religious people.[138]

Indeed, from a post-secular perspective, just as the dichotomy between faith and doubt can be dissolved so too can the equivalence between faith and belief be uncoupled. Faith and belief are not synonyms as the modern cognitivist view of religion would have it; belief is faith brought down to earth, brought within the realm of the possible. It is bound to knowledge through a series of (unverifiable) propositions, the unverifiability of which signal the residue of faith that still inheres within it. Faith, on the other hand, is unbound from knowledge, lies beyond its limits; it leaps into the abyss of the unknown and the unknowable and does not keep its feet on the ground. This is why for Caputo faith is 'unnervingly fragile':[139] because it is constituted by doubt, because it embraces the unknown and the impossible, it is *always* haunted by the possibility of its impossibility, even as that very embrace of *the* impossible is what makes it faith and not knowledge or belief. It is religious *belief* rather than religious faith that leads to conviction, to dogmatism, tied as it is to knowledge, unable as it is to take the leap into the dark of the unknown and unknowable. Shuttling between knowledge and faith (between that which is known and certain and its opposite) rather than faith and doubt, belief seeks comfort in the consolations of the knowable, even as it desires the impossible – rather like a person with vertigo who clings to a tower and cannot look down even as they feel the urge to throw themselves off. Belief is haunted by the *fear* of the unknown and unknowable, whereas faith embraces and desires it.

Of all the narratives in *The Satanic Verses*, it is the story of Ayesha the village prophetess that represents the novel's most sustained, sophisticated and apparently sympathetic engagement with the nature of religious faith. One of the reasons it appears to be a more successful treatment of the matter is that it dramatizes the religious passion for the impossible, both in terms of the pilgrims' faith that the Arabian sea really will part, and, at the narrative's end, through the maintenance of a careful ambiguity as to whether it did or not. Moreover, the magical realist form of the narrative enables the irruption of the miraculous into the mundane, such as the swarm of butterflies which guides the pilgrims and, at a crucial moment when the obstacles to their pilgrimage seem insurmountable, emboldens them by re-appearing (492). This passion for the impossible is not present in the other narratives, which situate the faith of the Prophet and the Imam within the frame of the political, in a secular context of 'the possible' (politics is, as the saying goes, the art of the possible).

The Ayesha narrative also demonstrates how certitude of belief cannot settle the questions that arise as a consequence of faith. As first the Sarpanch, then Mishal Saeed's mother, then the other villagers begin to doubt Ayesha when her conviction leads her to ever more extreme and inhumane callousness, the narrative illustrates, despite itself, how faith is not a settled condition of being, but an unsettled (and unsettling) *process*, for these questions and doubts arise *because* and not *despite* their faith, because of their passion for the impossible, without which they would not be on the pilgrimage in the first place. The narrative thus stages faith as a process of radical uncertainty, an excess that momentarily breaks apart a structure that seeks to contain it by presenting an uncompromising struggle between the prophetess Ayesha and the resolutely secular Mirza Saeed.

This structure, the purpose and trajectory of which seems to suggest that religious faith involves an inevitable movement towards certitude and absolutism, is bolstered by a series of other oppositions, such as that between the inhumane indifference of the absolute believer towards life and death, and the civilized humanity of the sceptics; 'By the end of the sixth week, she had forced the marchers to leave four more bodies where they fell . . . behind them, however, Mirza Saeed Akhtar gathered up the bodies and made sure they received a decent burial' (483) and, of course, the novel's governing opposition between faith and doubt. We are shown, ultimately, that faith, in order to sustain itself amidst doubt must harden and calcify in order to shore up its power.

The radical excess of the pilgrims' faith is also contained, firstly, by their amorphous passivity, such that faith appears not as an active process of questioning predicated on doubt, but the authoritarian inscription of Truth on the *tabula rasa* of their limitless credulity – they are led to the Truth by the certitude of others; secondly, by the staging of religious passion (albeit not of the pilgrims') as an indiscriminate zeal that is morally blind, as represented *in extremis* by the grotesque episode when a two-week-old baby is stoned to death by a mob raised to heights of fury by an unscrupulous Imam, aided and abetted by Ayesha's (im)moral righteousness. One cannot deny, of course, that there are many people who claim to be 'religious' who *do* believe that their faith demands a moral absolutism that in turn excuses (im)moral excesses undertaken 'in the name of God'. Nor can one deny that the 'worlding' of faith can lead, often leads, perhaps mostly leads, away from the restlessness and radical self-questioning that faith demands towards the stilled certitude of beliefs underwritten by demands of power – the move that, for Caputo, is represented by the shift from Augustine's *Confessions* to his *City of God*. However, the point is that *The Satanic Verses* denies the very possibility of faith being conceptualized and experienced otherwise, as an exposing of oneself 'to the radical uncertainty and open-endedness of life'.[140]

Finally, there is an apparent sting in the tale that, on closer inspection, turns out to be no such thing. At the narrative's end when Ayesha's secular opponent, Mirza Saeed Akhtar, at the moment of his death, makes 'a different choice' and opens himself up to faith in the impossible, he is granted a vision of the Arabian sea parting and the pilgrims walking across the ocean bed to Mecca. This closing scene, which maintains an artful ambiguity to the very end, clearly signals (or is meant to signal) a certain open-mindedness about faith that would seem to contradict and resist the closures discussed above. Yet this denouement does not actually dismantle the antinomy between faith and doubt. In fact, it reinforces it because Mirza Saeed's 'choice' can be taken only if there *is* a choice to be made. In preserving the trope of choice, the ending of this narrative can be contrasted with that of the moving and entirely secular story 'The Courter' where the narrator *refuses* to choose between his many identities.[141] That short story, which upholds Rushdie's unwavering commitment to secular hybridity, reflects back upon the earlier narrative and illuminates how, for Rushdie, religious faith can never occupy the hybrid space in which faith and doubt might co-exist.

The divergence between the secular and theological interests of the novel revealed by the trope of compromise speaks to a wider, more significant, discontinuity. Samir Amin defines as 'metaphysical' those forms of thought that seek 'totalization' by absorbing and superannuating the singular into the 'system', the particular into the general, and the concrete instance into the abstract concept.[142] From that perspective, the opposition between the religious and the secular is blurred because both secular and religious thought can be metaphysical. Secularism articulates its own metaphysical ambitions, for example, in such totalizing ideologies as nationalism, or in the fetishizing of a capitalized Reason, or in its invocation of historical Progress. In this respect, *The Satanic Verses* oscillates between the metaphysical and its opposite, the 'hermeneutic'; between the grand narrative, the global perspective, the totalizing gesture, and the suspicion, interrogation and dissolution of all these things, which is principally focused on the figure of the 'hybrid'.

Insofar as the novel approaches religion, however, the balance of emphasis tilts towards the metaphysical, for there is at its core a grand ambition, as we have seen, to dethrone God by mounting, in the name of a 'satanic' narrator, an adversarial attack on the foundational principle of divinity itself. It thus produces an anti-theology that seeks to displace religion *in its totality*. This totalizing gesture is profoundly metaphysical, as is its treatment of religious faith purely in terms of its claims to Truth. Religious 'faith' is defined by its *explicability* within a particular form of Reason rather than the multiplicity of (inexplicable) truths that might be derived from the singular, irreducible experience (or 'event') of faith. Thus, when Rushdie asks, 'if we accept that the mystic, the prophet is sincerely undergoing some sort of transcendental experience, but we cannot believe in a supernatural world, then what is going on?' we might, in turn, ask, 'what is *he* in fact *really* asking?'[143] In staging his exploration of religious faith in purely epistemological terms there is clearly a tension between exploring and empathetically understanding the sincerity of the experience in ontological terms (an empathy that is not actually upheld by the novel), and *explaining* the experience as an epiphenomenon of some other, deeper, more 'truthful' phenomenon that involves translating the singularity of the experience into a 'system' of knowledge. We can notice, too, that the tension itself involves precisely the separation of knowledge and experience, faith and reason, that characterizes post-Enlightenment thought.[144] Rushdie's exploration of faith, then, subscribes to the binary forms of thinking that establish and police the boundaries that, in other respects, he vigorously contests in the name of the 'hybrid', the 'postmodern' and the 'post-colonial'.

Ironically Rushdie's grand metaphysical ambition is bound to the very metaphysics it contests. Rushdie's method is to employ a 'satanic' narrator to provocatively induce 'sympathy for the devil' (the song, by The Rolling Stones, is referenced several times in the narrative) in order to confound and upset established notions of good and evil and thereby call into question the Divine *logos* on which they rest.[145] But engaging in a cosmic war against God suggests that this narrator is, in fact, a believer; he *must* believe in God for why would he oppose something he does not believe exists? I read this as symbolic of a wider filiative relation between the novel's secularism and the 'religion' it contests.

This is illuminated by an ethical problem that only arises because of the narrator's 'satanic' orientation. Put simply, it is this: the 'satanic' character, Saladin (who physically embodies the 'satanic' – and secular – ethic of the text) commits a diabolic act (the enunciation of his own 'satanic verses') that leads, eventually, to the deaths of Allie Cone, Whisky Sissodia and Gibreel. The text does not side-step or abjure his responsibility, 'how to explain his overwhelming feeling of guilt, of *responsibility*: how to tell her that these killings were the dark flowers he had planted long ago?' (542–3); however, not only is Saladin not punished, he is also the one major character who survives and, indeed, is *redeemed*, 'in spite of all his wrong-doing, weakness, guilt . . . he was getting another chance' (547). This poses a moral problem for a text that ultimately seeks to establish a framework of human existence, and a moral code, that is not founded on belief in a supernatural deity and the putatively rigid systems of thought and morality – the 'rules, rules, rules' (363) – that are derived from it (as symbolized in Baal's transition from polytheism to godlessness). For, despite the 'satanic' method, the ineluctable problem is that the text cannot espouse a 'satanic' ethics that exonerates Saladin's responsibility for the deaths of other human beings. This is a responsibility established by the same 'religious' moralities that are thrown into question by the text: 'Thou shall not kill'. The result is an *aporia* that is resolved by the paradoxical invocation of a religious gesture. When Gibreel Farishta puts the pistol through his mouth and pulls the trigger (whilst knowing full well of Saladin's ultimate responsibility for the downward spiral into which he has plunged), he commits an act of sacrifice that absolves Saladin of his 'sin'/guilt (and of having to 'explain' himself). It is only this return of the religious repressed that makes possible, and complete, Saladin's redemption and moral rehabilitation, although this is quickly repressed once more by a secular formulation: 'there was no accounting for one's good fortune' (547).

Thus, *The Satanic Verses* cannot divest itself of conventional (religious) morality, not least because 'religion' is an ineluctable part of human ethical development. Once this is admitted, it can only be dismissed by focusing purely on religion as an epistemological 'error', thereby excising its ethical dimension. In the Ayesha narrative, the effects of this displacement can be seen both in the way that religious faith is fetishized as an uncompromising dogmatism, and in the way that such certainty leads, inevitably, to inhumane and unethical behaviour, hence the grotesque stoning of the baby. This suggests that 'religion' is in a state of 'arrested development' ethically as well as historically; religious belief is shown to be inimical to even minimal standards of moral behaviour.[146]

Notwithstanding this rather uncompromising disavowal, the return of the religious repressed signals an inability to uphold secularism's governing oppositions between the religious and secular, between faith and reason – and, indeed, it exposes the fictitiousness of these oppositions. Not only does a religious sensibility return in the form of a redemptive sacrifice at the end of the novel, so too does it emerge in the form of several liberal humanist pieties that are revealed once the postmodern stylistic pyrotechnics of the novel are stripped away. Rushdie displaces faith in God only to replace it with his own articles of faith, not just in hybridity as a kind of ontology of history – it is its very nature – but also a belief in the redemptive power of a transcendental Love ('It all boiled down to love' (397)) and forgiveness. Such ideas about Love and forgiveness represent *continuities* with prevailing religious discourses and these tropes demonstrate how secularism, despite giving every appearance of being committed to a materialism that sees the world 'as it really is' and speaks, in Barthes' words, 'with the "Voice of Nature"' is, in fact, a system of belief with its own shibboleths, something that Nietzsche fully understood when he noted that 'we godless anti-metaphysicians still take our fire, too, from a faith that is thousands of years old'.[147]

The Satanic Verses is, therefore, a classic statement of secular liberal humanism. From that perspective, the radical excess of religious faith, as represented by Islam, is encircled and domesticated by a secular scepticism, the dominance of which is insistently reasserted over its efforts to empathetically represent the experience of religious belief. A novel that professes to be a 'love song to our mongrel selves' and a challenge to 'orthodoxies of all kinds' cannot imagine a hybrid position between the religious and the secular and ultimately re-inscribes and reinforces the categorical distinctions of secularist orthodoxy. Moreover, as we have seen, insofar as the figure of the hybrid in the novel also represents a post-colonial attempt to disrupt the master logic of western universalism, we must conclude by noting the ethical failure of a text that purports to speak up for difference but ultimately betrays that ambition.

Other verses, other choices

[E]very story one chooses to tell is a kind of censorship, it prevents the telling of other tales.

(Salman Rushdie, *Shame*, 73)

The unacknowledged essentialization of Islam, the complicity with Islamism, the inability to see, let alone dissent from, secularist orthodoxies – all of these represent the lineaments of Rushdie's ethical failure in *The Satanic Verses*.[148] Far from being written in good faith, the novel appears, in several respects, to be an act of bad faith. And there is one further ethical failure to note, one that, in some respects, stands above the others. Each of the failures suggested above constitutes a *self-transgression* for *The Satanic Verses* and its author explicitly declare themselves to be opposed to essentialism; to the ideologies that represent 'difference' as 'Other'; and to 'orthodoxies of all types' – all in the name of a post-colonial hybridity (it's 'love song to our mongrel selves') that was apparently meant to speak for the very people who subsequently turned against it. In each instance, however, the novel not only replicates and reinforces that which it opposes, but it does so without self-knowledge: its meta-fictional apparatus is, for all its sophistication, unable to reflect on these ethical limitations. Whilst some Muslims accused Rushdie of cultural betrayal, I would argue that, in fact, his greatest betrayal was of himself.[149]

Did it have to be this way? Ordinarily, I do not much care for the kind of criticism that laments the failure of the author to write the book the critic feels s/he *should* have written as opposed to the one they actually did. That kind of criticism is an abdication of the responsibility of the critic to engage with the work in front of them rather than the idealized version that exists only in their heads. Having said that, in this instance I would like to conclude by imagining some alternative narrative possibilities; if, as Rushdie himself has suggested, every text is a palimpsest that erases others which lie submerged within it, I would like to signpost some paths not taken which may have led to a more ethically appropriate intercultural encounter between Rushdie and Islam – a presumption, no doubt, but one that might be illuminating nonetheless. Indeed, these alternatives may in fact have delivered a much more radical critique of Islam than the one we find in *The Satanic Verses*, one that would have been true to Rushdie's own ethical principles whilst simultaneously observing an ethics of propriety with regard to its subject.

If, for instance, Rushdie was trying to argue against a dogmatic and uncompromising Islamist understanding of Islam then, rather than succumbing to such a characterization, might his riposte not have been more radical, more effective, and more ethically sound if it had articulated an alternative Islamic imaginary that draws on evidence within Islamic sources which suggest that compromise, far from being anathema to Islam, was in fact a major ethical value for the Prophet himself? In *The Satanic Verses*, Rushdie does, of course, present the Prophet as a man willing to compromise but only as an expedient. Had he chosen otherwise, Rushdie might instead have drawn upon evidence in the *Qur'an*, *hadith* and *sira* which suggests that the expedient compromise of the satanic verses appears anomalous within the overall Prophetic career. Although it is clear from the *Qur'an* that there can be no compromise concerning a Muslim's absolute commitment to monotheism, there are other verses that recommend compromise in other contexts. Thus, for example, within the context of fighting for God's cause, if opponents 'incline to peace, incline to it also' (8:61). Moreover, '[i]n the final analysis', writes Daniel Madigan, 'the *Qur'an* is concerned to assert God's tendency to forgive rather than condemn. More than five hundred times it characterizes God as forgiving', and the trope of forgiveness is clearly adjacent to the idea of compromise in both the *Qur'an* and *The Satanic Verses*, where it is aligned with the supposedly secular virtues of pragmatism, adaptability and love.[150]

A different understanding of the *Qur'an* might therefore have led to other narrative possibilities, as might a different reading of the early history of Islam. For it could be argued that the idea of compromise distinguished the nascent community of believers from the pagan Arabs. Rushdie gives pre-Islamic Mecca the name Jahilia, which has traditionally been taken to refer to the 'period of ignorance' – that is, the period before Islam. It is usually associated with the term *kufir*, which is translated as 'unbelievers'. Jahilia therefore refers to the period of the unbelievers, the pagans. In fact, both translations are misleading. *Kufir*, is based on the root KFR, whose primary connotation is 'ingratitude'. As Karen Armstrong points out, 'The Qur'an does not berate the *kafirun* for their lack of religious conviction, but for their arrogance.'[151] Indeed, in verse after verse of the *Qur'an*, the voice of Allah admonishes the Arabs not for their ignorance, but because they have been 'led astray' from the 'true path' (the *Shari'ah*). 'The chief vice of the *kafirun* was *jahiliyyah*', writes Armstrong, who argues that, 'although the root JHL has some connotations of "ignorance," its primary meaning is "irascibility": an acute sensitivity to honour and prestige; arrogance, excess, and above all, a chronic tendency to violence and retaliation'.[152] *Jahilia*, then, refers to the uncompromising tribalism of the pagan Arabs, captured well in the implacable hostility of Hind to her adversary. By contrast, Muslims are exhorted to observe the opposite of *jahilia*, the virtue of *hilm*, which referred to those who were 'forbearing, patient, and merciful'.[153]

It is on this basis that (most) Muslims claim that their religion is one of peace, and one expression of *hilm* in the realm of power is a willingness to compromise, which the *sira* shows to have consistently been the Prophet's first course of action. The classic moment in the *sira* tradition is at Hudaybiyah, just outside Mecca, when the Quraysh refuse the Prophet and the Muslims entry into Mecca to perform the *hajj*, and he accepts this in return for permission to return the following year, despite risking mutiny amongst his followers.[154] There is also an interesting literary foil throughout the *sira* in the zealotry of the uncompromising 'Umar (who would become the second caliph), which throws the moderation of the Prophet into sharp relief. And there is an interesting *hadith* on the origin of the number of prayers prescribed to Muslims. On his miraculous Night Journey to Jerusalem, when Muhammad is lifted by Gabriel to Heaven, Allah prescribes fifty prayers for the Muslims; on his descent he meets Moses who advises him to return and ask for a reduction, and it is duly reduced by half; each time Muhammad returns, Moses advises him to return to Allah until the number of prayers is reduced to five. The story clearly dramatizes the ethic of compromise within Islam.[155]

This alternative reading of *jahilia* also highlights other narrative possibilities open to Rushdie concerning Islam and hybridity. One reason to suppose that *jahilia* refers to the 'age of barbarism' rather than the 'age of ignorance' is the fact that the pagan Arabs were not ignorant of Allah, nor were they unaware of extant traditions of monotheism within the Arab tribes, known as *hanifiyya*, as well as those of the Christians and Jews, some of whom were also Arab. Watt writes that the *hanifiyya* signalled a 'vague monotheism' that was 'widespread' amongst the Arabs and 'was not so strict that the recognition of inferior divine beings was felt to be incompatible with it'.[156] This puts the incident of 'the satanic verses' in an altogether different context, one in which the development of Islamic metaphysics is an evolutionary process of negotiation, adaptation and evolution rather than a simple opposition between 'singularity' and 'multiplicity'. According to Peters, the 'unfolding' of Muhammad's 'new understanding of God' can be seen in the development of the divinity's appellation from 'Lord' to 'al-Rahman' – a 'name with a history, a history unconnected with Mecca' – to, eventually, 'the Allah of the Quraysh and, of course, the Jews and the Christians'.[157] It is possible that the Prophet's use of the term 'al-Rahman' here may have confused the Meccans by suggesting a devotion to an entirely different God, hence his eventual movement towards 'Allah', after which al-Rahman is never again used as a name for Allah, but becomes instead one if His attributes.[158] In other words, one might read this as demonstrating the historical development of the name of God Himself in Islam through a process of pragmatic adaptation and mutation, rather than a stable centre upon which Islam is unproblematically founded.

What would, in time, become known as 'Islam' has had a paradoxical and conflicted relationship to its antecedents. The *hanfiyya*, for instance, occupy a special place in the revelation and its subsequent exegesis: after his wife, Khadijah, the first to recognize Muhammad as a Prophet was acknowledged to be a Christian Arab called Waraqah, and even before

Muhammad received his first revelations, a Christian monk named Bahira, is shown to foretell his prophethood.[159] Chrisitans and Jews – 'the People of the Book' – are acknowledged throughout the *Qur'an*, their prophets are revered, and many other aspects of their respective traditions have been absorbed into Islam. The preference for Friday as the Muslim 'holy day' may have been due to the fact that the Jewish Banu Qaynuqa's *suq* (market) in Yathrib took place on that day; the Muslim feast day of Ashura may, in fact, have had its origins in a fast observed on the tenth day of the first month of the Jewish calendar, that is, Yom Kippur, although it was later 'severed from its Jewish prototype'; the idea that the *Qur'an* constituted a 'scripture' or Book of revelation on the Judeo-Christian model, that is, constituting, in its totality, a single revelation despite the 'occasional' and context-specific method by which it is revealed; and the idea of an angel, Gabriel, as an agent of revelation; all of these (and much more) may have worked their way into an evolving tradition that would, in time, neverthe-less come to see itself as 'a completely fresh start'.[160] This simultaneous acknowledgement and disavowal can be seen in the way Islam conceptual-izes itself on the one hand, as the 'original natural religion of Abraham' from which the Jews and Christians have strayed; it is therefore sent by God to 'confirm' once more these previous messages, thereby absorbing these antecedents within itself. On the other hand, the *Qur'an* insists its message is specific to *Muslims*, and it constantly *distances* the Jews and Christians, particularly with regard to its legislative aspects, 'this same sura [*sura* 5, which "confirmed Muhammad's status as a legislator"] expressed astonishment that the Jews should have recourse to Muhammad, "seeing they have the Torah, wherein lies God's judgement", while also enjoining Christians to seek guidance and advice in their Gospels'.[161]

The point is that a secular critique of Islam's 'ethic of purity' in the name of hybridity need not have essentialized Islam as the one-in-a-hundred time when something 'new' enters the world *ex nihilo*, thereby unwittingly corroborating its self-representation. The same could be said of the *hijrah*, which was as profoundly dislocating as well as dynamically creative for the early Muslims (and the Prophet especially) in much the same manner as the later migrations that have so much significance within Rushdie's work.[162] I would argue that these other interpretations of Islam represent opportu-nities for more radical narratives that are also more true to Rushdie's own 'ethic of impurity'.[163]

Of course, these alternative points of departure may not vouchsafe the integrity of the resulting literary work. An imaginative writer's relationship to his or her historical material is an open and dynamic one, and how they fashion a creative work from it depends on any number of choices available to them within the framework of their overall understanding of the subject. Nevertheless, as Edward Said reminds us, points of departure are significant because they determine what follows insofar as they orient the work towards certain possibilities and foreclose others.[164] A work like *The Satanic Verses* would obviously have been a very different novel to the one that exists, but it would have been no less critical for being less ethically compromised; indeed, the force of its critique would have been all the stronger. A work based on these understandings of Islam would, assuredly, have been avowedly refuted by orthodox, and perhaps many unorthodox, Muslims as a denial of the unique singularity of a perfect revelation as attested by tradition, and there will perhaps have been some, maybe many, who might have taken offence – after all, the ethics of propriety is a responsibility incumbent on readers as well as writers and not all readers and writers are prepared to assume it; but such a work might also have avoided the tropes and stereotypes that are to be found in western traditions of anti-Islamic polemic and, more importantly, would perhaps have delivered a more *historical* rather than essentialist understanding of Islam. True, the metaphysical ambition of *The Satanic Verses* may not have been so well served but that might not be such a bad thing because it is principally responsible for ethically compromising the novel's critique not only of Islam but also of nationalism and racism, for it is reductive and ahistorical to see all 'monological' ideological formations as equivalent to each other. Specifically with respect to its deconstruction of these latter ideologies, however, *The Satanic Verses* remains, in my view, unsurpassed as a work of moral and political imagination so it is unfortunate that the two aspects of the novel work against rather than with each other. With respect to its interrogation of Islam, however, it is a work that falls short of the integrity required to adequately address the task of generating the genuine intercultural dialogue and exchange through which mutual understanding might indeed be possible.

5

Visualism and Violence: On the Art and Ethics of Provocation in the *Jyllands-Posten* Cartoons and Theo Van Gogh's *Submission*

The controversy generated by the cartoons of the Prophet Muhammad in the Danish newspaper *Jyllands-Posten* closely resembles 'the Rushdie affair'. It followed a similar trajectory and observed a similar dynamic: initial protests by the Danish Muslim community were either ignored or rejected; the controversy 'proper' – which followed the publication and first protests after a hiatus of several months – was then exploited by both supporters of the newspaper and Muslim political organizations, and the internationalization of the controversy through the global media resulted in an escalation and polarization that, like the Rushdie affair, has never quite been resolved.[1] A continental counterpart to the absolutist defence of freedom of speech that accompanied the Rushdie affair also emerged. The phraseology of this discourse is an almost exact echo, using the same or similar motifs, tropes and arguments. A *Jyllands-Posten* editorial in February 2006 stated, 'we should only show concern for freedom of speech . . . If we say "freedom of speech, but", we have denounced the most basic foundation of democracy.'[2] This reprised the uncompromising tone of the Danish Prime Minister, Anders Fogh Rasmussen, who had earlier argued that 'freedom of speech is absolute. It is not negotiable.'[3]

Summoning the spirit of *Nineteen Eighty-Four*, the cultural editor of *Jyllands-Posten* and chief protagonist in the developing controversy, Flemming Rose, wrote that, 'It is no coincidence that people in totalitarian societies are imprisoned for telling jokes or for satirizing dictators. It is usually done with the argument that people's feelings have been hurt. Things have not gone that far in Denmark, but . . . we are on a *slippery slope* and nobody can predict where self-censorship will end.'[4] Robert A. Kahn has forensically examined the contradictions and sleights of hand involved in this comparison with totalitarianism,[5] but my interest here is in the way it evokes certain key tropes in liberal absolutist discourse: the idea of the 'embattled' defender of freedom; the 'speaking of truth to power'; the 'slippery slope' argument; and, as a prelude to the argument that in a free society 'everybody must be willing to put up with sarcasm, mockery and ridicule', the idea that unrestrained freedom of speech – 'It sounds so pretty that we should speak nicely to strangers and not provoke. But freedom of speech is not polite. It is raw and honest'[6] – is a good-in-itself. Indeed, far from hurting its targets, 'Rose . . . argues that insulting speech – in this case the cartoons – helps rather than harms [them],'[7] a point later amplified by Prime Minister Rasmussen when he claimed that 'this inclination to subject everything to critical debate . . . has led to progress in our society.'[8]

This liberal absolutism was most pronounced during the subsequent controversy over the re-publication of the cartoons in several European newspapers in 'solidarity' with *Jyllands-Posten* in the wake of the violence against Danish goods and property in the Middle East in February 2006.[9] Indeed, the issue of re-publication unsettled even those exceptionally attuned to Muslim sensitivities regarding the cartoons, thereby revealing the ethical limits of liberal thought concerning freedom of expression. Prefacing Jytte Klausen's *The Cartoons That Shook the World* are a 'Publisher's Statement' and 'Author's Statement' about the decision by Yale University Press not to re-publish the cartoons even in the context of an academic book about the controversy. The publishers cited security concerns, and in her 'Author's statement' Klausen says that she 'agreed with sadness to the Press's decision not to print the cartoons'. Although it would be difficult, even obtuse, to argue that re-publication in this instance would have constituted a provocation, what concerns me here is the regret ('with sadness') expressed by both Klausen and Yale University Press, for it is highly illustrative of the ways in which liberal accounts of expressive liberty ethically attenuate the very liberty they seek to defend. In truth, the inclusion of the cartoons in Klausen's book was neither here nor there, a sideshow: they are easily available on the internet, as are the other illustrations of the Prophet to which Klausen refers, and the author's citations are more than enough for those wishing to follow them up. Rather, the *angst* by which an irrelevance is made highly significant speaks to a more profound fact: given the availability of the cartoons online, there should have been no 'sadness' at making a 'judgment call', as Stanley Fish puts it, or deciding on the moral value of restraint over and above expression;[10] the regret, however, exposes an underlying conception of liberty in which restraint is indeed something to be regretted because it is seen as inimical to freedom – hence the ubiquitous use of the term self-censorship as a substitute for more appropriate terms like restraint, judgment, tact, politeness, consideration, sensitivity and so on. That some see such forms of judgment as a betrayal of freedom of speech only goes to show how free speech absolutism subverts the basis of freedom itself, namely the (relative) moral autonomy to make such a 'judgment call' as opposed to blindly submitting to some absolute abstract principle that carries the force of a commandment.

Compare the response of *Jyllands-Posten* with regard to the accusation of double-standards when it emerged that the paper had earlier refused to publish satirical cartoons of Jesus.[11] Jens Kaiser, the editor in question, said 'In the Muhammad drawings case, we asked the illustrators to do it. I did not ask for these cartoons. That's the difference . . . The illustrator thought his cartoons were funny. I did not think so. It would offend some readers, not much but some.' In other words, he made a 'judgment call', but in remarking on the difference between the unsolicited Jesus cartoons and the Muhammad cartoons, which had been commissioned to test the extent of 'self-censorship' in Denmark with respect to Islam, Kaiser inadvertently reveals the contrast between the restrictions that constitute 'normal' editorial procedure and the rhetoric of 'self-censorship'. This cannot be explained away by the supposed reason for undertaking the 'experiment' itself: the apparent inability of a children's book author to find illustrators willing to draw pictures of the Prophet. As Klausen has noted, the 'experimental' nature of the commission meant that normal editorial procedures could not apply 'for the obvious reason that it would have gone against the premise of the experiment . . . A normal process of editorial assessment . . . was out of the question because it would have seemed like censorship.'[12]

It is clear, then, that the premise of the experiment – based on a simple dichotomy between (self-)censorship and freedom – was highly problematic. Normal editorial procedures could not be applied not only because it would appear to be a form of censorship, but also because such procedures would dismantle the opposition on which the experiment rests: (self-)censorship would be shown to be located not outside but *within* 'freedom'. What is at stake, therefore, in any actually existing 'free society', is not a choice between freedom of speech and (self-)censorship but rather the nature, scope and basis of those restrictions that shape the kind of free speech that is practiced.

Moreover, as Joseph Carens has pointed out, the motives of the children's author, Kare Bluitgen, are themselves not entirely transparent, and yet they were taken, by most liberal and western commentators, as self-evident:

> Rhetorically, this reference to the origins of the conflict has made it appear as though an innocent exercise in intercultural communication was disrupted by the irrational reactions of an illiberal minority. But wait a minute. If the author knew anything about Islam, he must have known that many Muslims object to representations of Muhammad. And if he did not know this at the outset, he ought to have figured it out when the illustrators kept turning him down. So, why would someone deliberately present information to children about another religion in a way that the author knows will be offensive to many followers of the religion? Suddenly the author's agenda does not appear so benign.[13]

This fashioning of a rationale (Klausen notes how the *Jyllands-Posten* backstory to the 'experiment' began to 'fall apart' under close examination[14]) exposes the *performativity* of the cartoons, the attempt by the editors to use the cartoons and 'freedom of speech' as part of a larger political argument about Islam, Muslims, and their place in Danish society. In fact, the performativity of the cartoons lies not so much in their use as part of a wider political *argument* as in the way that argument is used to 'do' something: to *exclude* Muslims, symbolically, from Europe and Denmark.

Thus, we can see that the liberal absolutism that emerged in the wake of the Danish cartoon controversy, although overlapping with that which emerged after the Rushdie affair and the assassination of Theo van Gogh in 2004, has a specifically Danish provenance that distilled what Heiko Henkel has called the 'civilization-speak' of these antedecents into the prevailing concerns and lexicon of contemporary Danish political discourse.[15] The political performativity of the cartoons can only be understood against the backdrop of contemporary Danish concerns about immigration, and Muslim immigration in particular. As many commentators have observed, the ascendancy of Fogh Rasmussen's Liberal Party and its electoral alliance with the populist right-wing Danish People's Party (DPP), whose leader Pia Kjærsgaard is a vocal critic of Islam, has sustained 'the harsh tenor of Danish public debates on immigration and Muslims'.[16] For Kjærsgaard, Muslims are aliens with fundamentally irreconcilable norms and values that threaten the Danish way of life. The DPP is just one of a number of European populist parties that constitute what the Dutch sociologist Dick Pels calls a right-wing 'third way', a 'liberal fascism' that 'combine[s] liberalism with populism, articulated through the same sort of strong, charismatic leader [as traditional fascism].'[17] For Kjærsgaard in Denmark, read Pim Fortuyn in the Netherlands, and Jorg Haider in Austria. These parties have clearly appropriated liberalism in order to advance an exclusionary, intolerant and supremacist politics that rhetorically overlaps quite significantly with the discourse of liberal absolutism that has emerged in relation to the Muslim-related controversies over freedom of expression (despite the obvious and clear differences between their respective political agendas), not so much in every detail but certainly enough to suggest that this 'liberal facism' exposes the latent tendencies within more mainstream liberal thought concerning cultural difference, tendencies that traverse the left-right spectrum.

The politics being performed by the *Jyllands-Posten* cartoons, then, is an articulation of this form of liberal fascism that simultaneously excludes culturally different 'others' – in particular, Muslims – whilst also setting the terms of inclusion. It is here that we can see the rhetorical significance of the 'special considerations' being claimed by Muslims to which Flemming Rose refers in his essay accompanying the cartoons:

> The modern secular society is rejected by some Muslims. They demand a special position, special consideration of their own religious feelings. It

is incompatible with contemporary democracy and freedom of speech, where you must be ready to put up with insults, mockery and ridicule.[18]

In claiming that Muslims *set themselves apart*, Rose occludes the way in which they are in fact being *positioned* as 'outsiders'. Moreover, their claim to 'special consideration of their religious feelings' is characterized not as an argument over what kind of free speech is appropriate to a multicultural society, but as an argument *against* free speech per se. In so doing, Rose sets the terms of inclusion as being predicated upon Muslims accepting a particular kind of democratic culture, which is why his later claim that the cartoons were 'an act of inclusion. Equal treatment is the democratic way to overcome barriers of blood and soil for newcomers. To me, that means treating immigrants just as I would any other Danes', is not as obtuse as it might at first appear;[19] it is merely the other side of the coin to the act of exclusion, albeit a coin minted on the premise that difference should be subordinated to sameness, and the intrinsic supremacy of the Danish 'way of life' over those which the immigrants bring with them.

This is where the significance of the equation of democracy with 'insult, mockery and ridicule' lies: it is characteristic of what Robert Kahn calls 'the Danish idea of informal sociality', *hygge*. 'Sustaining *hygge* requires "quick repartee",' he writes, 'and an expertise in "teasing" . . . teasing is an effective way of ensuring that no-one remains "indefinitely in a mood or posture communicating separateness or isolation" because . . . "the individual cannot help effectively becoming part of the interaction."'[20] There is, clearly, an inclusive aspect to *hygge*, but there is also a 'harsher side to the practice' – although it 'reinforces a deeply held norm of democratic egalitarian informality', there is also a 'tendency toward "humiliation and ridicule for those who dare to stand out . . . ".'[21] It is summed up in one phrase by the Danish novelist Askel Sandemose, as 'Don't be different'. There is also a particular inflection that Sandemose describes as 'You shall not believe that you can teach *us* anything.' It is on this basis that one can read the assimilationist rhetoric of *Jyllands-Posten* editorials, 'We should be strong enough to say that we find our culture and civilization right for us around here, with our tradition; and that those who want part of it have to adjust themselves to it.'[22] This argument, *ipso facto*, renders even the peaceful Muslim protests against the cartoons invalid, thereby ironically denying them the right to freedom of speech that the *Jyllands-Posten* editors claim is characteristic of Denmark's democratic culture; not only are Muslims excluded, they are effectively silenced – they must 'put up or shut up'. There is no admitting the possibility that democratic citizenship might include the right to contest, challenge and revise the democratic culture itself in the name of an alternative kind of democracy, even though Fogh Rasmussen claims that the 'inclination to subject everything to critical debate' is its foundation.

The value of provocation

The *Jyllands-Posten* cartoons of Muhammad were clearly meant to be pro-vocative. They were accompanied by the headline 'The Face of Muhammad', which, as Jytte Klausen suggests, signals the editors' intent to break the taboo on representing the Prophet. The editor-in-chief's editorial in the main sec-tion of the paper (the cartoons were printed in the culture supplement) also explicitly stated that, 'Any provocation against one of these self-important imams or mad mullahs is instantly interpreted as a provocation against the Prophet himself or the holy book, the Koran, and then trouble ensues.'[23] But whilst many of the newspaper's opponents have argued that the cartoons should be condemned on this basis, provocation is, for an ethics of propri-ety, merely a point of departure rather than a self-evident conclusion. For it is not apparent that provocation is, in itself, always ethically compromised – that would bespeak an absolutism that is fundamentally at odds with the context-specific nature of ethical enquiry. Ethically speaking, the value of provocation rests on two things: the purpose or 'intentionality' behind it, and the manner in which it is done. In respect of the former, the purpose or intentionality of the cartoons is somewhat difficult to pin down because there were several stated motives all of which bear upon the (unstated) political performativity of the cartoons: to make a point about free speech; to conduct an experiment in order to test the extent of self-censorship in Denmark *vis à vis* Islam (as distinct from 'striking a blow for free speech', which would pre-judge the outcome of the experiment); to break a taboo; to satirize 'self-appointed' religious leaders; to 'educate' Muslims in the norms and values of 'democracy' and *hygge*; and to provoke self-criticism and 'pro-gress' among Muslims. Some of these might have ethical value in any given context, but the ethical as opposed to political effectivity of the provocation clearly rests on the visual semantics (the 'manner') of the cartoons them-selves, to which we shall turn in due course.

There are other, more general, considerations which might also redeem provocative speech acts. Defending the cartoons against accusations of racism, Andras Sajo writes, 'The Danish cartoons . . . addressed a religious belief. On what ground can you equate unchangeable race (skin color) and religion, if religion is a matter of choice?'[24] This of course rehearses several common liberal arguments that I have discussed at length in Chapters 2 and 3; but, properly speaking, the idea that speech acts, even provocative ones, are justified on the grounds that beliefs *need* to be criticized is also a point of departure and not a self-evident warranty of their ethical value. Two subsequent questions are particularly pertinent here: *what* and *whose* beliefs are being criticized? With respect to the former question, there are two broad beliefs that encompass most of the cartoons and the film *Submission*: that Islam is a violent religion, which justifies, condones or even encour-ages violence and aggression against unbelievers – a belief that encompasses its supposed rejection of pluralism and promotion of intolerance; and it is a misogynistic religion that justifies the oppression and violent abuse of women. But *whose* beliefs are these? Are these the beliefs of *all* Muslims *qua* Muslims? Of just *some* Muslims? Or are they, in fact, *European and non-Muslim* beliefs about Islam? The justification of the cartoons and *Submission* rests on the answers to these questions, which returns us to the 'manner' in which these 'texts' articulate them.

This is, in turn, predicated on the *visual* nature of these works. Saba Mahmood has argued that the incomprehension and incredulity of western secularists towards Muslim responses to the Danish cartoons arises from a divergence between their respective semiotic ideologies. The former 'presuppose a semiotic ideology in which signifiers are arbitrarily linked to concepts, their meaning open to people's reading in accord with a particular code shared between them', which is an 'impoverished understanding of images, icons, and signs' that 'fails to attend to the affective and embodied practices through which a subject comes to relate to a particular sign'.[25] This is a 'communicative or representational model' of the visual image, against which she posits the 'assimilative' model that characterizes the 'devout Muslim's relationship to Muhammad'; here, the 'mental image' or 'icon' establishes 'a form of relationality that binds the subject to an object or imaginary'.[26] Following W.J.T Mitchell's argument that the 'force' of an image emerges from 'a relationship that binds the image to the spectator', she cites Mitchell's insistence that 'Vision . . . is not reducible to language, or sign, or to discourse. Pictures want equal rights with language, not to be turned into language', and thus argues that any representational theory of language, such as post-Saussurean linguistics and deconstruction, is inadequate to the task of explaining the semiotic ideology of pious Muslims.[27] Naveeda Khan, however, notes that Mitchell had, in an earlier piece, rejected the idea that 'images are entirely distinct from words' because they are 'grounded in specific forms of life and accompanying conventions of language.'[28] On the other hand, she concurs that 'they are not entirely reducible to words either.'[29] Given that Mahmood's own distinction between 'representational' and 'assimilative' models of the image suggests that each rests on a semiotic convention that is not shared by other groups (that is, 'westerners' hold to the 'representational' convention, whilst pious Muslims share an 'assimilative' convention; one group finds certain images 'sacred' whereas the other group does not) it would seem that Saussurean theories of language are, in fact, not quite so inapplicable to analysis of the mental images held by pious Muslims as she suggests, because if that is the case then signifiers *are* arbitrarily linked to their signifieds through 'a particular code shared between them'. I would suggest, however, that Mahmood seems to be gesturing towards – without quite realizing it – Saussure's inability to account for diachrony. Although *in principle* (or at the structural level of *langue*) signs are arbitrarily linked to their referents, the important point is that they acquire meaning only through social *convention*, which introduces an element of temporality or diachrony into *la langue* that institutes *le parôle*. In lived practice, therefore, signs are weighted and attached to their denotative and connotative references. This is precisely why, in Chapter 1, I take issue with the liberatory potential of Judith Butler's politics of the performative.

The ways in which signs work in lived experience – as *le parôle* – *depends on the kinds of signs in question*: a street sign, for example, conforms much more readily to Saussure's model than an icon. The latter carries a connotative weight that is lacking in the former. Likewise, because they 'condense information in a special way', cartoons are also heavily weighted: 'they merge visual depictions with an array of cultural associations' and thus, like icons and other weighted images, carry a visceral force that arises from the ways in which the image 'sutures' itself to its connotations.[30] At the same time, as signs that depend on conventions of interpretation, and lacking the expansive ability of textuality to amplify, clarify, modulate and nuance their signification, images are paradoxically *more* open to interpretative plurality and instability – or 'liquidity' as Simon Weaver puts it[31] – even as the 'suture' renders them more stable and, in some cases, more opaque than textual signifiers. As we shall see, if the manner of these texts is crucial in assessing their ethical value, then this in turn depends on the *way* in which the force of the 'suture' operates in each of these images.

The cartoons

Jyllands-Posten published twelve cartoons, and not all of them were critical of or offensive towards Muslims and Islam. Four of them were, in fact, quite critical of the *Jyllands-Posten* editors, notably one that satirically re-interpreted the brief to draw 'the face of Muhammad as you see him' to mean not the Prophet, but rather a young immigrant Muslim boy called Muhammad pointing to some writing on a blackboard which states, in Farsi, '*Jyllands-Posten's* journalists are a bunch of reactionary provocateurs'. Ironically, the illustrator of this cartoon, Lars Refn, was the first to receive a death threat, which underscores the interpretative impropriety, amongst other things, of those who issue such threats. Another cartoon seems to have interpreted the brief quite literally, sketching a prophet figure in the desert. The illustrator drew on Christian rather than Muslim iconography and, according to Muller and Ozcan, may have thus inadvertently caused offence by associating the Prophet with a donkey, an animal that is held in low esteem among Muslims.[32] One shows a bearded figure with what appears to be a set of horns or, possibly, a halo. The question it seems to be asking is whether the Prophet is good or evil, angel or devil, and it remains pointedly equivocal. The remaining cartoons are all critical of the Prophet and, by implication, some or all Muslims. Some use motifs that clearly recall 'the language of anti-Semitic caricature used in Germany and elsewhere in Europe in the 1920s and 1930s'.[33] They all connote either violence or gender oppression, or sexual excess. This limited range of associations in itself represents the narrowness of vision within which Islam and Muslims are circumscribed. Nevertheless, within that narrow frame, not all of them are critical/offensive in the same way or to the same degree. Two distinguish the Prophet from his followers: one mistakes him for St. Peter at the gates of heaven telling a queue of suicide bombers 'Stop stop we ran out of virgins!'; the other depicts the Prophet as a sultan telling his followers, who carry swords, to 'Relax, folks, it is just a sketch made by a Dane from southwest Denmark.' Although both of these portray the Prophet as a moderating figure, the metonymic force of the suture is, in fact, merely displaced from the figure of the Prophet onto the followers: do these violent 'followers' represent *all* Muslims or just *some* of them? The visual nature of the images, and the lack of further clues, keeps that question open.

Here I want to focus on the most notorious of the cartoons, illustrated by *Jyllands-Posten*'s in-house cartoonist, Kurt Westergaard, which depicts a rather forbidding figure with bushy eyebrows and a prominent nose (it is one of those deploying anti-Semitic motifs) sporting a large turban in which is secreted a bomb with a lit fuse. On the bomb, in Arabic calligraphy, is the *shahada*, the Muslim profession of faith: *La illaha illalah Muhammad ur-Rasul Allah* (There is no God but Allah and Muhammad is His Messenger). Most if not all Muslims have interpreted it as suggesting that the Prophet Muhammad was a terrorist and thus, by metonymic extension, all Muslims are potential, if not actual, terrorists. At the very least, they argue, it suggests that Islam is a terroristic religion, and that violence is an integral aspect of the faith. Westergaard, on the other hand, claims otherwise:

> The cartoon is not about Islam as a whole, but the part that apparently can inspire violence, terrorism, death and destruction. And thereby the fundamentalist part of Islam. I wanted to demonstrate that terrorists get their spiritual ammunition from Islam.[34]

This has commonly been taken to mean that Westergaard is making a scrupulous distinction between Islam and Islamism or Islamic fundamentalism. But there is an ambiguity here that emerges when the statement is examined carefully. Westergaard could be suggesting that a 'fundamentalist' interpretation of Islam is only one among many (one part of the ensemble of positions that constitutes 'Islam') and that there is therefore no *necessary* connection between that interpretation and 'Islam' itself; that is, 'fundamentalists' may *use* 'Islam' to justify violence, but Islam could also be used to argue *against* violence, in the name of peace, etc. Or he could be suggesting that the 'part' of Islam that inspires violence is not merely one interpretation among others, but is in fact an integral part of a coherent and organic 'whole' called 'Islam'. The 'part' in this latter rendition is therefore *essential* rather than incidental, and Westergaard is suggesting that 'violence, terrorism, death and destruction' is *intrinsic* to Islam, a 'fundamental' element without which Islam would not be what it is. In any case, the key point here is that *the image itself offers no such ambiguity* precisely because it sutures the 'part' that inspires violence to the 'origin' or 'foundation' of Islam (as a whole), namely the figure of the Prophet Muhammad. Rather than making the *historical* point that violent forms of Islam are part of its history, the suture enables the image to make the *essentialist* point that Islam is, in its very nature, violent. In other words, Westergaard's image suggests that the militant and 'fundamentalist' interpretation of Islam is correct. This in turn raises the question of whose 'belief' Westergaard is representing. If it is indeed a 'correct' Islamic belief, then there can no difference of opinion between or amongst Muslims as to whether their faith does indeed justify violence and terrorism – it *must* (which is patently untrue unless one suggests that those who argue against violence are not 'true' Muslims). But, equally, one might ask where Westergaard gets this idea from – is it based on anything other than a belief, *on his part*, that it does?

This is where the concept of *jihad* needs to be addressed and interrogated. Just as Rushdie's interpretation of early Islamic history is complicit with Islamist accounts of the *salaf*, and thereby colludes in its embedding as the 'true' history of Islam, so too is Westergaard complicit with militant interpretations of *jihad* as the 'sixth pillar' of Islam, thereby colluding in its reinforcement, by Islamists and western liberals alike, as the only correct and 'true' interpretation of *jihad*. This is sometimes aided and abetted by western academic 'expertise' on the concept. David Cook's *Understanding Jihad*, for example, contests the usual means by which Muslims challenge militant interpretations of *jihad* by insisting that there is a distinction between the 'greater' and 'lesser' *jihad*, and that the former refers to 'spiritual' conquest, which is superior to the militant orientation of the 'lesser' *jihad*; furthermore, the latter is supposed to be defensive rather than aggressive. This 'creative re-interpretation', which is cited by modern Muslim 'apologists' and western scholars 'who want to present Islam in the most innocuous terms possible' as the basis for their 'nonviolent' interpretations of *jihad*, can be traced to the twelfth-century CE theologian al-Ghazali (d.1111), and it 'turns the focus radically away from the *original intent*', of the Qur'anic verse 9:29, part of a sura (chapter) revealed towards the end of the Prophet's life that effectively makes 'the final revelation a declaration of war' and 'explains the aggressiveness of the early Muslims'.[35] And yet, despite insisting that in the *Qur'an* 'we have a very martial and . . . well-developed religious justification for waging war against Islam's enemies', and that it 'was a powerful exponent of an aggressive jihad doctrine', that is 'unambiguously concrete and militant', Cook nevertheless admits that 'some' verses in the *Qur'an* 'appear to describe a purely spiritual striving' and 'other passages . . . similarly lend themselves to a nonviolent – or at least not exclusively violent – interpretation of *jihad*.[36] This is because of the 'inherent ambiguities' of the doctrine and 'difficulties of ascertaining the original meaning.'[37] At another point, he states that 'strictly speaking in the Qur'an the word jihad is used comparatively rarely for actual fighting (it appears only four times; other words such as *qital*, fighting, are more common)', but he still criticizes another scholar for 'ignoring the entirety of Muslim history and law with regard to jihad, which cites *dozens* of militant verses from the Qur'an'.[38] Presumably, then, these 'dozens' refer to verses other than the four that explicitly deploy the term *jihad*.

Such inconsistencies and contradictions seem to arise from Cook's limited hermeneutics, which, like the medieval jurists with whose work he is most familiar, treats the concept of *jihad* in isolation from the wider Qur'anic *ethos* – a method of interpretation that modern reformist Muslim scholars criticize on the basis of the *Qur'an's* own insistence on 'holistic' interpretation: 'Those who break the *Qur'an* into parts. Them, by thy Lord, we shall question' (15:91–2).[39] Thus, when Cook writes, 'Although Islam was not spread by the sword, as is commonly imagined, conquest and jihad created the preconditions for conversion, and conversion or proclamation was one of the goals of jihad', he neglects to set it against the Qur'anic injunction that there is no compulsion in religion (Q2:256).[40] In the absence of this wider ethical context, the rhetorical switchback in the sentence implies that the jihad of conversion is, in fact, predicated on the jihad of conquest – that they are two sides of the same coin, even as Cook acknowledges that Islam was not 'spread by the sword'. However, this formulation – which actually implies *forced* conversion – violates the foundational principle of Qur'anic ethics, derived from the fundamental premise of its theology (*tawhid*), which insists that only the moral autonomy of each human gives significance to the idea of *islam* itself: the *willing* surrender of oneself to Allah. Indeed, it would undercut it to the point where *jihad*, far from being an expression of the Qur'anic ethos, becomes its limit or even antithesis. This may be why *jihad* has so many dimensions and connotations, of which its militant aspect is but one. Richard Bonney notes that 'a modern holistic approach to reading the *Qur'an*, quite different from that of the jurists of classical times . . . suggests twelve senses of jihad which are to be found in the Qur'an and hadith', and that although '[t]here are 35 occurrences of the word jihad or its equivalent in the Qur'an . . . [t]here are just four verses which use derivation from jihad and are clearly "warlike" in intention . . . In contrast there are eleven verses which are pacific in intent . . . . Twenty of the verses are capable of different interpretations.'[41]

If Cook's intent is to establish that the meaning of *jihad* cannot be reduced *solely* to spiritual or nonviolent usage, then that is fair enough. But, conversely, given the martial culture prevailing among the Arab tribes during the *jahiliyya* period, what is remarkable is not that the concept of *jihad* in the *Qur'an* has a martial inflection nor that the Qur'anic ethos – with its emphasis on justice in both the secular and divine order – should have developed, over time, a military dimension in order to fight injustice, but rather that countervailing values in the Qur'anic ethos, such as restraint, moderation, forbearance, mercy, forgiveness and, indeed, peace, have enabled the idea of struggle in the path of Allah (*jihad*) to acquire a dual, even plural, provenance that is *not* exclusively militaristic. The point, then, is not whether it is 'legitimate', based on historical usuage and textual evidence, to interpret *jihad* as aggressive or militant warfare against non-Muslims. That it *can* be interpreted as such is not in question; what is at issue is the converse question: is it possible for *jihad* to be interpreted otherwise, to mean something other than militant warfare in a changed context where Muslim politics need no longer be pursued through war and conquest, which, after all, was the modus *operandi* of *all* political formations of the pre-modern period?

Even though Cook admits its theoretical possibility, he actually does his best to suggest that even asking that question is somehow unwarranted because all the 'evidence' from the 'history and experience' of Islam suggests it cannot be done. This effectively suggests that violent *jihad* is intrinsic to Islam. Ironically, despite the appeal to 'historical evidence', his is a very idealist position in which ideas fully determine actions. If we were to be properly historical, however, we might suggest that the historical context of Islam's emergence and consolidation, in which war and conquest was the way in which politics was executed, is what 'explains the aggressiveness of the early Muslims'.[42] Likewise, in a contemporary global context where other political modalities are not only possible but dominant, it is surely conceivable that *jihad* can be re-interpreted to meet the needs of our time, especially given its multiple meanings. Just as the classical jurists emphasized the concept's militancy, so too can contemporary reformers de-emphasize it. Whether they succeed or not is a political question, and in criticizing such efforts as 'ideological' and 'biased' Cook exposes his own ideological position in the process of laying claim to the 'unambiguous' and 'true' meaning of *jihad*.

Since we are talking about violence, it is difficult to imagine how it is possible to extract the concept of *jihad* out of the wider ethical context established by the *Qur'an* as well as the historical contexts of its emergence and development. But this is precisely how the classical jurists of medieval Islam, contemporary Islamists (particularly those with a militant orientation), and certain western commentators approach the matter, and it is how Westergaard's image represents it. The resulting complicity short-circuits the possibility of alternative interpretations of Islam and surreptitiously encodes a 'true' Islam that negates all others, a manoeuvre that serves the ideological agendas of both Islamists and secular-liberals alike.

Submission and the politics of polarization

On 2 November 2004 the well-known filmmaker and *provocateur* Theo van Gogh was assassinated by a young Dutch man of Moroccan descent, Mohammed Bouyeri.[43] He pinned a note to van Gogh's body, which indicated that the real target was a female Dutch member of parliament of Somali origin called Ayaan Hirsi Ali with whom van Gogh had collaborated in making a short film called *Submission*. The film had been broadcast on Dutch television a few months prior to the murder. Hirsi Ali was something of a skilled *provocateur* too, and had made a name for herself as a vocal critic of Islam, of the Muslim immigrant communities in the Netherlands, and in particular the treatment of women in Muslim societies. Although the assassination became *the* talking point in Dutch society for several months, and despite being an intervention in the politics of controversy, it was not itself controversial insofar as it was almost unanimously condemned by all parties. In contrast, the film *Submission* had generated considerable controversy upon its broadcast. But *Submission* was itself merely an intervention in a wider controversy concerning not just the integration of Muslim immigrants, as in Denmark, but also the nature, scope and viability of 'multiculturalism'. In contrast to the Danish suspicion of difference, the Dutch had convinced themselves that one of their virtues, as expressed through multiculturalism, was their ability to embrace and tolerate difference. But, increasingly, the limits of difference were becoming apparent to many, especially the difference of Islam. It is this wider question concerning Dutch identity, cultural difference and the limits of 'tolerance' that gives the controversy surrounding the film *Submission* its particular Dutch inflection.

In fact, the roots of this issue reach back as far as the establishment of the Dutch Republic in the sixteenth century. After the Reformation, the split between Protestants and Catholics in Dutch society was managed and reconciled by the development of a corporatist and 'consociational' system known as the *polder* (pillar) model.[44] Each group in society became a pillar and the number of pillars extended over time to include not just Catholics and Protestants, but also socialists and liberals. Each pillar had its own 'own media, social and sport clubs, and, to a large extent, segregated domiciles'.[45] 'While reinforcing segregation', writes Ron Eyerman, 'these pillars actually gave Dutch society an inherent structure, a form of stability under a surface fragmentation', because of an underlying common ground that constituted an 'imagined community of good Dutchmen'.[46] This ground was fashioned by certain myths relating to the heroic efforts to reclaim the literal ground on which Dutch society could be built: those who had wrested from the sea the land on which the Dutch stood were, despite their divisions and segregations, 'good Dutchmen'. This, suggests Eyerman, is the probable origin of the *autochthon/allochthon* (native/outsider) distinction that structures the vocabulary of Dutch identity to this day.[47] Following post-war immigration from the former Dutch colonies and the arrival of guest workers from Morocco and Turkey, multiculturalism emerged as an extension of the *polder* model, and the 'long tradition of tolerance' on which the Dutch pride themselves (a correlate of the *polder* system) was extended to the newcomers albeit in tension, now, with the *autochthon/allochthon* distinction that lay just beneath the surface.[48]

Concurrent with this extension of the *polder* system, the effects of a profound challenge to that very system were also beginning to be felt across society. This challenge was mounted by the student and counter-cultural rebellions of the 1960s that inaugurated what Peter van der Veer calls a 'silent revolution' that is 'celebrated in the Netherlands as a liberation, especially from obstacles to enjoyment.'[49] As the perceived origin of these obstacles, religion in particular was rejected and Dutch society experienced a widespread and precipitate secularization. According to van der Veer, 'A popular narrative among the Dutch is that during this decade [1960s] they finally liberated themselves from religion.'[50] This is the 'turning point' at which liberalism came to be seen as an alternative foundation for Dutch society as opposed to being one pillar among others – a recently 'invented tradition' that is most apparent in the reconstruction of Dutch identity articulated by the flamboyant Dutch populist politician Pim Fortuyn.[51]

Since the 1960s, then, two very different models of social life have been sitting somewhat uncomfortably alongside each other. The 'problem' of Islam, as both van Gogh and Hirsi Ali call it, has emerged in this context as a means by which post-1960s liberals have been able to mobilize an ideological offensive against multiculturalism, and thence against the corporatist *polder* model of which it is an extension. The 'anything-goes directness' of the 1960s that van Gogh, in particular, embodied in his cultural persona enabled him to perform a series of offensive remarks and gestures directed principally against Muslims (and Jews) but also against 'Dutch middle class conservatism'.[52] As for Hirsi Ali, her attachment to and zealous performance of what has been called, by her critics, an 'Enlightenment fundamentalism' is also an expression of this post-1960s liberal individualism. Eyerman notes that 'The issue of free expression in the service of cultural liberation is central to Ayaan Hirsi Ali's self-presentation . . . [which] is structured in the form of an emancipatory narrative, from submission to collective norms to liberation as an autonomous individual.'[53] In this narrative, derived from Kant, Islam is positioned as a 'backward' civilization which one must break free from if one is to integrate successfully into modern society.[54]

Interestingly, Ian Buruma notes that contemporary political conservatives, who are as much a product of the 'silent revolution' as their social democratic and neo-liberal counterparts, also gravitate towards the Enlightenment. 'Because secularism has gone too far to bring back the authority of the churches', he writes, 'conservatives and neo-conservatives have latched onto the Enlightenment as a badge of national or cultural authority. The

Enlightenment, in other words, has become the name for a new conservative order, and its enemies are the aliens, whose values we can't share.'[55] As a consequence, a new kind of 'civilization speak' which traverses the left-right political spectrum has emerged in relation to an Islam that has been transformed from an aspect of the 'cultures' that immigrants bring with them to a 'civilization' that defines these immigrants, and which is fundamentally irreconcilable to the Dutch way of life. For the post-1960s liberals, 'Muslims stand for the theft of enjoyment. Their strict sexual morals remind the Dutch too much of what they have so recently left behind', whereas for the conservatives, Muslims re-awaken the *autochthon/allochthon* distinction that lies just below the surface of Dutch social discourse: Islam is the quintessential alien civilization and Muslims the typical *allochtoons*.[56]

Thus, in the Netherlands, the politics of controversy surrounding Islam is not *just* a politics of inclusion and exclusion, but also a politics of polarization, which has domesticated the 'clash of civilizations' rhetoric within the particular dynamics of contemporary Dutch politics.[57] It is into this polarizing discourse that Hirsi Ali and Theo van Gogh inserted the semi-naked female body, inscribed with verses from the *Qur'an*, as a performative signifier of Islam's alien and 'backward' nature, an insertion that is ironic given that the female body (marshalled under the rubric of 'the liberation of women') is also made to bear the weight of an emancipatory narrative encoded in neo-colonial justifications for military intervention in the 'Muslim world'[58] – the irony being that '[f]ew people in Holland remember how recently emancipation of women came to the Dutch, or to other Europeans for that matter . . . Until 1954, women in government jobs were automatically fired when they got married.'[59] Of course, to the post-1960s liberals, this simply confirms the similarity between the conservatism of the *polder* model and 'backward' civilizations like Islam although such an equivalence between a quintessentially Dutch way of life and a quintessentially *allochtoon* one sits awkwardly, to say the least, within a polarizing civilization-speak that relies on essentializing difference.

Ayaan Hirsi Ali and the critique of Islamic misogyny in *Submission*

Unlike the Danish cartoons, there is a narrative of sorts in *Submission* as well as text, and it is the interplay between visual image (semi-naked and bruised female bodies) and the textual apparatus (the narrator recounting the tales of four fictional women that have been subjected to violent sexual, verbal and physical abuse; the words of four verses of the *Qur'an* that are projected onto the bodies) that gives the film its shocking – and, for most Muslims, offensive – force and constitutes the central point of controversy. Marc de Leeuw and Sonja van Wichelen have offered an insightful analysis of the visual and aural aspects of the film, noting that '[a]lthough we see the testifying witness, we do not see her mouth: this invisibility of the voice, turning the voice into voice-over, constitutes a voice "from nowhere and everywhere" . . . which echoes a theological and ideological realm.'[60] This realm is visually realized as a 'window-less dark inner space' that is culturally inscribed only through a prayer mat, the recognizable gestures of Muslim prayer, and the 'sounds of whips and Arabic music' that 'take turns in building up a dramatic and fearful atmosphere'.[61] Here I want to focus on the film's use of the four Qur'anic verses, which are (in the order they appear in the film): 24:2 ('The woman and the man guilty of adultery or fornication/ Flog each of them with a hundred stripes'); 2:222 ('You may approach them [wives] in any manner, time, or place ordained for you by Allah'); 4:34 ('As to those women on whose part ye fear/Disloyalty and ill-conduct/Admonish them (first), (Next) refuse to share their beds, (And last) beat them (lightly)'; 24:31 ('They should not display their beauty and ornaments').[62] Each of these verses is inserted into the testimonial accounts of the four women who, as devout Muslim women, have submitted to the will of Allah and are thus subject to their sanctions. It is worth noting, however, that the last of these verses relates to its narrative in a way markedly different from the others. Whereas the other three verses are used to demonstrate how Qur'anic injunctions legitimize the sufferings endured by the women, the verse on veiling is attached to a narrative about a women being raped by her uncle. Of course, no Qur'anic verse sanctions or even remotely legitimizes rape in any form, so its relevance is only established through an extended insinuation that veiling and seclusion create the opportunity and environment for such abuses by restricting women's liberty. This tortuous rationale for the use of this verse bespeaks an anxiety over its improper appropriation, but its real purpose is, perhaps, to evoke the *burqa/niqab* debate that has gripped Europe in recent years. In that respect, it is significant that the 'believing woman' who narrates all these accounts is dressed in a *niqab* (full face veil revealing only her eyes) and a chiffon *jilbab* (shroud) that simultaneously exposes her breasts.[63] This invokes the register of visibility and invisibility by which the 'liberation' of women is measured in current debates.[64] It is no surprise, then, that the two Danish cartoons that principally focus on this issue also invoke the *burqa/niqab*. One, which paradoxically appears to observe the taboo against figural representation, abstractly represents 'veiled' women (*hijab*, this time, not *burqa* or *niqab* – thereby illustrating how these are elided in the debate) using 'Islamic' and 'semitic' symbols (crescent moon, star of David); it is accompanied by the caption 'Prophet! Daft and dumb, keeping women under thumb.'

There is, then, a narrative suturing in the film that complements the more visceral visual suture realized through the projection of these verses (in Arabic) on semi-naked female bodies. Taken together, they achieve a suturing effect similar to the figure of the Prophet in the Danish cartoons. They 'stitch' a particular interpretation to a point of origin, thereby naturalizing it as the only or true interpretation. In this instance, the film is making the point that the *Qur'an* is not *used* to justify misogyny, patriarchal oppression and sexual abuse, but is itself the source of Muslim women's subordination. Throughout her highly visible career, Hirsi Ali has been at pains to emphasize this. In many interviews and articles, she speaks and writes of a 'true' or 'pure' Islam that 'can be found in the words of the Prophet Muhammad and in sacred texts, such as the Koran.'[65] She has even suggested that 'Mohammed is a perverse man. A tyrant . . . Mohammed is a role model for all Muslim men. Do you find it strange that so many Muslim men are violent?'[66] The performative offensiveness of such statements, like the Danish cartoons, rests on the wider rhetorical strategy of the 'suture'.

Muslim feminists have, however, strongly contested patriarchal interpretations of the *Qur'an* and the implications of the 'suture'. There are two particular methodologies that sustain their critique: historical and hermeneutical. The former is typified by Leila Ahmed's classic *Women and Gender in Islam*. Noting that the custom of female veiling, for instance, was a cultural practice dating back to antiquity across vast swathes of the Near east and Mediterranean (including classical Greeece, and Athens in particular); and that in the Qur'anic account there is 'no indication of the order in which the first couple was created', she observes, however, that veiling and the idea that Eve was created from Adam's rib (and thus secondary and subordinate to him) were 'easily and seamlessly' absorbed into the Islamic traditions after the early conquests. 'What is or is not unique, specific or intrinsic to Islam with respect to ideas about women and gender', she writes, 'has already, then, become a complicated question.'[67] Furthermore, with respect to veiling, only the Prophet's wives 'took the veil' during his lifetime (either in the sense of a veil, or seclusion or both), and the practice is not explicitly mentioned in the *Qur'an* at all; verse 24:31, which Hirsi Ali cites, is, even on a superficial reading, difficult to equate with veiling: typically, although she cites Abdullah Yusuf Ali's translation, Hirsi Ali omits the crucial qualifier 'except what (must ordinarily) appear thereof'; nor is it incontestable that 'beauty and ornaments' refers to the face or even the hair. Indeed, the inclusion of the verse indicates Hirsi Ali's uncritical and wholesale acceptance of the traditional patriarchal exegesis, which is ironic given her stated intention to institute a critical mindset among Muslims with respect to their traditions.

Ahmed also notes the remarkable fact that *ahadith* recounted 'on the authority of women' – usually but not exclusively the Prophet's wives, and Aisha in particular – 'became part of the official history of Islam and of the literature that established the normative practices of Islamic society'.[68] This, she reminds us, was unprecedented in the Abrahamic monotheisms, and it illustrates that women were key figures and significant players in the nascent Islamic community during and after the Prophet's lifetime. She also notes 'Islam's ethical vision, which is stubbornly egalitarian, including with respect to the sexes', and this is why 'Muslim women frequently insist, often inexplicably to non-Muslims, that Islam is not sexist.'[69] Verses such as 33:35 ('For believing men *and* women, For devout men *and* women, For true men *and* women . . . ') indicate the extent to which the *Qur'an* makes no distinction between the moral worth of either sex and, according to tradition, the explicit address to women as well as men was prompted by critical questioning by one of the Prophet's wives, who asked him why its early verses did not specifically address 'believing women' as well as men.[70] It is this disjuncture between the ethical voice of the *Qur'an* and its muting within the patriarchal tradition of Qur'anic interpretation that enables a discursive space for feminist exegesis of the *Qur'an*. Amina Wadud, for instance, argues that the *Qur'an*'s gender formulations are 'neutral' whilst Asma Barlas is bolder in arguing that the *Qur'an* is, in fact, 'antipatriarchal'.[71] Both have contested the traditional interpretations of each of the verses cited in *Submission* using a sophisticated hermeneutics of Qur'anic language, prising apart its polysemous syntax, grammar, concepts and terminology within the framework of a holistic understanding of its ethics and theology, principally the maxim that Allah does not oppress (*zulm*) anyone – which must mean, given the moral equality of men and women, that the words of Allah should not be used to oppress women – and Allah's total transcendence of temporality and spatiality, which renders all linguistic utterances (including Qur'anic utterances) relative to the historical conditions of their utterance. Only the ethical precepts of the divine self-disclosure, as tentatively signalled by the limited medium of human language in the *Qur'an*, are universal and eternal.[72]

Both the historical and hermeneutic methodologies are sustained by the fundamental importance of interpretation, and the need to distinguish all interpretations from the 'divine self-disclosure' itself. As Barlas puts it, 'collapsing God's Words with our interpretation of those Words not only violates the distinction Muslim theology has always made between Divine Speech and its "earthly realization" but it also ignores the Qur'an's warnings not to confuse it with its readings.'[73] She is referring here to 39:18, 'Those who listen to the Word, and follow the best (meaning) in it', which signals an irreducible interpretative pluralism; Hirsi Ali, with her emphasis on 'true' Islam discounts interpretation, and she ironically mimics the literalism of those she apparently criticizes. Hence the value of Qur'anic suture for her: as the 'direct word' of God it cannot be challenged. But, as the history of Qur'anic exegesis (*tafsir*) and even jurisprudence (*fiqh*) demonstrate, it is impossible to reduce the 'direct' word of God to the 'literal' word.[74] For one thing, 'the process by which Muhammad's recitations were transformed from oral materials into written texts was not as seamless as orthodox accounts declare . . . a number of different versions were evidently in circulation at the time of the compiling of the canonical version'; for another, since 'the Arabic letters used at this point were incomplete', without the diacritical marks that indicate which vowel should accompany the consonants, 'two or more readings' are always possible.[75] Thus, in Arabic, the same 'root' word can generate multiple meanings, not all of them congruent, depending on context, diacritical addition of vowels, and sonorization, and this gives the *Qur'an* its almost infinite capacity to be 'worked' exegetically, something that is borne out in Wadud and Barlas' extensive discussions of the various ambiguities and possible meanings of Q4:34. Furthermore, Wadud has recently advanced an even more radical interpretive methodology which enables interpretation to move along a three step process from assent to the 'literal' meaning, through re-interpretation and qualification ('Perhaps not') to, finally, a rejection ('No!') of verses that are no longer 'in concert with civilizational, or, better still, human development.'[76]

Hirsi Ali, however, is not interested in any of this even if she is aware of it. Despite her own self-positioning as 'daughter of the Enlightenment', and her supporters' claim that she is a new Voltaire inaugurating a critical reformation of Islam, she is clearly not very interested in reform.[77] Indeed, the strategy of Qur'anic suture precludes reform. If the *Qur'an* is the origin of misogyny and patriarchy, and if it cannot be challenged and re-interpreted, then what reform is possible? The call for reform is merely a rhetorical ruse, part of a wider strategy that finds 'suture' to be a highly effective technique in the performance of polarization. Its value lies in the way it effects an essentialism that makes it impossible to locate any common ground or common values that might enable Islam to be seen as a viable pillar in Dutch society. If the politics of polarization is part of an ensemble of performative exclusions, it makes exclusion all the more effective by declaring the impossibility of hybridity, reciprocity or mutual accommodation. This is why her claim that 'humiliation might be a good way to open up a group to discussion', and her disdainful dismissal of the objections of the very Muslim women on whose behalf she claimed to be speaking, speak so profoundly to the ethical impropriety of her engagement with Islam.[78]

I would like to conclude by briefly dwelling on a thread that runs through both the last chapter and this one. This is the complicity between Islamist and/or orthodox interpretations of Islam and those of their secular-liberal critics, a complicity apparent in *The Satanic Verses*, the Danish cartoons and *Submission*. This complicity is particularly damaging in the context of the internal contest over the interpretation of Islam being undertaken by Muslim feminists and progressives. It is not just that these secular-liberals reinforce the notion of a 'true' Islam against which all other interpretations are deemed 'inauthentic', they also uphold the Islamist/orthodox claim to authority as representatives of that 'true' Islam, and thereby give that 'true' Islam a consensual force in contemporary debates that excludes or marginalizes attempts to challenge it; this prevents the very reform they apparently seek. A certain disingenuousness, perhaps even duplicity, is thus apparent in the rhetoric of Rushdie, Rose, Hirsi Ali and the rest. This renders their provocations and interventions highly problematic from an ethical point of view. It is not ethical to claim that one is doing something when, in effect, one is doing its opposite (for example, to claim that one is criticizing the fundamentalist justification of violence by reference to 'Islam' when in fact endorsing that interpretation); nor is it ethical to claim to be representing the interests of some people (e.g. Hirsi Ali claiming to criticize misogyny in Islam on behalf of Muslim women) when in fact endorsing an interpretation of Islam that contradicts those interests. Nor is it ethical, indeed, to occlude the fact that the very mode of one's critique entails not so much reform of Islam but, in fact, a kind of cultural erasure of Islamic difference in order to advance a universalized reproduction of the secular-liberal subject. In this respect, their stated intentions count for very little if the intentionality of their texts suggest otherwise.

6
Romancing the Other: *The Jewel of the Medina* and the Ethics of Genre

The controversy, in 2008, surrounding the (non-)publication of a novel, *The Jewel of the Medina* (hereafter *Jewel*), about Aisha bint Abi Bakr, 'favourite' wife of the Prophet Muhammad, played itself out on a scale very different to the global protests over *The Satanic Verses* and the *Jyllands-Posten* cartoons, and the Dutch national trauma over *Submission* and the murder of Theo van Gogh.[1] Largely confined to Anglo-American literary and journalistic circles, it was one that barely left its mark on the wider public sphere on either side of the Atlantic. This was not the only difference for it was a Muslim-related controversy in which Muslims hardly figure, and to which Muslims have been almost unanimously indifferent (when, that is, they are even aware of it). It was, in fact, a controversy conducted almost entirely amongst those left-liberals and liberal-conservatives who constitute the social commentariat in the US and United Kingdom, and the debate focused on the issue of self-censorship and the putative fear of 'giving offence' that liberals now assume to be the dominant feature of 'politically correct' multiculturalist liberal-democracies (notwithstanding the fact that the ubiquity of such discussions over offensiveness, as discussed in Chapter 1, suggests otherwise). Muslims – in the form of a little-known extremist group seeing a chance to attain some publicity and notoriety, and perhaps even some recognition amongst fellow Islamists – only became involved *after* the initial controversy over the novel had become more generally known.

There are two other considerations pertinent to the difference between the controversy over *Jewel* and its antecedents, one a factor in explaining the muted reaction amongst Muslims to the novel (or, more accurately, the reports of it), the other a factor in determining the ethical context as well as content of the novel itself. Unlike the Prophet Muhammad, Aisha bint Abi Bakr is a controversial figure amongst Muslims. The daughter of Abu Bakr, she was therefore both the wife of Islam's prophet and the daughter of its first caliph, a dual relation that has ensured her pre-eminence amongst Sunni Muslims, but has also condemned her to calumny and vilification amongst Shi'a. As Denise Spellberg has observed, her legacy was embroiled in and, in fact, emerged out of the sectarian disputes over the politics of succession within the nascent Islamic polity. Moreover, Aisha was a participant in that politics, and her involvement as a woman in a realm that had become, in the course of time, thoroughly masculinized by patriarchal Muslim traditionists and exegetes meant that even amongst Sunnis her reputation emerged as a 'flawed ideal', a complex and 'multivalent historical persona [that] inspired praise and blame, defense and censure.'[2] With regard to its ethical status, *Jewel* is clearly not a 'provocative' text akin to some of the *Jyllands-Posten* cartoons and *Submission*, or even, more arguably, *The Satanic Verses*. Its author, Sherry Jones, has stated her 'respect for Islam', her recognition that Muhammad was 'a gentle, wise, and compassionate leader', and that her aim was to 'increase inter-cultural empathy and understanding' (344; 356).

However, as we have seen in previous chapters, the intentionality of a text exceeds its stated intentions such that its ethical *effects* may not, in fact, coincide with such intentions. With that in mind, I want to examine one particular, stated, intention of the text as a means by which to explore the ethics of representation at work in the novel. At several points, Jones signals the feminist credentials of her novel. She writes that '[a]s a feminist' she was 'disturbed' by reports of the mistreatment of women by the Taliban in Afghanistan following the US military intervention there in spring 2002 (355); that she was interested in 'women's crucial roles in the formation of the early Islamic community' (344); and that she hoped to 'empower women, especially Muslim women, by showing that Islam is, at its source, an egalitarian religion' (356). In addition to these paratextual elaborations, the early passages of the narrative orient the reader towards a feminist agenda; beginning Aisha's story *in media res*, the prologue opens with an account, from Aisha's perspective, of what is one of the two climactic moments in the representations of her life – the *hadith al-ifk* or 'affair of the lie', when the fourteen-year-old wife of the Prophet stood accused of adultery, thus precipitating a crisis in the Islamic community because of its implications for the Prophet's leadership. At the end of this prologue, there is a curious – and highly interesting – 'posthumous postscript' narrated by Aisha from the vantage point of an afterlife, '[w]here . . . all truth is known', which acknowledges how the scandal resonates '[c]enturies later' (10). Directly addressing the reader in the secular world using the second person, Aisha says:

> Where you are, men still want to hide the women away. You, in the now, they cover with shrouds or with lies about being inferior. We, in the past, they erase from their stories of Muhammad, or alter with false tales that burn our ears and the backs of our eyes . . . We cannot escape our destinies, even in death. But we can claim them, and give them shape . . . they don't know the truth: That Muhammad wanted to give us freedom

but that the other men took it away. That none of us is ever alive until we can shape our own destinies. Until we can choose. (10–11)

As I shall argue in due course, the ethics of the novel lies in the relations established here between the implied reader that is addressed as 'you' (who exactly is being addressed here?), the collective being of 'woman' signalled by 'we' and 'us' (who is the 'we' to which Aisha refers?), and the kind of feminism being substantiated from the absolute vantage point of a transcendental truth (what sort of freedom is being envisaged?). Whilst it seems that this passage is addressed to a contemporary *Muslim* woman ('you, in the now, they cover with shrouds'), we shall see that the implied readership of the novel is, in fact, 'western' and non-Muslim. What are the ethical implications of such a divergence?

Spellberg suggests that Aisha's 'legacy as a woman allows the historian access to the minds of medieval Muslim men', so that in 'studying Aisha, one studies male intellectual history, not a woman's history', and although Spellberg's authoritative work is not among the sources acknowledged at the end of the novel, the passage clearly responds to this historical exclusion and thereby aligns itself with what has become known as 'Islamic feminism', in particular its strategy of '"reinstating women into these dominant narratives [fashioned by men]" as a historical precedent for their own activism while also . . . exposing the problematic of Islamic knowledge production that led to women's textual marginality within, if not absence from, Islam's collective memory in the first place'.[3] Through this posthumous postscript we are meant to understand, then, that not only does Jones endorse the Islamic feminist goal of seeking gender equality principally, but not exclusively, through Islamic discourse itself, but that her own novel will pursue similar strategies towards recovering the egalitarian ur-text of the Qur'anic ethos from beneath the repeated historical over-inscriptions of patriarchal Muslim traditions.[4] Her reworking of Aisha's biography as fictional autobiography is thus adjacent to and in solidarity with, if not directly part of, the counter-hegemonic project of Islamic feminism, even if she is herself apparently unaware of the finer details of its theory and practice.

This raises some difficult ethical and political issues concerning her representational praxis since Jones is neither a 'believing woman' nor a secular, that is, cultural, Muslim. Her Aisha is far removed from her in time and space, differentiated by ethnicity, race and religion; she is an Other woman. This is not to imply there is any merit in the vulgar essentialism which claims that only Muslim women can represent and critique Islamic patriarchy for that rests on an entirely spurious claim to 'authenticity'. Rather, her relationship to her subject raises the kinds of questions concerning feminist representation that have been extensively explored by black, post-colonial and Islamic feminist critics who have interrogated the

theoretical and methodological assumptions underlying the universaliza-
tion of 'western' feminism. 'To what extent', asks Marnia Lazreg, 'can western feminism dispense with an ethics of responsibility when writing about
"different" women?'[5] It is a question to which Gayatri Spivak has offered a
particularly brilliant, if troubling, response in her essays on subalternity. If,
in response to her own question 'Can the Subaltern Speak?' she replies in
the negative, she nevertheless is at pains to point out the responsibilities
attendant upon representation in the sense of 'speaking for' and 'speaking
about' other women; whilst she has been criticized for establishing a paradox in which 'the non-subaltern must either maximally respect the Other's
radical alterity, thus leaving the status quo intact, or attempt the impossible
feat of "opening up" to the Other without in any way "assimilating" that
Other to his/her own subject-position, perspectives or identity', we might
open up an alternative reading of her intervention which focuses on the
ethics as opposed to the politics of representation (although the two are,
of course, related they are not continuous or identical to each other).[6] That
much is apparent in Spivak's positive assessment of Said's emphasis on
the 'critic's institutional responsibility' in 'Can the Subaltern Speak?' and,
indeed, much of the rationale for her extended discussion of the Deleuze-
Foucault dialogue which prefaces the essay rests on her exposure of the
intellectual's 'transparency' with regard to their representational practices,
which she argues is an abdication of such responsibility.[7] In the companion
essay 'Subaltern Studies: Deconstructing Historiography', the *ethical* basis
of Spivak's celebrated formulation of 'strategic essentialism' has often been
overlooked: 'a *strategic* use of positivist essentialism in a *scrupulously visible*
political interest'; the phrase is repeated with a difference a couple of pages
later – 'the historian then breaks his theory in a *scrupulously* delineated
"political interest"' – but in both cases it is the *ethical* aspect of the politics
of representation that is emphasized.[8] Taking our cue from the discussion
of Levinas' ethical maximalism in Chapter 3, we might therefore suggest
that the 'impossibility' of Spivak's paradox is akin to that which animates
Levinasian ethics, which relates to and shapes the necessity of ethical
minimalism in terms of political efficacy. The point is not to refrain from
representation altogether for fear of appropriating and thereby undermining
'difference' – that is unavoidable for it is intrinsic to the act of representation itself; rather, the point is to attend to the responsibility that 'difference'
inaugurates within one's representational praxis, that responsibility which,
as Derek Attridge has put it, encompasses both a 'responsibility to' and a
'responsibility for' the Other.[9] It is precisely this responsibility that 'western feminism' disavows in its arrogation of a universal vantage point from
which to speak about, and for, all women through its 'initial assumption of
women as a homogenous group or category'.[10]

    To the extent that Jones argues that she is 'qualified' to tell Aisha's story
because she is a 'woman' who thereby presumably 'know[s] the rivalries

and yearnings and heartaches' that *all* women 'experience in the name of love' (356), this troubling elision of the scrupulousness called for by Spivak in the name of an assumed universal womanhood offers an opening into which one might insert a set of questions pertaining to her specific representational practice as distinct from those pertaining to western feminism in general. The first concerns what might be termed an ethics of 'voice': what is at stake in a 'feminist' intervention by a non-Muslim, western woman into debates about gender politics in a culture whose gender normativities she does not herself share or inhabit, especially when that intervention is articulated in the 'first-person'? Whose voice is speaking? This 'voice' is, however, embedded in a literary representation, as a form of writing, so what is the ethical effect, then, of that form, particularly its genre? This we might term the ethics of genre.

Ethics of voice

Insofar as the act of narration establishes and governs the relations between objects, events, causes and effects within any given narrative, narratorial perspective is never ethically neutral. As Andrew Gibson puts it, narration is 'a mode of activity in which a subject takes another, others, the world as the object or objects of knowledge and claims possession of them', and thus 'the narration of a story appears as a particular kind of ethical concern. The important, formal distinctions between narratives or modes of narrative are not merely formalist'.[11] This is especially true of first-person narration, which involves the apparent erasure of the difference between authorial and narrating subjects, of speaking 'as' rather than 'for' or 'about' the Other, so that the Other appears to be the subject rather than object of the narrative discourse. Ethically speaking, it is a high-risk gamble because there is more at stake in the act of ventriloquism, especially when the narrating subject is an historical as opposed to merely fictional figure, and when there is significant differentiation (in terms geography, time, culture, race, religion, gender, sexuality, corporeal being and so on) between the subjectivities of the author and narrator. What does it mean, from an ethical point of view, for a western, non-Muslim woman in the twenty-first century to inhabit the persona of an Arab Bedouin girl in the seventh century, one who is venerated by billions of people whose culture and religion the author does not share? What is entailed in the apparent closure of this distance and difference in the very act of narration itself, and what does this reveal about the text's ethical intentions and effects? Such narration is subject to the demands of both ethical maximalism and minimalism: the impossibility of achieving its ambition is juxtaposed to the effectivity of its realisation. To what extent is the distance between self and other minimized by an empathetic imagination, and to what extent is the 'interest' of the author – whether political or not – rendered 'scrupulously visible'?

With this in mind it is worth noting that Jones is not the first to speak in Aisha's voice or, rather, make it appear as if she is speaking for herself. In early and medieval accounts of the *hadith al-ifk*, the accusation of adultery is accounted for by Aisha herself – she is allowed to tell her 'story'. According to Spellberg, '[t]here is an implied element of control given to A'isha by ceding to her the entire narrative and allowing her to detail it in the first person. A'isha thus appears to testify to her innocence on her own behalf in the historical record. Yet the nature of her narrative is clearly a carefully structured retrospective version of past events'.[12] This 'illusory' power to control the narrative is a consequence of the 'power of the written word over the spoken, of the scriptor over his subject'.[13] Insofar as all biography, indeed all autobiography, involves a similar retrospective 'working over' of the radically discontinuous material of a life in the service of what Barthes calls the 'counterfeit integration of the subject', the extent to which Jones' Aisha can escape this necessary deception and thus present herself to the reader as she 'really was' is moot;[14] the problem, however, is that Jones' Aisha makes precisely such a claim from the transcendental vantage point of the posthumous postscript, 'They never knew the truth – about me, about Muhammad, about how I saved his life and he saved mine. About how I saved all their lives . . . Of course, they know now. Where we are now, *all* truth is known' (10). It is precisely this literary conceit through which a claim is made for the absolute authenticity of Aisha's story which is ethically troubling, not least because it renders Jones' authorial intervention transparent. Even if one sets this aside, it is still troubling that this gesture involves the claim that Aisha *can* speak, that she *can* tell her own story, the impossibility of which is signalled in the *content* of that story as much as its form. As Spellberg observes, despite being apparently in charge of her own story, 'the written content underscores her vulnerability to the charge of adultery and her inability to convince her family or her husband of her innocence. Although she appears to have the final word regarding these events, her record of them definitively captures the fact that despite her protestations, her own words alone could not exonerate her from the charge of adultery'.[15] That is, within a context in which the 'honour' of the community is at stake when the reputation of its women are put into question, especially when that woman is the wife of a prophet claiming a direct divine mandate, Aisha simply does not have 'the power to vindicate herself'; she is subject to that divine mandate and is therefore the object rather than subject of 'divine vindication'.[16] She is, accordingly, exonerated only on the basis of a revelation testifying to her innocence. Jones simply cannot elude this constraint on her protagonist, which radically undermines her narrative authority, so despite vividly dramatizing 'the greatest performance of [her] life' (193) Jones' Aisha must, like her discursive antecedents, await divine deliverance; '*It's in your hands, al-Lah. I trust You to help me*' (ibid. original emphasis). Just like her Muslim male predecessors, Jones cannot extricate herself from the 'othering' that this involves.

There are, however, other troubling ways in which Jones' power as 'scriptor' overwhelms and manipulates Aisha's 'voice'. Firstly, Jones' Aisha exhibits a very modern sensibility, which is persistently represented through her attitude to gender relations (which I will discuss in more detail in the next section), and is periodically revealed in certain behaviours that signal her modernity; the opening paragraph of the narrative 'proper', for instance, shows her as a six year-old girl leaping out of bed with a very modern awareness of chronology, *'I'm late I'm late I'm late'*(12). This is part of the text's modernism which, at another level, makes a 'progressive' intervention into debates and controversies concerning Muhammad's marriage to his 'child-bride', a key trope in anti-Muslim polemics. Jones represents Aisha's betrothal, aged, six, and her marriage at puberty, aged nine. She thus follows the historicist explanation of the event in the Prophet's life, but goes much further, delaying the consummation until after the 'affair of the lie' and representing their relationship as paternal and platonic; indeed, it is Aisha herself, conscious of her disadvantage within *harem* politics should the fact of her unconsummated marriage become known, who is at pains to initiate the event. In this respect, the novel 'respects' the *Prophet's* legacy even if, by representing Aisha as a modern woman, it does not respect *her* historical alterity.

More significantly, the modernism of the text inscribes what might be termed a 'secular voice' that modulates and, indeed, overwhelms Aisha's account. As the novel progresses, this secular voice becomes increasingly apparent such that it displays an inability, except cursorily, to imagine how *faith* might have motivated these 'believing women' (and men). It is one thing to acknowledge and represent the secular context within which faith-inspired historical agents must necessarily act, and to highlight the secular dimension of their actions; it is another to imply that such persons were only concerned with instrumental calculations of personal interest and power, especially Aisha and the Prophet himself; '[p]ower was what drove them all, including Muhammad. In truth, it was what I desired, also' (197). Again, it is one thing to de-mythologize the early history of the Islamic *ummah* (although even a cursory glance at the earliest biographies of the Prophet demonstrates that these accounts were far from idealized), to show how the community was argumentative, divided and keenly aware of both its political vulnerability and, when the time came, its strength; it is quite another to give the impression that a community founded on faith in a divine power and its Prophet should only be concerned about its material interests. It is one thing to inscribe doubt into the practice of faith, to flesh out the rather one-dimensional caricatures of the Prophet's wives in the historical traditions and recuperate their independence of mind and feistiness; it is quite another to leave the reader unable to imagine how a man who founded a major world religion could have inspired any devotion amongst his wives let alone his other followers. At times, the Prophet comes across as an almost comical, hen-pecked figure; at others – such as when he does not acknowledge Aisha's (and his) longed-for pregnancy, 'He'd scoffed today when I'd told him I was carrying his child. "Desperate," he'd called me' (264) – he is self-absorbed, cruel, thoughtless and misogynistic, a figure barely distinguishable from the lusty lecher and power-hungry despot of western anti-Muslim stereotype. It is no wonder, then, that nearly all the characters seem to display a conspicuous *lack* of faith, especially Aisha. Only once does she willingly surrender herself to Allah and His Messenger – *the* definition of being a Muslim – when Muhammad offers her the choice to remain married to him or seek a divorce (on which more later); at other times, it is despite herself or in resignation (for example, after the 'affair of the lie'). To point out that this is because the narrative is seen from Aisha's point of view would not be a valid defence; in fact, it would underscore the point since it would suggest that her faith is 'really' cynical rather than sincere – how, then, can such a text respond and thus be responsible to Aisha as a 'believing woman'? These are aesthetic failures that expose ethical inadequacies.

Aisha's 'story' also succumbs to Jones' choice of narrative form, the genre of historical romance, which has very troubling ethical consequences. In making the first half of the novel a 'romance' in which Safwan ibn al-Mu'attal al-Sulami is not just Aisha's rescuer (as he is in the traditional accounts of the *hadith al-ifk*) but also her childhood 'sweetheart' and a generic 'romantic hero', the novel not only violates the historical record (in *Jewel*, Aisha is betrothed to marry Safwan before her father changes his mind and offers her to Muhammad whereas in fact she was betrothed to someone else, 'a young relative named Jubair'[17]) and, incidentally, libels an historical figure (Safwan was a devout Muslim, but in *Jewel* his role as romantic hero *objectively* propels him towards adultery with one of his Prophet's wives and, in addition, towards *apostasy* because, in the service of the 'elopement plot' he plans to join the Muslim community's Bedouin enemies);[18] more significantly, it is responsible for turning the 'affair of the lie' on its head.

In traditional Sunni accounts, the 'lie' refers to the slander perpetrated *against* Aisha by those accusing her of adultery; in *Jewel*, however, the 'lie' is told *by* Aisha in order to exonerate herself, 'Ali was insisting I tell my story . . . I closed my eyes, recalling the tale I and Safwan had fashioned on the ride home . . . I pressed on, spinning a tale . . . "In truth, it is a tale and nothing more." Ali spat on the dirt floor . . . Did he truly know the reason I had lost the caravan?"' (7). In a curious twist, one that occurs at the beginning rather than end of the book, she is no longer *al-siddiq*, the truthful; rather, it is her accusers who are 'the truthful'. In that moment, the text turns against itself; if Jones' decision to write Aisha's 'story' was to vindicate her against the 'lies . . . [and] false stories' that associate her name 'with treachery and shame' then she is clearly writing *against* the Shi'a or Alid narrative which, in contrast to the Sunni account, positions her [Aisha] as such. This is corroborated not only by the use of a first-person narrative voice to give 'her side of the story', but also by how that perspective counter-positions Ali (the Prophet's cousin and rival of Aisha's father for the position of caliph) as an 'enemy'. And yet, drawn inadvertently but inevitably into these sectarian debates for which Aisha acts as a lightning rod, Jones' text finds itself on the wrong side, undermining Aisha's integrity in the very act of defending it, an ideological and ethical confusion that results from her having blundered into 'an intense and deeply sensitive intellectual argument' with which she is unfamiliar.[19]

In fact, Jones' clumsy reworking of the 'affair of the lie' totally undermines the basis of Islamic theology, and thus undermines her 'respect' for Islam. If, in order to remain minimally faithful to the extant narrative accounts of Aisha's life – such that it remains recognizably 'Aisha's story' and not that of an entirely fictional character – Jones has no choice but to accept that Aisha's innocence is confirmed only by divine judgment, then this judgment is ironically rendered suspect by the fact that an omniscient Allah exonerates a liar. Again, the posthumous postscript to the Prologue is revealing, for the afterlife 'where all truth is known' is thrown into confusion because the 'truth' is not what her 'story' claims it to be. This impasse is only resolved by a 'technical' innocence that descends into absurdity (I hesitate to call it bathos). As she waits for Allah's judgment she consoles herself by affirming that '[a]t least I would die knowing I'd been true to Muhammad' (184). This, despite the fact that she had willingly eloped with her lover, kissed him and even reached the point of surrendering to his desire before losing her nerve when confronted with the reality, as opposed to the ideal, of absconding from her community. This is a 'technical' innocence in the sense that one cannot really say she had been 'true' to Muhammad, and such a justification would not really amount to much in the eyes of believing Muslims, even today, never mind the Muslim or Arab society of the time; indeed, even many contemporary secular, modernized 'western' individuals would find it difficult to conclude that Aisha's actions represent anything less than an irreparable breach of trust or, at the very least, the grounds for such a breach. The novel's confused attempt, therefore, to exonerate Aisha reveals a deeply problematic ethical relation to its subject, which is principally a consequence of Jones' attempt to rewrite Aisha's story in the genre of the contemporary 'oriental' historical romance, otherwise known as 'bodice-ripper'.

Ethics of genre

Since the late 1980s, the popular romance novel has undergone something of a critical re-appraisal. No longer seen as an automatic cipher through which bourgeois patriarchy is normalized, it has been recuperated by some feminists who have noted its complex and more sophisticated negotiations of gender roles and prospects for women's freedom.[20] As such, these critics claim it is a genre with feminist possibilities, which seems to be corroborated by the fact that almost every popular romance novel since the early 1980s 'either refers explicitly to feminism or deals implicitly with issues that feminism has raised'.[21] But it does seem, however, that it is hospitable to a particular type of feminism, namely liberal feminism. As many have noted, the genre encodes bourgeois-individualist values within its narrative conventions: the heroine's 'meeting with the hero occurs in a private realm which excludes all concerns but their mutual attraction', writes Ann Rosalind Jones, and, according to Rachel Blau Du Plessis, the 'quest' aspect of these romances portray 'the female characters [as] human subjects at loose in the world', embodying 'the liberal bourgeois ideology of the self-interested . . . individual agent.'[22]

This is especially true of the sub-genre of romance which emerged in the US in the 1970s that is described by Hsu-Ming Teo as the 'orientalist historical romance novel'. According to Teo, 'the sexualization of American women's popular culture', that followed in the wake of the second wave feminist movement was accompanied by 'an Orientalization of the female erotic imagination.'[23] The 'new heroine' of these novels 'is a descendant of *The Sheikh*'s Diana . . . who finds her greatest pleasure in horse riding. Quite often, she likes to swim and shoot as well. She is a passionate woman but she is not very eager to get married, fearing she will lose her freedom to do as she pleases. She will not marry simply to suit her family and friends. She has a temper and a penchant for getting her own way', and, if 'nothing breaks the new heroine's spirit', this quite simply reflects the liberal trope of the self-contained individual as a 'free spirit'.[24] Jones' Aisha bears a striking resemblance to Teo's description of the 'new heroine' of the orientalist historical romance, and there are a number of other generic indicators which immediately signal the genre. The cover art reproduces a famous orientalist painting, 'The Queen of the Harem' by Max Ferdinand Bredt (1868–1921), composed at the height of the fashion for orientalist representations of the 'eastern harem', one of the key tropes of gendered orientalism. As Jessica Taylor notes in relation to a related sub-genre, the contemporary sheikh romance, 'Cover art . . . acts to frame the novels as belonging to a particular subgenre', and, as if to underscore the point, the 'Author's note' which precedes the narrative begins thus: 'Join me on a journey to another time and place, to a harsh exotic world of saffron and sword fights, of desert nomads in camel's-hair tents, of caravans laden with Persian carpets and frankincense, of flowing colorful robes and kohl-darkened eyes and perfumed arms filigreed with henna.' All this, before the novel even begins, forms part of the elaborate generic scaffolding of the novel, and 'concrete' details here – which are elaborated and multiplied throughout the narrative – function

as 'props of authenticity' because 'accuracy in detail is the primary require-
ment of the oriental tale.'[25]

Once the novel actually begins other generic markers come into view:
Safwan, the 'romantic hero', has a 'smooth, sculpted face' and the 'strong
line of his jaw, the slant of his dark eyes and the long hair hanging like a
mane down his back made me think of an Arabian steed' (67); the heroine
dreams of 'riding on a horse with the wind in my hair and a sword in my
hand, free at last' (20), amongst the 'fierce, liberty-loving Bedouin' who had
been romanticized in popular orientalist tales from the nineteenth-century
onwards as an alternative to the 'decadent' Ottoman court.[26] There is a stock
generic convention which Pamel Regis calls 'the barrier' – in the form of
the rather inconvenient fact of marriage to the Prophet of Allah – which is
'anything that keeps the union of hero and heroine from taking place', but
which 'if the novel is a romance novel . . . will fall', and also a 'point of
ritual death', which is that 'moment in a romance novel when the union . . .
seems completely impossible. It is marked by death or its simulacrum
(for example, fainting or *illness*).'[27] At the moment of crisis, Jones' Aisha
suffers severe stomach cramps and vomits, but far from this being the point
at which the narrative moves inexorably towards its climactic union, this
is the very point at which *The Jewel of the Medina* departs from the generic
conventions of the romance, pulled back by other generic forces that set
limits on the liberties that can be taken in the name of romance, namely
'biography', 'historiography' and the pressure of recorded 'facts'. As a result,
the heroine does not, from this point, move towards union with the 'hero'
but rather towards the 'barrier', the Prophet, and the 'barrier' does not fall
but is, in fact, redefined as the lack of consummation and the arrival of each
new wife that threatens Aisha's position within the *harem*. Indeed, it would
be true to say that the crisis point in *Jewel* is also the climax of the romantic
element of the narrative (although vestiges of it remain); after the failed
elopement, the hold of the romantic genre on Aisha's story weakens
and *Jewel* begins to assume the shape of standard biographical accounts
of her life, conforming more to the details and form of these established
Islamic genres.

Nevertheless, the romance element of *Jewel* inscribes a particular kind of
secular-liberal feminism deep into the fabric of the text, and it is figured
in two principal ways: firstly, through an insistent emphasis on negative
liberty such that Aisha's romantic dreams are oriented towards the removal
of all social constraints so that she can 'escape' to the Bedouins, with whom
she would be 'unbridled' and 'free to live my life the way I wanted, to run
and yell and fight in battles and make my own choices' (23, 20). Secondly,
through the metaphor of the sword, which Aisha dreams of wielding in
battle alongside the men, and which she is symbolically bequeathed as an
inheritance from the Prophet himself, thereby aligning this liberal feminism with *Islamic* feminism. As Jones admits, the sword is a purely literary

symbol for there is no record of Aisha having participated in any martial endeavours, although some Arab women, including members of the first Muslim community, did fight on the battlefield. The symbolism is, however, problematic insofar as it speaks to the way that some forms of liberal feminism advocate a *neutralization* of gender as the principal means by which to overcome the 'gender system'. According to Sherry Okin, 'gender could no longer form a legitimate part of the social structure' in a just society, 'whether inside or outside the family.'[28] In contrast, Islamic feminists such as Asma Barlas and Amina Wadud have noted that gender and sexual differentiation is explicitly mentioned in the *Qur'an*, and they orient their hermeneutics towards demonstrating that this differentiation is in no way a mandate for patriarchal gender hierarchies. Whatever the merits and demerits of each position, there is a fundamental divergence between them that renders their alignment in *Jewel* somewhat problematic.

Moreover, the feminism encoded in *Jewel* is *secular*, which again problematizes the novel's claim that Aisha's story as represented in the novel might help empower Muslim women. This secularism is related to the 'secular voice' to which I have referred above, and it is most vividly illustrated by the novel's representation of a crisis within the Prophet's household, which resulted in an ultimatum offered to his wives – stay married to him and accept the restrictions and obligations this involves, or be released from marriage on good terms – that is marked in the *Qur'an* as the 'Verse of the Choice' (Q33:28–29).[29] The representation of this incident, or rather its *resolution*, both subtly inscribes a feminist intervention into this pivotal event and completely undermines Qur'anic theology. As the Prophet broods on what to do about the petty squabbles and intrigues within his *harem*, having withdrawn from his wives into the seclusion of his 'loft' for a month, Aisha slips past the guards and climbs up to his retreat and narrates to him the frustrations of a young, independent-minded woman condemned to living a *harem* life (295–6). In due course, the Prophet returns and, before offering Aisha the 'Verse of the Choice', he tells her, 'I had vowed to listen only to Al-lah, but He opened my ears to your words the other night' (305). This is a subtle rewriting of the extant traditions that inserts the figure of woman into the divine script, and in some ways it is analogous to the promptings of *shaitan* or the scribblings of Salman the Persian in *The Satanic Verses*, albeit from a very different perspective. The theological implications, however, are the same. It suggests the Qur'anic verse is the result of this fictional interpolation of a woman's words that apparently move the Prophet from 'ignorance' to an awareness of Aisha's suffering (the use of the word 'ignorance', with its connotations of *jahiliyya* is rather resonant and potentially explosive). But, according to Islamic theology, Allah is utterly transcendent and cannot be 'prompted' by man or woman; not even the Prophet has the power to do this for it would compromise Allah's transcendence and thus his *tawhid*. And yet Jones' reworking of this pivotal episode, which acts as a kind of second climax to the novel, suggests precisely that: secular agency trumps divine will.

Insofar as *The Jewel of the Medina* claims to narrate Aisha's story in order to intervene into debates about gender within Islam, and to assist in the recovery of Islam's gender egalitarianism, it does so by positioning Islamic gender equality simply as an extension of western liberal feminism's conceptions of gender subjectivity and liberty. It therefore does not speak 'to' Muslim women but rather speaks 'for' them. What the 'Muslim woman' sees in Jones' Aisha is a western-liberal subject inhabiting the guise of a venerated 'other' thereby projecting itself as universal. On the other hand, it is clear that the implied reader is not meant to be a 'Muslim woman' at all but rather a 'western' non-Muslim woman to whom the novel reflects back an image of themselves whilst purporting to educate them about 'other' women. Inside the jacket cover we read that the novel is '[e]xtensively researched' and 'a history lesson' as well as a 'love story'.[30] *The Jewel of the Medina* thus reproduces what has been termed 'Orientalist feminism', a discourse that, despite its often good intentions, appropriates the Other within the frame of a western narrative of history writ large as a universal account of humankind.[31] It therefore contributes to a hegemonic project. As Hsu-Ming Teo puts it:

> In many ways, these Orientalist romance novels represent white women's desires to promote liberal and multicultural agendas, and to foster interest in, and respect for, Middle Eastern cultures and peoples. These are no doubt often flawed and problematic attempts that not only reinstate Orientalism, but that also resurrect and attempt to reapply American modernization theory to the Middle East.[32]

An irruption of alterity

There is one moment in *Jewel* where this secular-liberal narrative frame is momentarily suspended, and an alternative non-liberal conception of freedom emerges. Although the liberal frame is quickly re-established, what is remarkable about this rupture is that this alterity is imagined as an alternative conceptualization of *liberty* thereby displacing the notion that only liberalism can offer a genuine account of it. After Aisha is offered the 'Verse of the Choice', she acknowledges that 'he'd given me the freedom and the power to choose my own destiny, the greatest gift anyone had ever given to me. In doing so, he had made me completely, utterly his own . . . "I choose you," I said' (306–7). There are two ways of reading this moment; the first is to suggest that it represents the triumph of liberalism, that it encodes into this pivotal moment in Islamic history the idea of an individual being able to control their destiny by being offered the liberty of 'free' choice.

Such a reading would be both aesthetically and philosophically facile, given that the entire force of the narrative up to this point has been to demonstrate that for a woman in the Arab society of that time – even someone as indomitable as Aisha – such a power is illusory *even if offered a 'free' choice in any given instance*. However, if the liberal notion that 'free' choice involves the ability to control one's 'destiny' is set aside, then the freedom of choice offered here is oriented toward a different end: the willing *surrender* of oneself – and one's destiny – to Allah, to his Prophet, and to the restraints and restrictions that define that submission, becomes not a negation of liberty but its very opposite, an embrace of what Allison Weir, in a sympathetic and perceptive critique of Saba Mahmood's *The Politics of Piety*, calls the 'substantive freedom' of 'inhabiting norms' and 'inhabiting connections'.[33] Of the former, she writes that 'freedom can be found through *inhabiting norms*: by focusing on an ideal or purpose you find freedom in that focus, which provides a structure within which free play is possible'.[34] For Muslims, this focus or purpose is Allah and serving Allah. Of the latter, she writes that this is a freedom to 'realize a self-in-connection . . . this experience of freedom is an experience of freedom in one's various relationships with others, with oneself, and with the world'.[35] For Muslims, this involves a 'connection with the source of life, with the sacred, or divine, or spirit, which gives one a center and by extension connects one with all beings, and with all of life. The common idea is that when one is focused on this connection, then one's daily life becomes lighter, and the lightness one feels is freedom'.[36] These 'communitarian' ideas of freedom 'are clearly opposed to a liberal individualist concept. But they do express a conception of freedom'.[37]

Weir acknowledges that '[t]he danger of such a conception of freedom . . . is that it can leave us open to quietism, to acceptance of domination and abuse', but she suggests that it need not be incompatible with 'practices of critique and resistance' if these are themselves reconceptualized as 'practices of *reworking and renegotiating connections*, and thereby renegotiating and transforming . . . identities', rather than 'simply as acts of resistance to norms, and . . . ways of inhabiting other norms'.[38] This radical alternative to liberal conceptions of liberty is akin to the eternal dialogue with the Other proposed in Chapter 3, the perpetual revision of one's relation to others and thus of one's self, and one example of it can be found in Amina Wadud's definition of *islam* as 'engaged surrender'.[39] For Wadud, if the act of submission to Allah is to have any moral significance then it must involve 'free will', but this act of freely surrendering does not imply a negation of one's freedom but rather an active moral engagement with one's responsibilities – to Allah, to others – which she defines as 'moral agency' (*khilafah*); as Khaled Abou El Fadl pithily puts it, to become a Muslim in this sense is 'to surrender meaningfully by gaining mastery and autonomy over oneself'.[40] Such agency is a particular form of freedom that is distinct from the liberal notion of an 'autonomous' individual ('autonomous', that is, from others as opposed to 'over oneself') insofar as it is the particular mode by which a subject negotiates his or her relation to others within a social environment, a negotiation that is circumscribed by the organization of social relations and the distribution of power between them, which 'shapes' the ways in which 'freedom' is experienced in any given social formation. One must acknowledge, then, this moment at which *Jewel*'s ethical relation to its subject does exceed its limitations, and alterity is both revealed and respected.

The ethics of genre and the literary market

Nevertheless, this irruption of alterity is quickly re-contained within the liberal frame and enveloped by the ethics of genre, which encompasses more than just purely literary considerations. Romance is by far the most popular and commercially lucrative of all literary genres. It is a multi-billion dollar market, and best-selling authors are substantially rewarded.[41] Were such financial considerations germane to Jones' choice of genre? If so, the ethics of *Jewel*'s representation of the Other woman is determined by its relationship to commercial interest: to what extent is Jones' Aisha a figure fashioned by a desire for commercial success, that is, by Jones' self-interest?[42] Although one cannot be certain about an author's exact intentions, the intentionality of the novel is clear. *Jewel* is not a completely conventional romantic fiction, but the importance of the genre is apparent in the way its impulses, motifs, tropes and conventions are pivotal to the creation and maintenance of whatever dramatic tension there is in the first half of the novel, up to the point of the narrative climax in the 'affair of the lie'. As such, it profoundly shapes the narrative as a whole, even after that point. And Jones does provide some paratextual indication of the commercial considerations at play. The novel has an afterword which comments on the decision by Random House to 'indefinitely postpone' (in their words) publication. She notes that '[Random House] had already placed my novel on the fast-track to best-sellerdom . . . selling foreign rights to several countries, landing deals with Book-of-the-Month Club and the Quality Paperback Book Club, and arranging an eight-city U.S. tour for me' (343). In the next paragraph, these commercial considerations are juxtaposed to a loftier ambition; she states that she was '[e]ager to bring my books into world while they are relevant – while they can contribute to an ongoing, worldwide discussion about Islam' (344). What is in question here, however, is the nature of that contribution, and indeed that ambition, and the ways in which it is compromised or otherwise by Jones' authorial choice to write in the manner she does. That choice was not incidental to her intervention but was foundational, and the ethical problems outlined above can be traced to it. In her defence, Jones cites the pieties of mainstream contemporary liberal understandings of freedom of speech – 'the best response to free speech is simply more speech in return' (345) – but it cannot be left at that because, as Kenneth Burke has noted, speech is never neutral; it is an articulation and effect of power, embedded in relations of domination and subordination, and these are determined by economic as well as political and cultural relations. The manner – in this instance, genre – in which one exercises the right to freedom of speech therefore matters because the meaning of speech acts are shaped as much by form as content. And it matters because the 'respond to speech with speech' argument is a trite idealist cliché: particular literary markets allow access to some forms of expression and exclude others, and therefore some utterances – and the attitudes, sensibilities and ideologies they encode – can be heard while alternative perspectives that do not meet the expectations of the market are silenced.

Part III

7

Satire, Incitement and Self-Restraint: Reflections on Freedom of Expression and Aesthetic Responsibility in Contemporary Britain

The *Racial and Religious Hatred Act 2006* finally received Royal Assent on 16 February 2006, although it did not come into force until 1 October 2007. This was the third attempt by the Labour government to introduce such legislation following the *Anti-Terrorism, Crime and Security Bill 2001–2*, and the *Serious Organized Crime and Police Bill 2004–5*.[1] On each previous occasion, parliamentary opposition in both the lower and upper houses led to the removal of the clauses relating to incitement of religious hatred. The Bill that passed in 2006, which amended the Public Order Act 1986, was significantly altered by four amendments to the Government's proposals: first, the provisions relating to incitement of religious hatred were to be separated from the existing provisions for the incitement of racial hatred; second, unlike the racial hatred provisions, the new offence would be confined to the use of 'threatening' words or behaviour, and not extend to words that were 'abusive and insulting'; third, the prosecution would need to prove the *intent* to stir up religious hatred rather than – as is the case with racial hatred – demonstrate that it was 'likely' to do so; fourth, a new clause was introduced explicitly protecting freedom of speech – 'Nothing in this Part shall be read or given effect in a way which prohibits or restricts discussion, criticism or expressions of antipathy, dislike, ridicule, insult or abuse of particular religions or the beliefs or practices of their adherents'.[2] In the course of what follows, I will discuss the significance of these amendments and what they reveal about contemporary understandings of expressive liberty in Britain, but I have neither the competence nor the desire to evaluate whether they improve or weaken the Act *as law*; rather if, as Valérie Amiraux suggests, the law makes social reality intelligible one of the ways it does this is by distilling the prevailing assumptions and ideas that might be circulating more or less nebulously within a particular discursive and moral economy in the process of encoding them.[3] It is an examination of this wider discursive economy that is my primary preoccupation in this chapter, and the Act provides a point of departure from which to do so.

To that end, we might begin by noticing that although the Act is meant to extend incitement legislation to cover religious as well as racial hatred, it does so by way of distinction rather than analogy. Each of the amendments – known as the 'Lester amendments', after Lord Lester, the main critic of the Bill in the House of Lords – distinguishes and distances the two: religious hatred is to have its own provisions; it is to be restricted to threatening words only; and the emphasis is on intent rather than effect (the removal of the 'likely limb', as it is known, was one of the most contentious disputes in the parliamentary deliberations). The fourth amendment, introducing a special reservation protecting freedom of expression, is, according to Lord Lester, 'a unique addition to the criminal code'.[4] This exceptionalizes the legislation still further, not only distinguishing it from incitement of racial hatred, but all legislation pertaining to the restriction of expression even though, according to Kay Goodall, it 'should have been unnecessary, given the emphasis on freedom of expression in prior law and given that [the Act] is now worded more restrictively than the law on racial hatred'.[5] Clearly, then, there is something exceptional about *religion* that induces an especially intense anxiety amongst contemporary legislators, and among wider constituencies of public opinion, about its relation to freedom of expression – something thrown into sharp relief when it is remembered that (arguably greater) restrictions on this freedom concerning the right to protest within the vicinity of Parliament and other locations were passed into law as part of the same Serious Organized Crime and Police Act from which the incitement to religious hatred provisions were dropped.[6]

As Nasar Meer notes, the central structuring principle of the discourse surrounding the Racial and Religious Hatred Bill – among supporters as well as opponents – was the distinction between 'voluntary' and 'involuntary' identities.[7] This is in turn premised, as I have discussed in Chapter 3, on the notion that religious identity is grounded in *belief*. Again, this was taken for granted by both supporters and opponents of the Bill. Indeed, the framing definition of 'religious hatred' in the Bill (and Act) is 'hatred against a group of persons defined by reference to religious belief or lack of religious belief'.[8] This opens up freedom of speech questions in a way that do not pertain to 'involuntary' identities such as 'race' because it rests on the idea that differences in religious identities are due to differences in beliefs that are voluntarily and therefore rationally and consciously professed rather than affectively experienced or 'confessed'. This in turn means that religious identity is open to rational 'debate' in the 'marketplace of ideas' in a way that racial identity is not, and so the harmful effects of restricting expression with regard to the former is therefore far more pronounced than it would be for the latter. As David Davis, the Shadow Home Secretary leading the Opposition to the Bill put it, 'Religion, unlike race, is a matter of personal choice and therefore appropriate for open debate', a view echoed in most of the opinion pieces and editorials opposing the Bill in the national press.[9]

But if religious identity – and therefore religious hatred – is grounded in belief then it becomes difficult to disentangle expressions of hatred from legitimate criticism. Unlike racial abuse and insults, which do not contribute to a debate but simply denigrate and subordinate their object, abuse and insult on religious grounds must, at least implicitly, offer a criticism of religious beliefs since these are the very basis of the identity that is being attacked. Hence the insistence, as the Bill passed through the Lords, on the removal of 'abuse and insult' from the provisions, leaving only 'threatening' words that are amply covered by existing restrictions on speech in any case. Conversely, it also becomes impossible to criticize religious beliefs without in some way offending against the person who holds them. Responding to the government claim that they are 'protecting the person and not the belief', Lord Hunt asked:

> [i]s it possible, however, to defend them from hatred as people while also preserving the right of others to criticise their beliefs? In other words, is it possible to draw a distinction between a group of people who share a religion or ideology and . . . the religion or ideology itself? If someone insults my beliefs, I can perfectly well argue that they insult me too . . . If we wish to apply criminal sanctions to protect people from feeling insulted or abused when someone criticises or attacks their beliefs, it is obvious that the beliefs themselves as well as the individual who feels insulted or abused are being protected.[10]

This was a central argument in the wider public discourse as well, and key to the anxiety that the Bill would have a 'chilling' effect on 'legitimate criticism' of religion even though it actually undermines the very distinction between legitimate and illegitimate criticism in the first place. The manner of the speech, its form, is negated as a basis for discriminating between legitimate and illegitimate criticism because they both potentially have the same effect – offence – and one cannot therefore really distinguish between reasoned criticism and abuse and insult because the latter *must*, on the basis of the first line of reasoning, contribute to 'open debate' as much as the former. Consequently, 'intent' becomes the only means of discriminating between legitimate and illegitimate forms of expression. What is occluded, of course, is the possibility that religious identity has, in fact, little or nothing to do with 'belief' for most people but instead involves what Allison Weir calls 'inhabiting connections' or modes of *belonging*.[11] Such connections might be established, for instance, by an intimate and deeply affective connection – identification – with the Prophet Muhammad.[12] The offensive force of a declaration that the Prophet was a paedophile (a common trope in anti-Muslim discourse) targets this connection, abusing the person by abusing the object of their affective relation. It is difficult to see how this involves any criticism of any belief held by any Muslim. Indeed, it returns us to the two questions posed in Chapter 5 – *whose* beliefs and *what* beliefs are at stake when someone abuses or insults another person? – and the fact that the beliefs in question may not be those held by the person being abused but rather those held by the *offender*. And even if it is held, in this instance, that the insult in fact criticizes the belief that the Prophet is worthy of veneration, if the basis of that veneration is affective rather than rational, it is difficult to see how the insult is a contribution to a 'debate' as opposed to merely a vehicle for denigration and subordination, thereby aligning it with the 'wounding' intent of racial abuse.

Both sides of the main argument advanced in opposition to the Bill – that abuse and insult are, in fact, forms of criticism of belief, and that it is impossible to criticize without insult or causing offence to believers – derive from the voluntarist assumption that people 'choose' their religious identity by subscribing to a set of beliefs. This, of course, implies that beliefs and the persons that hold them are separable, but it also leads, as we have seen, to the conclusion that they are also *not* separable. The grounding of religious identity in belief therefore constitutes an *aporia* that reveals the limits of secular-liberal thought about cultural and religious difference. Indeed, such is the extent to which these secular-liberal assumptions shape discourse about religion in contemporary society, even religious persons succumb to them. One significant anxiety that surfaced in the debate surrounding the Bill was the fear that it would effectively prohibit proselytizing activities that seek to convert people of other faiths and proscribe 'holy books' such as the Bible or the *Qur'an*, in spite of the acknowledgment of critics within Parliament, such as Lord Lester, 'that there was "not the slightest doubt" that reading from the sacred text of one of the main world religions could not in itself amount to an offence under the Bill, *even in its original draft*'.[13] Nevertheless, in wider public discussions, this anxiety circulated through a number of more or less alarmist (mis)interpretations. The Lawyers' Christian Fellowship issued a briefing suggesting that 'it is concerned that this measure could threaten the freedom to preach the Gospel of Jesus Christ because people with other beliefs could be offended by the message', and Andrew Myers, writing in the *New Law Journal*, suggested that reporting of activities by Hindu extremists, or documentaries about the discrimination of women under *Shari'a* law, would constitute criminal acts, and that booksellers would be committing an offence every time they sold a Bible or *Qur'an* – a reading that the legal scholar Kay Goodall claims is both 'extraordinary' and 'simply wrong'.[14] The columnist Polly Toynbee, writing in the *Guardian*, amplified this concern to a much wider readership in typically robust terms, 'the Bible and the Qur'an incite enough religious hatred to be banned outright', whilst the writer Kenan Malik offered an apparently more reasoned argument after the amended Bill had been passed: 'The irony of the campaign against *The Satanic Verses* is that Islam itself is a testament to the *necessity* for giving offence. The creation of the faith was shocking and viscerally offensive to the adherents of the pagan religion out of which it grew'.[15] Notwithstanding the fact that the pagan Arabs were well aware of several monotheisms which were circulating within the Arabian peninsula at the time, including Judaism and Christianity, or that what was truly shocking and even, perhaps, offensive to the tribal sensitivities of the pagan Meccans was not the *idea* or 'belief' in a single God but rather that *one of their own* should *abandon* the traditions, customs and practices of his ancestors, the underlying assumption is that it is simply not possible to profess one set of beliefs without criticizing other beliefs and, in so doing, offending and inciting 'hatred' against believers who hold alternative beliefs. This effectively rules out the possibility that religious believers might accept or even embrace pluralism because it reduces 'belief' to a zero-sum game: if my beliefs are true then yours cannot be.[16] Whilst for many religious persons this may indeed be true, it does not follow that it is structurally fundamental to religious identity as these accounts suggest it to be, nor does it require that one must therefore 'incite hatred' or cause 'offence' to other believers even if you believe their beliefs to be wrong. The *Qur'an*, for example, advises Muslims that 'they should speak in the most kindly manner [unto those who do not share their beliefs]: verily, Satan is always ready to stir up discord between men' (Q17:53). But in ruling out the possibility that religious identity is not a zero-sum game, that the *manner* of relating to other believers might, in fact, mean that the profession of one's beliefs does not *necessarily* lead to the giving of offence or incitement of hatred against others, this line of argument effectively reserves the idea of pluralism itself as a *secular* value that is truly enabled and vouchsafed only by the ideology of secular-liberalism because it can only emerge from a *lack* of belief.

This is why the aporia is so significant. Within the terms of their argument, it is entirely consistent for those who objected to the Racial and Religious Hatred Bill on these grounds to suggest that, in effect, there cannot be any such thing as incitement to *religious* as opposed to racial hatred; and those, such as Kenan Malik and Nick Cohen, who hold that *all* incitement legislation should be removed are merely extending this argument to its logical conclusion. But in so doing they either display a callous indifference to, and even incomprehension of, the physical and psychological harm that hate speech can inflict on its victims; or, in effect, they argue that such speech cannot have any such effects at all as it is 'only' speech (thereby ironically devaluing the importance of speech itself); or they espouse an idealist and naïve view that the power of speech alone is sufficient to contest such forms of expression and ameliorate its effects, and that any such progress as has been achieved in making such expression socially and morally unacceptable is the benighted consequence of the steady diffusion of more enlightened ideas about equality, tolerance and respect for others, as opposed to the determined political struggle of social agents to put these ideas into practice and direct state action towards these ends.

On the other hand, those who acknowledge the harm in hate speech, and also the reality that it can be expressed on *religious* grounds, were not wrong to propose legislation in order to restrict it. In the discourse surrounding the introduction of the Bill, these advocates recognize expressions of religious hatred when they see or hear them, but because they share the same underlying logic as their opponents, they find it extremely difficult to define and pin down in a manner that would exclude the possibility that protection of religious believers from such expressions of hatred would not, in fact, inadvertently result in the proscription of legitimate criticism of their beliefs. Thus critics such as Lord Lester repeatedly expressed a consensus on the need to do something about religious hatred, but also reservations about the means by which the Government's proposed legislation would tackle it; for her part Baronness Scotland, on behalf of the Government, stated that, 'I am sure that noble Lords will appreciate that squaring this particular circle is in no way easy', which concedes that there is a circle to be squared.[17] The ensuing compromise was a set of amendments that attenuated the effectivity of the Act to such an extent that it is, according to most legal commentators, a 'dead letter' – even without the redundant clause protecting freedom of expression. According to Kay Goodall, 'the Lords have pruned this statute so hard they have left it a stump'.[18]

If the removal of the 'abuse and insult' phrase from clause 29B(1) speaks to liberal uncertainties about how best to protect religious identities from unwarranted attack, the inclusion of the emphasis on 'intent' speaks equally profoundly to liberal confusions about the responsibilities attendant upon free expression. There is a double move here insofar as the clause does acknowledge such responsibility and even purports to give it the force of law, but in grounding this responsibility in the concept of intent the amendment effectively removes responsibility from the speaker by making it almost impossible to establish beyond reasonable doubt, other than in certain extreme cases already covered by existing public order provisions (e.g. 'direct' incitement presenting a 'clear and present danger' to public order). Perhaps inadvertently, the Act thus gravitates towards the position adopted by Kenan Malik that I examined in Chapter 3, and embodies the same contradictions. It bears repeating that this is because contemporary discourse sees something exceptional about offences against religious or 'voluntary' identities as opposed to 'involuntary' ones such as race insofar as this threshold of responsibility is not deemed appropriate for incitement to racial hatred (both Houses accepted that the incitement to racial hatred provisions should not be amended at all).

At the heart of this confusion is the vexed question of incitement, which is both acknowledged and abjured in liberal thought because, on the one hand, the effects of such forms of speech are all too evident (and there would be no point in having freedom of speech if it had no 'effects' in the world) while, on the other, there is a fear that it might lead to restrictions on speech that are unwarranted if the definition of incitement is extended too far. In the parliamentary debate, the rhetorical *over-extension* of the definition of incitement was used to underscore this point. Tony Wright MP attempted to vividly illustrate the danger by doing just that: 'I would like to incite people to hate bigotry, and I am worried about provisions that say I cannot go round inciting people in that way. That incitement – which, as we have heard, involves loathing and intense dislike – is integral to our tradition.'[19] Wright skilfully substitutes the word 'incite' for the more moderate – and semantically appropriate – term 'persuade' in order to achieve a catachrestic inversion that displaces the term 'incitement' from the margins, where it might relate to the effects of extreme speech acts such as expressions of hatred ('loathing and intense dislike') towards persons, to a more central position within the 'marketplace of ideas' (normally inhabited by the term it displaces, persuasion) where its restriction could be said to threaten 'open' debate; but in so doing Wright suggests that strong, emotive factors, rather than the cool rationality professed by Mill and others, constitute the marketplace of ideas itself such that *everyone* in fact exhibits a certain bigotry – those who oppose bigotry with 'loathing and intense dislike' as well as bigots themselves. Whilst superficially effective in highlighting a purported danger to freedom of expression, rhetorical interventions such as these in fact unwittingly expose the fact that the 'marketplace of outrage' is not the invention of thin-skinned religious believers (principally Muslim) overeager to take offence, but is rather a logical extension of a particular understanding of freedom of expression – which Wright suggests is 'integral to our tradition' – that any restriction on expression is, in principle, a threat to truly 'open' and 'free' debate even though *in practice* people such as Wright would be perfectly happy to accept all manner of other restrictions on that liberty. Whereas the idea of incitement and its prohibition is accepted in relation to public disorder, homicide, terrorism and racial hatred, it must, according to this view, be attenuated in relation to religious hatred to the point of nullity in order to prevent what is assumed will be an inevitable 'slippery slope' that leads, eventually, to the proscription of enquiry, criticism and satire – hence the emphasis on 'intent', which assumes the role of an unenforceable bulwark against any such slide.[20] Again, this confusion is revealed by the exceptionality of incitement to *religious* hatred, insofar as this is deemed to be an extension of the idea of incitement to the point where it encroaches on matters of belief, and thus onto the terrain of criticism and enquiry. This extension is therefore seen to undermine the foundations of expressive liberty and, for some, the foundations of liberty as a whole.

A law that is not prosecutable is, according to many, an unnecessary law. But, as Abigail Levin has argued, Acts of Parliament are performative speech acts authorized by the state and thus they possess more than just the symbolic force of 'deterrence' that Government ministers claimed for the Act following their defeat, an argument that rests on the assumption that laypersons will be deterred because they believe the law *will* be enforce-able. Rather, as a performative speech act articulated by the state, law has a material effectivity that goes beyond the question of enforceability insofar as it shapes the contours of the permissible, and therefore of freedom itself. This is the kind of effectivity with which I am concerned: the ethical signal of the law establishes a framework within which individual and collective understandings of moral responsibility can gather and take shape even if, as law, it fails to establish any specifically prosecutable legal responsibility. It is precisely in relation to the way legislation sculpts social reality that the liberal critique of the Racial and Religious Hatred Act reveals its full significance, for it was not just about opposing an attempt to criminal-ize certain forms of expression but also a response – and resistance – to a changing 'moral climate', from one in which 'religious believers may properly be offended, indeed deserve to be offended', to one in which they do not.[21] To put it another way, the opposition to the Bill and Act is illu-minating because it reveals *more* than just an antipathy to a change in the law; it reveals, in fact, a great deal about certain prevalent attitudes towards moral responsibility *as such*, especially amongst a stratum of well-known contemporary artists and intellectuals who led the opposition to the Bill outside Parliament. For them the Bill challenged certain assumptions about aesthetic responsibility that are paradigmatically represented in the writ-ings of Salman Rushdie, whose articulations on the matter were forged in the intense heat of the controversy that bore his name and was, in turn, the catalyst for the Muslim campaign to prohibit incitement to hatred on religious grounds.

Rushdie and responsibility

As discussed in Chapter 4, Rushdie justified himself in response to his critics by claiming to have written 'in good faith'. In so doing, he acknowledges a certain moral responsibility, but it is not at all clear to whom or what; the question of responsibility in his discourse about *The Satanic Verses* and the controversy surrounding it is fraught with inconsistencies, contradictions and evasions. He completely rejects any suggestion that a writer might be 'accountable to the community', howsoever that 'community' is defined, and he dismisses Rana Kabbani's 'Stalinist fervour' for having the temerity to suggest it, as if such responsibility involves an inherent totalitarianism – a comparison invoked by many others during the Rushdie affair in relation to the symbolic incineration of the novel by protestors in Bradford, and reprised a decade and a half later by the *Jyllands-Posten* editor Flemming Rose in relation to the Danish cartoons.[22] Insofar as readers constitute a community such a rejection implies a repudiation of any responsibility towards his readers. He even seems to disavow responsibility for his own text. In defending his use of strong language in the 'Jahilia' and 'Return to

Jahlia' sections of the novel, he states, 'It is quite true that the language here is forceful, satirical and strong meat for some tastes, but it must be remembered that the waking Gibreel is a coarse-mouthed fellow, and it would be surprising if the dream-figures he conjures up did not sometimes speak as rough and even obscene a language as their dreamer'.[23] This surprisingly naturalistic explanation from a writer of post-modern, magic-realist metafictions displaces the responsibility for the textuality of these passages onto his characters at the cost of negating the metaphysical weight these passages are clearly meant to bear, for this is not just a novel about a man losing his mind because of his loss of faith; rather, it is a novel that seeks to explore – among many other things – the very nature of faith itself, an objective most forcefully located in these dream episodes.[24]

Furthermore, Rushdie abjures any responsibility for the consequences that arose from the publication of his novel. *'The responsibility for violence lies with those who perpetrate it'*, he writes, and whilst this is indeed at least partially true, the characterization of 'responsibility' as indivisible is clearly meant to deflect attention away from any possibility that he might *also* have been indirectly responsible for such effects through incitement or provocation.[25] Indeed, this formulation renders the very idea of incitement impossible, an argument that is repeated in an almost identical fashion by Kenan Malik in his twentieth anniversary review of the Rushdie affair and its wider implications. As I argued in Chapter 3, for Malik (and therefore Rushdie), the speaker or author of a discourse bears no responsibility for their words because the relationship between 'deeds and words' is such that the concept of 'incitement' becomes a logical absurdity, assigning responsibility to the speaker of a discourse when it should rightfully be assigned only to those who respond to it.[26] In fact, it is impossible to read 'In Good Faith' without concluding that Rushdie sincerely believed that everyone else bore some responsibility for the 'Rushdie affair' but himself. But, like Malik, Rushdie accepts the idea of incitement in other circumstances. Just as Malik accepts the argument put forward by Oliver Wendell Holmes about crying 'Fire!' in a crowded theatre, so too does Rushdie, in an earlier passage of 'In Good Faith', lament the fact that '[i]ncitement to murder was tolerated on the nation's [Britain's] streets'; he also explicitly praises the US and European governments for 'swift action' that 'prevented such incitement at a very early stage'.[27] Indeed, in *The Satanic Verses* itself, the idea of 'incitement' appears to be absolutely central to the idea of art, and of literary art in particular. In a passage that has been often quoted for its tragic prescience, the poet Baal avers that 'A poet's work . . . To name the unnameable, to point at frauds, to take sides, start arguments, shape the world and stop it from going to sleep', to which the narrator adds, 'And if rivers of blood flow from the cuts his verses inflict, then they will nourish him'.[28] It is difficult to see how such a view of art can be severed from the notion of an artist's responsibility for the effects of his or her words in the world, but this doublethink does not appear to be peculiar to Rushdie himself: Malik uses the quote as an epigraph to the Introduction of *From Fatwa to Jihad*, even as he subsequently goes on to argue against the idea that a 'speaker' bears any responsibility for the incitement his or her words may effect.

Subsequently, Rushdie elaborated his ideas about the writer's role in the lecture 'Is Nothing Sacred?' This remains his most fully articulated pronouncement on the issue of writerly responsibility, and although what he says is often addressed specifically to 'literature' the arguments are, in fact, paradigmatic of modern conceptions of art in general, and have general purchase within the contemporary artistic and intellectual establishment. The lecture involves an initial sacralizing of aesthetics in general and 'the absolute freedom of the imagination', such that art 'becomes the third principle that mediates between the material and spiritual worlds . . . something that might even be called a secular definition of transcendence', but it then retreats from this quite obvious metaphysical, not to say religious, formulation because Rushdie 'cannot bear the idea of the writer as a secular prophet . . . We'll just have to get along without the shield of sacralization, and a good thing, too. We must not become what we oppose'.[29] He therefore concludes that the 'only privilege literature deserves – and this privilege it requires in order to exist – is the privilege of being the arena of discourse, the place where the struggle of languages can be acted out' (427). He then defends that privilege using a parable in which reality is compared to 'a large, rambling house' in which there a limitless number of rooms, and in some of which 'you can hear all kinds of voices', these being the 'arena' of literature. 'The reason for ensuring that that privilege is preserved', he suggests:

> is not that writers want the absolute freedom of the imagination to say and do whatever they please. It is that we, *all of us*, readers and writers and citizens and generals and godmen, *need* that little, unimportant-looking room. We do not need to call it sacred, but we do need to remember that *it is necessary*. (429, original emphasis and emphasis added)

Something very subtle is happening here. Rushdie initially acknowledges that writers should not enjoy 'absolute freedom to say and do whatever they please', (which was one of the main critiques put forward by his Muslim (and some non-Muslim) critics) and in so doing concedes that writers do have *some* responsibility to a wider community; he therefore recognizes some limit on the 'absolute freedom of the imagination' that he had earlier championed. The next sentence, however, qualifies and then negates this acknowledgment: writers do not claim such 'absolute freedom' because they *want to*, but rather because '*it is necessary*'. The right is – rather mysteriously – endowed upon them because of the special qualities inherent in 'literature', which is why it 'deserves' its 'privilege'. This, in turn, clarifies the precise nature of the responsibility Rushdie evokes, for writers do not just have the *right*, but also the *duty* to speak *without limit* because '[l]iterature is the one place in any society where . . . we can hear *voices talking about everything in every possible way*' (ibid. emphasis added). This responsibility to the 'absolute freedom of the imagination' and the duty incumbent upon writers to articulate it is grounded in some higher necessity, a metaphysical proposition that, in fact, returns to the view initially put forward by Rushdie that literature *is* sacred after all.

However, it would not be quite true to say that Rushdie sees literature in completely idealized terms; rather, there is an ambiguity in his championing, on the one hand, a Romantic notion of an artist being responsible only to his/her Imagination, and, on the other, his insistence that Literature is an oppositional force that resists, and speaks truth to, power, for 'if democracy no longer has communism to help it clarify, by opposition, its own ideas, then perhaps it will have to have literature as an adversary instead' (427). This is related to Rushdie's sacralization of 'Literature' as something 'holy' or 'set apart' because one of Literature's special qualities seems to be its inherent oppositionality, its radically subversive ability to undermine the grand narratives that underwrite claims to power and authority. This formulation of 'Literature', as if these were qualities typical of *all* literary works, is apparently further substantiated by Rushdie's reference to Foucault's definition of an 'Author' as someone 'to blame'. Citing the following passage from Foucault's essay 'What is an Author?' in which Foucault argues that 'texts, books and discourses really began to have authors . . . to the extent that authors became subject to punishment, that is, to the extent that discourses could be transgressive', and another in which he claims that 'discourse was not originally a product . . . it was essentially an act – an act placed in the bipolar field of the sacred and profane, the licit and illicit', and therefore 'a gesture fraught with risks', Rushdie draws two conclusions, the second of which is that 'literature is, of all the arts, best suited to challenging absolutes of all kinds', because 'in its origin' it is the 'schismatic Other of the sacred' (423–4). This echoes his invocation of another French postmodern philosopher, Jean-François Lyotard, some two pages earlier in order to bolster his claim that 'the rejection of totalized explanations is the modern condition' so 'the challenge of literature is to start from this point' (422). Notwithstanding the slippage from 'modern' to 'post-modern', conflating the two in a way that Lyotard never would, for it renders the *post-ness* of 'la condition postmoderne' superfluous, Rushdie's entire rhetorical strategy here begs several questions. Firstly, with respect to his use of Foucault, Rushdie identifies the 'origin' of 'literature' with that historical juncture that led to the emergence of the author, but what of works now thought of as 'literature' that predated this historical emergence? Are they still part of that formation known as 'literature', and do they exhibit the same inherently oppositional character? Secondly, with respect to the passage invoking

Lyotard, if the 'challenge of literature' is to start at the (postmodern) point where all 'totalized' explanations have broken down, what of those literary works that do *not* start from this point? Are they still to be considered 'literature' or not? If not, then why not? Why should the term 'literature' be reserved for a particular *kind* of literary work that is characteristically described as 'postmodern'? And if it is indeed the case that non-postmodern works *do* start from the same point as postmodern ones, then *all* literature must be 'postmodern', which makes the label somewhat redundant. Thirdly, why assume that *all* literature challenges absolutes? Here we might usefully return to the first conclusion that Rushdie draws from Foucault, *'that authors were named only when it was necessary to find someone to blame'* (424, original emphasis).

This interpretation is not wholly unwarranted, but it does rely heavily on one of the most questionable claims in Foucault's essay.[30] In the passage from which Rushdie quotes, Foucault suggests the 'author-function' emerges 'at the moment when a system of ownership and strict copyright rules were established (toward the end of the eighteenth and beginning of the nineteenth century)', but that 'its status as property is historically secondary to the penal code controlling its appropriation'.[31] He then makes the claim that Rushdie quotes about authors only becoming necessary when they become subject to punishment, substantiating this by offering the insight, which Rushdie also quotes, about discourse not being a 'thing' but an 'action . . . a gesture charged with risks'. While the first part of this passage – that modern authorship emerges at a particular historical conjuncture within the field of legal codifications assigning copyright – is specific and historically verifiable (although, as Simon During points out, the process began almost a century before Foucault says it did, with the 1709 English Copyright Act[32]), the second concerning punishment rests on a vague and general, ahistorical speculation about the 'transgressive properties always intrinsic to the act of writing'. This leads to a further speculation that the writer, who undertakes the risky gesture of discourse and is thus (always?) on the margins of the social order, has to pay a price for his acceptance into 'the social order' and the 'benefits of property' by 'reviving the older bipolar field of discourse in a systematic practice of transgression and by restoring the danger of writing'.[33]

According to this argument, the emergence of copyright laws and other legal codifications that created the modern concept of authorship constitutes a rupture that restores the transgressive properties of writing and locates them within a delimited field called 'literature', an argument that Rushdie completely adopts. But does this mean that these properties were suspended before that break? Was writing not deemed to have such threatening qualities in the earlier period? If not, why not given that it is 'intrinsic' to writing? Is this why there is no equivalent to the modern notion of authorship prior to modernity? Actually, on the very next page, Foucault describes a converse process: just as the 'author' emerges in the eighteenth century in relation to 'literature', s/he disappears in relation to 'scientific' texts, a process that, according to Foucault, took place some hundred years prior to its later 'literary' emergence. Whatever the historical merits of this claim, it suggests that the concept of the author did in fact predate its later emergence in relation to literature, only this time it is an 'index of truthfulness' rather than transgression.[34] This would seem to undermine the claim that the emergence of the author as a legal personality in the eighteenth century was *secondary* to its being subject to punishment on the basis of its 'intrinsic' transgressiveness. Indeed, it would seem more appropriate in the light of Foucault's own theoretical and methodological concerns to suggest that the transgressiveness ascribed to literature is an *effect* of the very process of codification that he identifies rather than something that is 'intrinsic' to the 'act of writing' as a whole. In other words, the emergence of the author as a figure in law subjects authors to the force of law as the corollary to the 'benefits of property' that are now endowed upon them; that is, in the process of acquiring rights they are also ascribed certain responsibilities, that 'owning one's book was synonymous with owning up to it'.[35] It is precisely in assuming the privileges of discourse that one becomes subject to the force of law and thus one risks transgressing it.

What we see in Foucault's formulation is an emphasis that reveals how a certain discourse of authorship and literariness speaks as much through Foucault as it does through Rushdie and others. This is the idea that the 'Author' and 'literature' are *objects* rather than subjects of power; even if one accepts Foucault's broader argument that subjectivity is itself a subject-*effect* of power rather than the property of a 'sovereign' subject, his emphasis in this passage would suggest that authors are primarily subject *to* as opposed to subjects *of* power.[36] Such a view overlooks how literature, and culture more generally, can be a servant of power as well as its adversary, as Marxist, feminist, post-colonial and queer analyses of literature's function as a purveyor of dominant ideologies attest. In other writings, Rushdie himself is well aware of this, as his celebrated critique of the Raj revivalism of the early 1980s demonstrates.[37] This is not to suggest, however, that literature and cultural praxis cannot be oppositional and subversive, but rather that its position in relation to power is contingent on the historical conjunctures determining each textual articulation as well its manner, style, form and content. Indeed, the same author and the same text can be *both* oppositional and complicit with dominant and dominating regimes of representation. In *The Satanic Verses*, the poet Baal makes his comment about 'a poet's work' at the very moment he becomes a literary mercenary, a pen for hire in the service of power; that he later becomes a critic of Mahound's power only underscores the point. There is nothing intrinsically transgressive or critical about his art, but the untenable opposition sustained throughout the novel between religion as an embodiment of power and literature as its transgressive 'other' suggests otherwise.

Nevertheless, the idea that art 'speaks truth to power' – and, therefore, that any form of restraint on the Imagination, whether moral or legal, constitutes an extension of power and a corresponding attenuation of liberty – has acquired common currency among artists and intellectuals in contemporary society, especially since the Rushdie affair. It is for this reason perhaps that satire acquired such prominence in the discourse surrounding both the Rushdie affair and the Racial and Religious Hatred Bill; another reason is that satire endows 'abuse and insult' with a moral seriousness that enables the argument for removal of that phrase to acquire a moral legitimacy that it might not otherwise have had, or, to put it another way, it provides a positive argument for the protection of abusive and insulting speech to augment the merely negative one that such forms of speech, though unpleasant, should not be criminalized.

Launching a public campaign against the Bill, the comedian Rowan Atkinson stated that '[t]here is an obvious difference between the behaviour of racist agitators . . . and the activities of satirists and writers who may choose to make comedy or criticism of religious belief, practices or leaders, just as they do with politics'.[38] Indeed, this close association of comedy and satire, as forms of art that purportedly critique power and folly, was a significant feature of the discourse on the Bill, on both sides of the debate. Responding to critics of the Bill, Lord Falconer argued in the Lords that the Bill 'will not stop the telling of jokes about religion or the ridiculing of faith . . . or stop artists from dealing with religious subjects'.[39] Despite this, the perception amongst a great many contemporary artists and intellectuals is that the Bill represents a new censoriousness about religion that *will* inhibit satire. Terry Jones of Monty Python, for example, wrote in the *Guardian* that he believed that the comic group would not dare to make a film such as *Life of Brian* in the current moral climate.[40] Such a view is not untypical of the concern within the contemporary liberal intelligentsia about the 'chilling' effect of the Act on religious satire, but it is unfounded. Indeed, as I will argue in due course, it may well be the case that the Act will, in fact, *enhance* rather than inhibit the quality of religious satire.

The prominence of satire in the discourse surrounding the Bill sits awkwardly, however, with the idea of the author as object rather than subject of power since satire is distinguished not by its formal qualities or elements – comedy, irony, wit, sarcasm, etc. are not peculiar to the form – but by its purpose and its attitude.[41] It is, of all genres, the most directly performative insofar as its articulation aims, to paraphrase Marx slightly, not merely to describe the world but also to change it.[42] Moreover, satire is performative in exactly the positional sense outlined in Chapter 1. For Arthur Pollard, the satirist sees himself (this gendering is deliberate, as we shall see below) as a 'guardian of ideals' and so, in John Clement Ball's words, 'satire measures deviation and deformity from an apparently superior position'.[43] This is the case even for those critics who argue that satire is powerless to effect real change in the world, such as Charles Knight and Leonard Feinberg. Knight argues, for instance, that satire is concerned with changing perception rather than behaviour, but the claim to a perception of things as they really are is a judgment based on an implicit superiority of vision, and Feinberg concludes that *in lieu* of material effectivity '[s]atire offers the reader the pleasures of superiority and safe release of aggression'.[44]

It does not follow, however, that satire necessarily speaks against or out-side power, as many assume it does, for it can be as conservative as it is radical, as often a howl of rage against a world perceived to be inexorably in decline as it is a call for change, renewal or revolution. One need only consider the perennial misogyny that underwrites the satiric tradition and its treatment of women as satiric victims – from Juvenal's sixth satire, which rails against the depravity of women who have the temerity to learn Greek, through the 'wiles of women' and their sexual licentiousness and lust, their irrationality, unpredictability and quixotic nature, as discussed by Chaucer, Pope, Congreve, Dryden and hundreds of lesser writers – to be disabused of the notion that satire is somehow inherently oppositional to power and orthodoxy.[45] Nevertheless, whatever its political orientation, satire's purpose is invariably moral, its attitude critical. And if that moral purpose is to have any significance it must induce – or at least seek to induce – some effects in the world. The satirist therefore wields power, and with that power comes a certain responsibility. The idea of a satirist who is not responsible for the effects of his or her satire is an odd formulation (not least because satirists themselves claim such responsibility as the counterpart to the serious moral intent behind their work) but this is precisely how the discourse surround-ing the Racial and Religious Hatred Act seems to conceive it. Beneath it lies a concept of satire in which anything becomes fair game regardless of its position in relation to power because power itself is discounted as a basis for discrimination between morally legitimate and illegitimate forms of satirical attack, which perhaps explains its prominence in discourses advocating an absolutist conception of free speech – satire becomes a sort of alibi excusing all offensive speech acts.

But if this is the case then satire is, in fact, divested of the very moral pur-pose that is its *raison d'être*, that which gives its offensiveness its moral value. For the issue is not offensiveness per se, as if all offensive speech acts are by definition morally illegitimate; rather, it turns on whom satire offends, how it goes about it and to what purpose. Writing about the celebrated court case involving the American pornographic magazine *Hustler*, which claimed First Amendment protection for its lurid sketch implying that the 'moral majority' leader Jerry Falwell enjoyed sexual relations with his mother on the basis that it constituted a legitimate satire of a powerful leader of a pow-erful lobby group, Stanley Fish has noted that while Falwell was a legitimate object of satirical attack the same cannot be said of his mother, whose sexual mores and therefore reputation was necessarily implicated in the attack on her son for no other reason than her relationship to him.[46] Quite apart from whether this should remove First Amendment protection, what is of interest to me here is the fact that, as a result, the sketch is reduced to a crudely abusive insult that annuls its satiric intent. The effectivity of satire, therefore, lies not in an insensitivity to the power of insult and abuse that abjures responsibility for the harm it causes, but in a serious appreciation of its power and an assumption of the responsibility that is attendant upon it – the responsibility to carefully delineate and distinguish the object of its attack. Arthur Pollard suggests as much when praising Pope over Juvenal; although both writers take aim against a wide range of targets, Juvenal 'seems to be too troubled over too little' such that he 'too often thrashes blindly around', whereas Pope 'destroys his victims by a relentless and penetrating finesse'.[47]

The satirist's responsibility is therefore both aesthetic and moral, which suggests that an ethics of propriety is especially relevant to discussions of satire, especially those satires that address, satirically, 'other' cultures. As I argued in Chapter 3, offensiveness is not always ethically inappropriate, and there are occasions when offensiveness is both morally and politically justified – if it is directed against the powerful. This, in turn, rests on the satirist's careful appreciation of the limits of his or her satirical intervention. As Pollard notes, 'the satirist is often a minority figure; he cannot, however, afford to be a declared outcast. For him to be successful his society should at least pay lip-service to the ideals he upholds'.[48] Charles Knight suggests that 'satire that is merely emotive – expressing the speaker's emotion without gaining the listener's agreement – is unsuccessful as satire . . . Satire usually demands an audience which either agrees with the propriety of the attack or is willing to do so for the purposes of entertainment'.[49] From a totally different theoretical perspective, that of linguistic stylistics, Paul Simpson notes that:

> As a discursive practice, satire is configured as a triad embodying three discursive subject positions . . . These are the *satirist* (the producer of the text), the *satiree* (an addressee, whether reader, viewer or listener) and the *satirized* (the target attacked or critiqued in the satirical discourse). Two of these three participants, the satirist and the satiree, are *ratified* within the discursive event. The third entity, the target, is *ex-colluded* and is not normally an 'invited participant' in the discourse exchange, even though the target is what provides the initial impetus for satire . . . Whereas satire which is successfully 'taken up' may draw closer the satirist and satiree, a failed or 'misfired' satire tends to destabilize and reshape the relationships in the triad by serving on the one hand to distance the satirist from the satiree, and on the other, by drawing together the satiree and the satirized target.[50]

Pollard, Knight and Simpson all emphasize the social relationality that determines the propriety of the satirical 'event'. But the norms and expectations shared by a satirist and his/her audience, which shape the limits of propriety, are usually impalpable and, since no society is homogeneous and undifferentiated, they are often contested. This is further complicated by cultural difference, and by the fact that one of satire's *formal* requirements seems to be a certain representational distortion involving such techniques as irony, reduction, caricature, exaggeration, parody, burlesque, grotesque, and tonal registers such as ridicule, sarcasm and invective. Together, these necessarily 'other' the object of attack thereby circumscribing still further the ethical basis of satire, rendering it that much more difficult.[51]

The satirical endeavour is, therefore, subject to a high degree of risk, which in turn demands a kind of precision and restraint that involves taking the care necessary to ensure that the attack is well-directed at the appropriate target, and that the attack itself is an appropriate one. The satirist cannot risk 'collateral damage' if s/he is to be successful, as Pollard notes when praising Dryden's satirical attack on the Puritans; 'he knew how far he could go to outrage the Puritans thoroughly without outraging his other contemporaries at all. This is the essence of successful satire – to get your victims "hopping mad" and your audience "laughing their heads off".'[52] In fact, the only time when the satirist *can* get away with carelessness and clumsiness is when the satirized is not only an 'other' within the representational frame of the satiric text, but also systematically 'othered' outside the text – when, that is, they are powerless to respond or object by virtue of their exclusion from or marginalization within the social relations that bind the satirist to his or her audience. In former times, this exclusion involved women, ethnic minorities, gays and lesbians and other 'minority' groups; in contemporary society, although some or all of these groups are still subject to some forms of exclusion, many of them have been increasingly drawn into the fold such that the satirical treatment of them *as groups* (rather than as individuals who happen to be part of those groups) is now more or less considered inappropriate. Instead, there are others who stand outside the orbit of secular-liberal values that constitute the norms of propriety in contemporary Britain, those whose culture, religion or beliefs mark them as 'alien' – principally Muslims. But in such instances, although the satire might not be deemed inappropriate within its particular social context, it nevertheless represents an ethical violation of the maximal responsibility to and for the Other that constitutes ethics itself; such is the satire of Mahound in *The Satanic Verses* (though not of the Imam), or of some of the cartoons published in *Jyllands-Posten*. On the other hand, although it is arguable that by virtue of its form satire can *never* observe an ethically maximal respect for the Other in general, ethically appropriate satires nevertheless operate within what I have called 'minimal ethics' insofar as they take what Simpson calls a 'calculated interactive risk' in order to pursue a calculable form of justice by violating and offending a powerful Other that is responsible for injustice, oppression, folly, corruption and vice. Such satires demonstrate what might be called a forensic sensitivity to the difficulties inherent in the discharging of their responsibilities, and they are successful ethically, as well as socially, politically and aesthetically. By way of example, I will offer a brief reading of two such satires: Chris Morris' *Four Lions* (2010) and *Monty Python's Life of Brian* (1979).

Satire and forensic sensitivity: *Life of Brian*

Prior to *The Satanic Verses*, two films generated considerable religious controversy amongst Christians in western Europe and north America. One, *The Last Temptation of Christ* (1988), was not a satirical work but a radical re-imagining of the life of Christ based on the novel by the Nikos Kazantzakis, originally published in 1953. The controversy it generated was largely confined to the United States, although there were some protests in Britain and Europe. The other, *Monty Python's Life of Brian* (1979) provoked widespread controversy in Britain, with influential public figures such as Mary Whitehouse, the journalist and broadcaster Malcolm Muggeridge, and the Bishop of Southwark condemning it as blasphemy. Several local authorities in the United Kingdom denied the film a public viewing licence, whilst others gave it an X certificate, restricting it to adults; the film was also banned in several European countries including Ireland and Norway.

I would argue that the reading of the film as blasphemous is careless as opposed to inappropriate because the film *is* a religious satire, but a careful reading of the film suggests that it takes great pains to distinguish its object of attack from either the figure of Jesus Christ, or the God he worships. When researching the film, the Pythons came to the view that Jesus of Nazareth was 'definitely a good guy' and that his teachings were not 'mockable' because 'it's very decent stuff'.[53] There are only a brace of scenes involving Jesus – the prefacing 'nativity' scene, which displays an 'aura' around the holy family, and haloes circling the heads of Jospeh and Mary; and the Sermon on the Mount, in which an actor plays Jesus 'straight'. The nativity scene makes it quite clear that Jesus and Brian are two separate persons who continue to be mistaken for one another throughout their lives, this slippage being one of the main themes of the film: the misrecognition and misinterpretation of the prophet's teachings by his followers, indexed at the outset by the scene representing the Sermon on the Mount. As the camera pans back from Jesus to focalize the view from the back of a large crowd, it becomes clear that Christ's audience are finding it difficult to hear the sermon, which is the cue for the punchline as one character interprets 'Blessed are the peacemakers' as 'Blessed are the cheesemakers'. Subsequent scenes amplify the point, leading to the climactic (mis)recognition of Brian as the Messiah. At this point, the satire becomes sharply focused on his 'followers' and their predilection for interpreting everything Brian says as a corroboration of their a priori belief that he is the 'chosen one'. When Brian tells them to 'Go away', one of them responds that 'Only the true Messiah would deny his divinity'; when he subsequently tells them to 'FUCK OFF!' they are, initially, shocked but then blind belief in Brian's status re-asserts itself, 'How should we fuck off, Master?' The satirical effectivity of the scene depends on the way it subsequently demonstrates that the closed-mindedness of such 'believers' rather than the teachings of the prophets is what results in zealotry and violence.

Terry Jones's assessment of the movie as 'heretical because it criticized the structure of the Church and the way it interpreted the Gospels' but *not* blasphemous would seem, therefore, to be apposite. Indeed, the subplot involving Brian's membership in a clandestine political group resisting Roman occupation suggests that although its principal target is organized religion and religious believers (though not religious belief), its more general concern is with unthinking believers in general, whether secular or religious, and the groupthink they exhibit. One of the most penetrating moments in the film (and also one of the funniest) is when a naked Brian opens his bedroom window to be confronted by his 'followers' who believe he is the Messiah. He beseeches them to think for themselves because 'you're all individuals'. 'Yes, we're all individuals', replies the crowd in unison. Related to this is the novel's critique of the ways in which religious and political organizations inevitably descend into schism, dogma and petty squabbles over obscure and irrelevant points of doctrine, as represented most forcefully in the 'splitters' scene by the various factions resisting the Romans, the 'People's Front of Judea', the 'Judean People's Front', 'The Popular Front for Judea' and the 'Campaign to Free Galillee'. This is paralleled by the fissure of Brian's followers between those who follow the 'gourd' and those who follow the 'shoe', and a subsequent fissure among the latter between those who believe Brian's true message is that shoes should be worn on the head and those who believe they should be waved in the air. Again, the point is carefully made. It is directed not so much at the fact that people must 'believe' in something, but rather at the way their belief is shaped by the exigencies of history, society, institutional power, ideology, interpretation and the inevitable slippages and mistranslations that this involves, as well as at the impact of dominant and dominating personalities such as Reg, whose leadership rests on his personal charisma, a penchant for bullying, and the credulity of his 'followers'. In the structure of the film, the 'true' prophet Jesus is paralleled on the one side by the reluctant Brian, whose journey leads him to question authority and the very notion of leadership itself, and on the other by the egomaniacal Reg who, one imagines, would very much like to be seen as a Messiah given the chance. The 'serious' message of the film is that one has to think for oneself in order to discriminate between the various claims to authority and leadership to which one is subjected – indeed, Brian does this very thing and, ironically, finds himself hoisted to a position of authority and leadership for doing so. The irony here is precise: such is the human need for belief in something that the truly original individual, whether religious or secular, cannot but become an object of veneration and therefore be hoisted by the group that venerates him or her onto a pedestal, at which point their 'originality' is no longer in their control but is in the hands of those who control and regulate 'the group'.

Satirically, perhaps the least successful scene is the crucifixion of Brian. Many Christians who objected to the film cited this concluding scene, with its comic and irreverent treatment of crucifixion, as proof that the film was indeed blasphemous. For them it mocked Jesus' suffering on the cross, and therefore a core tenet of Christian belief: that by suffering and dying, Jesus redeems humanity in the eyes of God. Instead of tragic seriousness, there is comic irreverence, and trivialization; the climax of Jesus' passion is reduced to parody, and the horror of death by crucifixion is belied by flippancy, 'See, not so bad when you're up.' In response, Terry Jones suggested that 'Any religion that makes a form of torture into an icon that they worship seems to me a pretty sick sort of religion.'[54] Although this demonstrates a secular disdain for, total incomprehension of, and insensitivity towards the significance of the crucifixion in Christian theology, he could more legitimately have pointed out that there are several dynamics in the scene that work towards a different interpretation. Firstly, and most obviously, this is a crucifixion of Brian not Jesus. Insofar as crucifixion was a regular method of execution, it is entirely plausible to claim that the crucifixion scene has nothing to do with Jesus (none of the narrative details of Jesus' crucifixion, such as the spearing of his side, are referenced, for instance). Secondly, the argument that the scene is nevertheless blasphemous would involve the logical supposition that *any* comic or irreverent treatment of *any* crucifixion necessarily mocks the Crucifixion of Christ, thereby evacuating crucifixion of its purchase as a historical phenomenon as opposed to theological symbol. Moreover, it advances a particular theological interpretation. The trope of Christ's suffering and death on the cross is, of course, fundamental to the Christian narrative. But is the particular mode of death intrinsic or incidental to the wider theological point? In other words, would the significance of Christ's passion be reduced if he had suffered and died in another fashion? Is the crucifixion per se central to Christian belief, or has the cross become the symbol of Christianity because that was, in fact, the manner in which Jesus was executed? If the former, then the charge of blasphemy may have some plausibility even though it would still be arguable; if not, then the charge of blasphemy simply misses the point. However, crucifixion has not been used as a common form of execution for nearly two millennia and in the absence of its everyday continuity, it has therefore become inextricably linked to Jesus Christ among both Christians and non-Christians. It is not possible to portray crucifixion, any crucifixion, without some subconscious reference to Jesus.[55] So the scene is, at the very least, ambiguous, which is why I do not feel the readings of the film as blasphemous were inappropriate in terms of an ethics of propriety; but, given the care and precision of the rest of the film, I am prepared to give the Pythons the benefit of the doubt.

Satire and forensic sensitivity: *Four Lions*

If *Life of Brian* was a careful and effective satire that nevertheless precipitated great controversy, *Four Lions* is one that was not as controversial as it might have been, precisely because of the same care it takes to mark out its targets with forensic sensitivity. It is a satiric treatment of contemporary global *jihadism*, that form of Islamist terrorism associated with Osama bin Laden and al-Qaeda. Conceived during the first decade of the twenty-first century, during the 'war on terror', its ostensible aim is to deflate the pretensions of those who see themselves engaged in a cosmic war, fighting in the name of Islam the forces of evil that, for them, are embodied in the 'bullshit, consumerist, godless, Paki-bashing, Gordon Ramsay "Taste the Difference" speciality cheddar, torture-endorsing, massacre-sponsoring, "Look at me dancing pissed with me knob out" Sky1 Uncovered, "Who gives a fuck about dead Afghanis?" Disneyland.' Part of its achievement lies in the way it demonstrates, through comic exaggeration and abstruse twists in logic, how the discourse of *jihadist* terrorism is in fact an empty discourse, devoid of reference and content and therefore, ultimately, a discourse that signifies nothing; it constantly over-inflates and hyper-extends, and then turns back on itself and collapses into incoherence and contradiction. The film, quite correctly, suggests that it is entirely valid *not* to treat this discourse at face value but to understand it as an elaborate, and entirely unselfconscious, exercise in absurdity. Its principal target is the *jihadi* terrorist cell, represented as comically inept buffoons, whose attraction to the cause and articulation of its discourse is purely performative insofar as it enables them to imagine themselves as part of a larger, more significant phenomenon that transcends the quotidian insignificance of their lives in a dreary northern English town, and also enables them to position themselves as morally superior not just to the *kuffars* but also their fellow Muslims. It is here that the greatest achievement of the film lies, one that accounts for the great enthusiasm with which it was received amongst young British Muslims. For it is the care and precision the film undertakes in not only distinguishing the *jihadi* terrorists from 'ordinary' Muslims, but also their discourse from other Islamic discourses that enabled such young men and women, beleaguered by the ubiquitous and surreptitious association of their faith and themselves with the terrorists, to both laugh at the terrorists and laugh along with a film that took great pains to ensure that they were *not* implicated in its satire.

One scene in particular embodies the film's scrupulous attention to the proper discriminations necessary in order to ensure that there is no collateral damage arising from the satire. It is a scene that builds on previous scenes that will have already disturbed the audience's expectations about Islamist *jihadi* terrorists: the leader of the group, Omar, is early on shown reviewing the group's farcical attempts at producing martyrdom videos along with his wife and son, and they all talk matter-of-factly about suicide bombing and violent *jihad*, including the young boy; later, we see Omar narrating a bedtime story to his boy in which characters from the Disney film *The Lion King* are transposed onto a narrative that tries to explain away Omar's abject failure at the training camp, and thereby assuage his shame. These episodes clearly signal and parody the close-knit 'modern' family familiar to sit-coms and soap operas, a family so familiar with American popular culture that it is the medium of choice through which it articulates anti-American *jihad*. If this ironic contradiction is destabilizing for an audience that is primed to see Muslims, particularly Muslim terrorists, as 'other' to the West, the pivotal scene to which I now turn further complicates and unsettles the prevailing discourse of a monolithic Islam. Omar is visited by his brother, Ahmed, a clearly devout Muslim who wears a skullcap and *shalwar-kameez*. The audience sees Ahmed refuse to enter the sitting room because he believes it is *haram* (forbidden) in Islam for him to share the same room as Omar's wife because she is a woman. Omar and his wife, Sofia, mock Ahmed's conservatism and misogyny, during an exchange in which it is revealed that Ahmed locks his wife in a small cupboard (formerly a toilet), and Omar sarcastically exclaims to Sofia 'Obey me wife!' By speaking sarcastically back to him in a broad Yorkshire accent, Sofia further confirms Ahmed's view that his brother's wife is 'out of control'. At the same time, Ahmed makes it clear that terrorist violence has no legitimacy in Islam, and the scene therefore carefully distinguishes *jihadi* Muslims not only from 'moderate' or 'progressive' modernists but also from conservative, often highly reactionary and misogynistic Muslims too, thereby drawing out, forensically, the multidimensionality of the ideological field within which attempts to capture the meaning of Islam are situated, a field that does not map easily onto the 'modern' equals 'progressive', conservative equals 'extremist' dyad, a point underscored by the scene in which the police ironically raid and arrest Ahmed's 'salafi' group, which abjures violence. Indeed, the effectivity of this scene rests on the careful editing of the sequence that leads the audience to expect a raid on Omar's group; the subsequent revelation that the police misrecognize conservatism for 'extremism' demonstrates how the security apparatus – and the wider public perception that informs it – *cannot* properly distinguish between 'good' and 'bad' Muslims because the suppositions on which such distinctions are based are themselves flawed.

Four Lions also tackles a much bigger, more powerful myth, one that is deployed as the rhetorical capstone of the security state during the war on terror: the metaphysicalization of terrorism as 'evil' rather than a form of politics. Evil is not a laughing matter; it is not hospitable to comedy. In representing terrorists as comically absurd, then, *Four Lions* punctures the discourse that obscures terrorism within a metaphysical aura, and it properly reduces terrorism to its human, and indeed secular, scale. In so doing it renders absurd the very phrase 'war on terror', the illogicality of which serves as a perfect vehicle for the metaphysical approach to terrorism. For terror is a mental state, not a political modality or even an adversary deploying that modality; to wage war on terror would seem to be the very epitome of utopianism, a moral endeavour as opposed to a political one. And in presenting to us the human scale of terrorism in the form of characters whose buffoonery does not so much provoke terror but rather its very opposite, *Four Lions* undermines the spurious rhetoric of the 'war on terror' through a judicious and entirely appropriate use of bathos.

Satire as an ethic of care

In *You Can't Read This Book*, Nick Cohen asks what he perceives to be a merely rhetorical question: if the target of your satire is a religious group how can you avoid satirizing its beliefs?[56] First of all, you have to take the question seriously and not assume, a priori, that it is not possible. Both *Life of Brian* and *Four Lions* demonstrate how this can be done, the former by prising apart the acts of believers, whether religious or secular, from the idea of belief itself. Some believers behave ridiculously and deserve ridicule, others do not. Moreover, it clearly satirizes a *process* as much as an 'object' (such as a 'belief' or a particular group). For its part, *Four Lions* scrupulously defines the particular group it wants to target and shows how its adoption of a religious discourse is merely a rhetorical performance; it also shows how the group's beliefs are contested and contradicted by other members of the religious group, thereby demonstrating that the object of the satire is not a metonym for the religion as whole. And what of the converse question? If you want to satirize a particular belief, how can you avoid offending its believers? The weight of this question is somewhat different because a belief might lead those who hold it to behave in a way you find ridiculous – in which case, the proper object of satire are those persons who behave ridiculously. The distinction between believers and their beliefs does not therefore arise. But what makes a *belief* ridiculous and appropriate for satire, and why should one ridicule a *belief* simply because it happens to be one that you do not hold? Here, one must acknowledge a distinction between beliefs relating to empirically verifiable (or refutable) ideas (such as a twenty-first century westerner believing in the flatness of the earth as an empirical fact) and those relating to myth and metaphysics. The boundary between them is, admittedly, porous; where might we place 'creationism', for example? This returns us to the question of *manner* because a satiric treatment of the idea of a flat earth or creationism could rest on their discursive displacement, that is, on their camouflaging of a metaphysical belief using the idiom of science. This would align it with the traditional satiric attack on hypocrisy, on the discrepancy between surface appearance and hidden reality. But is a *satire* of an unambiguously metaphysical concept such as the holy Trinity, for example, warranted? Does the idea that Jesus died to redeem humanity, or that God is one and indivisible as opposed to multiple or even non-existent deserve *ridicule*? One might find such beliefs incomprehensible, logically inconsistent or incoherent – absurd, even – but it is not at all clear that one should therefore ridicule someone for holding them. Insofar as these beliefs explicitly invoke faith rather than logic or reason, to consider them ridiculous *in themselves* would simply be to assert that variance from one's own assumed norm (rationalism, for example) is the problem; one would be ridiculing difference itself, which is not a position that liberals ought to adopt – but many do. In such instances, it may well be the case therefore that satire is not an appropriate form for the critique of beliefs as opposed to persons or groups.

Such questions prompt us to think fundamentally about what it is we are in fact trying to do when we undertake a critique or a satire of someone or something, and that in turn involves a certain *care* over what we are doing. Carelessness is the problem for it is symptomatic of a lack of scrupulous attention to the true object of one's attention. In cultural controversies such as those examined in this book, carelessness is not limited to those who produced the offending texts, but is also often characteristic of those who received them and took offence. The ethical dynamics of controversy is not a one-way street because the ethics of propriety is dialogic, rooted in mutual and shared responsibility of each to the other, addresser to addressee and vice versa. And carelessness is not just problematic ethically, but also aesthetically. Many contemporary artists and intellectuals know that with respect to aesthetics 'less is more', that restraint is a good thing, but they seem incapable of taking this insight beyond the text and translating it into the field of social relations, where any kind of restraint is seen as necessarily inimical to artistic freedom. Throughout this book I have argued, however, that certain kinds of restraint may in fact *enable* artistic freedom by *enhancing* the quality of aesthetic engagements with 'the world'. This is the pay-off for assuming the kind of responsibility demanded by an ethics of aesthetic propriety.

The kind of moral restraint that is at the core of this book's arguments about freedom of speech is, fundamentally, an ethic of care but, unfortunately, the discourse on freedom of speech among many contemporary artists and intellectuals is an absolutist one that has been characterized by

Glen Newey as follows: 'The idea that the only bad thing that can come of speech is its suppression sits best with a view of language-use as *blurting*. Talk matters mainly, on this view, not to get something across, but to get it out – a sort of psychic expectoration'.[57] Such a view of speech is particularly hostile to an ethic of care and the idea of 'social responsibility', and is in turn hospitable to carelessness, which in turn means that speech, in fact, matters *less* not more – it is 'only words'. Not all contemporary artists have succumbed to this view, however, but it is significant that they are often located in social contexts where the power of words and their consequences are recognized, either because they labour or have laboured within view of an authoritarian state that recognizes such power and does its very best to curb it through censorship, or in tenebrous and fragile social formations where the symbolic potency of language is often brutally manifest. Here is Vaclav Havel writing in support of Salman Rushdie and against the *fatwa*:

> alongside Rushdie's words we have Khomeini's. Words that electrify society with their freedom and truthfulness are matched by words that mesmerize, deceive, inflame, madden, beguile, words that are harmful – lethal, even. The word as arrow . . . words are a mysterious, ambiguous, ambivalent phenomenon. They are capable of being rays of light in a realm of darkness . . . They are equally capable of being lethal arrows. Worst of all, at times they can be the one and the other. And even both at once! . . . words are capable of betraying us – unless we are constantly circumspect about their use.[58]

In its emphasis on deliberation and care, Havel's support for Rushdie is qualified; its circumspection constitutes both a retort to Rushdie's own hyperbole and a warning against the sly complacency that sees language as neutral and transparent.

And if, in response to Khuswant Singh's warning to Penguin India that *The Satanic Verses* would be likely to cause trouble, Rushdie once believed that 'it would be absurd to think that a book could cause riots' (which underscores the point that those who appear to be most fervent in their support for freedom of speech paradoxically most underestimate the power of language) then another Indian, reflecting on the genesis of his novel, *The Shadow Lines*, was under no such illusions. In his essay 'The Ghosts of Mrs. Gandhi,' having elaborated in fine detail his experience of the day the then Prime Minister of India, Indira Gandhi, was assassinated, and the subsequent politically orchestrated civil disorder that led to the murder of several thousand Sikhs, Amitav Ghosh reflects on the challenge facing a writer who wishes to write about such events 'without recreating them as a panorama of violence', and reducing them to an 'aesthetic phenomenon'. Without the perspective and distance that would enable him to translate his direct experience of the riots into something that does not merely describe the violence, but finds a 'form – or a style or a voice or a plot – that could accommodate both violence *and* the civilized willed response to it', and thereby recuperate 'the meaning of such events and their effects on the individuals who live through them', the idea of writing fiction 'seemed obscene and futile' compared to the urgency of collecting and collating the facts and the testimonies of the victims.[59] Ghosh goes on to suggest that:

> The riots were generated by a cycle of violence, involving the terrorists in the Punjab, on the one hand, and Indian government on the other. To write carelessly, in such a way as to appear to endorse terrorism or repression, can add easily to the problem: and in such incendiary circumstances, words cost lives, and it is only appropriate that those who deal in words should pay scrupulous attention to what they say. It is only appropriate that they should find themselves inhibited.[60]

Ghosh's argument here acquires significance in the context of his quotation of the Bosnian writer Dzevad Karahasan, writing during the Balkan conflict, which 'makes a startling connection between modern literary aestheticism and the contemporary world's indifference to violence: "The decision to perceive literally everything as an aesthetic phenomenon – completely side-stepping questions about goodness and truth – is an artistic decision. That decision started in the realm of art, and went on to become characteristic of the contemporary world."'[61] Whether or not one agrees with Karahasan (I find the statement problematically idealist), there are nevertheless parallels here with the contemporary conceptualization of artistic responsibility that I have explored above. Insofar as, on the one hand, art is seen as a discourse that speaks 'truth to power' and is therefore oppositional and political, and yet, on the other, the artist claims responsibility only to the demands of the Imagination, such a view involves an aestheticization of politics as opposed to the politicization of aesthetics. And the result is indeed indifference – indifference to the effects of one's words on others.

Both Havel and Ghosh articulate a sense of responsibility that is not grounded in some transcendant Moral Law, such as deontological ethics, or in some abstract higher Good, as in consequentialist ethics; and they both acknowledge that their sense of responsibility is predicated not on an autochtonous individual, but on the irreducible *relationality* of human experience. Insofar as the moral value of expression emerges from the relative autonomy to speak freely, the responsibilities that accompany that freedom in turn rest on the relationships that are both established and represented in discourse. These are endowed on *all* parties to the discursive encounter through an infinitely recursive mutuality. Following the feminist theorists who have articulated most forcefully an ethics of care rooted in the primacy of social relationships, we could say that the purpose of freedom of speech is to develop mutual understanding and through that to create, nurture, sustain and, when necessary, recast and revise the irrevocable ties that bind us all to each other.[62] It is a difficult task, to be sure, but why should we expect it to be otherwise?

Notes and References

Introduction

1. Simon Lee, *The Cost of Free Speech* (London: Faber, 1990) p. ix.
2. The wonderfully judicious and precise phrase 'adequate to the predicament' is one of the gifts bequeathed by the late Seamus Heaney, in his collection *North*.
3. An example is Peter Jones's otherwise brilliant essay 'Respecting Beliefs and Rebuking Rushdie', *British Journal of Political Science*, 20:4, 1990, pp. 415–37.
4. Andrew Gibson, *Postmodernity, Ethics and the Novel: From Leavis to Levinas* (London: Routledge, 1999).
5. The phrase 'civilization-speak' is Heiko Henkel's. See his essay, '"The journalists of *Jyllands-Posten* are a bunch of reactionary provocateurs": The Danish Cartoon Controversy and the Self-Image of Europe,' *Radical Philosophy*, 137, 2006, p. 2.
6. Glen Newey, 'Unlike a Scotch Egg', *London Review of Books*, 35:23, 5 December 2013, p. 22.

1   From Blasphemy to Offensiveness: the Politics of Controversy

1. In using the term 'the Rushdie affair' as a shorthand for the controversy over *The Satanic Verses*, I concur with Paul Weller who notes the Muslim objections to it on the grounds that it seemingly trivialized what was, in fact, an event of momentous significance. It does retain, however, a certain currency even now and was the dominant marker at the time, used in many documents and sources that I will have occasion to quote. I will therefore use it alongside other descriptive terminology such as '*The Satanic Verses* controversy'.
2. Paul Weller, *A Mirror for Our Times: 'The Rushdie Affair' and the Future of Multiculturalism* (London: Continuum, 2009).
3. Rana Kabbani, *Letter to Christendom* (London: Virago, 1989) p. ix.
4. Ibid. pp. 11–12.
5. Salman Rushdie, 'In Good Faith' in *Imaginary Homelands: Essays and Criticism 1981–1991* (London: Granta, 1991) p. 406. 'The Courter' can be found in Salman Rushdie *East, West* (London: Jonathan Cape, 1994).
6. Norman Daniel, *Islam and the West: The Making of an Image* (Oxford: Oneworld, 2009 [1960]); R.W. Southern, *Western Views of Islam in the Middle Ages* (Cambridge, MA: Harvard University Press, 1962); Richard Fletcher, *The Cross and the Crescent: Christianity and Islam from Muhammad to the Reformation* (London: Allen Lane, 2003).
7. Samuel P. Huntington, 'The Clash of Civilizations?' *Foreign Affairs*, 72.3, 1993, pp. 22–49; *The Clash of Civilizations and the Remaking of the World Order* (New York: Simon and Schuster, 1996).
8. The first attack on the World Trade Centre in New York took place in February 1993, some months prior to the publication of Huntington's article in the autumn of that year. It may have been grist to its mill but it is unlikely that it prompted its composition.

9. Bernard Lewis, 'The Roots of Muslim Rage', *The Atlantic Monthly*, 266, September 1990, p. 60; *Time*, 15 June 1992, pp. 24–8.

10. See Inayat Bunglawala's articles on *Guardian's* 'Comment is free' website: 'I used to be a book-burner', 19 June 2007, http://www.guardian.co.uk/commentisfree/2007/jun/19/notsurprisinglytheawarding; and 'Words can never hurt us', 26 September 2008, http://www.guardian.co.uk/commentisfree/2008/sep/26/islam.religion

11. Andrew Anthony, 'How one book ignited a culture war', *Observer*, 11 January 2009. http://www.guardian.co.uk/books/2009/jan/11/salman-rushdie-satanic-verses

12. Lisa Appignanesi, 'No surrender', *Guardian: Comment is Free*, 14 February 2009. http://www.guardian.co.uk/commentisfree/2009/feb/12/religion-islam; Kenan Malik, *From Fatwa to Jihad: The Rushdie Affair and its Legacy* (London: Atlantic Books, 2009); Nick Cohen, *You Can't Read This Book: Censorship in an Age of Freedom* (London: Fourth Estate, 2012).

13. Salman Rushdie, 'In Good Faith' p. 396; 'Is Nothing Sacred?' in *Imaginary Homelands*, p. 429; p. 416.

14. Salman Rushdie, *Step Across this Line: Collected Non-Fiction 1992–2002* (London: Vintage, 2003). On the liberal 'backlash' against Islam, articulated through a dissatisfaction with multiculturalism, see Kenan Malik, *From Fatwa to Jihad*; Andrew Anthony, *The Fallout: How a Guilty Liberal Lost his Innocence* (London: Vintage, 2008); on the 'new atheism' see Arthur Bradley and Andrew Tate, *The New Atheist Novel: Fiction, Philosophy and Polemic after 9/11* (London: Continuum, 2010).

15. 'David Cameron tells Muslim Britain: stop tolerating extremists', *Guardian*, 5 February 2011. See also Anshuman A. Mondal, 'The Coalition Government and Muslims: Same Old, Same Old' http://anshumanmondal.wordpress.com/2011/02/05/the-coalition-government-and-muslims-same-old-same-old/

16. Appignanesi, 'No Surrender'. See also Jo Glanville, 'Respect for religion now makes censorship the norm' *Guardian*, 30 September 2008. http://www.guardian.co.uk/commentisfree/2008/sep/30/pressandpublishing.religion

17. Anthony, 'How one book ignited a culture war'.

18. Brian Winston, *A Right to Offend* (London: Bloomsbury Academic, 2012).

19. Alana Lentin and Gavan Titwell, *The Crises of Multiculturalism: Racism in a Neoliberal Age* (London: Zed Books, 2011); see also Arun Kundnani, *The End of Tolerance: Racism in 21st Century Britain* (London: Pluto Press, 2009).

20. Cohen, *You Can't Read This Book*, Kindle edition, ch. 1, p. 5 [loc 285].

21. This, in a nutshell, is Kenan Malik's argument in *From Fatwa to Jihad*, and rehearsed by Nick Cohen in *You Can't Read This Book*.

22. The phrase 'unthinking sheep' is from Ed Husain's *The Islamist* (London: Penguin, 2007) and he uses it in precisely this way. See Anshuman A. Mondal, 'Bad Faith: The Construction of Muslim Extremism' in Rehana Ahmed, Peter Morey and Amina Yaqin, eds. *Culture, Diaspora and Modernity in Muslim Writing* (London: Routledge, 2012) p. 44.

23. In addition to Malik, Lisa Appignanesi, Andrew Anthony and Aziz al-Azmeh have all advanced similar arguments. Al-Azmeh's position is more nuanced, but in focusing entirely on Islamist organizations' role in the protests he gives the impression that this was the only significant dimension to the Muslim protests. His article is anthologized in Lisa Appignanesis and Sara Maitland, eds. *The Rushdie File* (London: ICA, 1989) pp. 69–74.

24. Malise Ruthven, *A Satanic Affair* (London: The Hogarth Press, 1990) p. 73.

25. Cited in Daniel Allington, 'How to Do Things with Literature: Blasphemous Speech Acts, Satanic Intentions, and the Uncommunicativeness of Verses', *Poetics Today*, 29.3, 2008, p. 507.

26. Talal Asad notes that the Arabic term used during the controversy over the Danish cartoons was *isa'ah*, which refers to 'insult, harm, and offense' rather than *tajdif*, which is the word that is usually translated as 'blasphemy'. 'Free Speech, Blasphemy and Secular Criticism' in Talal Asad, Wendy Brown, Judith Butler, Saba Mahmood, *Is Critique Secular? Blasphemy, Injury and Free Speech* (Berkeley: Townsend Center for the Humanities, 2009) p. 38.

27. On *Behzti* see Weller, *A Mirror for Our Times*, pp. 155–6; and Sarita Malik, 'Censorship – Life after *Behzti*,' *ArtsProfessional*, 4 July 2005, http://www.artsprofessional. co.uk/magazine/article/censorship-life-after-behzti

28. Weller, *A Mirror for Our Times*, p. 157.

29. Malik, *From Fatwa to Jihad*, p. 156.

30. Cited in ibid. p. 157.

31. Ibid. p. 158.

32. Ibid. p. 161.

33. Ibid. p. 183.

34. Malik, *From Fatwa to Jihad*, p. 13.

35. Stanley Fish, 'Jerry Falwell's Mother, or, What's the Harm?' in *There's No Such Thing As Free Speech And It's A Good Thing Too* (New York: Oxford University Press, 1994) p. 126.

36. Ally Fogg, 'Political correctness gone bad' *Guardian: Comment is Free*, 19 July 2008. http://www.guardian.co.uk/commentisfree/2008/jul/19/wordsandlanguage

37. J.L. Austin, *How To Do Things With Words* (Oxford: Clarendon Press, 1962) p. 3.

38. Saba Mahmood has argued that Sausurre's model of language, which severs the signifier and signified is part of a 'semiotic ideology' that is rooted in Protestantism and is not wholly adequate for analysing the offensiveness of visual images, in particular, such as the Danish cartoons. I shall return to Mahmood's argument in more detail in Chapter 6. 'Religious Reason and Secular Affect: An Incommensurable Divide?' in *Is Critique Secular?* p. 72.

39. Austin, *How To Do Things With Words*, p. 52.

40. Ibid. pp. 4–11.

41. Judith Butler, *Excitable Speech: A Politics of the Performative* (London: Routledge, 1997) p. 18.

42. Ibid. pp. 11–12.

43. Ibid. p. 15.

44. Broadly speaking, Austin suggests a distinction between 'locutionary', 'illocutionary' and 'perlocutionary' speech acts. The first is involved when we say *anything* – the act *of* speaking itself; the second performs an action *in* the act of speaking; the last refers to the consequential effects that speech acts might have in the world, for example, on other people.

45. Cited in Bethan Benwell, James Procter and Gemma Robinson, 'Not Reading *Brick Lane*', *New Formations*, 73.2, 2011, p. 104.

46. This reading complements Benwell et al.'s interpretation of Newbie's post: 's/he is isolating evidence which supports or even came to define a community consensus over the novel's depiction of a particular ethnic group' (p. 105).

47. Butler, *Excitable Speech*, p. 5, p. 27, p. 34, pp. 36–7.

48. Judith Butler's elaboration of identity as performative contests this central liberal notion that at some level there is a singular 'true' identity. See *Gender Trouble: Feminism and the Subversion of Identity* (London: Routledge, 1992). Similarly, Homi Bhabha's concept of 'mimicry' involves the 'prodigious and strategic production of conflictual "identity effects" in the play of a power that is elusive because it hides no essence, no "itself".' 'Of Mimicry and Man: The

Ambivalence of Colonial Discourse', *October*, 28, 1984, p. 131 (reprinted in *The Location of Culture* (London: Routledge, 1995)).

49. On the purchase of the idea of substitutability in liberal discourse, see Chapter 2. See also Talal Asad, 'Free Speech, Blasphemy and Secular Criticism' in Talal Asad, Wendy Brown, Judith Butler, Saba Mahmood, *Is Critique Secular? Blasphemy, Injury and Free Speech* (Berkeley: Townsend Centre for the Humanities, 2009) pp. 24–5.

50. Cohen, *You Can't Read This Book*, 'Rules for Censors (1), p. 26 [loc 595]. David Aaronovitch, cited in 'The Right to Offend? Medhi Hasan denies the 'Absolute Right' To Freedom of Speech' *Huffington Post UK*, http://www.huffingtonpost.co.uk/2012/10/11/the-right-to-offend-mehdi-hasan-freedom-of-speech_n_1959512.html

51. 'The language that counters the injuries of speech, however, must repeat those injuries without precisely re-enacting them.' *Excitable Speech*, p. 40.

52. Butler, *Excitable Speech*, p. 39; p. 14.

53. Ibid., p. 37.

54. Abigail Levin, *The Cost of Free Speech: Pornography, Hate Speech, and their Challenge to Liberalism* (Basingstoke: Palgrave Macmillan, 2010) p. 148.

55. Butler, *Gender Trouble*, p. 190.

56. A similar logic of euphemism seems to be at work in arguments against multiculturalism, political correctness and respect, which enables some groups of people to be positioned as inferior without appearing to do so.

57. Rushdie, p. 422.

58. See Derek Attridge, 'The Impossibility of Ethics: On Mount Moriah' in *Reading and Responsibility: Deconstruction's Traces* (Edinburgh: Edinburgh University Press, 2011) p. 72: '[Ethical] Obligation happens to me most authentically when I am confronted not by the all-powerful, as Abraham was, but by the powerless.'

2   What is Freedom of Speech For?

1. These are articles 18 and 12, respectively, of the Universal Declaration of Human Rights. The latter states that 'No one shall be subjected to arbitrary interference with his privacy, family, home or correspondence, nor to attacks upon his honour and reputation. Everyone has the right to the protection of the law against such interference or attacks.' Although related, in the first instance, to libel and personal defamation laws, it is possible to argue that communal libel or group defamation laws can be derived from it. See Tariq Modood, *Multicultural Politics: Racism, Ethnicity and Muslims in Britain* (Edinburgh: Edinburgh University Press, 2005); Bhikhu Parekh, *Rethinking Multiculturalism: Cultural Diversity and Political Theory* 2nd edn. (Basingstoke: Palgrave Macmillan, 2006); and Simon Lee, *The Cost of Free Speech* (London: Faber, 1990), all of whom advance sensible arguments about this and would not endorse the 'right to be free from offence' *tout court* as a permissible right.

2. Nick Cohen, *You Can't Read This Book: Censorship in an Age of Freedom* (London: Fourth Estate, 2012) Kindle edition (all citations will be to this edition); Brian Winston, *A Right to Offend: Free Expression in the Twenty-First Century* (London: Bloomsbury Academic, 2012).

3. Cohen, *You Can't Read This Book*, ch. 3, p. 45 [loc 854].

4. Ibid. pp. 72–4 [loc 1261].

5. John Stuart Mill, *On Liberty* (London: Walter Scott Publishing Co., n.d [1859]) Kindle edition, ch. 2, [loc 430] (my emphasis).

6. Lisa Appignanesi, 'No surrender', *Guardian: Comment Is Free* 14 February 2009, www.guardian.co.uk/commentisfree/2009/feb/12/religion-islam.

7. Cohen, *You Can't Read This Book*, ch. 4, p. 111 [Loc 1843]. This, despite the fact that the absolutist position on freedom of speech enjoys overwhelming popular support in the United Kingdom, and in western societies more generally. A poll conducted for *Time Out* magazine in London in March 2009, during a controversy over the decision to withhold a visa to the controversial Islamophobic Dutch politician Geert Wilders, found that 73 per cent opposed the decision because 'free speech is vital' and only 23 per cent supported it on the grounds that 'spreading hate should not be tolerated'. Being an online poll inviting readers to vote, all the usual caveats apply about a self-selecting constituency, and multiple voting. True, readers of *Time Out* represent a very specific, metropolitan and liberal readership so we should not draw hard and fast conclusions. But it should also be pointed out that it is precisely this demographic that enjoys the greatest social, cultural and economic capital and thus constitutes a portion of the most powerful constituency of opinion in contemporary Britain. The wording of this particular poll is interesting because it explicitly links free speech with toleration of hate – speech – a position far more absolutist than the current legal provisions allow.

8. Ibid. p. 298 [loc 4568].

9. Winston, *A Right to Offend*, p. 255.

10. Ibid. p. 15.

11. See Paul Weller, *A Mirror for Our Times: 'The Rushdie Affair' and the Future of Multiculturalism* (London: Continuum, 2009) p. 61: 'Rafsanjani told the Majlis or Iranian Parliament that the Ayotollah Khomeini had delivered his fatwa not just because of the book itself but also because it was a focus of what he saw was a plot against Islam.'

12. Cohen, *You Can't Read This Book*, 'How to Fight Back', p. 228 [loc 3555]. Salman Rushdie, *Imaginary Homelands: Essays and Criticism 1981–1991* (London: Granta, 1991) p. 439.

13. Cohen, *You Can't Read This Book*, ch. 2, p. 29 [loc 621]; ch. 3, p. 111 [loc 1842] (my emphases).

14. Alan Haworth, *Free Speech* (London: Routledge, 1998) p. 27.

15. Ibid. p. 32.

16. Lee, *The Cost of Free Speech*, p. 34.

17. Cohen, *You Can't Read This Book*, 'How to Fight Back', p. 249 [loc 3864].

18. Lee, *The Cost of Free Speech*, p. 56.

19. See Bernard Williams, 'Which slopes are slippery?', *Making Sense of Humanity and Other Philosophical Papers 1982–1993* (Cambridge: Cambridge University Press, 1995) pp. 213–23.

20. Cohen, 'How to Fight Back' p. 228 [loc 3557].

21. Kenan Malik, *From Fatwa to Jihad: The Rushdie Affair and its Legacy* (London: Atlantic Books, 2009) p. 155.

22. George Orwell, *Nineteen Eighty-Four* (London: Penguin, 1989) p. 84.

23. Abigail Levin, *The Cost of Free Speech: Pornography, Hate Speech, and their Challenge to Liberalism* (Basingstoke: Palgrave Macmillan, 2010), p. 51.

24. Ibid. pp. 51–2. Levin also notes, however, that in fact liberty of thought must be founded on a more fundamental right, the right to security, since without security the benefits of freedom of thought cannot be actualized – we would spend our time worrying about our basic security rather than envisioning alternative conceptions of the 'good life'.

25. Ibid. p. 52.
26. Haworth, *Free Speech* p. 27.
27. Ibid. p. 25.
28. Ibid. p. 27.
29. Susan Mendus, 'The Tigers of Wrath and the Horses of Instruction' in *Free Speech: Report of a Seminar* (London: Commission for Racial Equality, 1990) p. 7.
30. Kent Greenfield, *The Myth of Choice* (New Haven and London: Yale University Press, 2011) Kindle edition, ch. 3.8 [loc 1015]; 3.5 [loc 904]; 6.5 [loc 2027].
31. Stanley Fish, *There's No Such Thing as Free Speech, and it's a Good Thing Too* (New York: OUP, 1994) p. 16.
32. Ibid.
33. Levin, *The Cost of Free Speech*, p. 47.
34. Catherine MacKinnon, cited in Levin, *The Cost of Free Speech*, p. 69 (original emphasis).
35. Ibid. p. 79.
36. Two examples: Malik, *From Fatwa to Jihad*, p. 172; p. 189. Cohen, 'How to Fight Back', p. 229 [loc 3566].
37. Fish, *There's No Such Thing as Free Speech*, p. 109.
38. Ibid. Actually, even the American courts recognize this. Citing the decision of the Seventh Circuit Court in the case of *American Booksellers Association, Inc* v. *Hudnut*, Fish notes that the court acknowledges that 'under present law "racial bigotry, anti-semitism," and other verbal assaults that "influence the culture" are protected even though "none is . . . answerable by more speech"' (Fish 122).
39. Cited in Levin, *The Cost of Free Speech*, p. 66.
40. Charles R. Lawrence III, ibid.
41. Fish, *There's No Such Thing as Free Speech*, p. 125. Idealism is so ubiquitous in liberal discourse that it would be futile to illustrate the point with reference to specific examples. My critique in this chapter and the next will return to this point repeatedly. It is, from my point of view, the key flaw in orthodox liberal thought.
42. See the discussion of Kenan Malik's notion of 'responsibility' in Chapter 3 below.
43. Frederick Schauer, cited in Levin, *The Cost of Free Speech*, p. 150.
44. Judith Butler, 'Ruled Out; Vocabularies of the Censor' in Robert Post, ed. *Censorship and Silencing: Practices of Cultural Regulation* (Los Angeles: Getty Research Institute, 1998) p. 249.
45. Levin, *The Cost of Free Speech*, p. 151.
46. Haworth, *Free Speech*, p. 7.
47. Ibid. p. 157: 'one function of a contract is to create a morally binding expectation where none had existed before'.
48. Winston, *A Right to Offend*, p. 256.
49. Haworth, *Free Speech*, p. 55.
50. Ibid. p. 83.
51. Ibid. p. 170.
52. Ibid. p. 164.
53. Ibid. p. 162.
54. Ibid. p. 170.
55. Ibid.
56. The phrase is Hannah Pitkin's, cited in ibid. p. 163.
57. Cohen, *You Can't Read This Book*, 'How to fight Back', p. 297 [loc 4556].
58. Haworth, *Free Speech*, p. 176.
59. Cohen, *You Can't Read This Book*, 'Rules for Censors(4)', p. 126 [loc 2065].

60. Note that this in effect makes freedom of religious belief equivalent to freedom of speech, a variety of the answer injurious speech with more speech.
61. Ibid. p. 204.
62. Ibid. p. 206.
63. Talal Asad, 'Freedom of Speech and Religious Limitations' in Crag Calhoun, Mark Jeurgensmeyer and Jonathan VanAntwerpen, eds. *Rethinking Secularism* (Oxford: Oxford University Press, 2012) Kindle edition, ch. 13 [loc 6813]. Asad suggests that this may be one reason why freedom of thought and conscience and the freedom to express oneself, as well as the idea of tolerance to which they are related, have acquired sacred value in the liberal tradition.
64. Ibid. [loc 6826].
65. This insistence on physical harm (Cohen explicitly rules out 'mental distress') would rule out psychological harms such as Post-traumatic Stress Disorder, for example. It is curious that the philosophical idealism of liberals like Cohen and Malik should co-exist with the denial of psychological harm as a valid form of injury. Nevertheless, the evidence suggests that hate speech does result in forms of physical as well as mental injury. Kevin Saunders cites critical race theorists Richard Delgado and Jean Stefancic, who have documented the following harms amongst victims of hate-speech: 'The immediate, short-term harms of hate speech include rapid breathing, headaches, raised blood pressure, dizziness, rapid pulse rate, drug-taking, risk-taking behavior, and even suicide.' This last claim has been supported by research conducted by psychologists Brian Miller and Joshua Smyth, who conclude their article 'Hate Speech Predicts Death' as follows: '[e]thnic immigrant groups subjected to more negative ethnophaulisms, or hate speech, were more likely to commit suicide. This pattern was obtained even after taking into account the previously established association between immigrant suicide rates and the suicide rates for those ethnic immigrant groups in their countries of origin.' Kevin W. Saunders, *Degradation: What the History of Obscenity Tells Us about Hate Speech* (New York: New York University Press, 2011), p. 2.
66. Fish, *There's No Such Thing as Free Speech*, p. 104. I will take this up in my discussion of Kenan Malik's notion of 'responsibility' in Chapter 3.
67. Ibid. p. 106 (my emphasis).
68. Ibid. p. 124; Levin, *The Cost of Free Speech*, p. 102.
69. Fish, ibid.
70. Haworth, *Free Speech*, pp. 132–3.
71. Cohen, *You Can't Read This Book*, 'How to Fight Back', p. 221 [loc 3457].
72. Ibid. p. 237 [loc 3681].
73. Malik, *From Fatwa to Jihad*, p. 151.
74. Fish, *There's No Such Thing as Free Speech*, p. 103.
75. Salman Rushdie, *Shame* (London: Picador, 1983) p. 71.
76. Fish, *There's No Such Thing as Free Speech*, p. 108.
77. Haworth, *Free Speech*, p. 88.
78. Flemming Rose, cited in Malik, *From Fatwa to Jihad*, p. 143.
79. Saunders, *Degradation*, p. 5.
80. Parekh, *Rethinking Multiculturalism*, pp. 316–17.
81. Thomas Babington Macaulay, 'Minute on Education in India' (1835), paragraph 10, Bureau of Education. *Selections from Educational Records, Part I (1781–1839)*. Edited by H. Sharp. Calcutta: Superintendent, Government Printing, 1920. Reprint. Delhi: National Archives of India, 1965, 107–17.

82. Jonathan Chaplin, 'How Much Cultural and Religious Pluralism can Liberalism Tolerate?' in John Horton, ed. *Liberalism, Multiculturalism and Toleration* (Basingstoke: Macmillan now Palgrave Macmillan, 1993) pp. 45–6.

83. Ibid. p. 47; p. 46.

84. Mendus, 'The Tigers of Wrath,' pp. 11–14. I will take up this issue in greater detail in Chapter 3.

85. Incidentally, liberalism's hegemony – at least within the cultural and political discourses of both the UK and the US, and to a greater or lesser extent in western Europe – is demonstrated by the fact that one could characterize contemporary conservativism as a liberalism emphasizing liberty (neo-liberalism), and left-liberalism as a discourse emphasizing equality, but at the core of both lies the centrality of the individual (this is even more apparent in the US than in the UK). In the UK, 'old fashioned' conservatism (Toryism), with its communitarian influences, only exists at the margins of the modern Conservative party as a kind of repressed presence that periodically excites frenzies and fantasies (particularly with regard to foreigners) that grow all the more frenzied and fantastical for being repressed. Left-wing non-liberalism has suffered an even more precipitous decline to the point of being not only marginal but virtually non-existent in official political discourse, although the ongoing economic crisis of the neo-liberal model since 2008 has initiated a return of the repressed from both the left and right, especially in continental Europe.

86. Cohen, *You Can't Read This Book*, 'Rules for Censors (1)', p. 27 [loc 610]; ch. 4, p. 102 [loc 1709].

87. Weller, *A Mirror for Our Times*, p. 17.

3 A Difficult Freedom: Towards Mutual Understanding and the Ethics of Propriety

1. See Stanley Fish, *There's No Such Thing as Free Speech And It's a Good Thing Too* (New York: Oxford University Press, 1994); Abigail Levin, *The Cost of Free Speech: Pornigraphy, Hate Speech, and their Challenge to Liberalism* (Basingstoke: Palgrave Macmillan, 2010); Kevin Saunders, *Degradation: What The History of Obscenity Tells Us About Hate Speech* (New York: New York University Press, 2011); Mari Matsuda, Charles R. Lawrence III, Richard Delgado and Kimberlé Williams Crenshaw, *Words that Wound: Critical Race Theory, Assaultive Speech, and the First Amendment* (Boulder, CO: Westview Press, 1993); Richard Delgado and Jean Stefancic, *Understanding Words That Wound* (Boulder, CO: Westview Press, 2004); and the various and extensive publications of Catherine MacKinnon.

2. Talal Asad, Wendy Brown, Judith Butler and Saba Mahmood, *Is Critique Secular? Blasphemy, Injury and Free Speech*, Townsend Papers in the Humanities no.2 (Berkeley: University of California Press, 2009); Stanley Fish, 'Crying Censorship', *Opinionator: Exclusive Online Commentary from the Times*, http://opinionator.blogs.nytimes.com/2008/08/24/crying-censorship/ [accessed 15 May 2013]

3. See Tariq Modood, *Multicultural Politics: Racism, Ethnicity and Muslims in Britain* (Edinburgh: Edinburgh University Press, 2005); Bhikhu Parekh, *Rethinking Multiculturalism: Cultural Diversity and Political Theory* 2nd edn. (Basingstoke: Palgrave Macmillan, 2006); and Simon Lee, *The Cost of Free Speech* (London: Faber, 1990).

4. Modood, *Multicultural Politics*; Parekh, *Rethinking Secularism*; Susan Mendus, 'The Tigers of Wrath and the Horses of Instruction' in *Free Speech: Report of a*

Seminar (London: Commission for Racial Equality, 1990) pp. 3–17; Peter Jones, 'Respecting Beliefs and Rebuking Rushdie', *British Journal of Political Science*, 20:4, 1990, pp. 415–37.

5. Talal Asad, *Genealogies of Religion: Discipline and Reasons of Power in Christianity and Islam* (Baltimore: Johns Hopkins University Press, 1993). For a more detailed discussion of Asad's genealogy of religion, see Chapter 4. See also Timothy Fitzgerald, *The Ideology of Religious Studies* (New York: Oxford University Press, 2004) and *Discourse on Civility and Barbarity: A Critical History of Religion and Related Categories* (New York: Oxford University Press, 2012).

6. Michael Ignatieff, 'Protect People, Not What They Believe' *Observer*, 11 February 1990. This, of course, contradicts the assumption that one cannot protect religious believers without protecting their beliefs. It is difficult to give an account of a contradictory discourse without appearing contradictory, and this is one of the key contradictions in contemporary freedom of speech discourse concerning religion. I will examine it in greater detail in Chapter 7.

7. Modood, *Multicultural Politics*, pp. 120–1.

8. Simone de Beauvoir, *The Second Sex*, new edn. (London: Vintage, 1997); Judith Butler, *Gender Trouble: Feminism and the Subversion of Identity*, new edn. (London: Routledge, 2006); Robert Miles, *Racism*, 2nd edn. (London: Routledge, 2003); Les Back and John Solomos, eds. *Theories of Race and Racism: A Reader* (London: Routledge, 1999).

9. Mendus, 'Tigers of Wrath' p. 11; p. 12.

10. Bernard Williams, 'Morality and the Emotions' cited in Mendus, ibid. p. 12.

11. Mendus, ibid. p. 15.

12. John Horton, 'Liberalism, Multiculturalism and Toleration' in John Horton, ed. *Liberalism, Multiculturalism and Toleration* (Basingstoke: Macmillan – now Palgrave Macmillan, 1993) pp. 2–3.

13. It might be suggested that the prevention of such crises is precisely the point of indictments against apostasy.

14. Mendus, 'Tigers of Wrath' p. 16.

15. Modood, *Multicultural Politics*, p. 125.

16. Ibid.

17. Ibid. p. 126.

18. Ibid.

19. Ibid. p. 130.

20. This animus against responsibility is apparent in the rhetorical inflation of a right to freedom of speech into a 'right' to offend. This is despite the fact that contractual theories of rights implicitly recognize attendant responsibilities because a contract creates 'a moral obligation where none had existed before' (Alan Haworth, *Free Speech*, p. 157).

21. This is, in fact, a very Gandhian formulation – it is, in effect, the basis for his key concept of *satyagraha* – and one that is perhaps too often overlooked as a way of creating conditions for mutual recognition and dialogue in western (and now, sadly, even Indian) multiculturalisms.

22. Modood, *Multicultural Politics*, p. 129. In Britain, arguments over the statutory underpinning of the press regulator so that its decisions would be legally binding and carry the force of law, as recommended by the Leveson report, demonstrate how politically (and legally) difficult such institutionalization might prove to be.

23. Lee, *The Cost of Free Speech*, p. 7.

24. Nick Cohen, *You Can't Read This Book: Censorship in an Age of Freedom* (London: Fourth Estate, 2012) Kindle edition, 'Rules for Censors (1)', p. 21 [loc 506–517].

25. See chapter 1.
26. Kenan Malik, *From Fatwa to Jihad: The Rushdie Affair and its Legacy* (London: Atlantic Books, 2009) p. 183.
27. Ibid. p. 190.
28. Ibid. p. 189; p. 190.
29. Ibid. p. 155.
30. They largely rely on Karl Popper's account of scientific method in his *The Logic of Scientific Discovery* (1934), which has been contested by Thomas Kuhn's *The Structure of Scientific Revolutions* (1962), as well as Michael Polanyi's *Personal Knowledge* (1972) and Rom Harre's 'Science as a Communal Practice' (1986) – these last two are cited by Wayne Booth in *The Company We Keep: An Ethics of Fiction* (Berkeley: University of California Press, 1988) p. 32. Booth writes, in a footnote: 'In recent decades many philosophers of science have argued forcefully that even the "hardest" sciences depend on primary acts of assent, faith, or trust.'
31. Scott Atran, *Talking to the Enemy: Faith, Brotherhood, and the (Un)Making of Terrorists* (New York: Ecco, 2010) p. 489.
32. Ibid. p. 452.
33. Ibid. p. 344; p. 382.
34. Ibid. p. 375.
35. Ibid. p. 385.
36. Ibid. p. 378.
37. Ibid. p. 379.
38. Richard Webster, *A Brief History of Blapsphemy: Liberalism, Censorship and 'The Satanic Verses'* (Southwold: Orwell Press, 1990).
39. Emmanuel Levinas, *Totality and Infinity: An Essay on Exteriority*, trans. Alphonso Lingis (Dordrecht: Kluwer, 1991) p. 42; p. 39.
40. Robert Eaglestone, *Ethical Criticism: Reading After Levinas* (Edinburgh: Edinburgh University Press, 1997) p. 135; Emmanuel Levinas, cited in ibid. p. 140.
41. Levinas, *Ethics and Infinity*, p. 90 cited in Eaglestone, *Ethical Criticism*, p. 124.
42. Ibid. p. 142.
43. Levinas, *Noms Propre*, p. 36, cited in Andrew Gibson, *Postmodernity, Ethics and the Novel: From Leavis to Levinas* (London: Routledge, 1999) p. 31.
44. Emmanuel Levinas, *Otherwise than Being Or Beyond Essence*, trans. Alphonso Lingis (Dordrecht: Kluwer, 1991) p. 117.
45. Eaglestone, *Ethical Criticism*, pp. 137–8.
46. Gibson, *Postmodernity, Ethics and the Novel*, p. 40.
47. Levinas, *Totality and Infinity*, p. 70.
48. Jacques Derrida, 'Violence and Metaphysics' cited in Eaglestone, p. 135.
49. Eaglestone, ibid.
50. Ibid. p. 142.
51. Ibid. p. 140 (citing Simon Critchley, *The Ethics of Deconstruction*, p. 7).
52. Ibid. p. 147.
53. Gibson, *Postmodernity, Ethics and the Novel*, p. 10.
54. Ibid. p. 11.
55. Ibid.
56. Ibid.
57. Ibid. p. 194.
58. Derek Attridge, *The Singularity of Literature* (London: Routledge, 2004) p. 101.
59. Ibid. p. 80.
60. Steven Connor, cited in Gibson, *Postmodernity, Ethics and the Novel*, p. 4.
61. Gibson, ibid. p. 15.

62. Jacques Derrida, *The Gift of Death*, trans. David Wills (Chicago: Chicago University Press, 1995).
63. Gibson, *Postmodernity, Ethics and the Novel*, p. 191.
64. David Parker, 'Introduction: the turn to ethics in the 1990s' in Jane Adamson, Richard Freadman and David Parker, eds. *Renegotiating Ethics in Literature, Philosophy and Theory* (Cambridge: Cambridge University Press, 1998) p. 8.
65. Derek Attridge, 'The Impossibility of Ethics: On Mount Moriah' in *Reading and Responsibility: Deconstruction's Traces* (Edinburgh: Edinburgh University Press, 2011) p. 58.
66. Derrida, *The Gift of Death*, pp. 68–9.
67. Attridge, 'Impossibility' p. 59.
68. Ibid. p. 62; p. 63.
69. Ibid. pp. 64–5.
70. Ibid. p. 65.
71. Ibid. p. 62.
72. Ibid. p. 63.
73. Ibid. p. 72.
74. Ibid. p. 71.
75. Derek Attridge, 'Posthumous Infidelity: Derrida, Levinas and the Third' in *Reading and Responsibility*, pp. 103–11.
76. Levinas, *Totality and Infinity*, p. 213, cited in ibid. p. 103.
77. Ibid. pp. 103–4.
78. Ibid. p. 104.
79. Emmanuel Levinas, 'Peace and Proximity' cited in Attridge, 'Posthumous Infidelity' p. 104.
80. Ibid.
81. Attridge, 'Posthumous Infidelity' p. 113.
82. Ibid. p. 109.
83. Ibid. p. 110.
84. Levinas, cited in ibid. p. 110.
85. Ibid.
86. Ibid. p. 112.
87. Derrida, cited in ibid. p. 111.
88. Gibson, *Postmodernity, Ethics and the Novel*, p. 174.
89. Simon Critchley notes that, for Levinas, 'ethics occurs as the putting into question of the ego, the knowing subject, self-consciousness' (*The Ethics of Deconstruction*, p. 5). James Meffan and Kim Worthington reasonably interpret Levinasian ethics, therefore, as '*self*-applied and not directed to the Other except as that Other effects the process of *self*-critique'. 'Ethics before Politics: J.M. Coetzee's *Disgrace*' in Todd F. Davis and Kenneth Womack, eds. *Mapping the Ethical Turn: A Reader in Ethics, Culture, and Literary Theory* (Charlottesville, VA: University Press of Virginia, 2001) p. 135.
90. This lack of a conceptualization of shared responsibility indicates the difficulty Levinas had in extracting himself from the thrall of phenomenology. I am indebted here to Hugh Silverman's account of Bernard Stiegler's critique of Levinas in his *Time and Technics*, which he presented at a seminar at Brunel University in 2008. This difficulty in accounting for shared responsibility also lays bare the convergence between liberalism and phenomenology. In *The Myth of Choice*, Kent Greenfield demonstrates how, for instance, legal systems in liberal democracies struggle to account for shared responsibility within the realm of calculable justice.

91. Gayatri Chakravorty Spivak, 'Reading *The Satanic Verses*,' *Public Culture*, 2.1, 1989, p. 87.
92. Adam Zachary Newton, *Narrative Ethics* (Cambridge, MA: Harvard University Press, 1995) p. 21.
93. Toni Morrison, cited in James Phelan, *Narrative as Rhetoric: Technique, Audiences, Ethics, Ideology* (Columbus, OH: Ohio State University Press, 1996) p. 174.
94. James Phelan, 'Sethe's Choice: *Beloved* and the Ethics of Reading' in Todd F. Davis and Kenneth Womack, eds. *Mapping the Ethical Turn*, p. 97.
95. Hans Robert Jauss, cited in Susan R. Suleiman, 'Introduction: Varieties of Audience-Oriented Criticism' in Susan R. Suleiman and Inge Crossman, eds. *The Reader in the Text: Essays on Audience and Interpretation* (Princeton, NJ: Princeton University Press, 1980) p. 35.
96. Booth, *The Company We Keep*, p. 89.
97. Wolfgang Iser, cited in Booth, *The Company We Keep*, p. 90.
98. Richard Cohen, *Face to Face with Levinas*, cited in Newton, *Narrative Ethics*, p. 28, fn. 45.
99. Dominick LaCapra, *Writing History, Writing Trauma* (Baltimore: Johns Hopkins University Press, 2001) p. 17.
100. Ibid. pp. 17–18.
101. Ibid. pp. 14–15, my emphases.
102. Bethan Benwell, James Procter and Gemma Robinson, 'Not Reading *Brick Lane*', *New Formations*, 73, 2011, p. 102.
103. Ibid. p. 95, 92.
104. Ibid. p. 95.
105. Salman Rushdie, *The Sunday Times*, 2 October 1994.
106. Booth, *The Company We Keep*, p. 91. Daniel Schwarz, 'A Humanistic Ethics of Reading' in Todd F. Davis and Kenneth Womack, eds. *Mapping the Ethical Turn*, p. 10.
107. Attridge, *Singularity of Literature*, p. 81.
108. There is some parallel here with how Derek Attridge defines 'literariness' as a kind of performance: 'the literary work exists only in *performance* . . . when, in conjunction with other modalities of reading, I respond to a text *as literature* . . . my pleasure and profit come from the experience of an event of referring, from a *staging* of referentiality . . . Literary fiction involves the performance of fictionality . . . Similarly, narrative becomes literary when it involves the performance of narrativity, metaphor when it involves the performance of metaphoricity, mimesis when it involves the performance of mimetivity, description when it involves the performance of descriptivity, and so on' *Singularity of Literature*, pp. 95–6.
109. This distinction between the 'text' and its 'manner' is, of course, merely a conceptual one. In terms of ethics, the experience of reading – as opposed to post-hoc analysis – observes no such distinction.
110. The phrase is Kenneth Burke's, cited by Booth in *The Company We Keep*, epigraph to chapter 4.
111. Malik, *From Fatwa to Jihad*, p. 153, 147, 145.
112. Attridge, *Singularity of Literature*, p. 29.
113. The philosopher Anthony Laden cautions against the term 'negotiation' insofar as it implies a bargaining from given positions, with each trying to maximize one's claim against those of the other. This precludes the sort of mutual vulnerability that each must feel before the other if what Jane Mansbridge calls 'altruistic trust' is to obtain. I take the point, but would suggest that the important

point about 'negotiation' is its dialogic character, and thus I feel it is still a suitable term to use here, with the above caveat in mind. Coming from a Kantian position, as opposed to the phenomenological tradition of continental philosophy that Levinas emerged from, Laden's position is nevertheless very hospitable to the kind of ethics I have outlined here – as indeed is mine to his.

114. Allison Weir, 'Feminism and the Islamic Revival: Freedom as a Practice of Belonging,' *Hypatia*, 28:2, 2013, pp. 323–40. See also my discussion of alternative conceptions of freedom in Chapter 6.

115. Attridge, *Singularity of Literature*, p. 34.

116. Christopher S. Taylor, 'Rushdie's Insensitivity', *The Christian Science Monitor*, 3 March 1989, cited in M.M. Ahsan and A.R. Kidwai eds. *Sacrilege versus Civility: Muslim Perspectives on* The Satanic Verses *Affair* (Leicester: Islamic Foundation, 1993) p. 87.

117. Modood, *Multicultural Politics*, p. 125.

118. Though not explicitly assigned to the field known as 'ethical criticism', trauma studies, as represented by Shoshana Felman, Dorothy Laub, Cathy Caruth, Dominick LaCapra and others, *is* a form of ethical criticism that is highly attendant to questions of writing, representation, and responsibility, as is the work of J.M. Coetzee, especially his Elizabeth Costello novels.

119. Séan Burke, *The Ethics of Writing: Authorship and Legacy in Plato and Nietzsche* (Edinburgh: Edinburgh University Press, 2008) pp. 36–7.

120. Ibid. p. 24.

121. Ibid. p. 34, fn.6.

122. Wayne Booth, 'Why Ethical Criticism Can Never Be Simple' in Davis and Womack, eds. *Mapping the Ethical Turn*, p. 21.

123. In his essay 'Free Speech, Blasphemy and Secular Criticism' (in *Is Critique Secular?*) Talal Asad cites a number of recent works tracing the development of legal copyright in the late eighteenth and nineteenth centuries which established the link between 'the literary work' and the 'proprietary author': Mark Rose, 'The Author as Proprietor: *Donaldson* v. *Becket* and the Genealogy of Modern Authorship', *Representations*, 23, 1988; Martha Woodmansee, 'The Genius and the Copyright: Economic and Legal Conditions of the Emergence of the "Author"' *Eighteenth-Century Studies*, 17.4, 1984; and in a later version of the essay published as 'Freedom of Speech and Religious Limitations' in Craig Calhoun, Mark Jeurgensmeyer and Jonathan VanAntwerpen, eds. *Rethinking Secularism* (New York: Oxford University Press, 2011) he also cites Jody Greene, *The Trouble with Ownership: Literary Property and Authorial Liability in England, 1660–1730* (Philadelphia: University of Pennsylvania Press, 2005). Characteristically, this enables him to make a brilliant insight which links these developments with developments in freedom of speech: 'It should be clear that the law of copyright is not simply a constraint on free communication but also a way of defining how, when and for whom literary communication . . . can be regarded as free, creative and inalienable. A person's freedom to say whatever he or she wants, how he or she wants, depends in part on a particular notion of property' (p. 32). See my related comments in Chapters 1 and 2 about the liberal notion of expression as self-expression.

124. Burke, *Ethics of Writing*, p. 30.

125. Phelan, *Narrative as Rhetoric*, p. 93, my emphases.

126. Ibid. p. 100.

127. Suleiman, 'Varieties of Audience-Oriented Criticism' p. 9.

128. Phelan, *Narrative as Rhetoric*, p. 147.
129. Parker, 'Introduction: the turn to ethics' pp. 9–10.
130. Booth, *The Company We Keep*, p. 143.
131. Gibson, *Postmodernity, Ethics and the Novel*, p. 209.
132. Thomas Docherty, cited by Gibson, ibid. p. 204.
133. Ibid. p. 207.
134. Derek Attridge, 'Responsible Reading and Cultural Distance', *New Formations*, 73, 2011, p. 119.
135. Ibid. p. 124.
136. Ibid.
137. Attridge, *Singularity of Literature*, p. 125.
138. Eaglestone, *Ethical Criticism*, p. 147.
139. Simon Critchley, *The Ethics of Deconstruction* (Oxford: Blackwell, 1992) p. 7.
140. Attridge, 'The Impossibility of Ethics' p. 70.
141. Ibid. p. 57.
142. Cited in Amina Wadud, *Inside the Gender Jihad: Women's Reform in Islam* (Oxford: Oneworld, 2006) p. 34.

4 The Self-Transgressions of Salman Rushdie: Re-Reading *The Satanic Verses*

1. Originally published in *Independent*, 1 February 1990, the essay was collected in *Imaginary Homelands: Essays and Criticism 1981–1991* (London: Granta, 1991) pp. 393–414.
2. Salman Rushdie, 'Is Nothing Sacred?' *Imaginary Homelands*, pp. 415–29.
3. Rushdie, 'In Good Faith,' p. 396, p. 395.
4. The exceptions include Roald Dahl, in a letter to *The Times*, 28 February 1989; Richard Webster, *A Brief History of Blasphemy: Liberalism, Censorship and 'The Satanic Verses'* (Southwold: The Orwell Press, 1990); Michael Dummett, 'An Open Letter', *The Independent on Sunday*, 11 February 1990; Talal Asad, 'Ethnography, Literature and Politics: Some Readings and Uses of Salman Rushdie's *The Satanic Verses*,' *Cultural Anthropology*, 5:3 (1990), pp. 239–69; Bhikhu Parekh, 'The Rushdie Affair and the British Press' in D. Cohn-Sherbrook, ed. *The Salman Rushdie Controversy in Interreligious Perspective* (Lewiston: E. Mellen Press, 1990) pp. 72–96 and *Rethinking Multiculturalism: Cultural Diversity and Political Theory* (Basingstoke: Palgrave Macmillan, 2006); and (partially) Pnina Werbner, 'Allegories of Sacred Imperfection: Magic, Hermeneutics and Passion in *The Satanic Verses*,' *Current Anthropology*, 37:1 'Supplement: Special Issue – Anthropology in Public', 1996, pp. S55–86.
5. This was the argument put forward by some of the principal Muslim interventions in the controversy: Shabbir Akhtar, *Be Careful with Muhammad!* (London: Bellew Publishing, 1989); Ziauddin Sardar and Merryl Wyn-Davies, *Distorted Imagination: Lessons from the Rushdie Affair* (London: Grey Seal, 1990); and some of the contributions collected in M.M. Ahsan and A.R. Kidwai, eds. *Sacrilege versus Civility: Muslim Perspectives on* The Satanic Verses (Leicester: Islamic Foundation, 1993).
6. Rushdie, 'In Good Faith', p. 395. Werbner, 'Allegories of Sacred Imperfection,' p. S57.
7. There have, to my knowledge, been three major attempts to read the novel from a 'Muslim' critical perspective whilst also acknowledging the novel's grounding in the protocols of western literary aesthetics: Shabbir Akhtar's *Be Careful*

with Muhammad!, Sardar and Wyn-Davies's *Distorted Imagination*, and more recently Amin Malak, *Muslim Narratives and Discourse of English* (New York: State University of New York Press, 2005). These place *The Satanic Verses* within the context of postmodernism and approach it accordingly using the methodologies of modern literary criticism. However, they do not subject *both* 'secular' and 'Islamic' perspectives to interrogation, but instead subject the former to the latter whilst deploying the former's critical methodologies. As described below, I shall attempt to move beyond 'singular' readings and attempt to fashion a 'dialogic' methodology that occupies neither ground, but rather a space *between* critical paradigms.

8. Edward Said, *Culture and Imperialism* (London: Chatto and Windus, 1993). For Said, there is a link between contrapuntal criticism and 'secular criticism', but whilst the equivalence between contrapuntal methodology and secularism in Said's work is problematic from the point of view of this essay, the idea of bringing into contact overlapping but discrepant histories and experiences without resolving the contradictions that emerge or imposing a singular overarching narrative is appropriate for the kind of post-secular encounter I am attempting to stage here.

9. Rushdie, 'In Good Faith', p. 394.

10. Ibid. p. 395.

11. Ibid. p. 393.

12. Salman Rushdie, 'Interview with *The Bandung File*,' 14 February 1989 [recorded 27 January 1989] in Lisa Appignanesi and Sara Maitland, eds. *The Rushdie File* (London: Fourth Estate, 1989), p. 28.

13. Salman Rushdie, 'Open Letter to Indian Prime Minister, Rajiv Gandhi' nd. in *The Rushdie File*, p. 44.

14. Rushdie, 'In Good Faith' p. 393.

15. Ibid. p. 408.

16. Jerome de Groot, *The Historical Novel* (London: Routledge, 2010).

17. See Hayden White, *Metahistory: The Historical Imagination in Nineteenth-Century Europe* (Baltimore: Johns Hopkins Universty Press, 1973), and *The Content of the Form: Narrative Discourse and Historical Representation* (Baltimore: Johns Hopkins University Press, 1987).

18. Rushdie, 'In Good Faith' p. 409.

19. In Chapter 7, I will examine at length the ambiguities and ambivalences that resonate throughout Rushdie's defence of literature and the imagination in his lecture 'Is Nothing Sacred?'

20. The notable exceptions relate to the problems involved in representing the Holocaust and other historical traumas, particularly the work of Dominick LaCapra, Shoshana Felman, and J.M. Coetzee's Elizabeth Costello novels. To be clear, I am not suggesting there is a dearth of ethical consideration within postmodernism in general, but rather within postmodern *historical* theory and practice.

21. Keith Jenkins, *Re-Thinking History* (London: Routledge, 1991) pp. 14–15.

22. Linda Hutcheon, *The Politics of Postmodernism* (London: Routledge, 1989) p. 77.

23. The phrase is from Hutcheon, ibid. pp. 73–4.

24. Beverley Southgate has a chapter entitled 'Fiction, history and ethics', in her book *History Meets Fiction* (Harlow: Pearson Education, 2009), but it is concerned with fiction's ability to undertake 'ethically oriented history' as opposed to my concern with the ethics of representation. As far as I am aware, none of the major

postmodern theorizations of history discuss the ethics of representation, and there is not even a single reference to ethics in the index of major introductory works on history and postmodernism, such as Richard Jenkins's *The Postmodern History Reader* (London: Routledge, 1997) and Alan Muslow's *The Routledge Companion to Historical Studies* (London: Routledge, 2000).

25. Salman Rushdie, 'Interview with *The Bandung File*,' p. 28.
26. Sometimes Rushdie sticks quite resolutely to certain 'orthodox' narrative renderings when it suits his purposes: at least one passage – the destruction of the idol of al-Uzza as the Prophet enters Mecca/Jahilia in triumph (*Satanic Verses*, pp. 372–3) – is a very close paraphrase, if not *verbatim* copy, from Martin Lings, *Muhammad: His Life Based on the Earliest Sources* (Cambridge: The Islamic Texts Society, 2001) pp. 303–4.
27. Salman Rushdie, *The Satanic Verses* (Delaware: The Consortium Inc., 1992), p. 22. Hereafter, all citations will be to this edition and cited in the text.
28. AnneMarie Schimmel, *And Muhammad is His Messenger: The Veneration of the Prophet in Islamic Piety* (Chapel Hill, NC: The University of North Carolina Press, 1985).
29. See Paula Richman, ed. *Many Ramayanas: The Diversity of a Narrative Tradition in South Asia* (Berkeley: University of California Press, 1991).
30. Jenkins, *Re-Thinking History*, p. 16.
31. I thank Dr Muhammad Mansur Ali, *hadith* scholar and Research Fellow at Cardiff University's Centre for the Study of Islam in the UK (Islam-UK) for this point.
32. Srinivas Aravamudan, '"Being God's Postman is No Fun, Yaar": Salman Rushdie's *The Satanic Verses*', *Diacritics*, 19:2 (1989), p. 12.
33. Tabari, *The History of al-Tabari*, vol. 6, trans. M.V McDonald and annotated by William Montgomery Watt (Albany: State University of New York Press, 1988) pp. 108–9, my emphasis. See also A.Guillaume, *The Life of Muhammad: A Translation of Ibn Ishaq's* Sirat Rasul-Allah (Oxford: Oxford University Press, 1955) p. 165.
34. It is little known that in the very early stages of the Muslim campaign against *The Satanic Verses*, the protestors wrote to Penguin requesting that the novel be prefaced by a statement clearly indicating its status as a fictional work. Penguin refused. See Paul Weller, *A Mirror for Our Times: 'The Rushdie Affair' and the Future of Multiculturalism* (London: Continuum, 2009) p. 17.
35. See, for instance, *The Quran*, trans. Tarif Khalidi (Oxford: Oxford University Press, 2008) 17:73–5 and 22:52.
36. Rushdie, 'In Good Faith' p. 399.
37. Nico Israel, *Outlandish: Writing Between Exile and Diaspora* (Stanford, CA: Stanford University Press, 2000), p. 135.
38. Talal Asad, 'Ethnography, Literature and Politics' p. 253; Sardar and Wynn-Davies, *Distorted Imagination*, p. 160; Robin Yassin-Kassab, 'Maps for Lost Lovers and Writerly Responsibility' *Qunfuz*, 6 February 2008, http://qunfuz.blogspot.com/2008/02/maps-for-lost-lovers-and-writerly.html (accessed 6 September 2012).
39. Peter Mandaville, *Global Political Islam* (London: Routledge, 2007) pp. 20–1, 49–95.
40. Sami Zubaida, *Law and Power in the Islamic World* (London: IB Tauris, 2003) p. 12.
41. W.M. Watt, *Muhammad at Medina* (Oxford: Oxford University Press, 1956) p. 293.
42. Ibid. p. 266.
43. Zubaida, *Law and Power*, p. 29.
44. Zubaida, *Law and Power*, pp. 10–11.

45. Ibid. p. 17
46. Ibid. p. 21, my emphasis.
47. S. Sayyid, *A Fundamental Fear: Eurocentrism and the Emergence of Islamism*, 2nd edn. (London: Zed Books, 2003) p. 53.
48. See Bukhari, *Sahih al-Bukhari*, trans. Muhammad Muhsin Khan, vol. 7, book 65, hadith 300 (Medina: Islamic University, nd.) p. 228, in which the believers eat a type of lizard in front of the Prophet even though he refuses to join them because of his dislike of the meat. See also hadiths 362, 363, p. 262: the Prophet's dislike of garlic is clearly another instance where Muslims have not felt obliged to demur to his likes and dislikes.
49. Zubaida, *Law and Power*, p. 10.
50. Ibid. p. 2.
51. Watt, *Muhammad at Medina*, p. 238; 271.
52. F.E. Peters, *Muhammad and the Origins of Islam* (Albany: State University of New York Press, 1994) p. 25.
53. Rushdie, 'In Good Faith' p. 396.
54. Ibid. p. 409, 413.
55. Salman Rushdie, 'One Thousand Days in a Balloon' in *Imaginary Homelands*, pp. 435–7. This gesture anticipates the 'good Muslim/bad Muslim' trope which has permeated post-9/11 public discourse in the US, Britain and Europe. See Mahmood Mamdani, *Good Muslim, Bad Muslim: America, the Cold War and the Roots of Terror* (New York: Doubleday, 2005) and Peter Morey and Amina Yaqin, *Framing Muslims: Stereotyping and Representation after 9/11* (Cambridge, MA: Harvard University Press, 2011).
56. Timothy Brennan, 'Rushdie, Islam and Postcolonial Criticism' *Social Text* 31/32 (1992) p. 273; Aamir Mufti, 'Reading the Rushdie Affair: An Essay on Islam and Politics' *Social Text*, 29 (1991) pp. 95–116; Sara Suleri, 'Contraband Histories: Salman Rushdie and the Embodiment of Blasphemy', *The Yale Review*, 78:4 (1989) pp. 604–24; Andrew Teverson, 'Fairy Tale Politics: Free Speech and Multiculturalism in *Haroun and the Sea of Stories*', *Twentieth Century Literature*, 47:4 (2001), pp. 444–66; Robert Spencer, 'Salman Rushdie and the "war on terror"', *Journal of Postcolonial Writing*, 46:3–4, p. 262.
57. Rushdie, 'In Good Faith' p. 396 (original emphasis).
58. Edward Said, *Orientalism: Western Conceptions of the Orient* (London: Penguin, 1991) p. 3.
59. Bhikhu Parekh, *Rethinking Multiculturalism: Cultural Diversity and Political Theory*, 2nd edn. (Basingstoke: Palgrave Macmillan, 2006) p. 299.
60. Tariq Modood, *Multicultural Politics: Racism, Ethnicity and Muslims in Britain* (Edinburgh: Edinburgh University Press, 2005) p. 123.
61. Rushdie, 'In Good Faith' p. 401.
62. Ali A Mazrui, 'Satanic Verses or a Satanic Novel?: Moral Dilemmas of the Rushdie Affair' *Third World Quarterly*, 12:1, 1990, p. 134.
63. Ibid. p. 133.
64. Ibid. p. 134.
65. Malise Ruthven, *A Satanic Affair* (London: Hogarth Press, 1990) p. 28; p. 162.
66. Rushdie, 'In Good Faith' pp. 401–2.
67. Norman Daniel, *Islam and the West: The Making of an Image*, Revised edn. (Oxford: Oneworld, 2009) p. 11; p. 326. See also R.W. Southern. *Western Views of Islam in the Middle Ages* (Cambridge, MA: Harvard University Press, 1962); Richard Fletcher, *The Cross and the Crescent: Christianity and Islam from Muhammad to*

the Reformation (London: Allen Lane, 2003); Edward Said, *Orientalism*; and Ian Almond, *The New Orientalists: Postmodern Representations of Islam from Foucault to Baudrillard* (London: I.B. Tauris, 2007).

68. The following works, amongst others, all demonstrate how medieval motifs continue to circulate in the most modern of media: Edward W. Said, *Covering Islam: How the Media and the Experts Determine How We See the Rest of the World*, 2nd edn (London: Vintage, 1997); Peter Morey and Amina Yaqin, *Framing Muslims: Stereotyping and Representation After 9/11* (Cambridge, MA: Harvard University Press, 2011); Elizabeth Poole, *Reporting Islam: Media Representations of British Muslims* (London: I.B. Tauris, 2002); The Runnymede Trust, *Islamophobia: a Challenge for Us All* (Stoke-on-Trent: Trentham Books, 1997) and *Islamophobia: Issues, Challenges and Action – A Report by the Commission on British Muslims and Islamophobia* (Stoke-on-Trent: Trentham Books, 2004). A particularly virulent strain of western anti-Islamic polemic that almost precisely rehearses the stock tropes and motifs of medieval Christian precursors has spread since the 1990s, and especially during the 'war on terror', in the writings of Orianna Fallaci, Bat 'Yeor, Robert Spencer (not be confused with the literary scholar who has published articles on Rushdie) and the proponents of the so-called 'Eurabian' thesis. The argument advanced by these writers, amongst others, is that large-scale immigration of Muslims into Europe will eventually 'Islamize' Europe within a couple of generations or perhaps slightly longer. The sociologist Eric Kaufmann has used demographic analysis to refute the 'Eurabian' hypothesis in 'Europe's Muslim Future' *Prospect*, 169, April 2010, http://www.prospectmagazine.co.uk/magazine/europes-muslim-future/ [accessed 4 December 2012]. For a critique of Kaufmann's article (whilst welcoming his critique of the Eurabian arguments) see my article 'The Tyranny of Numbers', partially published in *Prospect*'s letters page the following month, but available in full at http://anshumanmondal.wordpress.com/2010/05/25/the-tyranny-of-numbers-on-europes-muslim-future/ [accessed 4 December 2012].

69. Humbert of Romans, quoted in Daniel, *Islam and the West* p. 148. Daniel wryly adds a parenthesis: 'We have seen how fair a description Islamic practice this really was', having discussed the many deliberate provocations of Christian missionaries determined to martyr themselves for the cause of Christ and to demonstrate the truth of their characterization of Muslims: 'In all these stories the reluctance of the Muslim rulers to execute is obvious and it is difficult not to impute the ultimate violence to those who provoked it' (p. 146).

70. Ibid. p. 100.

71. Rushdie, 'In Good Faith' p. 403.

72. Webster, *A Brief History of Blasphemy*, p. 94.

73. Daniel, *Islam and the West*, p. 52.

74. The idea of the Qur'anic revelations being a pretence recurs again and again in the texts that Daniel examines, and it would be tedious to list all such instances here. This, in itself, is evidence of the importance of the idea in Christian anti-Islamic polemics.

75. Daniel, *Islam and the West*, pp. 112–13.

76. Al-Bukhari, *Sahih Bukhari*, vol. 6 chapter 240, hadith 311.

77. See, for instance, Lings, *Muhammad*, p. 77, pp. 244–5 and many others. Watt also notes an incident when Muhammad became suicidal because there was a period of time revelations were not appearing to him; this is known as the *fatrah*. See Watt, *Muhammad at Mecca*, p. 41 and p. 50. See also, Karen Armstrong,

Muhammad: Prophet for our Time (London: Harper Collins, 2006) p. 158 (citing Ibn Sa'd) and p. 182.

78. Ibid. p. 80, *fn*33 (p. 366).
79. For an alternative etymology, see Muhammad Asad, *The Message of The Qur'an*, trans. Muhammad Asad, vol. 2 (Bristol: The Book Foundation, 2003), footnote 10, p. 232.
80. *The Message of The Qur'an*, trans. Asad, vol. 1 p. 16. I have normally used Tarif Khalidi's translation, but in this instance Khalidi translates Iblis as Satan and thus exhibits the modern tendency to collapse the two; as the transliteration that accompanies Asad's text demonstrates, the Arabic text clearly does not support that tendency.
81. This is most strikingly apparent in *sura* 7:10–27, which refers at first to the angel Iblis, but then, at 7:20, refers to Satan as 'tempter', 'Thereupon Satan *whispered* unto the two . . . ' and again at 7:27, 'O Children of Adam! Do not allow Satan to seduce you in the same way he caused your ancestors to be driven out of the garden'. See also 2:30–9.
82. Wensinck, A.J.; Gardet, L. 'Iblīs.' *Encyclopaedia of Islam, Second Edition.* Brill Online, 2012, http://www.paulyonline.brill.nl/entries/encyclopaedia-of-islam-2/iblis-SIM_3021 [accessed 05 November 2012]
83. Henry Ansgar Kelly, *Satan: A Biography* (Cambridge: Cambridge University Press, 2006) pp. 2–3.
84. Ibid. p. 171.
85. Ibid. p. 172.
86. Ibid.
87. Ibid. p. 175.
88. 'Satan,' *Encyclopaedia of Religion*, 2nd. edn., ed. Lindsay Jones [Mircea Eliade], vol. 12 (Farmington, MI: Thomson Gale, 2005), p. 8124.
89. Ibid. pp. 175–9.
90. Ibid. pp. 197–8.
91. Ibid. p. 198.
92. 'Satan,' *Encyclopaedia of Religion*, vol. 12, p. 8124. On the rabbinical tradition in Persian Mesopotamia, see Tom Holland, *In the Shadow of the Sword: The Battle for Global Empire and the End of the Ancient World* (London: Hachette, 2012) p. 104ff.
93. D. Gimaret, 'Tawḥīd.' *Encyclopaedia of Islam, Second Edition.* Brill Online, 2012. http://referenceworks.brillonline.com/entries/encyclopaedia-of-islam-2/tawhid-SIM_7454 [accessed 06 November 2012]
94. Guy Monnot, 'Dualism.' *Encyclopaedia of Islam, THREE.* Edited by: Gudrun Krämer, Denis Matringe, John Nawas, Everett Rowson. Brill Online, 2012. http://www.paulyonline.brill.nl/entries/encyclopaedia-of-islam-3/dualism-COM_26100 [accessed 06 November 2012] Lings cites a *hadith* attributed by both Bukhari and Muslim to the Prophet which clearly illustrates the non-dualistic attitude to good and evil (p. 94).
95. 'Shayṭān.' *Encyclopaedia of Islam, Second Edition.* Brill Online, 2012. http://www.paulyonline.brill.nl/entries/encyclopaedia-of-islam-2/shaytan-COM_1054 [accessed 05 November 2012]
96. Annemarie Schimmel, *Mystical Dimensions of Islam* (Chapel Hill, NC: University of North Carolina Press, 1975) p. 195.
97. 'Iblis', *Encyclopaedia of Islam.*
98. Roger Clark, *Stranger Gods: Salman Rushdie's Other Worlds* (Montreal: MacGill-Queen's University Press, 2001) p. 129; p. 166.

99. Ibid. p. 131.
100. Salman Rushdie, 'Interview with Shrabani Basu' collected in Appignanesi and Maitland, eds. *The Rushdie File*, p. 41; Rushdie, 'In Good Faith' p. 396.
101. Rushdie, 'Is Nothing Sacred?' p. 417.
102. Rushdie, 'In Good Faith' p. 394.
103. Daniel Defoe, *The True-Born Englishman and other writings*, eds. P.N. Furbank and W.R. Owens (London: Penguin, 1997).
104. Rushdie, 'In Good Faith' p. 394.
105. Both Shabbir Akhtar and Bhikhu Parekh have attributed the phrase 'ethic of impurity' to a statement made by Rushdie in one of the publicity interviews he gave prior to the novel's publication; they did not, however, cite the source. See Akhtar, *Be Careful with Muhammad!*, p. 18; Bhikhu Parekh, 'The Rushdie Affair in the British Press' in Dan Cohn-Sherbrook, ed. *The Salman Rushdie Controversy in Interreligious Perspective* (Lampeter: Edwin Mellen Press, 1999,) p. 74. Rushdie speaks of the 'argument between purity and impurity' in 'In Good Faith' p. 394.
106. Roger Clark, *Stranger Gods*.
107. In *Shame*, Rushdie says, in one of the many meta-fictional asides, 'I, too, am a translated man. I have been *borne across*' (London: Picador, 1984) p. 29. He expands on this in the later, famous passage dealing with migration, roots and flight (pp. 85–6).
108. Rushdie is clearly not averse to essentializing gestures when it suits him, despite his ethic of impurity. He writes, '[i]n our beginnings we find our essences. To understand a religion, look at its earliest moments', in 'Is Nothing Sacred?' in *Imaginary Homelands*, p. 424.
109. Johannes Fabian, *Time and the Other: How Anthropology Makes its Object* (New York: Columbia University Press, 1983) p. 143.
110. See Talal Asad, *Genealogies of Religion: Discipline and Reasons of Power in Christianity and Islam* (Baltimore: Johns Hopkins University Press, 1993); and *Formations of the Secular: Christianity, Islam, Modernity* (Stanford: Stanford University Press, 2003).
111. Rushdie, 'In Good Faith' p. 409.
112. Jacques Derrida, 'Structure, Sign and Play in the Discourse of the Human Sciences' in *Writing and Difference*, trans. Alan Bass (London: Routledge, 2nd edn, 2001) pp. 278–94.
113. Asad, *Genealogies*, p. 48.
114. Ibid. p. 39 *fn*.22
115. Ibid. p. 39.
116. Ibid. p. 42.
117. Ibid. p. 40, p. 39.
118. Cited in ibid. p. 47.
119. Ibid. p. 48.
120. John Caputo, *On Religion* (London: Routledge, 2001) pp. 46–7.
121. Salman Rushdie, '"Imagine there's no Heaven": A Letter to the Six Billionth World Citizen' in *Step Across This Line: Collected Non-Fiction 1992–2002* (London: Vintage, 2003) p. 156.
122. Asad, *Genealogies*, p. 47.
123. Caputo, *On Religion*, p. 47. *The Qur'an* 36:36 would seem to support this, 'Limitless in His glory is He who has created . . . that of which [as yet] they have no knowledge' (Asad translation). The meaning of the verse clearly rests on the premise that the Qur'anic revelation does not represent 'the sum of all

knowledge', *contra* the Imam in *The Satanic Verses* (210), but is, in fact, a spur to the acquisition of further knowledge. Faith is the *beginning* not the end of knowledge, and as such is not antithetical to reason.

124. Mehdi Abedi and Michael M.J. Fischer, 'Bombay Talkies, the Word and the World: Salman Rushdie's *The Satanic Verses', Cultural Anthropology*, 5:2 (1990) p. 120.
125. Cited in Sardar and Wynn-Davies, *Distorted Imagination*, p. 65.
126. Caputo, *On Religion*, pp. 46–7.
127. Ibid. p. 2.
128. Ibid. pp. 8–9.
129. Ibid. p. 7.
130. Ibid. p. 8.
131. Ibid. p. 11, p. 9.
132. Ibid. p. 9, p. 14; my emphasis.
133. Ibid. p. 12.
134. Ibid. p. 11.
135. Ibid. p. 33.
136. This is the translation offered by Eric Peters in his *Muhammad and the Origins of Islam* (Albany, NY: SUNY Press, 1994) p. 156.
137. Caputo, *On Religion*, p. 124.
138. Ibid. p. 9.
139. Ibid. p. 118.
140. Ibid. p. 14.
141. Salman Rushdie, 'The Courter' in *East, West* (London: Jonathan Cape, 1994).
142. Samir Amin, *Eurocentrism* (London: Zed Books, 1988) p. 28.
143. Rushdie, 'In Good Faith' p. 408.
144. Caputo, *On Religion*, pp. 42–9.
145. Roger Clark, *Stranger Gods*, p. 129; p. 131.
146. Rushdie writes, 'To my mind religion, even at its most sophisticated, essentially infantilises our moral selves', in "Imagine There's No Heaven"' p. 157.
147. Roland Barthes, cited in Linda Hutcheon, *A Politics of Postmodernism*, London: Routledge, 1989, p. 3; Friedrich Nietzsche, *The Genealogy of Morals*, Book 3, 24, trans, by Maudemarie Clark and Alan J. Swensen (Indianapolis, IN: Hackett, 1998), p. 110. John Gray has systematically exposed the religious roots of secularism in *Black Mass: Apocalyptic Religion and the Death of Utopia*, London: Penguin, 2008, and *Al-Qaeda and What it Means to be Modern* (London: Faber, 2007).
148. Another orthodoxy to which Rushdie subscribes is his concept of 'fiction'. Ruvani Ranasinha has alerted us to the presumption that the 'fictional agreement' which sets 'fiction' apart from other forms of discourse is itself 'a literary judgment entrenched as normative and universal in liberal discourse,' but Rushdie's entire conceptualization of fiction as an aesthetic practice would collapse without it. Ruvani Ranasinha, 'The *fatwa* and its aftermath' in Abdulrazak Gurnah, ed. *The Cambridge Companion to Salman Rushdie* (Cambridge: Cambridge University Press, 2007) p. 52.
149. Sara Suleri, on the other hand, sees Rushdie's blasphemy as an act of cultural fidelity to 'his continuing obsession with the metaphors that Islam makes available to a postcolonial sensibility' ('Contraband Histories' p. 607). Nevertheless, whilst Rushdie may well be attempting to 'desecrate' Islam in order to renew its 'cultural materiality', that gesture – separating Islamic 'religiosity' from its 'culture' and 'civilization' – speaks to a more fundamental fidelity to the logic of secularism. Despite the brilliance of their readings, both Suleri and Mufti

(who also examines the politics of Rushdie's intervention in the name of open-ing the rubric of 'Islam' from those deployed by Islamists) overlook Rushdie's essentializing gestures, as does Robert Spencer's recent defence of *The Satanic Verses* ('Salman Rushdie').

150. Daniel A. Madigan, 'Themes and Topics' in Jane Dammen McAuliffe, ed. *The Cambridge Companion to the Qur'an* (Cambridge: Cambridge University Press, 2006) p. 91. See also Lings, *Muhammad.*

151. Karen Armstrong, *Muhammad*, p. 79.

152. Ibid.

153. Ibid. p. 80

154. Ibid. pp. 184–9. See also Lings, *Muhammad*, pp. 252–6.

155. Bukhari, *Sahih Bukhari*, 8:1, 345.

156. Watt, *Muhammad at Mecca*, p. 96; p. 104.

157. Peters, *Muhammad and the Origins of Islam*, pp. 156–7.

158. Ibid. pp. 157–8.

159. F.E. Peters, *Muhammad and the Origins of Islam*, p. 123; Lings, *Muhammad*, pp. 29–30.

160. Peters, p. 182; p. 204; p. 206; Watt, *Muhammad at Mecca*, p. 96.

161. Madigan, 'Themes and Topics', pp. 87–8; Alexander Knysh, 'Multiple Areas of Influence' in Jane Dammen McAuliffe, ed. *The Cambridge Companion to The Qur'an*, p. 216.

162. Karen Armstrong, *Muhammad*, pp. 108–9; Lings, *Muhammad*, p. 119. On the signifi-cance of migration to Rushdie, see my essay '*The Ground Beneath Her Feet* and *Fury*: The Reinvention of Location' in Abdurazak Gurnah, ed. *The Cambridge Companion to Salman Rushdie* (Cambridge: Cambridge University Press, 2007) pp. 169–83.

163. Tom Holland's recent account of the origins of Islam, *In the Shadow of the Sword*, does just this by placing Islam's origins within the wider context of religious developments in the Near East caused by the struggle between the Roman and Persian empires for supremacy. Although clearly inspired by the work of Michael Cook, Patricia Crone, John Wansborough and other radical western revisionists of early Islamic history, Holland neither goes so far as to argue that Muhammad himself was a post-facto contruction, or that the *Qur'an* is a composite work cob-bled together several generations after the lifetime of the Prophet. Nevertheless, Holland's account of the 'forging' of Islam in the late Umayyad period, although not unproblematic, is far more radical in its approach to Islam's origins than Rushdie's, and it generated some modest controversy when a television pro-gramme based on the book was screened in the UK in 2012.

164. Edward Said, *Beginnings: Intention and Method* (New York: Columbia University Press, 1975).

5   Visualism and Violence: On the Art and Ethics of Provocation in the *Jyllands-Posten* Cartoons and Theo Van Gogh's *Submission*

1. For a detailed account of the controversy, see Jytte Klausen, *The Cartoons That Shook The World* (London: Yale University Press, 2009).

2. Cited in Nasar Meer and Per Mouritsen, 'Political Cultures Compared: The Muhammad Cartoons in the Danish and British Press,' *Ethnicities*, 9:3, 2009, p. 340.

3. Sebastian C.H. Kim, 'Freedom or Respect? Public Theology and the Debate Over the Danish Cartoons,' *International Journal of Public Theology*, 1, 2007, p. 254.
4. Klausen, *The Cartoons That Shook The World*, p. 16, my emphasis.
5. Robert A. Kahn, 'Flemming Rose, The Danish Cartoon Controversy and the New European Freedom of Speech,' *California Western International Law Journal*, 40, 2010, pp. 253–90.
6. Cited in Meer and Mouritsen, 'Political Cultures Compared', p. 348.
7. Kahn, 'Flemming Rose' p. 257.
8. Kim, 'Freedom or Respect?' p. 254.
9. In examining the rationale behind *Le Monde*'s decision to republish the cartoons, Berkowitz and Eko suggest that '[its] aim was to separate the true believers in the Universal Declaration of Human Rights from the rest, and the act of republication of the Mohammed cartoons became the litmus test'. See Dan Berkowitz and Lyombe Eko, 'Blasphemy as Sacred Right/Rite: "The Mohammed Cartoons Affair" and maintenance of journalistic ideology', *Journalism Studies*, 8:5, p. 787. This was itself a response to the decision of most newspaper editors in Britain and the United States *not* to republish, a decision characterized by some as an act of cowardice and/or appeasement (evoking once more the Orwellian paradigm of the totalitarian threat). See Kahn, 'Flemming Rose' p. 274.
10. Stanley Fish, 'Crying Censorship' *Opinionator: Exclusive Online Commentary from The Times*, http://opinionator.blogs.nytimes.com/2008/08/24/crying-censorship/?_r=0 [accessed 24 September 2013].
11. Gwladys Fouché, 'Danish paper rejected Jesus cartoons' the *Guardian*, 6 February 2008. http://www.theguardian.com/media/2006/feb/06/pressandpublishing.politics[accessed 24 September 2013]
12. Klausen, *Cartoons That Shook The World*, p. 20.
13. Joseph H. Carens, 'Free Speech and Democratic Norms in the Danish Cartoons Controversy', *International Migration*, 44:5, 2006, p. 36.
14. Klausen, pp. 17–18.
15. Heiko Henkel, '"The journalists of *Jyllands-Posten* are a bunch of reactionary provocateurs": The Danish Cartoon Controversy and the Self-Image of Europe,' *Radical Philosophy*, 137, 2006, p. 2.
16. Klausen, p. 151.
17. Cited in Ron Eyerman, *The Assassination of Theo van Gogh: From Social Drama to Cultural Trauma* (Durham, NC: Duke University Press, 2008) p. 40.
18. Cited in Kenan Malik, *From Fatwa to Jihad: The Rushdie Affair and its Legacy* (London: Atlantic Books, 2009) p. 143.
19. Cited in Kahn, 'Flemming Rose' p. 254.
20. Ibid. p. 281.
21. Ibid. p. 283.
22. Cited in Meer and Mouritsen, 'Political Cultures Compared' p. 345.
23. Cited in Klausen, *Cartoons That Shook The World*, p. 13.
24. Cited in Saba Mahmood, 'Religious Reason and Secular Affect: An Incommensurable Divide?' in Talal Asad, Wendy Brown, Judith Butler, Saba Mahmood, *Is Critique Secular? Blasphemy, Injury and Free Speech* (Berkeley: UC Press, 2009), p. 80 fn. 34.
25. Ibid. pp. 69–70.
26. Ibid. p. 76, p. 74.
27. Ibid. p. 71.

28. Naveeda Khan, 'Images That Come Unbidden: Some thoughts on the Danish cartoons controversy,' *borderlands e-journal*, 9:3, 2010, p. 12. http://www.borderlands.net.au/issues/vol9no3.html [accessed 24 September 2013].

29. Ibid.

30. Marion G. Müller, Esra Özcan and Ognyan Seizov, 'Dangerous Depictions: A Visual Case Study of Contemporary Cartoon Controversies', *Popular Communication: The International Journal of Media and Culture*, 7:1, 2009, p. 28.

31. Simon Weaver, 'Liquid Racism and the Danish Prophet Muhammad Cartoons,' *Current Sociology*, 58:5, 2010, p. 678.

32. Marion G. Müller and Esra Özcan, 'The Political Iconography of Muhammad Cartoons: Understanding Cultural Conflict and Political Action,' *PS: Political Science and Politics*, 40:2, 2007, pp. 288–9.

33. Klausen, p. 22.

34. Cited in Weaver, 'Liquid Racism' p. 681.

35. David Cook, *Understanding Jihad* (Berkeley: University of California Press, 2005) p. 37, p. 10.

36. Ibid. p. 10; p. 19; p. 42; p. 32.

37. Ibid. p. 48; pp. 34–5.

38. Ibid. p. 43, my emphasis.

39. This is the Abdullah Yusuf Ali translation.

40. Cook, *Understanding Jihad*, p. 25.

41. Richard Bonney, *Jihad: From Qur'an to bin Laden* (Basingstoke: Palgrave Macmillan, 2004) pp. 26–7; p. 28.

42. See Hugh Kennedy, *The Great Arab Conquests: How the Spread of Islam Changed the World We Live In* (London: Weidenfeld & Nicolson) p. 39; more pertinently, 'The Islamic state could never survive as a stable Arab polity confined to Arabia and desert Syria . . . either the Islamic elite were to lead the Bedouin against the world beyond Arabia . . . or the Islamic polity would disintegrate into its warring constituent parts . . . the leadership had no choice but to direct the frenetic military energies of the Bedouin . . . against the non-Muslim world' (pp. 56–7).

43. The two most detailed accounts of the incident and its aftermath in English are Ron Eyerman's *The Assassination of Theo Van Gogh*, and Ian Buruma's *Murder in Amsterdam: The Death of Theo Van Gogh and the Limits of Tolerance* (London: Atlantic Books, 2006).

44. Peter van der Veer, 'Pim Fortuyn, Theo Van Gogh, and the Politics of Tolerance in the Netherlands,' *Public Culture*, 18:1, 2006, p. 118.

45. Eyerman, *Assassination*, p. 126.

46. Ibid.

47. Ibid. p. 108.

48. Van Der Veer, 'Pim Fortuyn,' p. 118.

49. Ibid.

50. Ibid.

51. The phrase 'invented tradition' was popularized by Eric Hobsbawm and Terence Ranger, eds. *The Invention of Tradition* (Cambridge: Cambridge University Press, 1992).

52. Eyerman, p. 97.

53. Ibid. p. 85.

54. Ibid. p. 104.

55. Buruma, *Murder in Amsterdam*, p. 34.

56. Van Der Veer, 'Pim Fortuyn' p. 119.
57. Eyerman, p. 138.
58. Marc de Leeuw and Sonja van Wichelen, 'Please, Go Wake Up!' *Feminist Media Studies*, 5:3, 2005, p. 333.
59. Buruma, p. 123.
60. De Leeuw and van Wichelen, 'Please, Go Wake Up!' p. 327.
61. Ibid.
62. I have used the Abdullah Yusuf Ali translation, which is used in the film. There are notable differences between the respective translations of each of these verses, which sometimes affect the most apparent meaning of the verse even to the unfamiliar reader.
63. This symbolic undermining of the garment's efficacy in *not* displaying the female body is, however, highly problematic because it concurrently evokes the visual semantics of 'soft porn'. Framing this critique of the 'depersonalization' of women in Islam within a 'Western misogynist image in which women's bodies are depersonalized', is, of course, a paradox because 'both stereotypes give little credit to woman [*sic*] as acting subjects'. De Leeuw and van Wichelen, p. 328.
64. Van der Veer indirectly indexes this register in his discussion of liberal Dutch attitudes to religious sexual mores, 'Pin Fortuyn' p. 120. In a recent paper, Valérie Amiraux has noted how (in)visibility is central to French discourses supporting the prohibition of the *burqa*, 'Headscarves and Burqas in Europe: how the religion of some became the public concern of others', presented at the 'Muslims, Multiculturalism and Trust: New Directions' conference held at SOAS, London, 1–2 June 2013.
65. Eyerman, p. 92.
66. Cited in de Leeuw and van Wichelen, p. 325.
67. Leila Ahmed, *Women and Gender in Islam: Historical Roots of a Contemporary Debate* (New Haven: Yale University Press, 1992) p. 5.
68. Ibid. p. 24.
69. Ibid. p. 63; p. 66.
70. Asma Barlas, *'Believing Women' in Islam: Unreading Patriarchal Interpretations of the Qur'an* (Austin: University of Texas Press, 2002) p. 20. See also Ahmed, *Women and Gender*, p. 72.
71. Amina Wadud, *Qur'an and Woman: Rereading the Sacred Text from a Woman's Perspective* (New York: Oxford University Press, 1999); Barlas, *'Believing Women'*.
72. See Wadud, *Qur'an and Woman*; see also Amina Wadud, *Inside the Gender Jihad: Women's Reform in Islam* (Oxford: Oneworld, 2006) p. 4, 43, 153, pp. 196–7, 202–5; Barlas, p. 14, pp. 157–60, 160–5, 184–9, 189–90.
73. Barlas, p. 10.
74. Ahmed, for instance, in examining the key differences between the legal schools on the matter of marriage and divorce notes that '[s]uch differences make plain that the injunctions . . . in the Qur'an are open to radically different interpretations even by individuals who share the assumptions . . . typical of Muslim society in the Abbasid period.' *Women and Gender*, p. 91.
75. Ibid p. 94.
76. Wadud, *Inside the Gender Jihad*, pp. 202–4.
77. Buruma, *Murder in Amsterdam*, pp. 178–9.
78. Eyerman (p. 90), Buruma (p. 117) and de Leeuw and van Wichelen (pp. 330–1) all find Hirsi Ali's supercilious dismissals of the objections voiced by the very Muslim women she claims to be 'saving' from themselves to be extremely illuminating.

6 Romancing the Other: *The Jewel of the Medina* and the Ethics of Genre

1. Sherry Jones, *The Jewel of the Medina* (New York: Beaufort Books, 2008). All references will hereafter be cited in the text.
2. Denise Spellberg, *Politics, Gender and the Islamic Past: The Legacy of 'A'isha bint Abi Bakr* (New York: Columbia University Press, 1994) p. 149.
3. Hibba Abugidieri, 'Revisiting the Islamic Past, Deconstructing Male Authority: The Project of Islamic Feminism,' *Religion & Literature*, 42.1–2, 2010, pp. 134–5.
4. Margot Badran, 'Islamic Feminism: what's in a name?' *Al-Ahram Weekly Online*, issue 569, 17–23, January 2002, http://www.ahram.org.eg/2002/569/cu1.htm [accessed 21 January 2014]; Leila Ahmed, *Women and Gender in Islam: Historical Roots of a Modern Debate* (Hew Haven, CT: Yale University Press, 1992).
5. Cited in Chandra Talpade Mohanty, 'Under Western Eyes: Feminist Scholarship and Colonial Discourses' in Patrick Williams and Laura Chrisman, eds. *Colonial Discourse and Post-Colonial Theory: A Reader* (Hemel Hempstead: Harvester Wheatsheaf, 1993) p. 251, fn50.
6. Bart Moore-Gilbert, cited in John McLeod, *Beginning Postcolonialism* (Manchester: Manchester University Press, 2000) p. 196.
7. Gayatri Chakravorty Spivak, *In Other Worlds: Essays in Cultural Politics* (London: Routledge, 1988) p. 280.
8. Ibid. p. 207, first emphasis original.
9. Derek Attridge, *The Singularity of Literature* (London: Routledge, 2004) p. 101.
10. Mohanty, 'Under Western Eyes' p. 213.
11. Andrew Gibson, *Postmodernity, Ethics and the Novel: From Leavis to Levinas* (London: Routledge, 1999) p. 24.
12. Spellberg, *Politics*, p. 66.
13. Ibid. p. 12.
14. Roland Barthes, cited in Spellberg, p. 201 fn53.
15. Spellberg, *Politics*, p. 66.
16. Ibid. p. 78.
17. Nabia Abbott, *Aishah – The Beloved of Mohammed* (London: Al-Saqi, 1985) p. 3.
18. Apostasy in Islam is not a lapsing of belief but rather something more akin to treachery; within the context of tribal politics, in which the Muslims constituted a 'tribe' that sought to transcend all tribes, the withdrawal from the community was a threat to the community itself, hence its punishment by death (not unlike the death penalty statutes for treason in many modern nations, including the US).
19. Lorraine Adams, 'Thinly Veiled' *New York Times*, 14 December 2008.
20. See Jean Radford, 'Introduction' in Jean Radford, ed. *The Progress of Romance* (London: Routledge, 1986) pp. 1–22; Ann Rosalind Jones, 'Mills and Boon Meets Feminism' in *The Progress of Romance*, pp. 195–218; Helen Taylor, 'Romantic Readers,' in Helen Carr, ed. *From My Guy to Sci-Fi: Genre and Women's Writing in the Postmodern World* (London: Pandora, 1989) pp. 58–77; and most notably, Pamela Regis, *A Natural History of the Romance Novel* (Philadelphia: University of Pennsylvania Press, 2003).
21. Jones, 'Mills and Boon' p. 197.
22. Ibid. pp. 198–9; DuPlessis cited in Regis, *Natural History*, p. 10.
23. Hsu-Ming Teo, *Desert Passions: Orientalism and Romance Novels* (Austin: University of Texas Press, 2012) p. 149.
24. Ibid. p. 154; p. 159.

25. Jessica Taylor, 'And You Can Be My Sheikh: Gender, Race, and Orientalism in Contemporary Romance Novels' *Journal of Popular Culture*, 40.6, 2007, p. 1039.
26. Teo, *Desert Passions*, p. 29.
27. Regis, *Natural History*, p. 14.
28. Cited in 'Liberal Feminism' *Stanford Encyclopaedia of Philosophy*, 2013, 1.2.1, http://plato.stanford.edu/entries/feminism-liberal/ [accessed 22 January 2014]
29. 'O Prophet, tell your wives: "If you desire this present life and its adornments, come let me provide for you and part with you amicably. But if you choose God and His Prophet and the Abode of the Hereafter, God has made ready for the righteous among a most glorious reward".' *The Qur'an*, trans. Tarif Khalidi (London: Penguin, 2008). The crisis is discussed in detail by Nabia Abbott, *Aishah*, pp. 48–59.
30. In a letter defending herself from charges that she effectively 'censored' *The Jewel of the Medina*, Denise Spellberg says, 'I do not espouse censorship of any kind, but I do value my right to critique those who abuse the past without regard for its richness or resonance in the present.' *Wall Street Journal*, 9 August 2008.
31. Teo, *Desert Passions*, p. 8.
32. Ibid. p. 25.
33. Allison Weir, 'Feminism and the Islamic Revival: Freedom as a Practice of Belonging' *Hypatia*, 28.2, 2013, pp. 329–30.
34. Ibid. p. 329 original emphasis.
35. Ibid.
36. Ibid.
37. Ibid. p. 330.
38. Ibid. p. 334; p. 336, original emphasis.
39. Amina Wadud, *Inside the Gender Jihad: Women's Reform in Islam* (Oxford: Oneworld, 2006) p. 23.
40. Ibid. pp. 35–6; Khaled Abou El Fadl, 'Foreword' to Amina Wadud, *Inside*, p. xi. One might note the similarities of this concept of freedom as 'self-mastery' to Gandhi's concept of *swaraj*, itself a non-liberal conceptualization of liberty and autonomy.
41. The Romance Writers of America website states that romance makes up the largest market share of the book market (16.7 per cent), that it generated $1.438bn in sales in 2012, that it was the top-performing category in the best-seller lists, and that 74.8 million people read at least one romance novel in 2008. See http://www.rwa.org/p/cm/ld/fid=580 [accessed 10 December 2013].
42. Spellberg raises such concerns in her letter to the *Wall Street Journal*: 'The combination of sex and violence sells novels. When combined with falsification of the Islamic past, it exploits Americans who know nothing about Aisha or her seventh-century world and counts on stirring up controversy to increase sales.'

7   Satire, Incitement and Self-Restraint: Reflections on Freedom of Expression and Aesthetic Responsibility in Contemporary Britain

1. In addition there was a Private Member's Bill, introduced to the House by Lord Avebury, the Religious Offences Bill 2002.
2. Racial and Religious Hatred Act 2006, 29J.
3. Valérie Amiraux, 'Headscarves and Burqas in Europe: How the religion of some became the public concern of others', Paper delivered to the *Muslims*,

Multiculturalism and Trust: New Directions conference, SOAS, University of London, 1 June 2013. See also her 'The "illegal covering" saga: what's next? Sociological Perspectives' *Social Identities: Journal for the Study of Race, Nation and Culture*, 19.6, 2013, pp. 794–806.

4. Kay Goodall, 'Incitement to Religious Hatred: All Talk and No Substance?' *Modern Law Review*, 70:1, 2007, p. 107.
5. Ibid.
6. Ivan Hare, 'Crosses, crescents and sacred cows: criminalizing incitement to religious hatred', *Public Law*, 2006, p. 523, fn.16.
7. Nasar Meer, 'The politics of voluntary and involuntary identities: are Muslims in Britain an ethnic, racial or religious minority?' *Patterns of Prejudice*, 42:1, 2008, pp. 61–81.
8. Schedule 29A.
9. *House of Commons Library Research Paper* 05/48, 16 June 2005, pp. 27–8. Nasar Meer cites other examples in 'The politics of voluntary and involuntary identities'.
10. Lucinda Maer, 'The Racial and Religious Hatred Act 2006', *House of Commons Library Standard Note* SN/PC/03768, 6 November 2009, p. 10.
11. Allison Weir, 'Feminism and the Islamic Revival: Freedom as a Practice of Belonging,' *Hypatia*, 28:2, 2013, pp. 323–40.
12. See Saba Mahmood, *The Politics of Piety: The Islamic Revival and the Feminist Subject* (Princeton: Princeton University Press, 2005).
13. Goodall, 'Incitement' p. 102, emphasis added.
14. Cited in Research Paper 05/48; Myers cited in Goodall, 'Incitement' p. 101.
15. Polly Toynbee, 'My right to offend a fool' *Guardian*, 10 June 2005, http://www.theguardian.com/politics/2005/jun/10/religion.politicalcolumnists [accessed 13 January 2014]; Kenan Malik, *From Fatwa to Jihad: The Rushdie Affair and its legacy* (London: Atlantic, 2009) p. 175.
16. Padraig Reidy, 'I'm going to heaven, you're not' *Guardian*, 31 January 2007, http://www.theguardian.com/commentisfree/2007/jan/31/imgoingtoheavenyourenot [accessed 13 January 2014].
17. House of Lords Debate, 8 November 2005, cited in Standard Note, p. 12.
18. Goodall, 'Incitement' p. 113. From an entirely opposing point of view, Ivan Hare comes to the same conclusion, 'Crosses, crescents and sacred cows,' p. 529.
19. House of Commons debate 21 June 2005, cited in Goodall, 'Incitement' p. 100.
20. Despite dire warnings of a flood of suits and counter-suits by opposing religious groups, by 2009 there had been only one prosecution (and I have not been able to establish if that led to conviction). This is not surprising. There have been few prosecutions and even fewer convictions under the incitement to racial hatred act in the nearly forty years since the *Race Relations Act 1976*, despite the presence of the 'likely' limb and the inclusion of 'abuse and insult' clauses; see Goodall, 'Incitement' p. 111. Indeed, the existing provisions against incitement to hatred in Northern Ireland introduced in the *Public Order (Northern Ireland) Act 1987*, which are largely comparable to the first, unamended, draft of the Racial and Religious Hatred Bill, led to *no* prosecutions at all between 1993 and 2003. Finally, one may turn to the Attorney General's advice to the government following the acquittal of the leader of the racist and Islamophobic British National Party (BNP) under existing racial incitement legislation. In the review that followed, the Attorney General informed the Home Secretary that the *Racial and Religious Hatred Act* was 'practically useless' and that 'the Crown Prosecution Service believes Mr Griffin would have walked free, even if he had

been prosecuted under the new Act'. See Standard Note, p. 5. This has led Kay Goodall to conclude that 'The greatest barrier to public enlightenment is likely to be pundits who will not be able to resist telling tall tales about the silencing of free speech' (p. 113).

21. Michael Dummett, 'An Open Letter,' *Independent on Sunday*, 11 February 1990.

22. Martin Amis, on the other hand, has rightly raised 'the accountability of the author in fiction' and asked, 'What does it mean morally? . . . Is one accountable for it?' Cited in Feroza Jussawalla, 'Resurrecting the Prophet: The Case of Salman, the Otherwise' *Public Culture*, 2:1, 1989, p. 116.

23. Rushdie, 'In Good Faith,' in *Imaginary Homelands: Essays and Criticism 1981–1991* (London: Granta, 1991) p. 399.

24. Rustom Bharucha pointedly asks, '[h]ow can one possibly accept that a writer could distance himself from the words his characters speak? Indeed, how can he not be responsible for his entire representation?' This is not to succumb to the fallacy that characters therefore 'represent' the author's point of view, but rather to mark the distinction between 'representation' and 'responsibility'. As Bharucha goes on to say, 'I am reminded in this context of a wise witticism relating to *Waiting for Godot* . . . Why do Vladimir and Estagon wait for Godot? We could come up with all kinds of mis(interpretations) [*sic*], but at least one answer could be simply this: they wait for Godot *because Beckett wants them to*.' Rustom Bharucha, 'The Rushdie Affair: Secular Bigotry and the Ambivalence of Faith,' *Third Text*, 11, 1990, p. 64.

25. Rushdie, 'In Good Faith', p. 411.

26. Malik, *From Fatwa to Jihad*, pp. 189–90.

27. Ibid. p. 406. Malik, *From Fatwa to Jihad*, p. 155.

28. Salman Rushdie, *The Satanic Verses* (Delaware: The Consortium, Inc., 1992) p. 97.

29. Rushdie, 'Is Nothing Sacred?' in *Imaginary Homelands*, p. 418, p. 420, p. 427. Subsequent citations are referred to in the text.

30. Simon During notes that this passage is 'not very convincing'. See his *Foucault and Literature: Towards a Genealogy of Writing* (London: Routledge, 1992) p. 124.

31. Michel Foucault, 'What is an Author?' in *Language, Counter-Memory, Practice: Selected Essays and Interviews*, ed. Donald F. Bouchard, trans. Donald Boucahrd and Sherry Simon (Ithaca, NY: Cornell University Press, 1977) pp. 124–5.

32. During, *Foucault and Literature*, p. 124.

33. Foucault, 'What is an Author?' p. 125.

34. Ibid. p. 126.

35. Jody Greene, *The Trouble with Ownership: Literary Property and Authorial Liability in England, 1660–1730* (Philadelphia: University of Pennsylvania Press, 2005). See also Mark Rose, 'The Author as Proprietor: *Donaldson* v. *Becket* and the Genealogy of Modern Authorship' *Representations*, 23, 1988, pp. 51–85.

36. This broader argument assumes more importance in the latter stages of Foucault's essay.

37. See 'Outside the Whale' in *Imaginary Homelands*, pp. 87–101.

38. Cited in Meer, 'The politics of voluntary and involuntary identities' p. 76.

39. Standard Note, p. 9.

40. Press Association, 'Life of Brian would be risky now, says Terry Jones,' *Guardian*, 10 October 2011. http://www.theguardian.com/film/2011/oct/10/life-of-brian-terry-jones [accessed 19 January 2014]

41. Charles Knight calls it the 'satiric frame of mind' in *The Literature of Satire* (Cambridge: Cambridge University Press, 2004).

42. Paul Simpson, *On the Discourse of Satire: Towards a Stylistic Model of Satirical Humour* (Amsterdam: John Benjamins Publishing Company, 2003). John Clement Ball notes the critics who see satire as 'ameliorative in its intention' – Linda Hutcheon, James Sutherland, Edward and Lillian Bloom – in *Satire and the Postcolonial Novel: V.S. Naipaul, Chinua Achebe, Salman Rushdie* (New York: Routledge, 2003) p. 35.

43. Arthur Pollard, *Satire* (London: Routledge, 1970) p. 3; Ball, *Satire and the Postcolonial Novel*, p. 22.

44. Knight, *Literature of Satire*, p. 3; Leonard Feinberg, cited in Ball, *Satire and the Postcolonial Novel*, p. 34.

45. Pollard, *Satire*, pp. 16–19; Felicity A. Nussbaum, *The Brink of All We Hate: English Satires on Women 1660–1750* (Lexington: University of Kentucky Press, 1984).

46. Stanley Fish, 'Jerry Falwell's Mother, Or, What's the Harm?' in *There's No Such Thing as Free Speech, and it's a Good Thing Too* (New York: OUP, 1994) pp. 120–33.

47. Pollard, *Satire*, p. 7.

48. Ibid. p. 3.

49. Charles Knight, cited in Ball, *Satire and the Postcolonial Novel*, p. 19.

50. Simpson, *On the Discourse of Satire*, p. 8 (original emphases).

51. Ball, *Satire and the Postcolonial Novel*, p. 22; p. 13.

52. Pollard, *Satire*, p. 12.

53. Graham Chapman, John Cleese, Terry Gilliam, Eric Idle, Terry Jones and Michael Palin with Bob MacCabe, *The Pythons Autobiography by The Pythons* (London: Orion, 2003) pp. 349–87.

54. *The Secret Life of Brian*, Channel 4, 1 January 2007.

55. I would like to thank my friend Reverend Nigel Dawkins for this point.

56. Nick Cohen, *You Can't Read This Book: Censorship in an Age of Freedom*, Kindle edition (London: Fourth Estate, 2012) p. 96 [loc 1630].

57. Glen Newey, 'Unlike a scotch egg' *London Review of Books*, 35.23, 5 December 2013, p. 22.

58. Cited in Simon Lee, *The Cost of Free Speech* (London: Faber, 1990) p. 20.

59. Amitav Ghosh, 'The Ghosts of Mrs Gandhi,' in *The Imam and the Indian: Prose Pieces* (Delhi: Permanent Black, 2002) p. 60.

60. Ibid. p. 61.

61. Ibid. p. 60.

62. See Virginia Held, *The Ethics of Care* (New York: Oxford University Press, 2006); Joan C. Tronto, *Moral Boundaries: A Political Argument for an Ethic of Care* (New York: Routledge, 1994); Allison Weir, 'Feminism and the Islamic Revival'.

Index

Aaronovitch, David, 26
Abou El Fadl, Khaled, 180
Abraham, 72–3, 92–3, 122–3, 145, 163, 215
accountability, 3, 65, 75, 240
Ahmed, Leila, 163
Aisha bint Abi Bakr, 7, 8, 119–20, 163, 167–9, 172–81, 238
Akedah (Binding of Isaac/Isma'il), 92–3
Allah, 93, 104–7, 118, 121, 129–30, 132, 134, 143–4, 155, 157–8, 162, 164, 174–5, 178, 180
allochronism, 130
allochthon *see also* autochthon, 159–61
Ali, Ayaan Hirsi, 4, 8, 34, 159–61, 163–6
Ali bin Abu Talib, 174–5
Ali, Monica, 20–1, 25, 80
Amin, Samir, 139
Amiraux, Valérie, 185, 236
Anthony, Andrew, 15, 17, 213
Appignanesi, Lisa, 15, 213
Armenian genocide, 16, 49
Armstrong, Karen, 143
Asad, Talal, 48, 50, 57–8, 107, 132–3, 214, 218
Asqalani, Ibn Hajar, 104
assaultive speech, 22–3, 43
assimilation, 17, 151
Atkinson, Rowan, 198
Atran, Scott, 65–6
Attridge, Derek, 6, 69–75, 81, 83–5, 89–92, 170
Augustine, 134, 138
Austin, J.L., 5, 22–3
authorial audience *see under* implied reader
authoritarianism, 4, 17, 35, 54
autochthon *see also* allochthon, 159–61
autonomy *see under* liberty

Badawi, Zaki, 19
Ball, John Clement, 198
Barlas, Asma, 164–5, 178
Baroness Scotland, 190

BBC, 19–20
Behzti, 19
belief, 47–8, 66, 87, 112, 127, 153, 156, 201, 204, 208
  moral, 59–60, 141
  nonce, 88
  rational defence of, 55, 60
  religious, 40, 48, 57–60, 93, 105, 128, 130–8, 140–1, 152, 185–191, 198, 203–4, 207–8
Bellow, Saul, 37
Benwell *et al.*, 25, 80–1
Bhagavad-Gita, 3
Bible, 92, 121–3, 188
  Book of Chronicles, 123
  Book of Job, 122
  New Testament, 121–2
  Old Testament, 122–3
Blair, Tony, 17, 40
blasphemy, 5, 20, 48, 57, 202, 204, 214, 232
  UK laws, 19–21
Bradford Council of Mosques, 19
Brand, Russell, 91, 21
Bonney, Richard, 157
Booth, Wayne C., 6, 69, 72, 78, 81, 85–6, 88
Bouyeri, Mohammed, 159
Boyle, Frankie, 21
Buddhism, 4
Bukhari, Muhammad, 104, 108
Bunglawala, Inayat, 15
Burke, Edmund, 4
Burke, Séan, 85–7
burqa *see under* veil
Buruma, Ian, 160
Butler, Judith, 5, 24–5, 27–8, 43, 82, 154, 214
  Excitable Speech, 25, 27
  Gender Trouble, 28

Cameron, David, 16
Caputo, John, 134–8
Carens, Joseph, 149

Printed and bound by CPI Group (UK) Ltd, Croydon, CR0 4YY